PROLEGOMENA

TO THE STUDY OF

HEGEL'S PHILOSOPHY

AND

ESPECIALLY OF HIS LOGIC

PROLEGOMENA

TO THE STUDY OF

HEGEL'S PHILOSOPHY

AND

ESPECIALLY OF HIS LOGIC

BY

WILLIAM WALLACE, M.A., LL.D.

FELLOW OF MERTON COLLEGE
AND WHYTE'S PROFESSOR OF MORAL PHILOSOPHY IN THE UNIVERSITY OF OXFORD

SECOND EDITION, REVISED AND AUGMENTED

NEW YORK / RUSSELL & RUSSELL

IN REMEMBRANCE OF

B. JOWETT

LATE REGIUS PROFESSOR OF GREEK

AND

MASTER OF BALLIOL COLLEGE

OXFORD

REPRINTED FROM A COPY IN THE COLLECTIONS OF
THE NEW YORK PUBLIC LIBRARY

REPRODUCED FROM THE SECOND EDITION, REVISED AND AUGMENTED
FIRST PUBLISHED IN 1894
REISSUED, 1968, BY RUSSELL & RUSSELL
A DIVISION OF ATHENEUM PUBLISHERS, INC.
L. C. CATALOG CARD NO: 68-15169
PRINTED IN THE UNITED STATES OF AMERICA

PREFACE

THE present volume of **Prolegomena** completes the second edition of my LOGIC OF HEGEL which originally appeared in 1874. The translation, which was issued as a separate volume in the autumn of 1892, had been subjected to revision throughout : such faults as I could detect had been amended, and many changes made in the form of expression with the hope of rendering the interpretation clearer and more adequate. But, with a subject so abstruse and complicated as Hegel's Logic, and a style so abrupt and condensed as that adopted in his *Encyclopaedia*, a satisfactory translation can hardly fall within the range of possibilities. Only the enthusiasm of youth could have thrown itself upon such an enterprise ; and later years have but to do what they may to fulfil the obligations of a task whose difficulties have come to seem nearly insuperable. The translation volume was introduced by a sketch of the growth of the *Encyclopaedia* through the three editions published in its author's lifetime : and an appendix of notes supplied some literary and historical elucidations of the text, with quotations bearing on the philosophical development between Kant and Hegel.

The **Prolegomena**, which have grown to more than twice their original extent, are two-thirds of them new matter. The lapse of twenty years could not but involve a change in the writer's attitude, at least in details, towards both facts and problems. The general purpose of the work, however, still remains the same, to supply an introduction to the study of Hegel, especially his *Logic*, and to philosophy in general. But, in the work of altering and inserting, I can hardly imagine that I have succeeded in adjusting the additions to the older work with that artful juncture which would simulate the continuity of organic growth. To perform that feat would require a master who surveyed from an imperial outlook the whole system of Hegelianism in its history and meaning ; and I at least do not profess such a mastery. Probably therefore a critical review will discern inequalities in the ground, and even discrepancies in the statement, of the several chapters. To remove these strains of inconsistency would in any case have been a work of time and trouble : and, after all, mere differences in depth or breadth of view may have their uses. The writer cannot always compel the reader to understand him, as he himself has not always the same faculty to penetrate and comprehend the problems he deals with. In these arduous paths of research it may well happen that the clearest and truest perceptions are not always those which communicate themselves with fullest persuasion and gift of insight. Schopenhauer has somewhere compared the structure of his philosophical work to the hundred-gated Thebes : so many, he says, are the points of access it offers for the pilgrims after truth to reach its central dogma. So—if one may parallel little things with his adventurous quest— even the less speculative chapters, and the less consecutive discourse, of these **Prolegomena** may prove helpful to some individual mood or phase of mind. If—as I suspect— the Second Book should elicit the complaint that the reader has been kept wandering too long and too deviously in the *Porches of Philosophy*, I will hope that sometimes in the course of these rovings he may come across a wicket- gate where he can enter, and—which is the main thing— gather truth fresh and fruitful for himself.

Fourteen chapters, viz. II, XXIV, and the group from VII to XVIII inclusive, are in this edition almost entirely new. Three chapters of the first edition, numbered XIX, XXII, XXIII, have been dropped. For the rest, Chaps. III–VI in the present correspond to Chaps. II–V in the first edition : Chap. XIX to parts of VII, VIII : Chaps. XX–XXIII to Chaps. IX–XII : Chaps. XXV–XXX to Chaps. XIII–XVIII : and Chaps. XXXI, XXXII to Chaps. XX, XXI. But some of those nominally retained have been largely rewritten.

The new chapters present, amongst other things, a synopsis of the progress of thought in Germany during the half-century which is bisected by the year 1800, with some indication of the general conditions of the intellectual world, and with some reference to the inter-connexion of speculation and actuality. Jacobi and Herder, Kant, Fichte, and Schelling have been especially brought under succinct review. In the first edition I did Kant less than justice. I have now, so far as my limits allowed, tried to rectify the impression ; and even more perhaps, by a clear palinode, to tender my apology for the meagre and somewhat inappreciative notice I gave to the great names of Fichte and Schelling. For like reasons, and from a growing perception how much post-Kantian thought owed to the pre-Kantian thinkers, Spinoza and Leibniz have been partly brought within my range. If, furthermore, I may seem to have transgressed the due amount of allusions and comparisons drawn from Plato and Aristotle, Bacon and Mill, the excuse must be sought in that fixture of philosophical horizon which can hardly but creep on after a quarter of a century spent in teaching philosophy under the customs and ordinances of the Oxford School of Classical Philology.

It would be to mistake the scope of this survey to seek in it a history of the philosophers of the period I have named. They have been presented, not in and for themselves, but as *momenta* or constituent factors in producing Hegel's conception of the aim and method of philosophy. To do this it was necessary to lay stress on their inner purport and implications : to treat the individual thinker in subordination to the general movement of ideas : to give, as far as was possible, a constructive conception of them rather than an analysis and chronicle. Yet as the picture had to be done, so to say, with a few vigorous touches, and made characteristic rather than descriptive, it cannot have that fairness and completeness which only patient study of every feature and untiring experiment in reconstruction can enable even the artist to produce. I may have seemed to confine the environment too exclusively to continental thinkers : but this is not, I think, due to any anti-patriotic bias. English (by which term, I may explain to my countrymen, I mean English-writing) thought, if it has its own intrinsic value, has after all been only an occasional influence, of suggestion and modification, in Germany. It is not therefore an integral portion of my theme. Even in Kant's case, too much may be made of the stimulus he received from Hume.

Even twenty years ago, my translation could hardly be described literally as a voice crying in the wilderness. But since that time there has been a considerable out-put of history, translation, and criticism referring to the great age of German philosophy, and a comparatively numerous group of writers, more or less familiar with the aims and principles of that period, have treated various parts of philosophy with notable independence and originality. To these writers it has sometimes been found convenient to give the title of Neo-Kantians, or Neo-Hegelians. The prefix suggests that they do not in all points reproduce the ideal or the caricature which vulgar tradition fancied, and perhaps still fancies, to be implied in German ' transcendentalism '. And that for the good reason that the springs of the movement lie in the natural and national revulsion of English habits of mind. Slowly, but at length, the storms of the great European revolution found their way to our intellectual world, and shook church and state, society and literature. The homeless spirit of the age had to reconsider the task of rebuilding its house of life. It may have been that some of the seekers, in the fervour of a first impression, spoke unadvisedly, as if salvation could and would come to English philosophy only by Kant and Hegel. Yet, there was a real foundation for the belief that the insularity—however necessary in its season, and however admirable in some of its results—which had secluded and narrowed the British mind since the middle of the eighteenth century, needed something deeper and stronger than French ' ideology ' to bring it abreast of the requirements of the age. Whatever may be the drawbacks of transcendentalism, they are virtues when set beside the vulgar ideals of enlightenment by superficialisation. Mill has well pointed out how the spirit of Coleridge was for the higher intellectual life a needful complement to the spirit of Bentham. Yet the spirit of Coleridge had but caught some of the side-lights and romantic illuminations : it had not dared to face the central sun either in literature or philosophy. The scholar who has given us excellent versions of Fichte's lighter works, those who have translated and expounded Kant, and the great author who opened German literature to the British public, have brought us nearer the higher teaching of Germany. In Germany itself it has always been the possession only of the few. Even at the height of the classical period there were littérateurs who vended thousands of their books for Goethe's hundreds, and the great philosophers had ten opponents to one follower even amongst the teachers of their day. Yet Goethe and not Kotzebue gave the permanent law to literature ; Hegel, and not Krug or Fries, has influenced philosophy. To have had the resolution to learn in this school is the merit of ' Neo-Hegelianism '. It has probably not found Kant free from puzzles and contradictions, or Hegel always intelligible. But the example of the Germans has served to widen and deepen our ideas of philosophy : to make us think more highly of its function, and to realise that it is essentially science, and the science of supreme reality. And it has at least familiarised many with the heresy that dilettantism and occasional fits of speculativeness are worth as little in philosophy as elsewhere. To have striven for dignity in its scope, and scientific security in its method, is something. If the Neo-Hegelian has not given philosophy a settled language, it may be urged that a philosophical language cannot be created by the easy device of inventing a few Hellenistic-seeming vocables.

I could have wished to make these volumes a worthier contribution to the work whereby these and other writers have recently enriched our island philosophy. Not least because of the honoured name I have ventured to write on the dedication-page. If, as Epicurus said, we should above all be grateful to the past, the first meed is from the scholar due to the teachers of earlier years, and not least those who have now entered into their rest. I do not forget what I, and others, owed to T. H. Green, my predecessor in the Chair of Moral Philosophy ; that example of high-souled devotion to truth, and of earnest and intrepid thinking on the deep things of eternity. But at this season the memory of my Oxford tutor and friend is naturally most prominent. The late Master of Balliol College was more than a mere scholar or a mere philosopher. He seemed so idealist and yet so practical : so realist and yet so full of high ideals : so delicately kind and yet so severely reasonable. You felt he saw life more steadily and saw it more whole than others : as one reality in which religion and philosophy, art and business, the sciences and theology, were severally but elements and aspects. To the amateurs of novelty, to the slaves of specialisation, to the devotees of any narrow way, such largeness might, with the impatience natural to limited minds, have seemed indifference. So must appear those who on higher planes hear all the parts in the harmony of humanity, and with the justice of a wise love maintain an intellectual *Sôphrosyne*. On his pupils this secret power of an other-world serenity laid an irresistible spell, and

PREFACE

bore in upon them the conviction that beyond scholarship and logic there was the fuller truth of life and the all-embracing duty of doing their best to fulfil the amplest requirements of their place.

In earlier days Jowett had been keenly interested in German philosophy, and had made a version (most of which was still extant in 1868) of the Logic I have translated. But Greek literature, and above all Plato, drew him to more congenial fields. It was on his suggestion,—or shall I say injunction ?—at that date, that the work I had casually begun was some years later prosecuted to completion. It was his words, again, two years ago, that bade me spare no labour in the work of revision.

OXFORD,
December, 1893.

FROM THE PREFACE TO THE FIRST EDITION

THE ' Logic of Hegel ' is a name which may be given to two separate books. One of these is the ' Science of Logic ' (Wissenschaft der Logik), first published in three volumes (1812–1816), while its author was schoolmaster at Nüremberg. A second edition was on its way, when Hegel was suddenly cut off, after revising the first volume only. In the ' Secret of Hegel ', the earlier part of this Logic has been translated by Dr. Hutchison Stirling, with whose name German philosophy is chiefly associated in this country.

The other Logic, of which the present work is a translation, forms the First Part in the ' Encyclopaedia of the Philosophical Sciences '. The first edition of the Encyclopaedia appeared at Heidelberg in 1817 ; the second in 1827 ; and the third in 1830. It is well to bear in mind that these dates take us back forty or fifty years, to a time when modern science and Inductive Logic had yet to win their laurels, and when the world was in many ways different from what it is now. The earliest edition of the Encyclopaedia contained the pith of the system. The subsequent editions brought some new materials, mainly intended to smooth over and explain the transitions between the various sections, and to answer the objections of critics. The work contained a synopsis of philosophy in the form of paragraphs, and was to be supplemented by the *viva voce* remarks of the lecturer.

The present volume is translated from the edition of 1843, forming the Sixth Volume in Hegel's Collected Works.

FROM THE PREFACE TO THE FIRST EDITION

It consists of two nearly equal portions. One half, here printed in more open type, contains Hegel's Encyclopaedia, with all the author's own additions. The first paragraph under each number marks the earliest and simplest statement of the first edition. The other half, here printed in closer type, is made up of the notes taken in lecture by the editor (Henning) and by Professors Hotho and Michelet. These notes for the most part connect the several sections, rather than explain their statements. Their genuineness is vouched for by their being almost verbally the same with other parts of Hegel's own writings.

The translation has tried to keep as closely as possible to the meaning, without always adhering very rigorously to the words of the original. It is, however, much more literal in the later and systematic part, than in the earlier chapters.

The Prolegomena which precede the translation have not been given in the hope or with the intention of expounding the Hegelian system. They merely seek to remove certain obstacles, and to render Hegel less tantalizingly hard to those who approach him for the first time. How far they will accomplish this, remains to be seen.

Oxford,
September, 1873.

CONTENTS

BOOK I

OUTLOOKS AND APPROACHES TO HEGEL

CONTENTS

BOOK II

IN THE PORCHES OF PHILOSOPHY

CONTENTS

BOOK III

LOGICAL OUTLINES

BOOK I

OUTLOOKS AND APPROACHES TO HEGEL

CHAPTER I

WHY HEGEL IS HARD TO UNDERSTAND

'THE condemnation,' says Hegel, 'which a great man lays upon the world, is to force it to explain him.'[1] The greatness of Hegel, if it be measured by this standard, must be something far above common. Interpreters of his system have contradicted each other, almost as variously as the several commentators on the Bible. He is claimed as their head by widely different schools of thought, all of which appeal to him as the original source of their line of argument. The Right wing, and the Left, as well as the Centre, profess to be the genuine descendants of the prophet, and to inherit the mantle of his inspiration. If we believe one side, Hegel is only to be rightly appreciated when we divest his teaching of every shred of religion and orthodoxy which it retains. If we believe another class of expositors, he was the champion of Christianity.

These contradictory views may be safely left to abolish each other. But diversity of opinion on such topics is neither unnatural, nor unusual. The meaning and the bearings of a great event, or a great character, or a great work of reasoned thought, will be estimated and explained in different ways, according to the effect they produce on different minds and different levels of life and society. Those effects, perhaps, will not present themselves in their true character, until long after the original excitement has passed away. To some minds, the chief value of the Hegelian system will lie in its vindication of the truths of natural and revealed religion, and in the agreement of the elaborate reasonings of the philosopher with the simple

[1] Hegel's *Leben* (Rosenkranz), p. 555.

aspirations of mankind towards higher things. To others that system will have most interest as a philosophical history of thought,—an exposition of that organic development of reason, which underlies and constitutes all the varied and complex movement of the world. To a third class, again, it may seem at best an instrument or method of investigation, stating the true law by which knowledge proceeds in its endeavour to comprehend and assimilate existing nature.

While these various meanings may be given to the Hegelian scheme of thought, the majority of the world either pronounce Hegel to be altogether unintelligible, or banish him to the limbo of *a priori* thinkers,—that bourne from which no philosopher returns. To argue with those who start from the latter conviction would be an ungrateful, and probably a superfluous task. Wisdom is justified, we may be sure, of all her children. But it may be possible to admit the existence of difficulties, and agree to some extent with those who complain that Hegel is impenetrable and hard as adamant. There can be no doubt of the forbidding aspect of the most prominent features in his system. He is hard in himself, and his readers find him hard. His style is not of the best, and to foreign eyes seems unequal. At times he is eloquent, stirring, and striking : again his turns are harsh, and his clauses tiresome to disentangle : and we are always coming upon that childlikeness of literary manner, which English taste fancies it can detect in some of the greatest works of German genius. There are faults in Hegel, which obscure his meaning : but more obstacles are due to the nature of the work, and the pre-occupations of our minds. There is something in him which fascinates the thinker, and which inspires a sympathetic student with the vigour and the hopefulness of the spring-time.

Perhaps the main hindrance in the way of a clear vision is the contrast which Hegelian philosophy offers to our ordinary habits of mind. Generally speaking, we rest contented if we can get tolerably near our object, and form a general picture of it to set before ourselves. It might almost be said that we have never thought of such a thing as being in earnest either with our words or with our thoughts. We get into a way of speaking with an uncertain latitude of meaning, and leave a good deal to the fellow-feeling of our hearers, who are expected to mend what is

defective in our utterances. For most of us the place of
exact thought is supplied by metaphors and pictures, by
mental images, and figures generalised from the senses.
And thus it happens that, when we come upon a single
precise and definite statement, neither exceeding nor falling
short in its meaning, we are thrown out of our reckoning.
Our fancy and memory have nothing left for them to do :
and, as fancy and memory make up the greater part of
what we loosely call thinking, our powers of thought seem
to be brought to a standstill. Those who crave for fluent
reading, or prefer easy writing, something within the pale
of our usual mental lines, are more likely to find what they
seek in the ten partially correct and approximate ways
commonly used to give expression to a truth, than in the
one simple and accurate statement of the thought. We
prefer a familiar name, and an accustomed image, on which
our faculties may work. But in the atmosphere of Hegelian
thought, we feel very much as if we had been lifted into
a vacuum, where we cannot breathe, and which is a fit
habitation for unrecognisable ghosts only.

Nor is this all. The traveller, as his train climbs the
heights of Alps or Apennines, occasionally, after circling
in grand curve upon the mountain-side, and perhaps
after having been dragged mysterious distances through
the gloom of a tunnel, finds himself as it would seem back
at the same place as he looked forth from some minutes
before ; and it is only after a brief comparison that he
realises he now commands a wider view from a point some
hundreds of feet higher. So the student of Hegel—(and it
might be the case with Fichte also) as the machinery of the
dialectical method, with its thesis, antithesis, and synthesis,
carries him round and round from term to term of thought—
like the *Logos* and the Spirit, which blow us whithersoever
they list—begins to suffer from dizziness at the apprehension that he has been the victim of phantasmagoria and
has not really moved at all. It is only later—if ever—that
he recognises that the scene, though similar, is yet not
altogether the same. It is only later—if ever—that he
understands that the path of philosophy is no wandering
from land to land more remote in search of a lost Absolute,
a vanished God ; no setting forth of new and strange facts,
of new Gods, but the revelation in fuller and fuller truth of
the immanent reality in whom we live, and move, and have

our being,—the manifestation in more closely-knit unity and more amply-detailed significance of that Infinite and Eternal, which was always present among us, though we saw but few, perhaps even no, traces of its power and glory.

To read Hegel often reminds us of the process we have to go through in trying to answer a riddle. The terms of the problem to be solved are all given to us : the features of the object are, it may be, fully described : and yet somehow we cannot at once tell what it is all about, or add up the sum of which we have the several items. We are waiting to learn the subject of the proposition, of which all these statements may be regarded as the predicates. Something, we feel, has undoubtedly been said : but we are at a loss to see what it has been said about. Our mind wanders round from one familiar object to another, and tries them in succession to see whether any one satisfies the several points in the statement and includes them all. We grope here and there for something we are acquainted with, in which the bits of the description may cohere, and get a unity which they cannot give themselves. When once we have hit upon the right object, our troubles are at an end : and the empty medium is now peopled with a creature of our imagination. We have reached a fixed point in the range of our conception, around which the given features may cluster.

All this trouble caused by the Hegelian theory of what philosophy involves—viz. really beginning at the beginning, is saved by a device well known to the several branches of Science. It is the way with them to assume that the student has a rough general image of the objects which they examine ; and under the guidance, or with the help of this generalised image, they go on to explain and describe its outlines more completely. They start with an approximate conception, such as anybody may be supposed to have ; and this they seek to render more definite. The geologist, for example, could scarcely teach geology, unless he could pre-suppose or produce some acquaintance on the part of his pupils with what Hume would have called an ' impression ' or an ' idea ' of the rocks and formations of which he has to treat. The geometer gives a short, and, as it were, popular explanation of the sense in which angles, circles, triangles, &c. are to be understood : and then by the aid of these provisional definitions we come to a more

scientific notion of the same terms. The third book of
Euclid, for example, brings before us a clearer notion of
what a circle is, than the nominal explanation in the list
of definitions. By means of these temporary aids, or, as
we may call them, leading-strings for the intellect, the
progress of the ordinary scientific student is made tolerably
easy. But in philosophy, as it is found in Hegel, there is
quite another way of working. The helps in question are
absent : and until it be seen that they are not even needed,
the Hegelian theory will remain a sealed mystery. For that
which the first glance seemed to show as an enigma, is only
the plain and unambiguous statement of thought. Instead
of casting around for images and accustomed names, we
have only to accept the several terms and articles in the
development of thought as they present themselves. These
terms merely require to be apprehended. They stand in no
immediate need of illustration from our experience. What
we have to bring to the work, is patience, self-restraint, the
sacrifice of our cherished habits of mind, the surrender of
the natural wish to see at once what it all comes to, what
it is good for, how it squares with other convictions. As
Bacon reminded his age, Into the kingdom of philosophy,
as into the kingdom of heaven, none can enter, *nisi sub
persona infantis* : i. e. unless he at least steadfastly resolve
to renounce that world which lieth in the Evil.

Ordinary knowledge consists in referring a new object to
a class of objects, that is to say, to a generalised image
with which we are already acquainted. It is not so much
cognition as re-cognition. ' "What is the truth ? " ' asked
Lady Chettam of Mrs. Cadwallader in *Middlemarch*. ' " The
truth ? he is as bad as the wrong physic—nasty to take,
and sure to disagree." " There could not be anything
worse than that," said Lady Chettam, with so vivid a conception of the physic that she seemed to have learned
something exact about Mr. Casaubon's disadvantages.'
Once we have referred the new individual to a familiar
category or a convenient metaphor, once we have given it
a name, and introduced it into the society of our mental
drawing-room, we are satisfied. We have put a fresh object
in its appropriate drawer in the cabinet of our ideas : and
hence, with the pride of a collector, we can calmly call it
our own. But such acquaintance, proceeding from a
mingling of memory and naming, is not the same thing as

knowledge in the strict sense of the term.[1] ' What is he ?
Do you know him ? ' These are our questions : and we
are satisfied when we learn his name and his calling. We
may never have penetrated into the inner nature of those
objects, with whose *tout ensemble*, or rough outlines, we are
so much at home, that we fancy ourselves thoroughly
cognisant of them. Classifications are only the first steps
in science : and we do not understand a thought because
we can view it under the guise of some of its illustrations.

In the case of the English reader of Hegel some peculiar
hindrances spring from the foreign language. In strong
contrast to most of the well-known German philosophers,
he may be said to write in the popular and national dialect
of his country. Of course there are tones and shades of
meaning given to his words by the general context of his
system. But upon the whole he did what he promised to
J. H. Voss—the translator of Homer, and the poet of the
Luise, in a letter written from Jena in 1805. He there says
of his projects : ' Luther has made the Bible, and you
have made Homer speak German. No greater gift than
this could be given to the nation. So long as a nation
is not acquainted with a noble work in its own language,
it is still barbarian, and does not regard the work as its
own. Forget these two examples, and I may describe my
own efforts as an attempt to teach philosophy to speak in
German.' [2]

Yet, in this matter of nationalising or Germanising philosophy, he only carried a step further what Wolff and
even Kant had begun ; just as, on the other hand, he falls
a long way short of what K. C. F. Krause, his contemporary,
attempted in the same direction. Such an attempt, by its
very nature, could never command a popular success. It
runs directly counter to that tendency already noted, to
escape the requirement to think and think for ourselves, by
taking refuge under the shadow of a familiar term, which
conceals in its apparent simplicity a great complex of ill-
apprehended elements. The ordinary mind—and the more
readily perhaps the more vulgar it is—flees for ease and
safety to a cosmopolitan term, to the denationalised vocable
of learned origin, to the language of general European

---

[1] ' Das Bekannte überhaupt ist darum, weil es bekannt ist, nicht
erkannt.' *Phenomenologie des Geistes*, p. 24.

[2] *Vermischte Schriften*, vol. ii. p. 474.

culture. To such an ordinary mind—and up at least to a certain extent we all at times come under that heading— the effort to remain in the pellucid air of our unadulterated mother-tongue is too embarrassing to be long continued. Nor, after all, is it more than partially practicable. The well of German undefiled is apt to run dry. Hegel himself never shrinks when it is needful to appropriate non-Teutonic words, and is in the habit of employing the synonymous terms of native and of classical origin with a systematic difference of meaning.[1]

Hegel is unquestionably *par excellence* the philosopher of Germany,—German through and through. For philosophy, though the common birthright of full-grown reason in all ages and countries, must like other universal and cosmopolitan interests, such as the State, the Arts, or the Church, submit to the limits and peculiarities imposed upon it by the natural divisions of race and language. The subtler *nuances*, as well as the coarser differences of national speech, make themselves vividly felt in the systems of philosophy, and defy translation. If Greek philosophy cannot, no more can German philosophy be turned into a body of English thought by a stroke of the translator's pen. There is a difference in this matter, a difference at least in degree, between the special sciences and philosophy. The several sciences have a de-nationalised and cosmopolitan character, like the trades and industries of various nations ; they are pretty much the same in one country and another, especially when we consider the details, and neglect the general subdivisions. But in the political body, in the works of high art, and in the systems of philosophy, the whole of the character and temperament of the several peoples finds its expression, and stands distinctly marked, in a shape of its own. If the form of German polity be not transferable to this side of the Channel, no more will German philosophy.

---

[1] e. g. *Dasein* and *Existenz : Wirklichkeit* and *Realität : Wesen* and *Substanz*. It is the same habit of curiously pondering over the tones and shades of language which leads him to something very like playing on words, and to etymologising, as one may call it, on unetymological principles : e. g. the play on *Mein* and *Meinung* (vol. ii. 32 : cf. *Werke*, ii. 75) : the literal rendering of *Erinnerung* (*Encycl.* §§ 234 and 450) ; and the abrupt transitions, as it would seem, from literal to figurative use of such a term as *Grund*. At the same time it is well not to be prosaically certain that a free play of thought does not follow the apparently fortuitous assonance of words.

Direct utilisation for English purposes is out of the question : the circumstances are too different. But the study of the great works of foreign thought is not on that account useless, any more than the study of the great works of foreign statesmanship.

Hegel did good service, at least, by freeing philosophy from that aspect of an imported luxury, which it usually had,—as if it were an exotic plant removed from the bright air of Greece into the melancholy mists of Western Europe. ' We have still,' he says, ' to break down the partition between the language of philosophy, and that of ordinary consciousness : we have to overcome the reluctance against thinking what we are familiar with.' [1] Philosophy must be brought face to face with ordinary life, so as to draw its strength from the actual and living present, and not from the memories or traditions of the past. It has to become the organised and completed thinking of what is contained blindly and vaguely in the various levels of popular intelligence, as these are more or less educated and ordered. It must grow naturally, as in ancient Greece, from the necessities of the social situation, and not be a product of artificial introduction and nurture : the revelation by the mind's own energy of an implicit truth, not the communication of a mystery sacramentally received. To suppose that a mere change of words can give this grace, would be absurd. Yet where the national life pulses strong, as that of Germany in those days did at first in letters and then in social reform, the dominant note will make itself felt even in the neutral regions of speculation. It was a step on the right road to banish a pompous and aristocratic dialect from philosophy, and to lead it back to those words and forms of speech, which are at least in silent harmony with the national feeling.

[1] Hegel's *Leben* (Rosenkranz), p. 552.

CHAPTER II

WHY TRANSLATE HEGEL?

' BUT,' it is urged, ' though it be well to let the stream of foreign thought irrigate some of our philosophical pastures, though we should not for ever entrench ourselves in our insularity—why try to introduce Hegel, of all philosophers confessedly the most obscure ? Why not be content with the study and the " exploitation " of Kant, whom Germans themselves still think so important as to expound him with endless comment and criticism, and who has at length found, after some skirmishes, a recognised place in the English philosophical curriculum ? Why seek for more Teutonic thinking that can be found in Schopenhauer, and found there in a clear and noble style, luminous in the highest degree, and touching with no merely academic abstruseness the problems of life and death ? Or—as that song is sweetest to men which is the newest to ring in their ears—why not render accessible to English readers the numerous and suggestive works of Eduard von Hartmann, and of Friedrich Nietzsche—not to mention Robert Hamerling ? [1] Or, finally, why not give us more and ever more translations of the works in logic, ethics, psychology, or metaphysics, of those many admirable teachers in the German universities, whom it would be invidious to try to single out by name ? As for Hegel, his system, in the native land of the philosopher, is utterly discredited ; its influence is extinct ; it is dead as a door-nail. It is a pity to waste labour and distract attention, and that in English lands, where there are plenty of problems of our own to solve, by an attempt, which must perforce be futile, to resuscitate these defunctitudes ? '

That Hegelianism has been utterly discredited, in certain

---

[1] A book by V. Knauer published last year (*Hauptprobleme der Philosophie*), a series of popular lectures, gives one-sixth of its space to the ' Atomistic of Will ' by the Austrian poet Hamerling.

quarters, is no discovery reserved for these later days.
But on this matter perhaps we may borrow an analogy. If
the reader will be at the trouble to take up two English
newspapers of opposite partisanship and compare the
reports from their foreign correspondents on some question
of home politics, he may, if a novice, be surprised to learn
that according to one, the opinion e. g. of Vienna is wholly
adverse to the measure, while, according to the other, that
opinion entirely approves.   It is no new thing to find
Hegelianism in general obloquy.   Even in 1830 the Catholic
philosopher and theologian Günther [1]—an admirer, but by
no means a follower of Hegel—wrote that, ' for some years
it had been the fashion in learned Germany to look upon
philosophy, and above all Hegelian philosophy, as a door-
mat on which everybody cleaned his muddy boots before
entering the sanctuary of politics and religion.'   What is
true as regards the alleged surcease of Hegelianism is that
in the reaction which from various causes turned itself
against philosophy in the two decennia after 1848, that
system, as the most deeply committed part of the ' metaphysical ' host, suffered most severely.   History and
science seemed to triumph along the whole line.   But it
may be perhaps permissible to remark that Hegelianism
had predicted for itself the fate that it proved had fallen
on all other philosophies.   After the age of Idealism comes
the turn of Realism.   The Idea had to die—had to sink as
a germ in the fields of nature and history before it could
bear its fruit.   Above all it is not to be expected that such
a system, so ambitious in aim and concentrated in expression, could find immediate response and at once disclose all
its meaning.   His first disciples are not the truest interpreters of any great teacher.   What he saw in the one
comprehensive glance of genius, his successors must often
be content to gather by the slow accumulation of years,
and perhaps centuries, of experience.   It is not to Theo-
phrastus that we go for the truest and fullest conception of
Aristotelianism ; nor is Plato to be measured by what his
immediate successors in the Academy managed to make
out of him.   It is now more than a century since Kant gave
his lesson to the public, and we are still trying to get him
focussed in a single view : it may be even longer till Hegel
comes fully within the range of our historians of thought.

[1] Hegel's *Briefe*, ii. 349.

Aristotelianism too had to wait centuries till it fully entered the consciousness even of the thinking world.

It is to be said too that without Hegel it would be difficult to imagine what even teachers, like Lotze, who were very unlike him, would have had to say. It does not need a very wide soul, nor need one be a mere dilettanist eclectic, to find much of Schopenhauer's work far from incompatible with his great, and as some have said, complementary opposite. It is not indeed prudent as yet for a writer in Germany who wishes to catch the general ear to affix too openly a profession of Hegelian principles, and he will do well to ward off suspicion by some disparaging remarks on the fantastic methods, the overfondness for system, the contempt for common sense and scientific results which, as he declares, vitiate all the speculations of the period from 1794 to 1830. But under the names of Spinoza and of Leibniz the leaven of Hegelian principles has been at work : and if the Philistines solve the riddle of the intellectual Samson, it is because they have ploughed with his heifer,— because his ideas are part of the modern stock of thought, —not from what they literally read in the great thinkers at the close of the seventeenth century. Last year saw appear in Germany two excellent treatises describable as popular introductions to philosophy,[1] one by a thinker who has never disguised his obligations to Hegel, the other by a teacher in the University of Berlin who may in many ways be considered as essentially kindred with our general English style of thought. But both treatises are more allied in character to the spirit of the Hegelian attempts to comprehend man and God than to the formalistic and philological disquisitions which have for some years formed the staple of German professorial activity. And, lastly, the vigorous thinker, who a quarter of a century ago startled the reading public by the portent of a new metaphysic which should be the synthesis of Schelling and Schopenhauer, has lately informed us [2] that ' his affinity to Hegel is, taken all in all, greater than his affinity to any other philosopher ' ; and that that affinity extends to all that in Hegel has essential and permanent value.

[1] J. Volkelt, *Vorträge zur Einführung in die Philosophie der Gegenwart* (München 1892) : F. Paulsen, *Einleitung in die Philosophie* (Berlin 1892).

[2] E. v. Hartmann, *Kritische Wanderungen*, p. 74.

But it is not on Eduard von Hartmann's commendation that we need rest our estimate of Hegelianism. We shall rather say that, till more of Hegel has been assimilated, he must still block the way. Things have been altered greatly in the last twenty years, it is true ; and ideas of more or less Hegelian origin have taken their place in the common stock of philosophic commodities. But it will probably be admitted by those best qualified to speak on the subject, that the shower has not as yet penetrated very deeply into the case-hardened soil, still less saturated it in the measure most likely to cause fruitful shoots to grow forth. We have to go back to Hegel in the same spirit as we go to Kant, and, for that matter, to Plato or Descartes : or, as the moderns may go back—to borrow from another sphere—to Dante or Shakespeare. We do not want the modern poet to resuscitate the style and matter of *King Lear* or of the *Inferno*. Yet as the Greek tragedian steeped his soul in the language and the legend of Homeric epic, as Dante nurtured his spirit on the noble melodies of Mantua's poet ; so philosophy, if it is to go forth strong and effective, must mould into its own substance the living thought of former times. It would be as absurd, and as impossible to be literally and simply a Hegelian,—if that means one for whom Hegel sums up all philosophy and all truth—as it is to be at the present day in the literal sense a Platonist or an Aristotelian. The world may be slow, the world of opinion and thought may linger : *e pur si muove*. We too have our own problems—the same, no doubt, in a sense, from age to age, and yet infinitely varying and never in two ages alike. New stars have appeared on the spiritual sky ; and whether they have in them the eternal light or only the flash and glare of a passing meteor, they alter the aspects of the night in which we are still waiting for the dawn. A new language, born of new relations of ideas, or of new ideas, is perforce for our generation the vehicle of all utterances, and we cannot again speak the dialect, however imposing or however quaint, of a vanished day.

And for that reason there must always be a new philosophy, couched in the language of the age, sympathetic with its hopes and fears, conscious of its beliefs, more or less sensible of its problems—as indeed we may be confident there always will be. But, perhaps, the warrior in that battle against illusion and prejudice, against the sloth

which takes things as they are and the poorness of spirit
which is satisfied with first appearances, will not do wisely
to disdain the past. He will not indeed equip himself with
rusty swords and clumsy artillery from the old arsenals.
But he will not disdain the lessons of the past,—its methods
and principles of tactics and strategy. Recognising perhaps some defects and inequalities in the methods and aims
of thought most familiar to him and current in his vicinity,
he may go abroad for other samples, even though they be
not in all respects worth his adoption. And so without
taking Hegel as omniscient, or pledging himself to every
word of the master, he may think from his own experience
that there is much in the system that will be helpful, when
duly estimated and assimilated, to others. There is—and
few can be so bigoted or so positive-minded as to regret
it—there is unquestionably a growing interest in English-
speaking countries in what may be roughly called philosophy—the attempt, unprejudiced by political, scientific,
or ecclesiastical dogma, to solve the questions as to what
the world really is, and what man's place and function is.
' The burthen of the mystery, the heavy and the weary
weight of all this unintelligible world ' is felt—felt widely
and sometimes felt deeply. To the direct lightening of that
burthen and that mystery it is the privilege of our profoundest thinkers and our far-seeing poets and artists to
contribute. To the translator of Hegel there falls the
humbler task of making accessible, if it may be, something
of one of the later attempts at a solution of the enigma of
life and existence,—an attempt which for a time dazzled
some of the keenest intellects of its age, and which has at
least impressed many others with the conviction, born of
momentary flashes from it of vast illuminant power, that
—*si sic omnia*—there was here concealed a key to many
puzzles, and a guard against many illusions likely to beset
the inquirer after truth.

CHAPTER III

ENGLISH PHILOSOPHY AND HEGEL

ALTHOUGH we need not take too seriously Hegel's remark (vol. ii. p. 13) on the English conception of philosophy, it may be admitted that, by the dominant school of English thought, philosophy, taken in the wide sense it has predominantly borne abroad, was, not so very long ago, all but entirely ignored. Causes of various kinds had turned the energy of the English mind into other directions, not less essential to the common welfare. Practical needs and an established social system helped to bind down studies to definite and particular objects, and to exclude what seemed vague and general investigations with no immediate bearing on the business of life. Hence philosophy in England could hardly exist except when it was reduced to the level of a special branch of science, or when it could be used as a receptacle for the principles and methods common to all the sciences. The general term was often used to denote the wisdom of this world, or the practical exhibition of self-control in life and action. For those researches, which are directed to the objects once considered proper to philosophy, the more definite and characteristic term came to be Mental and Moral Science.

The old name was in certain circles restricted to denote the vague and irregular speculations of those thinkers, who either lived before the rise of exact science, or who acted in defiance of its precepts and its example. One large and influential class of English thinkers inclined to sweep philosophy altogether away, as equivalent to metaphysics and obsolete forms of error ; and upon the empty site thus obtained they sought to construct a psychological theory of mind, or they tried to arrange and codify those general remarks upon the general procedure of the sciences which are known under the name of Inductive Logic. A smaller, but not less vigorous, school of philosophy looked upon their business as an extension and rounding off of science into a complete unification of knowledge. The first is illustrated by the names of J. S. Mill and Mr. Bain : the second is the doctrine of Mr. Herbert Spencer.

The encyclopaedic aggregate of biological, psychological, ethical and social investigation which Mr. Spencer pursues, under the general guidance of the formula of evolution by differentiation and integration, still proceeds on its course : but though its popularity—as such popularity goes —is vast and more than national, it does not and probably cannot find many imitators. Very differently stand matters with the movement in psychology and logic. Here the initiative has led to divergent and unexpected developments. Psychology, which at first was partly an ampler and a more progressive logic, a theory of the origin and nature of knowledge, partly a propaedeutic to the more technical logic and ethics, and pursued in a loosely introspective way, has gravitated more and more towards its experimental and physiological side, with occasional velleities to assume the abstractly-mathematical character of a psycho-physical science. Logic, on the other hand, has also changed its scope. Not content to be a mere tool of the sciences or a mere criterion for the estimation of evidence, it has in one direction grown into a systematic effort to become an epistemology—a system of the first principles of knowledge and reality—a metaphysic of science ; and in another it has sought to realise the meaning of those old forms of inference which the logicians of half a century ago were inclined to pooh-pooh as obsolete. Most remarkable—and most novel of all—is the vast increase of interest and research in the problems of ethics and of what is called the philosophy of religion—subjects which at that date were literally burning questions, apt to scorch the fingers of those who touched them. In all of this, but especially marked in some leading thinkers, the ruling feature is the critical—the sceptical, i. e. the eager, watchful, but self-restrained—attitude towards its themes. Ever driving on to find a deeper unity than shows on the surface, and to get at principles, the modern thinker—and in this we see the permanent and almost overwhelming influence of Kant upon him—recoils from the dogmatism of system, at the very moment it seems to be within his grasp.

Thus the recent products of English thought have been, as Mr. Spencer has taught us to say, partly in the line of differentiation, partly of integration. At one moment it seems as if the ancient queen of the sciences sat like Hecuba, *exul, inops*, while her younger daughters enjoyed the freedom and progress of specialisation. The wood seems lost behind the trees. And at another, again, the centripetal force seems to preponderate: every department, logic, ethics, psychology, sociology, rapidly carries its students on and up to fundamental questions, if not to fundamental principles. Philosophy—the one and undivided truth and quest of truth—emerges fresh, vigorous, and as yet rather indeterminate, from the mass of detailed investigations. That the position is now altered from what it was in times when knowledge had fewer departments, is obvious. The task of the ' synoptic ' mind—which Plato claims for the philosopher—grows increasingly difficult : but that is hardly a reason for performing it in a more perfunctory way. It seems rather as if in such a crisis one of the great reconstructive systems of a preceding age might be in some measure helpful.

If we consult history, it is at once clear that philosophy, or the pursuit of ultimate reality and permanent truth, went hand in hand with scientific researches into facts and their particular explanations.

In their earlier stages the two tendencies of thought were scarcely distinguishable. The philosophers of Ionia and Magna Graecia were also the scientific pioneers of their time. Their fragmentary remains remind us at times of the modern theories of geology and biology,—at other times of the teachings of idealism. The same thing is comparatively true of the earlier philosophers of Modern Europe. The seventeenth and eighteenth centuries, in spite of Bacon and Newton, endeavoured to study the mental and moral life by a method which was a strange mixture of empiricism and metaphysics. In words, indeed, the thinkers from Descartes to Wolff duly emphasise, perhaps over-emphasise, the antithesis between the extended and the intellectual. But in practice their course is not so clear. Their mental philosophy is often only a preliminary *medicina mentis* to set the individual mind in good order for undertaking the various tasks awaiting a special research. They are really eager to get on to business, and only, as it were, with regret spend time in this clearance of mental faculty. And when they do deal with objects, the material and extended tends to become the dominant conception, the basis of reality. The human mind, that *nobilissima substantia*, is treated only as an aggregate, or a receptacle, of ideas, and the *mens*,—with them all nearly as with Spinoza,—is only an *idea corporis*, and that phrase not taken so highly as Spinoza's perhaps should be taken. In the works of these thinkers, as of the pre-Socratics, there is one element which may be styled philosophical, and another element which may be styled scientific,—if we use both words vaguely. But with Socrates in the ancient, and with Kant in the modern epoch of philosophy, an attempt was made to get the boundary between the two regions definitively drawn. The distinction was in the first place accompanied by something like turning the back upon science and popular conceptions. Socrates withdrew thought from disquisitions concerning the nature of all things, and fixed it upon man and the state of man. Kant left the broad fields of actually-attained knowledge, and inquired into the central principle on which the acquisition of science, the laws of human life, and the ideals of art and religion, were founded.

The change thus begun was not unlike that which Copernicus effected in the theory of Astronomy. Human personality, either in the actualised forms of the State, or in the abstract shape of the Reason,—that intellectual liberty, which is a man's true world,—was, at least by implication, made the pivot around which the system of the sciences might turn. In the contest, which according to Reid prevails between Common Sense and Philosophy, the presumptions of the former have been distinctly reversed, and Kant, like Socrates, has shown that it is not the several items of fact, but the humanity, the moral law, the thought, which underlies these doctrines, which give the real resting-point and true centre of movement. But this negative attitude of philosophy to the sciences is only the beginning, needed to secure a standing-ground. In the ancient world Aristotle, and in the modern Hegel (as the inheritor of the labours of Fichte and Schelling), exhibit the movement outwards to reconquer the universe, proceeding from that principle which Socrates and Kant had emphasised in its fundamental worth.

Mr. Mill, in the closing chapter of his Logic, has briefly sketched the ideal of a science to which he gives the name of Teleology, corresponding in the ethical and practical sphere to a *Philosophia Prima*, or Metaphysics, in the theoretical. This ideal and ultimate court of appeal is to be valid in Morality, and also in Prudence, Policy and Taste. But the conception, although a desirable one, falls short of the work which Hegel assigns to philosophy. What he intended to accomplish with detail and regular evolution was not a system of principles in these departments of action only, but a theory which would give its proper place in our total Idea of reality to Art, Science, and Religion, to all the consciousness of ordinary life, and to the evolution of the physical universe. Philosophy ranges over the whole field of actuality, or existing fact. Abstract principles are all very well in their way ; but they are not philosophy. If the world in its historical and its present life develops into endless detail in regular lines, philosophy must equally develop the narrowness of its first principles into the plenitude of a System,—into what Hegel calls the Idea. His point of view may be gathered from the following remarks in a review of Hamann, an erratic friend and fellow-citizen of Kant's. ' Hamann would not put himself to the trouble, which in an higher sense God undertook. The ancient philosophers have described God under the image of a round ball. But if that be His nature, God has unfolded it ; and in the actual world He has opened the closed shell of truth into a system of Nature, into a State-system, a system of Law and Morality, into the system of the world's History. The shut fist has become an open hand, the fingers of which reach out to lay hold of man's mind, and draw it to Himself. Nor is the human mind a self-involved intelligence, blindly moving within its own secret recesses. It is no mere feeling and groping about in a vacuum, but an intelligent system of rational organisation. Of that system Thought is the summit in point of form : and Thought may be described as the capability of going beyond the mere surface of God's self-expansion,—or rather as the capability, by means of reflection upon it, of entering into it, and then when the entrance has been secured, of retracing in thought God's expansion of Himself. To take this trouble is the express duty and end of ends set before the thinking mind, ever since God laid aside His rolled-up form, and revealed Himself.' [1]

[1] *Vermischte Schriften*, vol. ii. p. 87.

Enthusiastic admirers have often spoken as if the salvation of the time could only come from the Hegelian philosophy. ' Grasp the secret of Hegel,' they say, ' and you will find a cure for the delusions of your own mind, and the remedy which will set right the wrongs of the world.' These high claims to be a panacea were never made by Hegel himself. According to him, as according ·to Aristotle, philosophy *as such* can produce nothing new. Practical statesmen, and theoretical reformers, may do their best to correct the inequalities of their time. But the very terms in which Bacon scornfully depreciated one great concept of philosophy are to be accepted in their literal truth. Like a virgin consecrated to God, she bears no fruit.[1] She represents the spirit of the world, resting, as it were, when one step in the progress has been accomplished, and surveying the advance which has been made. ' Philosophy is not,' says Fichte, ' even a means to *shape* life : for it lies in a totally different world, and what is to have an influence upon life must itself have sprung from life. Philosophy is only a means to the *knowledge* of life.' Nor has it the vocation to edify men, and take the place of religion on the higher levels of intellect. ' The philosopher,' Fichte boldly continues, ' has no God at all and can have no God : he has only a concept of the concept or of the Idea of God. It is only in life that there is God and religion : but the philosopher as such is not the whole complete man, and it is impossible for any one to be *only* a philosopher.' [2] Philosophy does not profess to bring into being what ought to be, but is not yet. It sets up no mere ideals, which must wait for some future day in order to be realised. Enough for it if it show what the world *is*, if it were what it professes to be, and what in a way it must be, otherwise it could not be even what it is. The subject-matter of philosophy is that which is always realising and always realised—the world in its wholeness as it is and has been. It seeks to put before us, and embody in permanent outlines, the universal law of spiritual life and growth, and not the local, temporary, and individual acts of human will.

Those who ask philosophy to construe, or to deduce

[1] *De Augm. Scient.* iii. 5.
[2] The passages occur in some notes (written down by F. in reference to the charge of Atheism) published in his *Werke*, v. pp. 342, 348.

a priori a single blade of grass, or a single act of a man, must not be grieved if their request sounds absurd and meets with no answer. The sphere of philosophy is the Universal. We may say, if we like, that it is retrospective. It is the spectator of all time and all existence : it is its duty to view things *sub specie aeternitatis*. To comprehend the universe of thought in all its formations and all its features, to reduce the solid structures, which mind has created, to fluidity and transparency in the pure medium of thought, to set free the fossilised intelligence which the great magician who wields the destinies of the world has hidden under the mask of Nature, of the Mind of man, of the works of Art, of the institutions of the State and the orders of Society, and of religious forms and creeds :— such is the complicated problem of philosophy. Its special work is to comprehend the world, not try to make it better. If it were the purpose of philosophy to reform and improve the existing state of things, it comes a little too late for such a task. ' As the thought of the world,' says Hegel, ' it makes its first appearance at a time, when the actual fact has consummated its process of formation, and is now fully matured. This is the doctrine set forth by the notion of philosophy ; but it is also the teaching of history. It is only when the actual world has reached its full fruition that the ideal rises to confront the reality, and builds up, in the shape of an intellectual realm, that same world grasped in its substantial being. When philosophy paints its grey in grey, some one shape of life has meanwhile grown old : and grey in grey, though it brings it into knowledge, cannot make it young again. The owl of Minerva does not start upon its flight, until the evening twilight has begun to fall.' [1]

[1] *Philosophie des Rechts*, p. 20 (*Werke*, viii).

CHAPTER IV

HEGEL AND THEOLOGY

EVEN an incidental glance into Hegel's Logic cannot fail to discover the frequent recurrence of the name of God, and the discussion of matters not generally touched upon, unless in works bearing upon religion. There were two questions which seem to have had a certain fascination for Hegel. One of them, a rather unpromising problem, referred to the distances between the several planets in the solar system, and the law regulating these intervals.[1] The other and more intimate problem turned upon the value of the proofs usually offered in support of the being of God. That God is the supreme certitude of the mind, the basis of all reality and knowledge, is what Hegel no more put in question, than did Descartes, Spinoza, or Locke. What he often repeated was that the *matter* in these proofs must be distinguished from the imperfect *manner* in which the arguers presented it. Again and again in his Logic, as well as in other discussions more especially devoted to it, he examines this problem. His persistence in this direction might earn for him that title of ' Knight of the Holy Ghost ', by which Heine, in one of the delightful poems of his ' Reisebilder ', describes himself to the maid of Klausthal in the Harz. The poet of Love and of Freedom had undoubted rights to rank among the sacred band : but so also had the philosopher. Like the Socrates whom Plato describes to us, he seems to feel that he has been commissioned to reveal the truth of God,

---

[1] Hegel's *Leben*, p. 155. It was in his dissertation *de Orbitis Planetarum*, that the notorious contretemps occurred, whereby, whilst the philosopher, leaning to a Pythagorean proportion, hinted —in a line—that it was unnecessary to expect a planet between Mars and Jupiter, astronomers in the same year discovered Ceres, the first-detected of the Planetoids. A good deal has been made out of this trifle ; but it has not yet been shown that the corroboration was anything but the *luck* of the other hypothesis.

and quicken men by an insight into the right wisdom. Nowhere in the modern period of philosophy has higher spirit breathed in the utterances of a thinker. The same theme is claimed as the common heritage of philosophy and religion. A letter to Duboc,[1] the father of a modern German novelist, lets us see how important this aspect of his system was to Hegel himself. He had been asked to give a succinct explanation of his standing-ground : and his answer begins by pointing out that philosophy seeks to apprehend in reasoned knowledge the same truth which the religious mind has in its faith.

Words like these may at first sight suggest the bold soaring of ancient speculation in the times of Plato and Aristotle, or even the theories of the medieval Schoolmen. They sound as if he proposed to do for the modern world, and in the full light of modern knowledge, what the Schoolmen tried to accomplish within the somewhat narrow conceptions of medieval Christianity and Greek logic. Still there is a difference between the two cases. While the Doctors of the Church, in appearance at least, derived the form of exposition, and the matter of their systems, from two independent and apparently heterogeneous sources, the modern Scholastic of Hegel claims to be a harmonious unity, body finding soul, and soul giving itself body. And while the Hegelian system has the all-embracing and encyclopaedic character by which Scholastic science threw its arms around heaven and earth, it has also the untrammeled liberty of the Greek thinkers. Hegel, in short, shows the union of these two modes of speculation : free as the ancient, and comprehensive as the modern. His theory is the explication of God ; but of God in the actuality and plenitude of the world, and not as a transcendent Being, such as an over-reverent philosophy has sometimes supposed him, in the solitude of a world beyond.

The greatness of a philosophy is its power of comprehending facts. The most characteristic fact of modern times is Christianity. The general thought and action of the civilised world has been alternately fascinated and

---

[1] *Vermischte Schriften*, vol. ii. p. 520. Duboc was a retired hatter, of French origin, who had settled at Hamburg (Hegel's *Briefe*, ii. 76 seqq.).

repelled, but always influenced, and to a high degree permeated, by the Christian theory of life, and still more by
the faithful vision of that life displayed in the Son of Man.
To pass that great cloud of witness and leave it on the
other side, is to admit that your system is no key to the
secret of the world,—even if we add, as some will prefer,
of the world as it is and has been. And therefore the
Hegelian system, if it is to be a philosophy at all, must be
in this sense Christian. But it is neither a critic, nor an
apologist of historical Christianity. The voice of philosophy is as that of the Jewish doctor of the Law : ' If this
council or this work be of men, it will come to nought :
but if it be of God, ye cannot overthrow it.' Philosophy
examines what is, and not what, according to some opinions,
ought to be. Such a point of view requires no discussion
of the ' How ' or the ' Why ' of Christianity. It involves
no inquiry into historical documents, or into the belief in
miracles : for to it Christianity rests only incidentally on
the evidence of history ; and miracles, as vulgarly explained,
can find no reception in a philosophical system. For it
Christianity is ' absolute religion ' : religion i. e. which has
fully become and realised all that religion meant to be.
That religion has, of course, its historical side : it appeared
at a definite epoch in the annals of our race : it revealed
itself in a unique personality in a remarkable nation. And
at an early period of his life Hegel had tried to gather up
in one conception the traits of that august figure, in his
life and speech and death. But, in the light of philosophy, this historical side shrivels up as comparatively
unimportant. Not the personality, but the ' revelation
of reason ' through man's spirit : not the annals of a
life once spent in serving God and men, but the words
of the ' Eternal Gospel ', are henceforth the essence of
Christianity.

Thus the controlling and central conception of life and
actuality, which is the final explanation of all that man
thinks and does, has a twofold aspect. There is, as it
were, a double Absolute—for under this name philosophy
has what in religion corresponds to God. It is true that in
the final form of his system the Absolute Spirit has three
phases—each as it were passing on into and incorporated
with the next—Art working out its implications till it
appears as Religion, and Religion calling for its perfection

in Philosophy. But in the *Phenomenology*, his first work, the religion of Art only intervenes as a grade from ' natural ' religion to religion manifest or revealed ; and in the first edition of the *Encyclopaedia* what is subsequently called Art is entitled the Religion of Art. It is in entire accordance with these indications when in the Lectures on Aesthetics [1] it is said ' the true and original position of Art is to be the first-come immediate self-satisfaction of Absolute Spirit ' ; though in our days (it is added) ' its form has ceased to be the highest need of the spirit '. It is hardly too much then to say that, for Hegel, the Absolute has two phases, Religion and Philosophy.

The Hegelian view presents itself most decisively, though perhaps with a little lecture-like over-insistance, in the Philosophy of Religion. [2] ' The object of religion as of philosophy is the eternal truth in its very objectivity,—God and nothing but God,—and the " explication " of God. Philosophy is not a wisdom of the world, but cognition of the non-worldly : not a cognition of the external mass of empirical existence and life, but cognition of what is eternal, what is God, and what flows from His nature. For this nature must reveal and develop itself. Hence philosophy " explicates " itself only when it " explicates " religion ; and in explicating itself it explicates religion. . . . Thus religion and philosophy coincide : in fact, philosophy is itself a divine service, is a religion : for it is the same renunciation of subjective fancies and opinions, and is engaged with God alone.'

Again, it may be asked in what sense philosophy has to deal with God and with Truth. These two terms are often synonyms in Hegel. All the objects of science, all the terms of thought, all the forms of reality, lead out of themselves, and seek for a centre and resting-point. They are severally inadequate and partial, and they crave adequacy and completeness. They tend to organise themselves ; to call out more and more distinctly the fuller reality which they presuppose,—which must have been, otherwise they could not have been : they reduce their first appearance of completeness to its due grade of inadequacy and bring out their complementary side, so as to constitute a system or universe ; and in this tendency to a self-correcting unity

[1] *Werke*, x. 1, p. 131.   [2] Ibid., xi. p. 21.

consists their progress to truth. Their untruth lies in
isolation and pretended independence or finality. This
completed unity, in which all things receive their entireness
and become adequate, is their Truth : and that Truth, as
known in religious language, is God. Rightly or wrongly,
God is thus interpreted in the Logic of Hegel.

Such a position must seem very strange to one who is
familiar only with the sober studies of English philosophy.
In whatever else the leaders of the several schools in this
country disagree, they are nearly all at one in banishing
God and religion to a world beyond the present sublunary
sphere, to an inscrutable region beyond the scope of scientific
inquiry, where statements may be made at will, but where
we have no power of verifying any statement whatever.
This is the common doctrine of Spencer and Mansel, of
Hamilton and Mill. Even those English thinkers, who
show some anxiety to support what is at present called
Theism, generally rest content with vindicating for the
mind the vague perception of a Being beyond us, and
differing from us incommensurably. God is to them a
residual phenomenon, a marginal existence. Outside the
realm of experience and knowledge there is not-nothing—
a something—beyond definite circumscription : incalculable,
and therefore an object, possibly of fear, possibly of hope :
the reflection in the utter darkness of a great What-may-it-
not-be ? He is the Unknown Power, felt by what some of
these writers call intuition, and others call experience.
They do not however allow to knowledge any capacity of
apprehending in detail the truths which belong to the
kingdom of God. Now the whole teaching of Hegel is the
overthrow of the limits thus set to religious thought. To
him all thought, and all actuality when it is grasped by
knowledge, is from man's side, an exaltation of the mind
towards God : while, when regarded from the divine standing-point, it is the manifestation by God of His own nature
in its infinite variety.

It is only when we fix our eyes clearly on these general
features in his speculation, that we can understand why
he places the maturity of ancient philosophy in the time of
Plotinus and Proclus. Not that these Neo-Platonists are,
as thinkers, of power equal to their master of Athens.
But, in the realm of the blind the one-eyed may be king.
The later thinkers set their vision more distinctly and

persistently on the land that is eternal—' on the further side of being ', to quote Plato's phrase.   It is for the same reason Hegel gives so much attention to the religious or semi-religious theories of Jacob Böhme and of Jacobi, though these men were in many ways so unlike himself.

CHAPTER V

PSEUDO-IDEALISM : JACOBI

It is hazardous to try to sum up the net result of a philosophy in a few paragraphs. Since Aristotle separated the pure ' energy ' of philosophy from the activities which leave works made and deeds done behind them, it need scarcely be repeated that the result of a philosophical system is nothing palpable or tangible,—nothing on which you can put your finger, and say definitely : Here it is. The spirit of a philosophy always refuses to be incarcerated in a formula, however deftly you may try to charm it there. The statement of the principle or tendency of a philosophical system tells not what that system is, but what it is not. It marks off the position from contiguous points of view ; and on that account never gets beyond the border-land, which separates that system from something else. The method and process of reasoning is as essential in knowledge, as the result to which it leads : and the method in this case is thoroughly bound up with the subject-matter. A mere analysis of the method, therefore, or a mere record of the purpose and outcome of the system, would be, the one as well as the other, a fruitless labour, and come to nothing but words. Thus any attempt to convey a glimpse of the truth in a few sentences and in large outlines seems fore-closed. The theory of Hegel has an abhorrence of mere generalities, of abstractions with no life in them, and no growth out of them. His principle has to prove and verify itself to be true and adequate : and that verification fills up the whole circle of circles, of which philosophy is said to consist.

It seems as if there were in Hegel two distinct habits of mind which the world—the outside observer—rarely sees except in separation. On one hand there is a sympathy with mystical and intuitional minds, with the upholders of immediate knowledge and of innate ideas, with those who find that science and demonstration rather tend to distract from the one thing needful—who would 'lie in Abraham's bosom all the year ',—those who would fain lay their grasp upon the whole before they have gone through the drudgery of details. On the other hand, there is within him a strongly ' rationalising ' and non-visionary intellect, with a practical and realistic bent, and the full scientific spirit. Schelling, in an angry mood, could describe him as ' the quintessence of all that is prosaic, both outside and in '.[1] Yet, seen from other points of view, Hegel has been accused of dreaminess, pietism, and mystical theology. His merging of the ordinary contrasts of thought in a completer truth, and what would popularly be described as his mixing up of religious with logical questions, and the general unfathomableness of his doctrine,—all seem to support such a charge. Yet all this is not inconsistent with a rough and incisive vigour of understanding, a plainness of reason, and a certain hardness of temperament. This philosopher is in many ways not distinguishable from the ordinary citizen, and there are not unfrequent moments when his wife hears him groan over the providence that condemned him to be a philosopher.[2] He is contemptuous towards all weakly sentimentalism, and almost brutal in his emphasis on the reasonableness of the actual and on the folly of dreaming the might-have-been ; and keeps his household accounts as carefully as the average head of a family. And, perhaps, this convergence of two tendencies of thought may be noticed in the gradual maturing of his ideas. In the period of his ' Lehrjahre ', or apprenticeship, from 1793 to 1800, we can see the study of religion in the earlier part of that time at Bern succeeded by the study of politics and philosophy at Frankfort-on-the-Main.

His purpose on the whole may be termed an attempt to combine breadth with depth, the intensity of the mystic who craves for union with Truth, with the extended range and explicitness of those who multiply knowledge. ' The depth of the mind is only so deep as its courage to expand and lose itself in its explication.' [3] It must prove its profundity by the ordered fullness of the knowledge which it has realised. The position and the work of Hegel will not

[1] *Aus Schellings Leben* (Plitt.), ii. 161.
[2] Hegel's *Briefe*, ii. 377.
[3] *Phenomenologie des Geistes*, p. 9.

be intelligible unless we keep in view both of these antagonistic points.

The purpose of philosophy—as has been pointed out—is, for Hegel—to know God, which is to know things in their Truth—to see all things in God—to comprehend the world in its eternal significance. Supposing the purpose, capable of being achieved, what method is open to its attainment? There is on one hand the method of ordinary science in dealing with its objects. These are *things*, found as it were projected into space before the observer, lying outside one another in *prima facie* independence, though connected (by a further finding) with each other by certain ' accidents' called qualities and relations. Among the objects of knowledge, there are included, by the somewhat naïve intellect that accepts tradition like a physical fact, certain ' things' of a rather peculiar character. One of these is God : the others, which a historical criticism has subjoined, are the Soul and the World. And whatever may be said of the thinghood, reality, or existence of the World, there is no doubt that God and the Soul figure, and figure largely, in the consciousness of the human race as entities, differing probably in many respects from other things, but still possessed of certain fundamental features in common, and thus playing a part as distinct realities amongst other realities.

Given such objects, it is natural for a reflecting mind to attempt to make out a science of God and a science of the Soul, just as of other ' things '. And to these a system-loving philosopher might add a science of the world (Cosmology).[1] It was felt, indeed, that these objects were peculiar and unique. Thus, for example, as regards God, it was held necessary by the logician who saw tradition in its true light to prove His ' existence ': and various arguments to that end were at different times devised. With regard to the human Soul, similarly, it was considered essential to establish its independent reality as a thing really separate from the bodily organism with which its phenomena were obviously connected,—to prove, in short, its substantial existence, and its emancipation from the bodily fate of dissolution and decay. With reference to the World, the problem was rather different : it was felt that the name

[1] Cf. Notes and Illustrations in vol. ii. 396, and chapter iii. of the *Logic*.

suggested problems for thought rather than denoted reality. How can we predicate of the whole what is predicable of its parts ? This or that may have a beginning and a cause, may have a limit and an end : but can the totality be presented under these aspects, without leading to self-contradiction ? And the result of these questions in the case of ' Cosmology ' was to shed in the long run similar doubts on ' Rational ' Theology and ' Rational ' Psychology.

Practically this metaphysical science—which is so called as dealing with a province or provinces of being *beyond* the ordinary or natural (*physical*) realities—treated God and the Soul by the same terms (or *categories*) as it is used in dealing with ' material ' objects. God e. g. was a force, a cause, a being ; so, too, was the Soul. The main butt of Kant's destructive *Criticism of pure Reason* is to challenge the justice of including God and the Soul among the objects of science,—among the things we can know as we may know plants or stars. To make an object of knowledge (in the strict sense), to make a thing, the prerequisite, Kant urges, is perception in space and time. Without a sensation— and that sensation, as it were, laid out in place and duration —an object of science is impossible. No mere demonstra-tion will conjure it into existence. And with that require-ment the old theology and psychology, which professed to expound the object-God and the object-soul, were ruled out-of-order in the list of sciences, and reduced to mere dialectical exercises. The circle of the sciences, therefore, does not lead beyond the ' conditioned ', beyond the regions of space and time. It has nothing to say of a ' first cause ' or of an ultimate end.

Such was the result that might fairly be read from Kant's *Criticism of pure Reason,*—especially if read without its supplementary sequels, and, above all, if read by those in whom feeling was stronger than thought, or who were by nature more endowed with the craving for faith than with the mind of philosophy. Such a personality appeared in J. H. Jacobi, the younger brother of a poet not undistinguished in his day. Amid the duties of public office and the cares of business, he found time to study Spinoza, the English and Scotch moralists, and above all to follow with interest the development of Kant from the year 1763 onwards. His house at Düsseldorf was the scene of many literary reunions, and Jacobi himself maintained familiar

intercourse with the leaders of the literary and intellectual
world, such as Lessing, Hamann, Goethe. His first considerable works were two novels, in letters,—Allwill, begun in
a serial magazine in 1775, and Woldemar, begun in another
magazine in 1777 ; both being issued as complete works in
1781. Both turn on a moral antithesis, and both leave the
antithesis as they found it. *Here* pleads the advocate of
the heart : ' it is the heart which alone and directly tells
man what is good ' : ' virtue is a fundamental instinct of
human nature ' : the true basis of morals is an immediate
certainty ; and the supreme standard is an ' ethical genius '
which as it were discovered virtue and which still is a
paramount authority in those exceptional situations in life
when the ' grammar of virtue ' fails to supply adequate rules,
and where, therefore, the immediate voice of conscience
must in a ' licence of sublime poesy ' [1] dare, as Burke says,
to ' suspend its own rules in favour of its own principles '.
There, on the other hand, is the champion of reason, who
declares all this sentimentalism ' a veritable mysticism of
antinomianism and a quietism of immorality ' : [2] ' To
humanity,' he says, ' and to every man (every complete
man) principles, and some system of principles, are indispensable.' Woldemar concludes with the pair of mottoes :
' Whosoever trusts to his own heart is a fool,' and ' Trust
love : it takes everything, but it gives everything.'

    In 1780 Jacobi had his historic conversation with Lessing
at Wolfenbüttel.[3] The talk turned on Spinoza. For many
years the philosophy of Spinoza had seemed to vanish from
the world. His name was only heard in a reference of
obloquy, as if it were dangerous to be even suspected of
infection with the taint of Atheism. But both Lessing and
Jacobi had found him out. The former saw in him an ally
in that struggle for higher light and wider views which he
undertook in a spirit and with a scope hardly surmised by
those he usually wrought with. Jacobi, on the contrary,
saw in him personified the conjunction of all those irreligious
tendencies which all philosophy in some degree exhibited :
the tendency to veil or set aside God and personality.
' I believe,' says Jacobi, as he began the conversation, ' in
an intelligent personal cause of the world.' ' Then I am
going,' replied Lessing, ' to hear something quite new ' : and

---

[1] Jacobi's *Werke*, v. 79, 111, 115, 417.   [2] Ibid., i. 178.
[3] Ibid., iv. i. Abth. p. 55 seqq.

he dryly put aside the other's rhapsody on the ' personal extra-mundane deity ' with the remark ' Words, my dear Jacobi, words.' Jacobi's work *Letters on the doctrine of Spinoza* (it appeared in 1785) was the beginning of a controversy in which Mendelssohn and Herder took part, and in which Goethe took an interest under Herder's tutorship. To the exact philological study of Spinoza it did not contribute much : for the Spinoza whom Herder and Goethe saw as their spiritual forefather was transfigured in their thought to a figure to which Leibniz had almost an equal right to give his name. He upheld to them the symbol of the immanence of the divine in nature : he was the leader in the battle against ' philistine ' deism and utilitarianism.

With the Kantian criticism of the pseudo-science of theology Jacobi had in one way no fault to find. That reasoning by its demonstration cannot find out God, was to him an axiomatic belief. But the ' man of feeling ' felt uneasy at the trenchant methods of the Königsberg man of logic. He seemed to see the world of men and things passing under Kant's manipulation into a mere collection of phenomena and ideas of the mind. Still more was he sensible to the loss of his God. That surrogate of an argument for theism which Kant seemed to offer in the implications of the Moral Law did not give what Jacobi wanted. Mere morality is a cold and mechanical principle— he thinks—compared with that infinite life and love which we deem we have in God. The son of man, he felt, was, in virtue of an indwelling genius of conscience, supreme over the moral law : how much more, then, the Absolute and Eternal on a higher grade of being than its mechanical regularities !

If the way of reasoning will not carry us to the Absolute, still less (and that is whither Jacobi wishes to reach) to God, there must be another way : for something in him, which may be called Faith or Feeling, Spiritual Sense or Reason, proclaims itself certain of the reality both of God and Nature. There *is* an objective reality—outside and beyond him—yet somehow to be reached by a daring leap,— whereby, out of sheer force of will, he, shutting his eyes to the temporal and the mechanical, finds himself carried over the dividing gulf into the land of eternal life and love. ' I appeal ' he says in his latest utterances [1] ' to an imperative

---

[1] Jacobi's *Werke*, iv. 1, p. xxi.

an invincible feeling as the first and underived ground
of all philosophy and all religion,—to a feeling which lets
man become aware of and alive to the fact that he has a
sense for the supersensuous.'   ' As it is religion which makes
man man,' he continues, ' and which alone lifts him above
the animals, so it also makes him a philosopher.'   Such an
organ for the supersensuous is what in his later writings he
calls *Vernunft* (Reason) and distinguishes from *Verstand*
(Understanding).   ' This reason,' says Coleridge (to whom
we owe this use of the terms in English) in the *Friend*, ' is
an organ bearing the same relation to spiritual objects as
the eye bears to material phenomena.'   It is ' that intuition
of things which arises when we possess ourselves as one with
the whole ', and is opposed to that ' science of the mere
understanding ' in which ' transferring reality to the negations of reality (to the ever-varying framework of the
uniform life) we think of ourselves as separated beings, and
place nature in antithesis to the mind, as object to subject,
thing to thought, death to life.'   But this Reason is even
more than this.   It is the direct contact with reality, which
it affirms and even *is*.   It apprehends the *me* and the *thee*,
it apprehends above all the great *Thee*, God : apprehends,
and we may even say appropriates.[1]   And it apprehends
them at one bound—in one *salto mortale*—because it
is really in implicit possession of them.   Call the step a
miracle, if you will : you must admit, he adds, that
' some time or other every philosophy must have recourse
to a miracle '.[2]

And yet the asseveration rings false—it shows a womanish
wilfulness and weakness in its reiteration.   He has the
reality ; yet he has it not.   ' Were a God known,' he says
in one place, ' He would not be God.'   He yearns with passionate longing to find the living and true : he feels himself
and the Eternal clasped in one : his faith effects the reality
of things hoped for.   But, he adds, ' We never see the
Absolute ' : the primal light of reason is but faint.   It is
but a presage—a pre-supposition—of the Everlasting.   This
reason, in short, needs discipline and development, it needs
the ethical life to raise it : ' without morality no religiosity,'
he says.   ' Light,' he complains, ' is in my heart,' but at
the moment I want to bring it into the understanding, the
light goes out.'   And yet he knows—and Coleridge repeats

[1] Jacobi's *Briefwechsel*, i. 330.   [2] Jacobi's *Werke*, iii. 53.

—' the consciousness of reason and of its revelations is only possible in an understanding.'

There seem to be one or two motives acting upon Jacobi. The ' plain man ', especially if he be of high character and of ' noble ' religiosity, has a feeling that the lust of philosophising disturbs the security of life, and endangers things which are deservedly dear to him. In such an one the ' enthusiasm of logic '—the calm pursuit of truth at all costs, so characteristic of Lessing—is inferior to the ' enthusiasm of life ',—a passion in which the terrestrial and the celestial are inextricably blended, where one clings to God as the stronghold of self, and sets personality—our human personality—in the throne of the Eternal. He will be all that is noble and good, if only he be not asked utterly to surrender self. So, too, Jacobi's God—or Absolute (for he leaves his ' non-philosophy ' so far as to use both names), is rather the final aim of a grand, overpowering yearning, than a calm, self-centred, self-expanding life which carries man along with it. It would be, he feels, so very terrible, if at the last there were no God to meet us—to find the throne of the universe vacant. Avaunt philosophy therefore ! Let us cling to the faith of our nature and our childhood, and refuse her treacherous consolations !

With the central proposition of Jacobi, Hegel, for one, is not inclined to quarrel. He too, as he asks and answers the question as to the issues of this and of the better life, might say

' Question, answer presuppose
Two points : that the thing itself which questions, answers,—*is*, it knows ;
As it also knows the thing perceived outside itself—a force
Actual ere its own beginning, operative through its course,
Unaffected by its end,—that this thing likewise needs must be ;
Call this—God, then, call that—Soul, and both the only facts for me.
Prove them facts ? that they o'erpass my power of proving proves them such :
Fact it is, I know, I know not something which is fact as much.'

But when Jacobi goes on to say that it is the supreme and final duty of the true sage ' to unveil reality ',— meaning thereby that, given the feeling, he has only to

' Define it well
For fear divine Philosophy
Should push beyond her mark and be
Procuress to the Lords of Hell,'

Hegel withdraws. It is the duty of philosophy to labour to make the perception—the fleeting, uncertain, trembling perception—of faith, a clear, sure, inwardly consistent knowledge : to show, and not merely to assert, that ' the path of (this world's) duty is the way to (that world's) glory '. There is, Hegel himself has said more than once, something opposed to ordinary ways of thinking in the procedure of the philosopher. To the outsider, it seems like standing on your head. It involves something like what, in religious language, is termed conversion—a new birth—becoming a new man. But though such a change always seems to culminate in a moment of sudden transformation,—as if the continuity of old and new were disrupted, the process has a history and a preparation. Of that pilgrim's progress of the world-distracted soul to its discovery of its true being in God, philosophy is the record : a record which Hegel has written both in the *Phenomenology of Mind*, and, more methodically, in his *Encyclopaedia*. The passage from nature to God—or from man's limitations to the divine fullness—must be made, he urged, in the open day and not in the secret vision when sleep falls upon men. When the aged Jacobi read these requirements of Hegel, he wrote to a friend : ' He may be right, and I should like once again to experiment with him all that the power of thinking can do alone, were not the old man's head too weak for it.' [1]

' For a philosophy like this,' says Hegel,[2] ' individual man and humanity are the ultimate standpoint :—as a fixed invincible finitude of reason, not as a reflection of the eternal beauty, or as a spiritual focus of the universe, but as an ultimate sense-nature, which however with the power of faith can daub itself over here and there with an alien supersensible. Let us suppose an artist restricted to por-trait-painting ; he might so far idealise as to introduce in the eye of a common-place countenance a yearning look, and on its lips a melancholy smile, but he would be utterly debarred from depicting the Gods, sublime over yearning and melancholy—as if the delineation of eternal pictures were only possible at the cost of humanity. So too Philo-sophy—on this view—must not portray the Idea of man, but the abstraction of a humanity empirical and mingled

[1] Jacobi's *Briefwechsel*, ii. 468.
[2] Hegel's *Werke*, i. 15.

with short-comings, and must bear a body impaled on the stake of the absolute antithesis ; and when it clearly feels its limitation to the sensible, it must at the same time bedeck itself with the surface colour of a supersensible, and point the finger of faith to a something Higher.

' But the truth cannot be defrauded by such a consecration if finitude be still left subsisting ; the true consecration must annihilate it. The artist, who fails to give actuality the true truth by letting fall upon it the ethereal illumination and taking it completely in that light, and who can only depict actuality in its bare ordinary reality and truth (a reality however which is neither true nor real) may apply the pathetic remedy to actuality, the remedy of tenderness and sentimentality, everywhere putting tears on the cheeks of the commonplace, and an O God ! in their mouth. No doubt his figures in this way direct their look over the actual heavenwards, but like bats they belong neither to the race of birds nor beasts, neither to earth nor heaven. Their beauty is not free from ugliness, nor their morals without weakness and meanness : the intelligence they haply may show is not without banality : the success which enters into it is not without vulgarity, and the misfortune not without cowardice and terror ; and both success and misfortune have something contemptible. So too philosophy, if it takes the finite and subjectivity as absolute truth in the logical form habitual to her, cannot purify them by bringing them into relation with an infinite : for that infinite is not itself the true, because it is unable to consume finitude. But where a philosophy consumes the temporal as such and burns up reality, its action is pronounced a cruel dissection, which does not leave man complete, and a forcible abstraction which has no truth, above all no truth for life. And such an abstraction is treated as a painful amputation of an essential piece from the completeness of the whole : that essential piece, and absolute substantiality being believed to consist in the temporal and empirical, and in privation. It is as if a person, who sees only the feet of a work of art, were to complain, should the whole work be unveiled to his eyes, that he was deprived of the privation, that the incomplete was decompleted.'

Jacobi has been spoken of as the leader of this ' Un-philosophy ' of faith. As such his allies lie on one side

among philosophers who hold by the deliverances of
'common sense', by the consciousness of the unsophisticated
man shrinking from the waywardness of an idealism that
deprives him of his solidest realities. The type of such
a philosopher has been drawn by Hegel [1] in Krug. But,
on the other side, Jacobi touched hands—though not in a
sympathetic spirit—with a somewhat motley band which
also had set its face to go to the everlasting gates, but had
turned aside to aimless wandering on the Hill Difficulty,
or sought too soon the repose of the Delectable Mountains,
without due sojourn in the valley of Humiliation or descent
under the Shadow of Death. Like Wordsworth, they felt
that the world is too much with us : that our true self is
frittered away into fragments and passing stages, in which
we are not ourselves,—whereby we also lose the true
perception of the essential life of nature. Gradually we
have sunk into the deadening arms of habit, reduced ourselves to professional and conventional types, and lost the
freer and larger mobility of spiritual being. We have grown
into *verständige Leute*—people of practical sense and worldly
wisdom. To such, philosophy would come—if it could
come—as the great breath of life—of 'reason' (*Vernunft*)
which transcends the separations inevitable in practical will
and knowledge. But to this band—which has been styled
the Romantic School of Germany—the liberation came in
ways more analogous to that craved for by Jacobi. Their
way was the way of Romance and Imagination. The
principle of Romance is the protest against confining man
and nature to the dull round of uniformities which custom
and experience have imprisoned them in. Boundless life,
infinite spontaneity is surging within us and the world,
ready to break down the dams convention and inertia have
established. That inner power is an ever-fresh, ever-restless
Irony, which sets up and overthrows, which refuses to be
bound or stereotyped, which is never weary, never exhausted,
—free in the absolute sense. It is the mystic force of
Nature, which they seemed to see ever on the spring to
work its magic transformations, and burst the bulwarks of
empirical law. It is the princely *jus aggratiandi*, the
sportive sovereignty of the true artist, who is able at any
moment to enter into direct communion with the heart
of things.

[1] Hegel's *Vermischte Schriften*, i. 50.

The beginning of the nineteenth century in Germany, as well as in England, was a period of effervescence :—there was a good deal of fire, and naturally there was also a good deal of smoke. Genius was exultant in its aspirations after Freedom, Truth, and Wisdom. The Romantic School, which had grown up under the stimulus of Fichte's resolve to enact thought, and had for a time been closely allied with Schelling, counted amongst its literary chiefs the names of the Schlegels, of Tieck, Novalis, and perhaps Richter. The world, as that generation dreamed, was to be made young again,—first by drinking, where Wordsworth led, from the fresh springs of nature,—afterwards when, as often has happened, doubts arose as to where Nature was really to be found, by an elixir distilled from the withered flowers of medieval Catholicism and chivalry,

'Since the Mid-Age was the Heroic Time'

and even from the old roots of primeval wisdom. The good old times of faith and harmonious beauty were to be brought back again by the joint labours of ideas and poetry.—

'So, all that the old Dukes had been, without knowing it,
This Duke would fain know he was without being it.'

To that period of incipient and darkling energy Hegel stands in very much the same position as Luther did to the pre-Reformation mystics, to Meister Eckhart, and the unknown author of the 'German Theology'. It was from this side, from the school of Genius and Romance in philosophy, that Hegel was proximately driven, not into sheer re-action, but into system, development, and science.

To elevate philosophy from a love of wisdom into the possession of real wisdom, into a system and a science, is the aim which he distinctly set before himself from the beginning. In almost every work, and every course of lectures, whatever be their subject, he cannot let slip the chance of an attack upon the mode of philosophising which substituted the strength of belief or conviction for the intervention of reasoning and argument. There may have been a strong sympathy in him with the end which these German contemporaries and, in some ways, analogues to Coleridge, Shelley, Wordsworth, and Byron had in view. No

one who reads his criticism of Kant can miss perceiving his
bent towards the Infinite. But he utterly rejects the vision
of feeling, whether as longing faith or devout enjoyment,
as an adequate exposition of the means to this end. Whereas
these fantastic seers and sentimentalists either disparage
science as a limitation to the spirit, in the calm trust of
their life in God, or yearn throughout life for a peace which
they never quite reach, Hegel is bent upon showing men
that the Infinite is not unknowable, as Kant would have it,
and yet that man can not, as Jacobi would have it, naturally
and without an effort enjoy the things of God.[1] He will
prove that the way of Truth is open, and prove it by
describing in detail every step of the road. Philosophy for
him must be reasoned truth. She does not visit favoured
ones in visions of the night, but comes to all who win her by
patient study.

' For those,' he says, ' who ask for a royal road to science,
no more convenient directions can be given than to trust
to their own sound common sense, and, if they wish to
keep up with the age and with philosophy, to read the
reviews criticising philosophical works, and perhaps even
the prefaces and the first paragraphs in these works themselves. The introductory remarks state the general and
fundamental principles ; and the reviews, besides their
historical information, contain a critical estimate, which,
from the very fact that it is such, is beyond and above
what it criticises. This is the road of ordinary men : and
it may be traversed in a dressing-gown. The other way
is the way of intuition. It requires you to don the vest-
ments of the high-priest. Along that road stalks the
ennobling sentiment of the Eternal, the True, the Infinite.
But it is wrong to call this a road. These grand sentiments
find themselves, naturally and without taking a single
step, centred in the very sanctuary of truth. So mighty
is genius, with its deep original ideas and its high flashes of
wit. But a depth like this is not enough to lay bare the
sources of true being, and these rockets are not the empyrean. True thoughts and scientific insights are only to be
gained by the labour which comprehends and grasps its
object. And that thorough grasp alone can produce the
universality of science. Contrasted with the vulgar vagueness and scantiness of common sense, that universality is

[1] Compare pages 121–142 of the *Logic*.

a fully-formed and rounded intellect ; and, contrasted with the un-vulgar generality of the natural gift of reason when it has been spoilt by the laziness and self-conceit of genius, it is truth put in possession of its native form, and thus rendered the possible property of every self-conscious reason.'[1]

These words which were taken to heart (unnecessarily, perhaps) by the patron of the *Intellectual Intuition* rung the knell to the friendship of Hegel with his great contemporary Schelling. Yet this hard saying is also the keynote to the subsequent work of the philosopher. In Hegel we need expect no brilliant *aperçus* of genius, no intellectual legerdemain, but only the patient unraveling of the clue of thought through all knots and intricacies : a deliberate tracing and working-out of the contradictions and mysteries in thought, until the contradiction and the mystery disappear. Perseverance is the secret of Hegel.

This characteristic of patient work is seen, for example, in the incessant prosecution of hints and glimpses, until they grew into systematic and rounded outline. Instead of vague anticipations and guesses at truth, fragments of insight, his years of philosophic study are occupied with writing and re-writing, in the endeavour to clear up and arrange the masses of his ideas. Essay after essay, and sketch after sketch of a system, succeed each other amongst his papers. His first great work was not published before his 37th year, after six years spent in university work at Jena, following as many spent in preliminary lucubration. The notes which he used to dictate some years afterwards to the boys in the Gymnasium at Nürnberg bear evidence of constant remodelling, and the same is true of his professorial lectures.

Such insistance in tracing every suggestion of truth to its place in the universe of thought is the peculiar character and difficulty of Hegelian argument. Other observers have now and again noticed, accentuated, and, it may be, popularised some one point or some one law in the evolution of reason. Here and there, as we reflect, we are forced to recognise what Hegel termed the dialectical nature in thought,—the tendency, by which a principle, when made to be all that it implied, when, as the phrase is, it is carried to extremes, recoils and leaves us confronted by its anti-

[1] *Phenomenologie des Geistes*, p. 54 (*Werke*, ii).

thesis. We cannot, for example, study the history of ancient thought without noting this phenomenon. Thus, the persistence with which Plato and Aristotle taught and enforced the doctrine that the community was the guide and safeguard of the several citizens, very soon issued in the schools of Zeno and Epicurus, teaching the rights of self-seeking and of the independent self-realisation of the individual. But the passing glimpse of an indwelling discord in the terms, by which we argue, is soon forgotten, and is set aside under the head of accidents, instead of being referred to a general law. Most of us take only a single step to avoid what has turned out wrong, and when we have overcome the seeming absoluteness of one idea, we are content and even eager to throw ourselves under the yoke of another, not less one-sided than its predecessor. Sometimes one feels tempted to say that the course of human thought as a whole, as well as that branch of it termed science, exhibits nothing but a succession of illusions, which enclose us in the belief that some idea is all-embracing as the universe,—illusions, from which the mind is time after time liberated, only in a little while to sink under the sway of some partial correction, as if it and it only were the complete truth.

Or, again, the Positive Philosophy exhibits as one of its features an emphatic and popular statement of a fallacy much discussed in Hegel. One of the best deeds of that school has been to protest against a delusive belief in certain words and notions ; particularly by pointing out the insufficiency of what it calls metaphysical terms, i. e. those abstract entities formed by reflective thought, which are little else than a double of the phenomenon they are intended to explain. To account for the existence of insanity by an assumed basis for it in the ' insane neurosis ', or to attribute the sleep which follows a dose of opium to the soporific virtues of the drug, are some exaggerated examples of the metaphysical intellect which is so rampant in much of our popular, and even of our esoteric science. Positivism by its logical precepts ought at least to have instilled general distrust of abstract talk about essences, laws, forces and causes, whenever they claim an inherent and independent value, or profess to be more than a reflex of sensation. But all this is only a desultory perception, the reflection of an intelligent observer. When we come to Hegel, the Comtian perception of the danger lying in the terms of metaphysics is replaced by the Second Part of Logic, the Theory of Essential Being, where substances, causes, forces, essences, matters, are confronted with what Mr. Bain has called their ' suppressed correlative '.[1]

[1] *Practical Essays*, p. 43.

CHAPTER VI

THE SCIENCES AND PHILOSOPHY

By asserting the rights of philosophy against the dogmatism of self-inspired ' unphilosophy ', and by maintaining that we must not feel the truth, with our eyes as it were closed, but must open them full upon it, Hegel does not reduce philosophy to the level of one of the finite sciences. The name ' finite ', like the name ' empirical ', is not a title of which the sciences have any cause to be ashamed. They are called empirical, because it is their glory and their strength to found upon experience. They are called finite, because they have a fixed object, which they must expect and cannot alter ; because they have an end and a beginning,—presupposing something where they begin, and leaving something for the sciences which come after. Botany rests upon the researches of chemistry : and astronomy hands over the record of cosmical movements to geology. Science is interlinked with science ; and each of them is a fragment. Nor can these fragments ever, in the strict sense of the word, make up a whole or total. They have broken off, sometimes by accident, and sometimes for convenience, from one another. The sciences have budded forth here and there upon the tree of popular knowledge and ordinary consciousness, as the interest and needs of the time drew attention closer to various points and objects in the world surrounding us.

Prosecute the popular knowledge about any point far enough, substituting completeness and accuracy for vagueness, and especially giving numerical definiteness in weight, size, and figure, until the little drop of fact has grown into an ocean, and the mere germ has expanded into a structure with complex interconnexion,—and you will have a science. By its point of origin this luminous body of facts is united to the great circle of human knowledge and ignorance. Each special science is a part, which presupposes a total of much lower organisation, but much wider range than itself : each branch of scientific knowledge grows out of the already existent tree of acquaintance with things. But the part very soon assumes an independence of its own, and adopts a hostile or negative attitude towards the general level of unscientific opinion. This process of what we may, from the vulgar point of view, call abnormal development, is repeated irregularly at various points along the surface of ordinary consciousness. At one time it is the celestial movements calling for the science of astronomy : at another the problem of dividing the soil calling for the geometrician. Each of these outgrowths naturally re-acts and modifies the whole range of human knowledge, or what we may call popular science ; and thus, while keeping up its own life, it quickens the parent stock with an infusion of new vigour, and raises the general intelligence to a higher level and into a higher element.

The order of the outcome of the sciences in time, therefore, and their connexions with one another, cannot be explained or understood, if we look only to the sciences themselves. We must first of all descend into the depths of natural thought, or of general culture, and trace the lines which unite science with science in that general medium. The systematic interdependence of the sciences must be chiefly sought for in the workings of thought as a whole in its popular phases, and in the action and reaction of that *general* human thought with the sciences, those definite organisations of knowledge which form sporadically round the *nuclei* here and there presented in what would superficially be described as the inorganic mass and medium of popular knowledge. Thus, by means of the sciences in their aggregate action, the material of common consciousness is expanded and developed, at least in certain parts, though the expansion may be neither consistent nor systematic. But so long as this work is incomplete, so long, that is to say, as every point in the line of popular knowledge has not received its due elaboration and equal study, the sciences merely succeed each other in a certain imperfect sequence, or exist in juxtaposition : they do not form a total. The whole of scientific knowledge will only be formed, when science shall be as completely rounded and unified, as in its lower sphere and more inadequate element the ordinary consciousness of the world is now.

Up to a certain point the method of science is but the method of ordinary consciousness pursued knowingly and steadily. But ere long the method acquires a distinctive character of its own. It shakes off the pressure of that immediate subservience in which ordinary knowledge stands to man's needs, wishes and interests. Knowledge is pursued —within a wide range—for its own sake, and by a class more or less definitely set apart by humanity for its scientific service,—which is thus performed more systematically and continuously. But the great step which carries ordinary knowledge into its higher region is the discovery, due to reflection and comparison, that there is a double grade of reality—a permanent, essential, uniform, substantial being, which is contrasted with an evanescent, apparent, varying and accidental. To know a thing is in all cases to *relate it* to something else : to know it in the higher sense—*vere scire*—is to relate it to its essence, its substantial or universal form, its permanent self. Ordinary knowledge, e. g., fixes a thing by referring to its antecedents : scientific knowledge refers it to its ' invariable ', ' unconditional ' or ' essential ' antecedent,—to something which contains it implicitly, and necessarily, and is not merely by accident or juxta-position associated with it. To discover this permanent, underlying substance or reality comes to be the problem of science—a problem which may be taken in the widest generality, or restricted to some one group of existences. What is asked for, e. g., may be the uniformity and essence in the appearance of the diurnal journey of the sun, or it may be the underlying, invisible, nature which displays itself in all the variety of minerals, and in animal and plant life. The one-and-the-same in a diversity of many ; the type-form in individuals : the cause which is the key to understanding an effect that always and unconditionally follows it ; the force which finds different expression in actions—are what Science seeks.

In that search two points emerge as regards the method. The first is the importance of quantitative statements or numerical appreciations, and the general law that variations in the qualitative are in some ratio concomitant with variations in the quantitative. Mathematics, in a word, is found to be an invaluable instrument for recording with ac-curacy the minutest as well as the most immense differences of quality. First, it is seen that qualitative differences within a given range, e.g. various colours or various musical notes, can be accurately expressed by a numerical ratio.

But, secondly, it soon appears that even greater divergences of quality, e. g. those of colour and of chemical quality, may possibly be reduced to stages on one quantitative scale. It is not unnatural that such experiences should give rise to a hope—and in sanguine minds, an assurance—that all the phenomena of nature are ultimately phases of some common nature—some elementary being—which runs through an infinite gamut of numerically defined adjustments.

But the numerical prepossession—as we may call it—creates another assumption. Every number consists of units : every cube can be regarded as an aggregation of smaller cubes, and in measurement is (implicitly at least) so regarded. Transferring this to the physical world, every object is regarded as a composite—a Large, made up by the addition and juxtaposition of many (relatively) Littles. The essentials of the composite are here the elements that compose it : these, by a natural tendency, we proceed to conceive as remaining always unchanged, and giving rise by their peculiar juxtaposition to certain perceptions in the human being. You whirl rapidly a blazing piece of wood, and instead of a discontinuous series of flashes you see one orbit of luminous matter : or, let falling rain-drops take up a particular position in reference to your eyes and the sun, and a rainbow is visible. In both cases there is what may be called an illusion—the illusion, above all, of unity and continuity. Now what is in these cases obviously and demonstrably seen, is, as Leibniz in particular has reminded us, the general law of all matter as such. In the extended and material world there is nowhere a real unity discoverable. The small is made up of the smaller *ad infinitum*.[1] But the conclusion (which Leibniz drew)—that unity belongs only to Monads and never by any possibility to a material substance, was not that commonly reached or accepted. There are—or there must be,—said the prevalent creed, ultimates, indivisibles, indecomposables, simples, atoms. These are the final bricks of reality, out of which the apparent universe is built : each with a maximum,—a *ne plus ultra*—of resistibility, hardness, fullness, and unsqueezable bulk.

[1] Leibniz, ed. Gerhardt, iii. 507 : ' Les atomes sont l'effet de la foiblesse de nostre imagination, qui aime à se reposer et à se hâter à venir à une fin dans les sous-divisions et analyses : il n'en est pas ainsi dans la nature qui vient de l'infini et va à l'infini.'

Into further details of these ultimate irreducibles we need not enter. It is sufficient to denote the general purport of the conception, and the tendency it implies. In these ultimates supreme reality is understood to lie ; and on them at last, and indeed always, rests whatever reality truly exists in any object. All else is secondary—and, comparatively speaking, illusory,—unreal. Any phenomena that may be noted only affect the surface or show of these reals : the inner reality continues one and unchanged. Outside them, around them, is the void—emptiness, non-entity. Yet null and void as it may be, we may, in passing, reply,— this circumambient is the source of all that gives these masses of atoms any distinctive reality—any character of true being. Space may be empty enough,—a mere spectre-shell ; and yet it is their differences in spatial circumstance that bring out and actualise what they implicitly are. These '*individua*', these units of reality, these atoms, are real and knowable only in their relations. So too Time may be contemptuously treated as a passive receptacle : yet it is only by its connexions in the past and the future that the present moment has any actuality it may claim. And time and space are potent agencies—in popular mode of utterance —whatever the mechanical philosophy may say.

But all of these relations are in the realm of unreality. The atoms alone *are* : and yet the void, which ought *not* to *be*, in an unmistakable way *is* also. To this mysterious vacuum which lies outside (and yet not outside) reality, to this not-being which *is*, there can only be given a half-negative and baffling name. Let it be called Chance—or let it be called Necessity ; let it be called inexplicable Law of co-existence and sequence,—the Force which is the beginning of motion. It is the ultimate key to the mystery —but it is at least a key which no human hand can use, or even lay hold of. It is enough for science if, leaving this ultimate inexplicability untouched, it trace in each separate instance the exact equation between the sum of the constituents and the total which they compose,—if it prove that the several items when put together exactly give the sum proposed. Identification—the establishment of quantitative equations—is the work of science. Identity is its canon, working on the presumption or axiom that there can be nothing in the result which was not in the antecedents or conditions. *Ex nihilo nihil fit*. The quantity of energy must always be the same, though its phases may vary, or temporarily avoid detection. Matter, i. e. the ultimate reality, is indestructible. In short, the method of analysis and synthesis, as that of addition and subtraction, is a calculus which takes the form of an equation.

So far the inorganic, inanimate world has been mainly in view. If we now turn to the organisms, we find the popular creed expressed in the adage *Omne vivum e vivo*. No eye has ever seen—though fanatical observers have sometimes so deluded themselves as to think they saw—a living being directly emerge from inorganic stuff. The saner student of physiology contents himself with leaving for the while the crux of the genesis of Life, and examining only the building up of the living creature out of its constituents. Here the atom is called the cell : every organism is a synthesis of cells, and in the cell we have the primary element of organic reality : *Omnis cellula e cellula*. In the atom we have the ultimate element ; in the cell a relative element,—the absolute beginning of a new order of things,—which we may, if we like, choose to treat (though only for logical simplicity's sake) as a gradual development from the other and more primitive, but which, so far as experience and history teach, is equally ultimate in its kind. But be the final constituent (physical) atom, or (physiological) cell, the relation of these constituents is at first conceived by science only as composition, or mechanical synthesis. It is only gradually that science begins to have doubts as to the inviolability and unalterableness of the elements. When the idea—not altogether new—of a 'latent meta-schematism' and latent process within the constituents is entertained and carried out in earnest, science has passed on to a new stage : from mechanical atomism to a dynamic and organic theory of existence. And the governing ideas of scientific logic have then ceased to be co-existence, and sequence, correlation and composition : the new category is intus-susception, development, adaptation not only external but internal.

Divide et impera is the motto of Science. To isolate one thing or one group of facts from its context,—to penetrate beneath the apparent simplicity, which time and custom have taught ordinary eyes to see in the concrete object, to the multitude of underlying simple elements,—to leave everything extraneous out of sight,—to abolish the teleology which imposes upon Nature a permanent tribute (direct or indirect) towards the supply of human wants,—and to take, as it were, one thing at a time and study it for itself disinterestedly ; that is the problem of the sciences. And to accomplish that end they do not hesitate to break the charmed links which in common vision hold the world together,—to disregard the spiritual harmony which the sense of beauty finds in the scene,—to strip off the relations of means and end, which reflection has thrown from thing to thing, and the sensuous atmosphere of so-called 'secondary' qualities in which human sense has enveloped each ; and finally to sever its connexion by which

> ' the whole round world is every way
> Bound by gold chains about the feet of God '.

In those days when reflection had not set in,—when humanity had not yet found itself a stranger in the house of Nature, and had not yet dared to regard her as a mere automatic slave, men had no doubts as to the meaning of things. They lived sympathetically her life.

> ' Man, once descried, imprints for ever
> His presence on all lifeless things : the winds
> Are henceforth voices, wailing or a shout,
> A querulous mutter, or a quick gay laugh.'

To the extent of his abilities and his culture, indeed, man has in all ages read himself into the phenomena external to him. Such readings, in times when he feared and loved his kinsfolk of Nature, were fetichism and anthropomorphism. Gradually, however, forgetting his community, he claimed to be the measure and master of all things : to decree their use and function. But in course of time, when the sciences had emancipated themselves from the yoke of philosophy, they refused to borrow any such help in reading the riddle of the universe, and resolved to begin, *ab ovo*, from the atom or cell, and leave the elements to work out their own explanation. Modern science in so doing practises the lessons learned from Spinoza and Hume. The former teaches that all conception of order, i. e. of adaptation and harmony in nature, and indeed all the methods by which nature is popularly explained, are only modes of our emotional imagination, betraying how imperfect has been in most of us the emancipation of

human intellect from the servitude to the affections.[1]
The latter points out that all connexions between things
are solely mental associations, ingrained habits of expectation, the work of time and custom, accredited only by
experience.[2] There must be no pre-suppositions allowed
in the studies of science, no help derived prematurely from
the later terms in the process to elucidate the earlier.
Let man, it is said, be explained by those laws, and by the
action of those primary elements which build up every
other part of nature : let molecules by mechanical union
construct the thinking organism, and then construct
society. The elements which we find by analysis must be
all that is required to make the synthesis. Thus in modern
times science carries out, fully and with the details of
actual knowledge in several branches, the principles of the
atom and the void, which Democritus suggested.

The scientific spirit, however, the spirit of analysis and
abstraction (or of ' Mediation ' and ' Reflection '), is not
confined in its operations to the physical world. The
criticism of ordinary beliefs and conventions has been
applied—and applied at an earlier period—to what has
been called the Spiritual world, to Art, Religion, Morality,
and the institutions of human Society. Under these
names the agency of ages, acting by their individual minds,
has created organic systems, unities which have claimed
to be permanent, inviolable, and divine. Such unities or
organic structures are the Family, the State, the works of
Art, the forms, doctrines, and systems of Religion, existing
and recognised in ordinary consciousness. But in these
cases, as in Nature, the reflective principle may come
forward and ask what right these unities have to exist.
This is the question which the ' Encyclopaedie ', the
' Aufklärung ', the ' Rationalist ' and ' Freethinking '
theories, raise and have raised in the last century and the

---

[1] Spinoza, *Ethica*, i. 36, App. ' *Quoniam ea nobis prae ceteris grata
sunt quae facile imaginari possumus, ideo homines ordinem confusioni
praeferunt : quasi ordo aliquid in natura praeter respectum ad nostram
imaginationem esset . . . Videmus itaque omnes rationes quibus vulgus
solet naturam explicare modos esse tantummodo imaginandi.*' Cf. *Eth.*
iv. praef. : Epist. xxxii.

[2] ' This transition of thought from the Cause to the Effect proceeds not from Reason. It derives its origin altogether from Custom
and Experience.' Hume, Essay V. (Enquiry concerning Human
Understanding.) ' All inferences from Experience therefore are
effects of Custom.' (Ibid.)

present. What is the Family, it is said, but a fiction or
convention, which is used to give a decent, but somewhat
transparent covering to a certain animal appetite, and
its probable consequences ? What is the State, and what
is Society, but a fiction or compact, by which the weak
try to make themselves seem strong, and the unjust seek
to shelter themselves from the consequences of their own
injustice ? What is Religion, it is said, but a delusion
springing from the fears and weakness of the crowd, and
the cunning of the few, which men have fostered until it
has wrapped humanity in its snaky coils ? And Poetry,
we are assured, like its sister Arts, will perish and its
illusions fade away, when Science, now in the cradle, has
become the full-grown Hercules. As for Morality and
Law, and the like, the same condemnation has been prepared
from of old. All of them, it is said, are but the inventions
of power and craft, or the phantoms of human imagination,
which the strength of positive science and bare facts is
destined in no long time to dispel.

When they insisted upon a severance of the elements in
the vulgarly-accepted unities of the world, Science and
Freethinking, like Epicurus in an older day, have believed
that they were liberating the world from its various super-
stitions, from the bonds which instinct and custom had
fastened upon things so as to combine them into systems
more or less arbitrary. They denied the supremacy and
reality of those ideas which insist on the essential unity
and self-sameness in things that visibly and tangibly have
a separate existence of their own, and branded these ideas
comprehensively as mysticism and metaphysics. They
sought to disabuse us of spirits, vital forces, divine right
of governments, final causes, *et hoc genus omne.* They were
exceedingly jealous for the independence of the individual,
and for his right to demand satisfaction for the questioning,
ground-seeking faculty of his nature. But while they did
so they hardly realised how entirely the spectator is the
part, the product of what he surveys, and while surveying
treats as if it were but a spot or mark on the circumference
of the circle that lies—some way off—around him. ' Pheno-
menalism,' as this mode of looking at things has been called,
is false to life, and would cut away the ground from philosophy.[1]

[1] J. Grote, *Exploratio Philosophica.*

To some extent philosophy returns to the position of the wider consciousness, to the general belief in harmony and symmetry. It reverts to the unity or connexion, which the natural presumptions of mankind find in the picture of the world. The *nolo philosophari* of the intuitivist, in reaction from the supposed excesses of the sciences, simply reverted to the bare re-statement of the popular creed. If science, e. g., had shown that the perception of an external world pre-supposed for its accomplishment an unsuspected series of intermediate steps, the mere intuitivist simply denied the intermediation by appealing to Common Sense, or to the natural instincts and primary beliefs of mankind. Conviction and natural instinct were declared to counter-balance the abstractions of science. But philosophy which seeks to comprehend existence cannot take the same ground as the intuitional school, or neglect the testimony of science. If the spiritual unity of the world has been denied and lost to sight, mere assertion that we feel and own its pervading power will not do much good. It is necessary to reconcile the contrast between the wholeness of the natural vision, and the fragmentary, but in its fragments elaborated, result of science.

The sciences break up the rough generalisations or vulgar concepts of everyday use, and make their fixed distinctions yield to analysis. They thus render continuous things which were looked at as only separate. But they tend again to substitute the results of their analysis as a new and permanent distinction and principle of things. They are like revolutionists who upset and perturb an old order, and set up a new and minuter tyranny in its place. Gradually, the general culture, the average educated intelligence, gathers up the fruit of scientific research into the total development of humanity : and uses the work of science to fill up the *lacunae*, the gaps, which make popular consciousness so irregular and disconnected. A sort of popular philosophy comes to sum up and estimate what science has accomplished · and therein is as it were the spirit of the world taking into his own hand the acquisitions won by the more audacious and self-willed of his sons, and investing them in the common store. They are set aside and preserved there, at first in an abstract and technical form, but destined soon to pass into the possession of all, and form that mass of belief and instinctive or implanted knowledge whence a new generation will draw its mental supplies. Each great scientific discovery is in its turn reduced to a part of the common stock. It leaves the technical field, and spreads into the common life of men, becoming embodied in their daily beliefs,—a seed of thought, from which, by the agency of intelligent experience, new increments of science will one day spring.

Philosophy properly so called is also the unification of science, but in a new sphere, a higher medium not recognised by the sciences themselves. The reconciliation which the philosopher believes himself to accomplish between ordinary consciousness and science is identified by either side with a phase of its antagonist error. Science will term philosophy a modified form of the old religious superstition. The popular consciousness of truth, and especially religion, will see in philosophy only a repetition or an aggravation of the evils of science. The attempt at unity will not approve itself to either, until they enter upon the ground which philosophy occupies, and move in that element. And that elevation into the philosophic ether calls for a tension of thought which is the sternest labour imposed upon man : so that the continuous action of philosophising has been often styled superhuman. If anywhere, it is in pure philosophy that proof becomes impossible, unless for those who are willing to think for themselves.[1] The philosophic lesson cannot be handed on to a mere recipient : the result, when cut off from the process which produced it, vanishes like the palace in the fairy tale.

' The whole of philosophy is nothing but the study of the specific forms or types of unity.' [2] There are many species and grades of this unity. They are not merely to be enumerated and asserted in a vague way, as they here and there force themselves upon the notice of the popular mind. Philosophy sees in that unity neither an ultimate and unanalysable fact, nor a deception, but a growth (which is also a struggle), a revealing or unfolding, which issues in an organism or system, constructing itself more and more completely by a force of its own. This

---

[1] Cf. vol. ii. p. 4.

[2] *Philosophie der Religion*, i. p. 97 : ' Die ganze Philosophie ist nichts Anderes als das Studium der Bestimmungen der Einheit.' See especially *Encycl.* § 573 (Philosophy of Mind, pp. 192 seqq.).

system formed by these types of the fundamental unity is called the ' Idea ', of which the highest law is development. Philosophy essays to do for this connective and unifying nature, i. e. for the thought in things, something like what the sciences have done or would like to do for the facts of sense and matter,—to do for the spiritual binding-element in its integrity, what is being done for the several facts which are more or less combined. It retraces the universe of thought from its germinal form, where it seems, as it were, an indecomposable point, to the fully matured system or organism, and shows not merely that one phase of pure thought passes into another, but how it does so, and yet is not lost, but subsists suspended and deprived of its narrowness in the maturer phase.

CHAPTER VII

ANTICIPATORY SKETCH OF THE SCOPE OF PHILOSOPHY

THE psychology of the Greeks has to all appearance given the mere intellect an undue pre-eminence, if it has not even treated it as man's essential self. Whether the appearance is altogether sound might be a profitable inquiry for those who most criticise it. At any rate, a later psychology has taught us to regard man as at once a cognitive, an emotional, and a volitional being. It has arrived at this conclusion as it looked at the division that parted off the systems of science from the sphere of conduct and social life, and both from the inner life of sentiment, of love, admiration and reverence. And the inference was justifiable, in the same way as Plato's when, as he surveyed the triple sphere into which the outward world of his contemporary society was divided, he concluded a triplicity of the soul. If it was justifiable, it was also, as in his case, somewhat misleading. In the outward manifestation, where the letters are posted up on a gigantic scale, one tends to forget that they only spell one word. Their difference and distance seem increased, and we fail to note that, though there are three aspects, yet there is only one power or soul, which exhibits itself under one or other of the three tones or modes. In the actual human being, cognition is always of some emotional interest and always leads up to some practical result. From different points of view one or other is occasionally declared to be primary and original ; the others derivative and secondary. At any rate we may say that in the ordinary human being who is still in the garden of preparation and has not yet stepped forth on one of the separate routes of life, his knowledge, his emotional and his active life are in a tolerable harmony, and that each in its little development is constantly followed by the other.

But with the outward differentiation an inward went hand in hand. In some cases the intellectual or scientific, in others the emotional, in others the active faculties became predominant. Human nature in order to attain all its completeness had first of all, as it were, to lose its life in order to gain it. The individual had to sacrifice part of his all-sided development in order that he might gain it again, and in a larger measure, through the medium of society. This process is the process of civilisation : the long and, as it often seems, weary road by which man can only realise himself by self-sacrifice : can only reach unity through the way of diversity, and must die to live. It is a process in which it is but too easy to notice only one stage and speak of it as if it were the whole. It is possible sometimes to identify civilisation with the material increase in the means of producing enjoyment, or with the progress of scientific teaching as to the laws of those material phenomena on which material civilisation is largely dependent. It is possible sometimes to take as its test the stores of artistic works, and the extension of a lively and delicate love of all that is beautiful and tasteful. One may identify it with a high-toned moral life, and with an orderly social system. Or one may maintain that the real civilisation of a country presupposes a lofty conception and reverent attitude to the supreme source of all that is good, and true, and beautiful.

The question is important as bearing on the relation of philosophy to the special sciences. Philosophy is sometimes identified with the sum of sciences : sometimes with their complete unification. Philosophy, says a modern, is knowledge completely unified. It is of course to some extent a question of words in what sense a term is to be defined. And no one will dispute that the scientific element is in point of form the most conspicuous aspect of philosophy. Yet if we look at the historical use of the term, one or two considerations suggest themselves. Philosophy, said an ancient, is the knowledge of things human and divine. Again and again, it has claimed for its task to be a guide and chart of human life—to reveal the form of good and of beauty. But to do this, it must be more than a mere science, or than a mere system of the sciences. Again, it has been urged by modern critics that Kant at last discovered for philosophy her true province—the study of the conditions and principles of human knowledge. But though epistemology is all-important, the science of

knowledge is not identical with philosophy : nor did Kant
himself think it was.   Rather his view is on the whole in
accord with what he has called the ' world's (as opposed
to the scholar's) conception of philosophy ',[1] as the science
of the bearing of all ascertainable truths on the essential
aims of human reason—*teleologia humanae rationis*,—in
accord, too, with the world's conception of the philosopher
as no mere logician, but the legislator of human reason.

This, it need hardly be added, is the conception of
philosophy which is implicitly the basis of Hegel's use.
Let us hear Schelling.   ' A philosophy which in its principle
is not already religion is no true philosophy.'[2]   Or again,
as to the place of Ethics :   ' Morality is God-like disposition,
an uplifting above the influence of the concrete into the
realm of the utterly universal.   Philosophy is a like elevation, and for that reason intimately one with morality,
not through subordination, but through essential and
inner likeness.'[3]   But, again, it has more than once been
felt that philosophy is kindred with Art.   It has been
said—not as a compliment—that philosophy is only a form
of gratifying the aesthetic instincts.   Schopenhauer has
suggested—as a novelty—that the true way to philosophy
was not by science, but through Art.   And Schelling before
him had—while asserting the inner identity of the two—
even gone so far as to assert [4] that ' Art is the sole, true
and eternal organon as well as the ostensible evidence of
philosophy '.

Philosophy, therefore, is one of a triad in which the
human spirit has tried to raise itself above its limitations
and to become god-like.   And philosophy is the climax ;
Art the lowest ; Religion in the mean.   But this does not
mean that Religion supersedes Art, and that Philosophy
supersedes religion ; or, if we retain the term ' supersede ',
we must add that the superseded is not left behind and
passed aside : it is rather an integral constituent of what
takes its place.   Philosophy is true and adequate only as
it has given expression to all that religion had or aimed at.
So, too, Religion is not the destruction of Art : though
here the attitude may often seem to be more obviously
negative.   A religion which has no place for art is, again,

---

[1] Kant's *Kritik d. r. Vernunft* : Methodenl. Architektonik d. r.
Vern.
[2] Schelling's *Werke*, v. 116.   [3] Ibid. v. 276.   [4] Ibid. iii. 267.

no true religion. And thus again, Philosophy becomes a reconciler of Art and Religion : of the visible ideal and the invisible God. Art, on the other hand, is a foretaste and a prophecy of religion and philosophy.

But Art, Religion, and Philosophy, again, rest upon, grow out of, and are the fulfilment of an ethical society —a state of human life where an ordered commonwealth in outward visibility is animated and sustained by the spirit of freedom and self-realisation. And that public objective existence of social humanity in its turn reposes on the will and intelligence of human beings, of souls which in various relations of discipline and interaction with their environment have become free-agents, and have risen to be more than portions of the physical world, sympathetic with its changes, and become awake to themselves and their surroundings. Such is the mental or spiritual life as it rises to full sense of its power, recognises its kindred with the general life, carries out that kindred in its social organisation, and at length through the strength social union gives floats boldly in the empyrean of spiritual life, in art, religion, and philosophy.

But, what about the special relationship of philosophy to the sciences ? Undoubtedly the philosophers of the early years of the century have used lordly language in reference to the sciences. They have asserted—from Fichte downwards—that the philosophical construction of the universe must justify itself to itself—must be consistent, continuous, and coherent—and that it had not to wait for experience to give it confirmation. Even the cautious Kant [1] had gone so far as to assert that the ' understanding gives us nature '—i.e. as he explains, *natura formaliter spectata*, viz., the order and regularity in the phenomena— that it is the source of the laws of nature and of its formal unity. The so-called proofs of natural laws are only instances and exemplifications, which no more *prove* them, than we prove that $6 \times 4 = 24$, because 6 yards of cloth at 4s. must be paid for by 24 shillings. To assert that this instance is no proof, is not to reject experience—still less to refuse respect to the new discoveries of science. But it is unquestionably to assert that there is something prior to the sciences—prior, i.e. in the sense that Kant speaks of the *a priori*, something which is fundamental to them,

[1] Kant, *Kritik d. r. Vern.*, Deduction of the Categories, Sect. III.

and constitutes them what they are—something which is assumed as real if their syntheses (and every scientific truth is a synthesis) are to be possible. The analysis and exhibition in its organic completeness of this Kantian *a priori* is the theme of the Hegelian Logic.

The Philosophy of Nature stands in the Hegelian system between Logic and Mental or Spiritual Philosophy. Man—intelligent, moral, religious and artistic man—rests upon the basis of natural existence : he is the child of the earth, the offspring of natural organisation. But Nature itself—such is the hypothesis of the system—is only intelligible as the reflex of that *a priori* which has been exhibited in Logic. The whole scheme by which the natural world is scientifically held together, apprehended by ordinary consciousness and elaborated by mathematical analysis, presupposes the organism of the categories—these fundamental habits of thought or form of conception which are the framework of the existence we know. Yet Nature never shows this intelligible world—the Idea—in its purity and entirety. In the half-literal, half-figurative phrases of Hegel, Nature shows the Idea beside itself, out of its mind, alienated, *non compos mentis*. ' It is a mad world, my masters.' ' The impotence of nature—*Ohnmacht der Natur*[1] —is a frequent phrase, by which he indicates the a-logical, if not illogical, character of the physical world. Here we come across the negation of mind : chance plays its part : contingency is everywhere. If you expect that the physical universe will *display* unquestioning obedience to the laws of reason and of the higher logic, you will be disappointed. What you *see* is fragmentary, chaotic, irregular. To the bodily sense—even when that sense has been rendered more penetrating by all the many material and methodical aids of advanced civilisation—the Idea is in the natural world presented only in traces, indications, portions, which it requires a well-prepared mind to descry, still more to unite. Yet at the same time the indications of that unity are everywhere, and the hypothesis of the logical scheme or organisation of the Idea is the only theory which seems fully to correspond with the data. Nature,[2] says Hegel, is the Idea as it shows itself in sense-perception, not as it shows itself in thought. In thought a clear all-comprehending total ; in sense a baffling fragment. The Idea—

---

[1] *Encyclopaedie*, § 250.   [2] *Encycl.* Sect. 244 (*Logic*, p. 379).

the unity of life and knowledge—is everywhere in nature, but nowhere clearly, or whole, or otherwise than a glimpse ; not a logical scheme or compact theory. Nature is the sensible in which the intelligible is bound—the reality which is the vehicle of the ideal. But the ideal treasure is held in rough and fragile receptacles which half disclose and half conceal the light within. Nature in short contains, but disguised, the idea, in fainter and clearer evidences : it is the function of man, by his scientific intelligence and ethical work, building up a social organisation, to provide the ground on which the ultimate significance and true foundation of the world may be deciphered, guessed, or believed, or imaginatively presented. The verification of the guess or deciphering, of course, lies in its adequacy to explain and colligate the facts. The true method and true conception is that which needs no subsequent adjust-ments—no epicycles to make it work—which is no mere hypothesis useful for subjective arrangement, but issues with uncontrollable force and self-evidence from the facts.

What Hegel has called the 'impotence of nature', Schopenhauer has styled the irrational Will, and it is from that end, so to speak, that Schopenhauer's philosophy begins. Nature—the basis of all things—the fundamental prius—is an irresistible and irregular appetite or craving to be, to do, to live,—but an *appetitus* or *nisus* which ascends from grade to grade—from mere mechanical forces acting in movement up to the highest form of animal activity. But as this 'Will' or blind lust of being and instinct of life gets above the inorganic world, and manifests itself in the animal organism, there emerges a new order of existence—the intellect, or the ideal world. Seen from the underside, indeed, all that has appeared now in the animal is a brain and a nerve-system—a new species of matter. But there is another side to the Mind which has thus awakened out of the sleep of natural forces. This intellect is unaware and can never be made aware that it is a child of nature : it acknowledges no superior, and no beginning or end in time. Its natal day is infinitely beyond the age when the cosmic process began its race ; before stars gathered their masses of luminosity, and the earth received the first germs of life. As the genius of Art, it arrests the toiling struggle of existence to produce new forms and destroy old ones ; it sets free in typical forms of eternal beauty the great ideas that nature vainly seeks to embody, and as moral and religious life its aim is to annihilate the craving and the lust for more and ever more being and to enter in passionless and calm union with the One-and-All.

Thus it is, if not absurd, at least misleading, to speak of Hegel's system as Panlogism. Strictly speaking, it is only of the Logic that this is the proper name : there, unquestionably, reason is all and in all. Yet to hold that reason is the very life and centre of things is for philosophy the cardinal article—the postulate which must inspire her first and last steps and guide her throughout. But the Logical Idea, if put at the beginning, is at first only put as a presupposition, which it is the task of human intelligence to work out and organise. If it be the key which is to explain nature and render it intelligible, it is a key which has only been gained in the process—the long process—by which man has risen from his natural origin—never however parting company with it—to survey and comprehend himself and his setting. The faculty of ' pure thinking ', which is the pre-condition of Logical study, is the result of a gradual development in which animal sense has grown and metamorphosed, and worked itself up to be a free intelligence and a good will capable of discerning and fulfilling the universal and the eternal. Thus in the Logic the system constructs the pure Idea—the ideal timeless organisation of thoughts or λόγοι on which all knowledge of reality rests—the diamond net which suffers nothing to escape its meshes : in the Philosophy of Nature it tries to put together in unity and continuity the phases and partial aspects which the physical universe presents in graduated exemplification of the central truth : and in the Philosophy of Mind it traces the steps by which a merely natural being becomes the moral and aesthetic idealist in whom man approaches deity.

It is indeed Hegel's fundamental axiom that actuality is reasonable. But the actuality is not the appearance—the temporary phases—the succession of event : it is the appearance rooted in its essence—the succession concentrated (yet not lost) in its unity. There is room for much so-called irrationality within these ranges. For, when human beings pronounce something irrational, they only mean that their practical intelligence would have adopted other methods to arrive at certain conclusions. They judge, in fact, by their limited understandings and not *ex ordine universi*. Hegel's doctrine is after all only another way of stating the maintenance of the fittest ; and it is liable to the same misconception by those who employ their personal aims as the standards of judgment.

So too there is reason—there is the Idea—in Nature. But it is there only for the artist, the religious man, and the philosopher ; and they see it respectively by the eye of genius, by the power of faith, by the thought of reason. They see it from the standpoint of the absolute—*sub specie quadam aeternitatis*. It is therefore a recalcitrant matter in which Nature presents the Idea : or, if recalcitrant suggests a positive opposition, let us say rather a realm in which the Idea fails to come out whole and clear, where unity has to be forced upon and read into the facts. Science, says one writer, is an ideal construction : it implies an abstraction from irregularities and inequalities : it smoothes and sublimates the rough and imperfect material into a more rounded and perfect whole. Its object, which it terms a reality, is a non-sensible, imperceptible reality : what one might as well call an ideality, were it not that here again the popular imagination twists the word into a subjective sense to mean the private and personal ideas of the student.

But the obvious individual reality never quite in its obviousness equals the ' golden mediocrity ' of the ideal. Its myriad grapes must be crushed to yield the wine of the spirit.

' It 's a lifelong toil till our lump be leavened '

—till the ore be transformed into the fine gold. But the gold is there, and in the great laboratory of *natura naturans* is the principle and agent of its own purification. ' Nature is made better by no mean, but nature makes that mean '— for nature is spirit in disguise.

It is on this side that a certain analogy of Hegel's and Schelling's philosophy of nature with the Romantic school comes out. Nature is felt, as it were, to be spirit-haunted, to give glimpses of a solidarity, a design, a providentiality, which runs counter to that general outward indifference in which part seems to have settled beside part, each utterly indifferent to the other. Romance is the unexpected coincidence, the sudden jumping together of what seemed

set worlds apart and utterly alien.   It was the sense of this
Romance which wove its wild legends of nymph and cobold,
of faun and river-god, of imp and fairy, wielding the powers
of the elements and guiding the life of even the so-called
inanimate world.   But it is no less the theme of the fairy
tale of science.   Even in the austere demonstrations of
geometry, and the constructions of mechanics, the un-
looked-for slips upon us with gipsy tread.   Who has not—
in his early studies of mathematics—been fain to marvel
at the almost unexpected consilience of property with
property in a figure, suddenly placing in almost ' eery ' relief
the conjunction of what was apparently poles asunder ?   It
is not a mere form of words to speak of beautiful properties
of a conic section or a curve.   Custom perhaps has blunted
our sense for the symmetries of celestial dynamics, but they
are none the less admirable, because we are otherwise
engrossed.   To the first generation of our century the
phenomena of chemistry, magnetism and electricity appealed—as they have never since done—with a tangible
demonstration of that *appetitus ad invicem*, that instinct of
union Bacon speaks of ;   and this time in a higher form
than in mere mechanism.   Polarity—the bifurcation of
reality into a pair of opposites which yet sought their complement in each other—eternally dividing only eternally
to unite, and thus only to exist—became a process pressed
into general service.   Lastly, what more admirable than
that adaptation of the individual to the environment—and
of the environment to the individual—of the organs in him
to his total, and of his total to his organs.   One in all and
All in one :   one life in perpetual transformation, animals,
plants, and earth and air ;   one organism, developing in
absolute coherence.   This was the vision which the genius
of Schelling and his contemporaries saw—the same vision
which, by accumulation of facts and pictorial history,
Darwin and his disciples have impressed in some measure
even on the dullest.

But there is a profound difference between the spirit of
a Philosophy of Nature and the aggregate of the physical
sciences.   Each science takes the particular quarry which
accident or providence has assigned to it, and does its best
to ' put out ' every piece of rock it contains.   But it seldom
goes, unless by constraint, and in these days of specialisation
it does so less and less, to examine the neighbouring excava-

tion, and see if there be any connexion between the strata. Even within its own domain it is ashamed to put forward too much parade of system. Its method is often like that of the showman in the travelling menagerie : ' And now, please pass to the next carriage.' It respects the compartmental arrangement into which it finds the world broken up, and often thinks it has deserved well if it has filled the compartment fuller than before, or succeeded in creating a few sub-compartments within the old bounds. Even the so-called mental and moral sciences when they lose their philosophical character tend to imitate these features. Yet in every science there is an outlook and an outlet, for whosoever has the will and the power, to emerge from his narrow domain on the open fields and free prospect into the first fountains and last great ocean of being. Always, and not least in our own day, the physicist, the chemist, the physiologist, the psychologist, the sociologist, and the economist, have made their special field a platform where they might discourse *de omnibus rebus*, and become for the nonce philosophers and metaphysicians. It would be a silly intolerance and a misconception of the situation to exclaim *Ne sutor ultra crepidam.* In the organic system of things ' each " moment " even independent of the whole is the whole ; and to see this is to penetrate to the heart of the thing.' We need hardly go to Hegel to be told that to know one thing thoroughly well is to know all things. The finite, which we inertly rest content with, would, if we were in full sympathy with it, open up its heart and show us the infinite. And yet if the specialist when he rises from his shoe-making, with a heart full of the faith that ' there is nothing like leather ', should proclaim his discovery of it in regions where it was hitherto unsurmised, one may smile incredulous and be no cynic.

Philosophy then keeps open eye and ear—as far as may be no doubt for the finer shades and delicate details—but essentially for the music of humanity and the music of the spheres—for the general purpose and drift of all sciences—from mathematics to sociology—as they help to make clear the life of nature and further the emancipation of man. It will seem occasionally to over-emphasise the continuity of science and to make light of its distinctions : it will seem occasionally more anxious as to the order than as to the contents of the sciences : it will remind the sciences of the hypothetical and formal character of much of their method and some of their principles : and sometimes will treat as unimportant, results on which the mere scholar or dogmatist of science lays great weight. From his habit of dealing with the limitations and mutual implication of principles and conceptions, the philosopher will often be able—and perhaps only too willing—to point out cases where the mere specialist has allowed himself to attribute reality to his abstraction. He will tell the analyst of the astronomical motions that he must not take the distinction of centrifugal and centripetal force, into which mechanics disintegrate the planetary orbit, as if it really meant that the planet was pulled inward by one force and sent on spinning forward by another.[1] And the scientist, proud of his mathematics, will resent and laugh at the philosopher who lets fall a word about the planets moving in grand independence like ' blessed gods '. The philosopher will hint to the chemist that his formulae of composition and decomposition of bodies are, as he uses them, somewhat mythological, picturing water as atom of oxygen locked up with atom of hydrogen ; and the chemist will go away muttering something about a fool who does not believe in the well-ascertained chemical truth that water is composed of these two gases. If the philosopher further hints that it is not the highest ideal of a chemical science to be content with enumerating fifty or sixty elements, and detecting their several properties and affinities ;[2] that it would be well to find some principle of gradation, some unity or law which brought meaning into meaningless juxtaposition, the mere dogmatist, whose chemistry is his living and who shrinks from disendowment, will scent a propensity towards the heresy which sinks all elements in one. And yet, even among chemists, the instinct for law and unity begins to demand satisfaction.

A still richer store of amazing paradox and perplexing analogies awaits anyone who will turn over the volume in Hegel's *Werke* (vii. 1) and select the plums which lie thick in the lecture-notes. He will find a great deal—and probably

---

[1] *Encyclop.* §§ 266, 269 ; cf. the lecture-note as given in *Werke* vii. 1. p. 97. A large number of paradoxical analogies from Hegel's *Naturphilosophie* has been collected by Riehl in his *Philosophischer Criticismus*, ii. 2, 120.

[2] See notes and illustrations in vol. ii. 419.

more, the less he really knows of any of the subjects under discussion—that he cannot make head or tail of : language where he cannot guess whether it should be taken literally or figuratively. For Hegel seriously insists on the essential unity and identity of all the compartments of the physical universe ; he will not keep time and space on one level, matter and motion on another, and senses, suns, plants, passions, all in their proper province. Going far beyond the theory which supposes that all the complex difference of organisation has grown up in endless, endless ages from a primitive indistinctness, so that the gap of time acts as a wall to keep early and late apart, Hegel insists upon their essential unity to-day. And that sounds hard—the herald of anarchy, of the collapse of the ordered polity of the scientific state. It is no doubt probable that Hegel, like other men, made mistakes ; that he over-estimated the supposed discoveries of the day : that he indulged in false analogies, and that he was attracted by a daring paradox. All this has nothing to do with his main thesis : which is, that the natural realm is as it stands an a-logical realm where reason has gone beside itself, and yet containing an instrument—man, and that is mind—by which its rationality may be realised and restored. In that point at least he and Schopenhauer are at one.

CHAPTER VIII

THE SCEPTICAL DOUBT: HUME

WE have seen that an innate tendency leads the human
mind to connect and set in relation,—to connect, it may be
erroneously, or without proper scrutiny, or under the influence of passions or prejudices,—but at any rate to
connect. Criticism occasionally has impatiently banned
this tendency as a mere fountain of errors. The human
mind, says Francis Bacon, always assumes a greater
uniformity in things than it finds ; it expects symmetry, is
bold in neglecting exceptional cases, and would fain go
beyond all limits in its everlasting cry, Why and To what
end. It varies in individuals between a passion for discovering similarities and an intent acuteness to every shade
of unlikeness. But notwithstanding these warnings of the
hen, the ugly duckling Reason *will* go beyond what is given :
it knows no insuperable limitation. It may be guilty of
what Bacon calls ' anticipation '—an induction on evidence
insufficient—or it may subdue itself to the duty of ' interpretation ' of nature by proper methods : in either case, it
is an act of association, synthesis, unification. For Νοῦς *is*
ἀρχή, and knows that it is : it will not yield to clamour or
mere rebuke : it, too, cannot be commanded, unless by first
obeying it : and Bacon, having duly objurgated the ' mind
left to itself ', is obliged to let it go to gather the grapes
before they are quite ripe, and to indulge it with a ' prerogative ' of instances. As Mr. Herbert Spencer and many
others are never weary of telling us : ' We think in relations.
This is truly the form of all thought : and if there are any
other forms they must be derived from this.' [1] Man used
to be defined as a thinking or rational animal : which means

[1] *First Principles*, p. 162. It may be as well to remark that Relation
is scarcely an adequate description of the nature of thought as
a whole. We shall see when we come to the theory of logic, that
the term is applicable—and then somewhat imperfectly—only to the
second phase of thought, the categories of reflection, which are the
favourite categories of science and popular metaphysics.

that man is a connecting and relation-giving animal ; and from this, Aristotle's definition, making him out to be a ' political ' animal, is only a corollary, most applicable in the region of Ethics. Here is the ultimate point, from which the natural consciousness, and the energies of science, art, and religion equally start upon their special missions.

In ordinary life we attach but little importance to this machinery of cognition. We incline to let the fact of synthesis drop out of sight, as if it required no further study or notice, and we regard the things connected as exclusively worth attending to. The interest centres on the object—on the matter : the formal element—the connective tissue—is *only* an instrument of no importance, except in view of the end it helps us to. We use general and half-explained terms, such as development, evolution, continuity, as bridges from one thing to another, without giving any regard to the means of locomotion on their own account. Some one thing is the product of something else : we let the term ' product ' slip out of the proposition as unimportant : and then read the statement so as to explain the one thing by turning it into the other. Things, according to this opinion, are all-important : the rest is mere words. These relations between things are not open to further investigation or definition : they are each *sui generis*, or peculiar : and even if the logician in his analysis of inference finds it advisable to deal with them, he will be content, if he can classify them in some approximate way, as a basis for his subdivision of propositions. This is certainly one way of getting rid of Metaphysics—for the time.

But there are epochs in life, and epochs in universal history, when the mind withdraws from its immersion in active life, and reflects upon its own behaviour as on the proceedings of some strange creature, of which it is a mere spectator. At such seasons when we stop to reflect upon the partial scene, and close our eyes to the totality, doubts begin to arise, whether our procedure is justified when we unify and combine the isolated phenomena. Have we any right to throw our own subjectivity, the laws of our imagination and thought, into the natural world ? Would it not be more proper to refrain altogether from the use of such conceptions ?

Philosophy, said one of the ancients,[1] begins in wonder,

[1] Arist. *Metaph.* i. 2. 26.

and ends in wonder. It begins from the surprise that something could *be* what it purports to be : it ends in the marvel of our having *thought* anything else possible. Such a phrase well becomes the naïve age in which the soul goes freely forth, wandering from one novelty to another, curious to find out all that can be known,—like the young wanderer on the sea-shore whom fresh pebbles and new shells tempt endlessly to fill his basket. But as the ages roll on, and the accumulations of the past grow heavier in the receptacle, the need of a re-examination of the stores becomes imperative. The bright colours have faded—and generally they fade soon : there has been much picked up in the inexperience of youthful enthusiasm which maturer reflection hardly can think worth carrying further.

The duty of doubt and of re-examination of what tradition has bequeathed has been enforced by philosophy in all ages. For it is the cardinal principle of philosophy to be free—to possess its soul—never to be a mere machine or mere channel of tradition. But, in some ages, this assertion of its freedom has had for the soul a pre-eminently negative aspect. It has meant only freedom *from*—and not also freedom *in* and *through*—its environing, or rather constituting, substance. Such an epoch was seen in the ancient world when the *New Academy*, with its sceptical abstention from all objective assertions, had to protest against the dogmatism of the Stoic and Epicurean schoolmen. In modern times the initial shudder before plunging in has been a recurrent crisis. Each thinker—as he personally resolved to thread his way through the wilderness of current opinion to the realm of certified truth—has had to remind himself (and his contemporaries) that in knowledge at least no possessions are secured property unless they have been earned by the sweat of their owner's brow. This is the common theme of Bacon's aphorisms in the beginning of the *Novum Organum*, of Descartes' *Discourse of Method*, and of Spinoza's unfinished essay on the *Emendation of the Intellect*. There is indeed a discrepancy in these utterances as to the measure in which they severally think it needful to insist as preliminary on a kind of moral and religious consecration of life to the service of truth. But a more compelling division arises. The maxim may be understood to say, ' Divest thy mind of its ill-gotten gains, its evil habits, prejudices, and system, and in childlike simplicity prepare thine eye

and ear to receive in pure vessels the stores of truth which
are ready to stream in from the world.'   Or it may rather
be held to say, ' Remember that thou art a conscious,
waking mind, and that every idea thou hast is thine by
thine own assent : insist upon thy right of free intelligence,
and give no place to any belief which thou hast not raised
into full light of consciousness, and found to be completely
consistent with the whole power and content of thy clearest
thought.'   And, we may add, if the maxim be obeyed too
exclusively in either way, it will be obeyed amiss.

   With Locke the question comes into even greater prominence.   On what conditions can I have knowledge ?
How can I be certified that my ideas—the subjective
images in *my* mind—have a reference to something objective
and real ?   Locke's answer is, not unnaturally perhaps,
somewhat prolix, and wanting in fundamental precision of
principles.   After dismissing the view that, even before
experience, there are certain common ideas spontaneously
and by original endowment present in all human beings, he
goes on to show how we can sufficiently account for the ideas
we actually find by supposing in us an almost unlimited
power of joining and disjoining, of comparing, relating, and
unifying the various elementary ' ideas ' which make their
way into the empty chambers of our mind by the senses.
As to the source, the channel, and the nature of these
sense-ideas, Locke is obscure and apparently inconsistent :
though clearly it should be all-important to know how an
idea can be caused by, or spring from, a material thing.
When in his fourth book he comes to the question of what is
the reality, or the *meaning* of our ideas, he does not really
get beyond a few—rather dubiously reasoned-out—conclusions that, although strictly we cannot go beyond ' the
present testimony of our senses employed about the particular objects that do affect them ', we may for practical
purposes allow a good deal to the presumptions of general
probability.

   But Locke had also begun to criticise our ideas, in his
account of their formation out of the ' simpie ideas '—
(which neither Locke nor any other atomist of mind has
succeeded in making clear)—which the several senses give,
and by observing or reflecting on what goes on or is present
in *our* minds, *we* ' form ', he says, various ideas.   In a style
of discussion which is on the borderland between vulgar

and philosophical analysis—(never quite false, but nearly always inadequate, because it almost invariably assumes what it ostensibly proposes to explain),—Locke tells us how we get one idea by ' enlarging ', another by ' repeating ', as we please, the bounteous data of the touch and sight. But amongst the compounds there are some of more disputable origin. There are some—e.g. ideas of punishable acts or legalised states—which are ' voluntary collections of ideas put together in the mind independent from any original patterns in nature '. These, though entirely subjective, are entirely real, because they only serve as patterns by which we may judge or designate things so and so. It is worse with the idea of power, which we only ' collect ' or ' infer ', and that not from matter, where it is invisible, but only in a clear light when we consider God and spirits. Still worse, perhaps, is it with the idea of substance, which is a ' collection ' of simple ideas with the ' supposition ' of an ' incomprehensible ' something in which the collection ' subsists '.

Hume put all this rather more pointedly. We have ' impressions ', i.e. lively perceptions by sense. We have also ' ideas ', i.e. fainter images of these, but otherwise identical. An idea *should* be a copy of an impression. If you cannot point out any such impression, you may be certain you are mistaken when you imagine you have any such idea. There is prevalent in the mental world a kind of association ; a ' gentle force ' connects ideas in our imagination according to certain relations they possess. This ' mind ' or this ' imagination ' is only a bundle or collection of impressions and ideas ; but a collection which is continually and rapidly changing in its constituents, and in the scale of liveliness possessed by each constituent. When an idea is particularly fresh and forcible, it is a *belief*, or it is believed in : when faint, not so. Or, otherwise put, the object of an idea is *said* to *exist*, when the idea itself is vividly *felt*.[1] Really there is no such thing as ' external existence ' taken literally. ' Our universe is the universe of the imagination : ' all existence is for a consciousness.

Impressions arise in certain orders of sequence or co-existence. When two impressions frequently recur and always in the same order, the custom binds them so closely together, that, should one of them only be given as impres-

[1] *Treatise of Human Nature* (Understanding), iii. 7 and ii. 6.

sion, we cannot help having an idea of the other, which, growing more vivid by the contagion of the contiguous impression, creates, or is, a belief in its reality. Between the perceptions as such, there is no connexion ; they are distinct and independent existences. They only get a connexion through *our feeling* ; *we feel* a ' determination ' of our thought to pass from one to another. The one impression has no power to produce the other ; the one thing does not cause the other. ' We never have any impression that contains any power or efficacy.'[1] Hence the power and necessity we attribute to the so-called causal agent and to the connexion are an illegitimate transference from our feeling, and a mistranslation of *our* incapacity to resist the force of habitual association into a real bond between the two impressions *themselves*. The necessity is in the mind— as a habit-caused compulsion—not in the objects.

As with the relation of cause and effect, so it is with others. The identity of continued existence is only another name—an objective transcript—of the feeling of smooth uninterrupted succession of impressions in which our thought glides along from one in easy transition to another. And here the coherence and continuity of perceptions need not be absolute. A vivid impression of unbroken connexion in a part will, if predominant, by association fill up the gaps and weak points, and behind the admitted breaks in the line of our ideas will suppose—invent—or create an imperceptible but *real* continuity in the supposed things. And by this fiction of a continuous existence of our perceptions, we easily lapse into the doctrine that our perceptions have an independent existence as objects or things in themselves : —a doctrine which according to Hume is contrary to the plainest experience.

But if the world is always the world of imagination—of *Vorstellung*—of mental representation, Hume is aware that we must admit two orders or grades of such representation. We must distinguish, he remarks,[2] ' in the imagination betwixt the principles which are permanent, irresistible and universal (such as the customary transition from causes to effects and from effects to causes), and the principles which are changeable, weak, and irregular. The former are the foundation of all our thoughts and actions.' There are, in

---

[1] *Treatise of Human Nature* (Understanding), iii. 14.
[2] Ibid. iv. 4.

other words, normal and general laws of association—such
as the relation of cause and effect—which persuade us of
real existence. By its own laws, therefore, within the realm
of *Vorstellung* or Mental idea, there grows up a permanent,
objective world for all, contrasted with the temporary,
accidental perception of the individual and of the moment ;
and this serves as the standard or the one common measure
by which occasional perturbations are to be measured.
Within the limits of the subjective in general there arises
a subjective of higher order, which is truly objective.
This same change of front—as it may be called—Hume
makes in morals.   There the mind can modify and control
its passions according as it can feel the objects of them near
or far ; and though each of us has his ' peculiar position ',
we can—so creating the ethical basis—' fix on some steady
and general points of view, and always in our thoughts place
ourselves in them, whatever may be our present situation : [1]
we can ' choose some common point of view ', and from the
vantage-ground of a permanent principle, however distant,
we have a chance of gaining the victory over our passion,
however near.

Thus far Hume had gone in the development of idealism.
Whether his theory is consistent from end to end, need not
be here discussed.   But it is evident that Hume was not
lost in the quagmire of subjective idealism.   The objective
and the subjective are with him akin : the objective is the
subjective, which is universal, permanent, and normal.
The causal relation has, in the first instance, only a subjective necessity ; but through that subjective necessity
or its irresistible belief, it generates an objective world. But
it has been and is the fortune of philosophers to be known
in the philosophical world by some conspicuous red rag of
their system which first caught the eye of the bull-like
leaders of the human herd.   It was so notably with Hobbes
and Spinoza ; and most of the thinkers whose names
appear in the pages of Kant suffer from this curtailment.
Descartes, Locke, Leibniz, Berkeley, Hume, are *there* not
the real philosophers, discoverable in their works, but the
creatures of historic reputation and of popular simplification
who do duty for them.

Kant's Hume is therefore a somewhat imaginary being :
the product, partly of imperfect knowledge of Hume's

[1] *Treatise of Human Nature* (Morals), iii. 1.

writings, partly of prepossessions derived from a long previous training in German rationalism. Such a Hume was—or would have been, had he existed—a philosopher who ' took the objects of experience for things in themselves ', who ' treated the conception of cause as a false and deceptive illusion ', who did not indeed venture to assail the certainty of mathematics, but held—as regards all knowledge about the existence of things—' empiricism to be the sole source of principles ', founding his conclusion mainly on an examination of the causal nexus.[1]   This ' note of warning ' sounded against the claims of pure reason— as he calls Hume's *Enquiry*—was what about 1762 broke Kant's dogmatic slumber and forced him to give his researches in speculative philosophy a new direction.   His first step was to generalise Hume's problem from an inquiry into the origin of the causal idea into a general study of the synthetic principles in knowledge.   His next was to attempt to fix the number of these concepts and synthetic principles. And his third was to ' deduce ' them : i. e. to prove the reciprocal implication between experience or knowledge and the concepts or categories of intelligence.

[1] Kant, *Prolegomena* to Metaph. Introduction and *Crit. of Practical Reason* (on the Claim of Pure Reason, *Werke*, viii. 167).

CHAPTER IX

THE ATTEMPT AT A CRITICAL SOLUTION : KANT

THE *Criticism of Pure Reason* has been described by its author as a generalisation of Hume's problem. Hume, he thought, had treated his question on the 'relations of ideas' in their bearing upon 'matters of fact' mainly with reference to the isolated case of cause and effect. Kant extended the inquiry so as to comprise all those connective and unifying ideas which form the subject-matter of metaphysics. In his own technical language—which has lost its meaning for the present day—he asked, 'Are Synthetic judgments *a priori* possible ? '—a question which in another place he has translated into the form, 'Is the metaphysical faith of men sound, and is a metaphysical science possible ? ' By a metaphysics he meant in the first instance the belief in a more than empirical reality, and secondly the science which should give real knowledge of God, Freedom and Immortality,—a science whose objects would be God, the World, and the Soul. From a comparatively early date (1762-4) Kant had been inclined to suspect and distrust the claims of metaphysics to replace faith, and to give knowledge of spiritual reality ; and he had tried to vindicate for the moral and religious life an independence of the conclusions and methods of the metaphysical theology and psychology of the day. But it was not till some years later—in 1770—that he formulated any very definite views as to the essential conditions of scientific knowledge : and it was not till 1781 that his theory on the subject was put together in a provisionally complete shape.

What then are the criteria of a science ? When is our thought knowledge, and of objective reality ? In the first place, there must be a given something—a sense-*datum*—an 'impression' as Hume might have said. If there be no impression, therefore, there can be no scientific idea, no real knowledge. There must be the primary touch—the feeling—the affection—the *je ne sais quoi* of contact with reality. Secondly, what is given can only be received if taken up by the recipient, and in such measure as he is able to appropriate it. The given is received in a certain mode. In the present case, the sensation is apprehended and perceived under the forms of space and time. Perception, in other words, whatever may be its special quality or its sensuous material, is always an act of dating and localisation. The distinction between the mere lump of feeling or sensibility and the perception is that the latter implies a field of extended and mutually excluding parts of space, and a series of points of time, both field and series being continuous, and, so far as inexhaustibility goes, infinite. Thirdly, even in the reception of the given there is a piece of action and spontaneity. If the more passive recipiency be called Sense, this active element in the adaptation may be termed Intellect. Intellect is a power or process of choice, selection, comparison, distinguishing and dividing, analysis and synthesis, affirmation and negation, numeration, of judgment and doubt, of connexion and disjunction, differentiation and integration. Its general aspect is by Kant sometimes described as Judgment—the act of thought which correlates by distinguishing ; sometimes as Apperception, and the unity of apperception. It is, i. e., an active unity and a synthetic energy ; it unifies, and always unifies. It links perception to perception, correlating one with another—interpreting one by another ; estimating the knowledge-value of one by the rest. It thus ' ap-perceives '. It is a faculty of association and consociation of ideas. But the association is inward and ' ideal ' union : the one idea interpenetrates and fuses with the other, even while it remains distinct.

Kant's work may be described—in its first stage—as an analysis and a criticism of experience. The term Experience is an ambiguous one. It sometimes means what has been called the ' raw material ' of experience : the crude, indigested mass of poured-in *matter*-of-knowledge. If there be such a shapeless lump anywhere,—which has to be considered presently—it, at any rate, is not on Kant's view properly entitled to the name of Experience. The Given must be felt and apprehended : and—to put the point paradoxically—to be felt it must be more than felt,— it must be perceived. It must, in other words, be projected—set in space and time : let out of the mere dull

inner subjectivity of feeling into the clear and distinct
outer subjectivity of perception. But, again, to be perceived, it must be apperceived : to be set in time and
space, it must first of all be in the hands of the unifying
consciousness, which is the lord of time and space. For
in so far as space and time mean a place and an order—
in so far as they mean more than an empty inconceivable
receptacle for bulks of sensation, in the same degree do
they presuppose an intellectual, synthetic genius, which
is in all its perceptions one and the same,—the fundamental,
original unity of consciousness. And this analysis of
experience is ' transcendental '. Beginning with the assumed datum—the object of or in experience—it shows
that this object which is supposed to be *there*—to exist by
itself and wait for perception—is created by and in the
very act which apprehends it. Climbing up and rising
above its habitual absorption *in* the *thing*, consciousness
(that of the philosophic observer and analyst) sees the
thing in the act of making, and watches its growth.

We have seen that Kant made free use of the metaphor
of giving and receiving. But it is hardly possible to use
such metaphors and retain independence of judgment.
The associations customarily attached to the figurative
language carry one away easily, and often for a long way,
on the familiar paths of imagination. The analogy is used
even where—if all were looked into—its terms become
meaningless. No reader of Locke can have failed, e. g., to
notice how he is misled by his own images of the dark
room and the empty cabinet :—images, useful and perhaps
even necessary, but requiring constant restraint in him
who would ply them wisely and to his reader's good.
From what has been said above it will be clear that the
acquisition of experience, the growth of knowledge, is a
unique species of gift and acceptance. The consciousness
which Kant describes may be the consciousness of John
Doe or Richard Roe : but as Kant describes it, the limitations of their personality, i. e. of their individual body and
soul, have been neglected. It is consciousness in general
which is Kant's theme, just as it is granite in general—and
not the block in yonder field—which is the theme of the
geologist. Once get that clear, and you will also see
clearly that consciousness is at once giver and recipient—
neither or both : at once receptivity and spontaneity

But—you may reply—does not the material object *act* (chemically, optically, mechanically, &c.) on the sense-organ on the periphery of my body, does not the nerve-string *convey* the impression to the brain ; and is not perception the *effect* of that process, in which the material object is the initial *cause* ?

In this exposition—which is not unknown in vulgar philosophy—there is a monstrous, almost inextricable, complication of fact with inference, of truth with error. So long as there is an uncertainty—and metaphysicians themselves, we may be reminded, are not agreed upon the matter—as to what we are to understand by cause, effect, and act, what an impression is, and how brain and intelligence mutually stand to each other, it is hardly possible to pronounce judgment upon this mode of state-ment. Yet perhaps we may go so far as to say that while the terms quoted bear an intelligible meaning when applied within the physiological process they are vain when used of relations of mind to body. There is a sense in which we may speak of the action of mind on body, and of body on mind : but what we mean would perhaps be more unmistakably expressed by saying that the higher intel-lectual and volitional energies are never in our experience entirely independent of the influences of the lower sensitive and emotional nature. In the metaphysical sense which the terms are here made to bear, they mislead. Action and re-action can only take place in the separateness of space, where one is here and another there : (though, be it added, they cannot take place even on these terms, unless the here and the there be somehow unified in a medium which embraces both). *Mens*, said Spinoza, is the *idea corporis* : [1] he would hardly have said *Corpus habet ideam*. What he meant would scarcely have been well described by calling it a *parallelism* or mutual independence, yet with harmony or identity, of body and mind. Apart from body, no doubt, mind is for him a nullity : for body is what gives it reality. But, on the other hand, Mind is the enveloping and including ' Attribute ' of the two : idealism overlaps realism.

This was the fundamental proposition which Kant contended for ; what he spoke of as his own Copernican discovery : though, in reality, for the *student* of the history

[1] Spinoza, *Eth.* ii. 7-13.

of philosophy it was only the re-statement, in some respects the clearer statement, of the idealism which even Hume, not to mention Spinoza and Leibniz, had maintained. The world of experience—the empirical, objective, and real world—is a world of ideas, of representations which have place only in mind, of appearances. Space and time are subjective : the forms of thought are subjective : and yet they constitute phenomenal or empirical or real objectivity. Such language is—it would seem inevitably—misunderstood : and in his second edition, Kant—besides many other minor modifications of statement,—had to defend himself by inserting a ' confutation of idealism ', i. e. of the theory which holds that the existence of objects outside us in space is doubtful, if not even impossible. But no end of argument will ever confute the view that Kant's doctrine is such idealism : until people can be got to rise to a new view of what is subjectivity—what is an idea— and what is existence outside us.

By ' subjective ' the world is in the way of understanding what is due to personal prepossession, void of general acceptability, a product of individual feeling, peculiar and inexplicable tastes. By subjective Kant means what belongs to *the* subject or knowing mind as such and in its generality : what is constitutive of intelligence in general, what sense and intellect are *semper et ubique*. Into the question how the human being came to have such an intellectual endowment—the question which Nativist psychology is supposed to settle in one way, and Evolutionism in another—Kant does not enter ; he merely says where there is knowledge, there is a knower,—a knowing subject *so* constituted. It comes after all to the tautology that the reality we know is a known reality : that knowledge is a growth in the knower, and not an accidental product due to things otherwise unknown. The predicate (or category) ' *is* ' is contained, implicit, in the predicate ' *is known* ', or what ' *is* ' puts implicitly, ' *is known* ' puts explicitly and truly.

By ' appearance ' the world understands a sham, or at least somewhat short of reality. By appearance Kant understands a reality which has appeared : or, as that is going too far, a something which is real so far as it goes (a *prima facie* fact), but only a candidate for admission into the circle of reals. And such reality depends on nothing more than its thorough-going coherence with other appearances, its explaining the rest, and being in turn explained by them,—its absolute adaptation to its environment. And this environment all lies in the common field of consciousness, and in the one correlating and unifying apperceptivity of the ego,—that Ego which is the inseparable comrade, vehicle, and judge, of all our perceptions. It is the appearance—but as yet not the appearance *of* something,—but rather an appearance *to* or *for* something.

By an ' idea ' the world in general understands what it is sometimes ready to call a *mere* idea. And by a mere idea is meant something which is *not* reality, but a peculiarity of an individual mind, or group of minds—a fancy, without objective truth :—something, we may even add, which for many people is located in their own head or brain, cut off by blank bone-walls from the open air of real being. By idea (representation, *Vorstellung*) Kant meant that an object is always and essentially the object of a mind : always relative to a subject consciousness, and implying it, just as a subject consciousness always implies an object.

And by ' existence outside us ' the world probably means —for it is imprudent to define and refine too much in this hazy medium of words where we all drowse—existence of things on an independent footing beyond the limits of our personal, i.e. bodily and sentient, self. As regards *our own* trunk and limbs, most of us, except in some most strange insanity, are not likely ever to be in doubt, and are indeed more likely, after Schopenhauer's model, to take the knowledge of these *personalia* as the one thing immediately and intuitively certain. We talk freely enough, it is true, about existence outside our own minds ; but it is only a drastic method of stating the difference between a fancy and a fact. And probably we labour under a half-unconscious hallucination that our minds are localised in some material ' seat ', somewhere in our bodily limits, and more especially in the central nerve-organs.

But, as has been said elsewhere,[1] the point of view under which Mind is regarded by Kant is that of Consciousness, and especially perceptive consciousness. He describes, as

[1] *Encyclopaedia*, §§ 415, 420. Consciousness is only as it were the surface of the ocean of mind ; and reflects only the lights and shadows in the sky above it.

we have put it above, the steps or conditions under which the single sense-observation is elevated into the rank of an experience claiming universality and necessity. But the whole machinery of consciousness—the form of sensibility and the category of intellect—is originally set in motion by an impetus from without : or at least the manipulating machinery requires a raw material on which to operate. Consciousness, or the observer who takes this point of view, feels that it is being played upon by an unknown performer—or that it is attempting to apprehend something, which, because the act of apprehension is also to some extent (and to what extent, who can say ?) a transmutation, it must for ever fail to apprehend truly. It is haunted by the phantom of a real,—a thing in its own right, which can only appear in forms of sense and intellect, never in its own essential being. It is only a short step further—and Kant, if one may judge him by several isolated passages, has more than once crossed the interval, —to treat, after the manner of uneducated consciousness and of popular science, the thing in its independent being as the cause which produces the sensation, or as the original which the mental idea reproduces under the distortions or modifications rendered necessary by the sensuous-intellectual medium. For, if under the terms of one analogy the perception is an *effect* of the thing, under those of another it is an *image* or copy of external reality.

If this be Kantian philosophy—and it can quote chapter and verse in its favour—Kantian philosophy is one version of the great dogma of the relativity of knowledge. That unhappy phrase seems to have many meanings, but none of absolutely catholic acceptation. It may mean that knowledge of things states their relations—the way they behave in reference to this or that, in these or those circumstances ; and that of an utterly unrelated and *absolutely* isolated thing, our knowledge is and must be *nil*. Of a thing-in-itself we can know nothing ; for there is nothing to know. It may mean that knowledge is relative to the recipient or the knower,—that it is not a product which can stand by itself, but needs a vehicle and an object in close relation. In this way, too, knowledge is relative to age and circumstances : grows from period to period, and may even decay. And thirdly, the relativity of knowledge may be taken to mean that we (and all human beings) can

never know the reality ; because we can only know the
phenomenon, i.e. the modified, transmuted, reflected thing
which has reconstituted an image of itself after passing the
interfering medium.   For, first of all, we must strip it—
this ' image ' so-called (the vulgar call it the ' thing ')—of
the secondary qualities (sound, colour, taste, resistance)
which it has in the consciousness of a being dependent on
his sense-organs :   and then, we must get rid also of those
quantitative attributes (figure, number, size) which it has
in the consciousness of a spatially and temporally perceptive being ;—and then ;—but the prospect is too horrible
to continue further and face the Gorgon's head in the outer
darkness, where man denudes appearance in the hope to
meet reality.

The fact is, there are too many strands in the web which
Kant is weaving, for him or perhaps for any man to keep
them all well in hand and lose none of the symmetry of
the pattern he designs.   To be just, we must, in dealing
with him as with any other philosopher, try to keep in
view the unity of that design instead of insisting too
minutely and too definitely upon its occasional defects.
It is easy to work the pun that a ' critical ' philosophy
must itself expect to be criticised ;   it is more important
to remember that by a criticism Kant meant an attempt
to steer a course between the always enticing extremes of
dogmatism and scepticism,—an attempt to be fair, i.e. just
to both sides, and yet neither to sink into the systematised
placidity of the former, nor to rove in a mere guerilla
warfare with the latter.   And it is the mere privateer who
in the popular sense of the word is the mere critic.

Of Kant we must remember that he has the defects
of his qualities.   He prides himself on his distinctions of
sense and intellect, of imagination and understanding, of
understanding and reason ;   and with justice :   but his
distinctions are sometimes so decisive that it is hard work
both for him and for his reader to reconstitute their unity.
He is fond of utilising old classifications to embody his
new doctrine :   and occasionally the result is like what we
have been taught to expect from pouring new wine into
old bottles.   He draws hard and fast lines, and then has
to create, as it seems, supplementary links of connexion,
which, if they operate, can only do so because they are the
very unity he began by ignoring.   One gets perfectly lost

in the multitude of syntheses, in the labyrinth of categories, schemata, and principles, of paralogisms, antinomies, and ideals of pure reason. One part of this formalism *may* be set down to the pedantry and pipeclay of the age of the Great Frederick—pedantry, from which, as we console ourselves, our modern souls are freed. But it arises rather from the necessity of pursuing the battle ·between truth and error through every complicated passage in that great fortress which ages of scholasticism had—on various plans—gradually constructed. Kant is always a little of the martinet and the schoolmaster ; but it is because he knows that true liberty cannot be secured without forms and must capture the old before it can plant the new. The forms as they stand in his grouping may often appear stiff and lifeless : but a more careful study, more sympathetically intent, will find that there is latent life and undisplayed connexion in the terms. Unfortunately the classified cut-and-dried specimens are more welcome to the collector, and can more easily be put in evidence in the examination-room.

Thus the original question, Are synthetic judgments *a priori* possible ? is answered—somewhat piecemeal—in a way that leads the reader to suppose it is a question of psychology. He hears so much of sense, imagination, intellect, in the discussion, that he fancies it is an account of a process carried on by the faculties of an individual mind. And of course nobody need suppose these processes are ever carried on otherwise than by individual thinkers, human beings with proper names. But scientific investigation is concerned only with the essential and universal. For it, really, sense, imagination, &c. are not so many faculties in a thinking agent : they are grades and aspects of consciousness,—' powers ' in a process of gradual mental complication (involution). Kant is really dealing with a ' normal ' thought with its distinguishable constituent aspects. Only—he fails to make this explicit and clear. The individualism—the un-historical prepossession—of his age is upon his phraseology, if not upon his thought : and one hardly realises that he is really engaged on human thought and knowledge as a substantial subject of itself apart from its individual vehicles,—on that thought, which lives and grows in social institutions and products,—in language, science, literature, and moral usage,—the common stock which one age bequeathes to the next, but which the later-comer can only inherit if he works for and creates it afresh. If it be a psychology, therefore, it is a psychology which does not assume a soul with qualities, but which expounds the steps in the constitution of a normal intelligence.

One may note, without insisting on them too much, the defects of his treatment of the forms of thought. It may be said that, in the *first* place, the table of the categories was incomplete. It had been borrowed, as Kant himself tells us, from the old logical subdivision of judgments, derived more or less directly from Aristotle and the Schoolmen. Now many of the relations occurring in ordinary thought could not be reduced to any of the twelve forms, without doing violence to them. But Kant expressly disclaims exhaustiveness in detail. He could, if he would : but that is for another season. In the *second* place, the classification did not expressly put forward any principle or reason, and gave ground for no development. That there should be four fundamental categories, each with three divisions, making twelve in all, seems as inexplicable as that there should be four Athenian tribes in early times and twelve Phratriai. The twelve patriarchs of thought stand as if in equal authority, with little or no bearing upon one another. We have here, in short, what seems an artificial and not a natural classification of the types of thought. But Kant himself has given some explanation of the triad, and a sympathetic interpretation has shown how the four main groups are steps in the solution of one problem.[1] In the *third* place, the question as taken up seems largely psychological, or subjective, concerning the constitution of the human mind as a percipient and cognitive faculty. But this is necessary, perhaps, to the restricted nature of Kant's problem. He is dealing with the elements that form our objective or scientific consciousness of the physical world. The deeper question of the place and work of mind in life in general, in law and morality and religion, does not at this stage come before him. That problem in fact only gradually emerges with the Criticism of the Moral Faculty and the Aesthetic Judgment. Logic—

---

[1] It is not the least of the merits of the exposition in Caird's *Critical Philosophy* of Immanuel Kant, vol. i. to have brought out this.

as the doctrine of the *Logos* which is the principle of all things, even of its own Other—had to wait for its preparation till it could be matured.

In Hegel the question assumes a wider scope, and receives a more thorough-going answer. In the *first* place the question about the Categories is transferred from what we have called the epistemological or psychological, to what Hegel terms the logical, sphere. It is transferred from the Reason subjectively considered as a mere receptive and synthetic human consciousness to the Reason which is in the world and in history,—a Reason, which our Reason, as it were, touches, and so becomes possessed of knowledge. In the *second* place, the Categories become a vast multitude. The intellectual telescope discovers new stars behind the constellations named in ancient lore. There is no longer, if there ever was, any mystic virtue supposed to inhere in the number twelve : while the triadic arrangement is made radical and everywhere recurs. The modern chemist of thought vastly amplifies the number of its elementary types and factors, and proves that many of the old Categories are neither simple nor indecomposable. *Thirdly*, there is a systematic development or process which links the Categories together, and shows how the most simple, abstract, and inadequate, inevitably lead up to the most complex and adequate. Each term or member in the organism of thought has its place conditioned by all the others : each of them is the germ, or the ripe fruit of another.

CHAPTER X

KANT'S answer to his question was briefly this. Intelligence is essentially synthetic, always supplementing the given by something beyond, instituting relationships, unifying the many, and thus building up concrete totalities. In pure mathematics this is obvious : the process of numeration shows it creating number out of units, and geometry shows elementary propositions leading on to complicated theorems. In abstract physics it is hardly less obvious : there, e.g., the principle of reason and consequent or the persistence of substance are rational and legitimate steps beyond the mere datum. The more important question follows. How are these ' pure ' syntheses applicable to real fact ? To that Kant replies : They apply, because in all that we call real or objective fact there is a subjective element or constituent. What appears to be purely given, and independent of our perceptions, is a product of perceptual and conceptual conditions,—is constituted by a synthesis in perception, imagination, conception. Our world is a mental growth— not our individual product, but the work of that common mind in which we live and think, and which lives and thinks in us. Anyhow it is not an isolated self-existing un-intelligent world for ever materially outside us—an other world, eternally separate from us ; but bone of our bone, flesh of our flesh, the work realised by our great ' elder brother ',—the Idea of human collectivity—the Reason or Spirit in which we are all one soul. It is therefore no unwarranted step on to a foreign property when we apply the categories of thought and forms of sense to determine objective reality : for objective reality has been for ever made, and is now making, objective and reality by the conscious or unconscious syntheses of perception and imagination.

There remains the answer to the same question as regards

the objects of Metaphysics. These objects are according to Kant inferences, and illegitimate inferences. They are not necessary elements or factors in the constitution of experience. In order that there should be experience, knowledge, science, there must be an endless hold of space and time in which to stow it clearly and distinctly away : and there must also be ties and relations binding it part to part, links of reference and correlation, a sort of logical elastic band that will stretch to include infinitely copious materials. But each real knowledge attaches to a definite assignable perception, in a single place and time. From this point we can travel—by means of like points—practically without limit in any direction. But though the old margin fades forever and forever as we move, a new margin takes its place : the limitation and finitude remain : and new acquisitions are always balanced in part by the loss of the old. Yet the heart and the imagination are clamorous, and the intellect is ready to serve them. Such an intellect Kant has called Reason, and its products (Platonic) ' Ideas '. The (Platonic) Idea expresses not so much an object of knowledge as a postulate, a problem, an act of faith. The ' Vaulting ambition ' Intelligence ' o'erleaps itself and falls on t'other '. Unsatisfied with a bundle of sensations and ideas, it demands their abiding unity in a substantial Soul. To simplify the endlessness of physical phenomena, it sums them up in a Universe. To gather all mental and physical diversities and divisions into one life, it creates the ideal of God.

Each single experience, and the collected aggregate of these experiences, is felt to fall short of a complete total : and yet this complete total, the ultimate unity, is itself not an experience at all. But, if it be no object of experience, it is still an idea on which reason is inevitably driven : and the attempt to apprehend it, in the absence of experience, gives rise to the theories of Metaphysics. Everything, however, which can be in the strict sense of the word known, must be perceived in space and time, or, in other words, must lie open to experience. Where experience ends, human reason meets a barrier which checks any efficient progress, but refuses to recognise the check as due to a natural limit which it is really impossible to pass. The idea of complete-ness, of a rounded system, or unconditional unity, is still left, after the categories of the understanding have done their best : and is not destroyed although its realisation or explication is declared to be impossible.

There is thus left unexplained a totality which encompasses all the single members of experience—a unity compared to which the several categories are only a collection of fragments—an infinite which commands and regulates the finite concepts of the experiential intellect. But in the region of rational thought there is no objective and independent standard by which we can verify the conclusions of Reason. There are no definite objects, lying beyond the borders of experience, towards which it might unerringly turn ; and its sole authentic use, accordingly, is to see that the understanding is thorough and exact, when it deals in the co-ordination of experiences. In this want of definite objects, Reason, whenever it acts for itself, can only fall into perpetual contradictions and sophistries. Pure Reason, therefore, the faculty of ideas, the organ of Metaphysics, does not of itself ' constitute ' knowledge, but merely ' regulates ' the action of the understanding.

By this rigour of demonstration Kant dealt a deadly blow, as it seemed, to the dogmatic Metaphysics, and the Deism of his time. Hume had shaken the certainty of Metaphysics and thrown doubt upon Theology : but Kant apparently made an end of Metaphysics, and annihilated Deistic theology. The German philosopher, as Hegel has said and Heine has repeated, did thoroughly and with systematic demonstration what Voltaire did with literary graces and not without the witticisms with which the French executioner gives the *coup de grâce*. When a great idea had been degraded into a vulgar doctrine and travestied in common reality, the Frenchman met its inadequacies with graceful satire, and showed that these half-truths were not eternal verities. The German made a theory and a system of what was only a sally of criticism ; and rendered the criticism wrong, by making it too consistent and too logical.[1]

Science—such is Kant's conclusion—is of the definite and detailed, of the conditioned. It goes from point to point, within the enveloping unity of what we call experience, and which rests upon the transcendental and original unity of consciousness. But a knowledge of the whole—of the enveloping unity—is a contradiction in terms. To know is

[1] Hegel's *Werke*, vol. i. p. 140.

to synthetise : you cannot synthetise synthesis. Knowledge is of the relative : but an absolute and unconditional totality has no relations. We may therefore, possibly, feel, believe in, presuppose the absolute : but know it in the stricter sense, we cannot. It may be the object of a rational faith. But as for knowledge, we can get on in psychology without the invisible and immortal soul : we can carry out sciences of the physical universe, without troubling ourselves about the ' cosmological' questions of ultimate atoms or ultimate void, of first beginning and final end : and no proofs will ever prove the *existence* of that ' ideal ' of reason —briefly termed God—which transcends and completes and creates all existence. Not that such Ideas are useless even in science. They represent—if not without risks—the faith and the presupposition which underlie the spirit of scientific progress, and set before it an ideal perfection which it will do well to strive after, though it can never get beyond approximations. What is perhaps more important : this faith of reason science is as little competent to disprove, as it is incompetent to prove it. Science is not all in all : we are more than mere theoretical and cognitive beings. The logic of science is not the sole code of our spiritual or higher intellectual life ;

> ' We live by admiration, hope, and love.'

The sequel and development of the first Criticism are found in Kant's works on ethics, aesthetics, teleology and religion. Only in one supplementary chapter, and in casual indications as need arises, has Kant made any pronouncement on his view of Philosophy as a whole and as a system. That it is and can only be a system, when it really engages on reconstruction in theory, was of course his fundamental insight. But in his stage of *Zetesis*,[1] of testing and sifting the sound from the professed, he has confined himself to breaking up the mass piecemeal, and leaving each result in its turn to corroborate and correct the other. Sense and intellect may spring from a common stem ; but let us, he says, deal with them in their apparent separateness. Reason practical must no doubt be identical at bottom with reason theoretical : all the more convincing will be the

---

[1] Kant from 1762 onwards continues to insist on the necessity for philosophy taking up an analytic and critical attitude to current conceptions : see especially *Werke*, i. 95 and 292.

undesigned coincidence between the results of an inquiry into the principles of science, and one into the principles of morals. We have seen that science ultimately rests—though it does not discuss it and would indeed be incompetent to do so—on a faith, a hope, a postulate of the ultimate supremacy of intelligence,—the faith of reason in its own power (not verifiable indeed by an exhaustive list of actual results)—or in the rationality of the world. For science—though a kind of action and a part of conduct—is a sort of inactive action : an *enclave* in the busy world, a period of preparation for the battle of life. In the field of conduct the ultimate presupposition, which was for the luxury of science called a reasonable faith or faith of reason, makes itself felt in the more forcible form of a categorical imperative.

Or, at least, so it seems on first acquaintance. The command of duty, addressed to the sensuously-conditioned nature, brooks no opposition and condescends to no reasons in explanation or promises by way of attraction. The moral law claims unconditional authority : towards its sublime aspect reverence and sheer obeisance is due, utter loyalty to duty for duty's sake. Nothing short of this absolute identification with the Ought and a willingly willed self-surrender of the whole self to it can entitle an agent to the full rank of moral goodness. Such is the form—the synthetic link which joins the sensuous will indissolubly with the will reasonable of moral law. Now for its explanation. Humanity, though in the world of appearance and experience always subject to sensuous conditions, is also a power of transcending these conditions. Man is more than he can ever show in visibly single act. He has in him the hope, the faith, the vision of absolute perfection and completeness : but has it not as positive attained vision, but as the perpetual unrest of unsatisfied endeavour, as the feeling and the anticipation of an unachieved idea. And that perfection, that completeness he believes himself to be ; he even in some sense is. Lapses and ill-success cannot quench the faith : for so long as there is life, there is hope.

As he pictures out this invisible self, it may assume various forms more or less imaginative. At times it may seem a far away, and yet intimately near, being of beings,—the common father of all souls, the eternal self-existent centre of life and love, the omnipresent bond of nature, the omniscient heart of hearts,—on whom he can lean in closest communion ; though he is only too well aware how often he lives as if God were not, and human beings were roaming specks in chaos. At other times, he looks up to it as to an inner and better self, his conscience, the true and permanent being, which controls his choices and avoidances, which approves and disapproves, commands and condemns : his soul of soul, genius, and guardian spirit. In such a mood to be true to his own self—to follow the very voice of his nature—is to realise his law of life. His Ego is the absolute ego—the reason which is all things. And lastly, there are times when he conceives this better self and true essence as the community of the faithful, as the congregation of reasonable beings, of all perfected humanity.

In Kantian phraseology, man under one visible form is the union of an intelligence and a sensibility, of a noümenal with a phenomenal being. He is, indeed, says Kant, the former only in idea : it is only a standpoint which he assumes. But it is a standpoint he always does assume, if he is to be practical, i.e. if he is to move and modify the world he finds around him. And what standpoint is that ? What is the law that has to govern his action, the law of the spiritual world ? Its supreme law is the law of liberty ; and that law is autonomy. Action—always under law— but that law a self-imposed one. So act that thy will may be thy law, and with thy will the law of all others whatso- ever ; so act that no other human being may by thy act be deprived of full freedom and treated merely as a thing : so act as to respect the dignity of every human being as implicitly a sovereign legislative. In other words, Morality is a stage of struggle and of progress which bears witness to something beyond. The ' I ought ' represents a transition stage towards the ' I will ', or rather it is the translation of it into the language of the phenomenal world.[1] Morality, in a sense-being, always presents itself as a contest between the good and the evil principle : but in the transcendent and noümenal being which such a being essentially is,—in the reasonable or good will, the victory is already won by the good. Good is the law which governs the world, and

[1] Foundation of Metaph. of Eth. (*Werke*, viii. 82, 89) : ' Dieses Sollen ist eigentlich ein Wollen.'

which is the strength of the individual life. To the sensuous imagination, indeed, which here is apt to usurp the place of reason, things appear under a somewhat different aspect. There the certainty of self-conquest is forced by the difficulties of apparent failure to veil itself under the picture of a perpetual approximation through endless ages towards the standard of perfect goodness : the confidence that the world is reasonable is presented under the conception of a God who makes all things work together for good to the righteous : and the autonomy of reason presents itself as the postulate of freedom to begin afresh, absolutely untrammeled by all that has gone before. Thus the kingdom of reason is represented as having its times and seasons ; as making determinate starts, and working up to a consummation in the end of ages. But implicitly Kant's idea of reason's autonomy,—of the ' I ought ' as in its supreme truth an ' I will ',—is an eternal truth. The ' standpoint ', so to call it after Kant, is the standpoint which explains life and conduct and which makes conduct possible. It is the assertion that the completeness *is*, and is my inmost being, the source of my action, my chief good, and that chief good not a gratification or satisfaction to be looked forward to as reward, but essential life and self-realisation. And this joy is what is hidden under the austere gravity of the categorical imperative.

The Criticism of the Judgment-faculty is Kant's next step towards providing a completer philosophy. Ostensibly it owes its origin to the need of supplementing the treatment of Understanding and Reason by a discussion of Judgment, and of considering our emotional as well as our cognitive and volitional appreciations. What it really does is to minimise still further the gulf left between the intellect and nature—between the natural and the spiritual world. The intellect, said the first criticism, makes nature : it makes possible the general outlines of our conception of the world around us as a causally-connected system, in which a permanent being undergoes perpetual alteration, and manifests phenomena subject to mathematical conditions. Intellect, in short, has staked out the world which is the object of the practical man, and of his adviser the scientist. But there is another world—the world of beauty and sublimity—the world which art imitates and realises. The interpretation Kant gives to the aesthetic world is as

follows. The fact of beauty is a witness to the presence in
the mere copiousness of sensible existence of a sub-conscious
symmetry or spirit of harmony which realises without
compulsion and as if by free grace all the proportion and
coherence which intellect requires. Nature itself has something which does the work that intellect was charged with,
and does it with a subtle secret hand which does not suggest
the artificer. The fact of sublimity, on the other hand,
indicates the presence of an even greater spirit. For beauty
may seem—from what has been said—to be only an un-
bought accrement to the commodities of life—facilitating
the task of the practical intellect. But the sublime in
nature speaks of something which is greater than human
utilities and practical conveniences. It reveals a something
which is in sympathy with our essential and higher self, and
therefore stirs within us the keen rapture of the traveller
who sees from afar his home in ' rocky Ithaca ', but a something which is cold to daily wants and vulgar satisfactions,
and therefore strikes upon us a gelid awe.

Another world yet remains, which appeals neither to our
utilitarian science, nor to our higher sentiments of artistic
perfection. This is the world as the home of organic life,
and perhaps itself an organism. The organism is apt to be
a poser for the ordinary categories of mechanical science.
Here the part contains the whole, not less than the whole
contains the part : the cause is an effect, as well as cause,
of its effect. One thing is in another, and the other in it :
' the present is charged with the past, and pregnant of the
future,'—as the great founder of modern teleology often
said. In the plant and the animal the natural world has to
a certain degree reached an ideal unity which is also real.
Reason—the syllogism—is here not merely introduced from
without, as when man manipulates, but is the immanent
law of a natural life,—the end working out itself by its own
means and act. The fact admitted in these creatures
suggests extending the conception of organism (or teleology)
to nature as a whole. From this point of view Nature may
almost be said to have a history—because it is almost conceived as having one abiding self which in apparent unconsciousness wonderfully simulates the purposive adaptation
of conscious life. The older vulgar teleology was somewhat
mechanical : it regarded the natural world outside of—or
as it said, below—man as having no end of its own, but in

its series subserving man's commodities. In the teleology
of Kant the supreme end is still in a way man, and still
there is a little of the mechanical about it : but it is not
to promote man's happiness, understood as that probably
must be in a selfish sense, but to produce in him the
worthiest agent to carry on to its highest the rational
process of development. The struggles and pains of natural
existence, the laws of life, the competition of rivals, are all
means in the hands of nature to produce an autonomous
being. Kant says, a moral agent. But a moral agent has
been already explained as an intelligence certified unto
truth and a self-centred will whose law is the law of the
cosmos,—whose plan of life, if we so put it, is essentially
a concentration in miniature and in individuality of the
system ordained by the all-present God.

It is true that Kant, after all these soarings, checks
enthusiasm by the words ' not that we can know this, or
that it is so : but our nature with unmistakable tendency
bids us act *as if* it were so. Logic will hardly justify it—
but life seems to demand it.' And some have replied : ' let
us trust the larger hope.'

CHAPTER XI

SYNTHESIS AND RECONSTRUCTION : FICHTE

To get the full effect of a new doctrine it must be brought into contact with a mind unshackled by those traditional prepossessions which clung to its original author. Kant, essentially by training a man of the school, was by heart and character essentially a seeker after the wider ends of the larger world. His lesson is on one hand the scholar's disproof of pretended science, and on another an appeal and an example to the mere scholar to make his philosophy ample for the whole life, and co-extensive with the whole field of reality. His first disciples who stand forward as teachers caught only the first part of his message, and sought to set theoretical philosophy on a sounder basis. Johann Gottlieb Fichte—perhaps the least professional of great philosophical professors—with a resolute will, a passion for logical thoroughness, and great impulse to force mankind to be free and to realise liberty in an institution—was the first who really grappled with the searching questions that arose out of Kant's message to his age. His was a Kantism, not certainly always of the letter, nor indeed always of the spirit : yet for all that, there was substantial justice in his claim that his system supplied the presupposition which gives meaning and interconnexion to Kant's utterances.[1] It is, says the proverb, the first step that costs. And Fichte took that step. Before his impetuosity the cautelous clauses which besmirched the great purpose of Criticism shrunk away, the central truth was disengaged from its old-fashioned swaddling clothes, and openly announced itself as a renovating, almost a revolutionary principle.

But, as was to be expected, the unity and force are paid for by a considerable surrender of catholicity. If Kant's utterances are fused into comparative simplicity, the unification does not embrace the whole of the Kantian gospels. What Fichte did in his earlier stage—the stage by

[1] Cf. notes and illustrations in vol. ii. p. 399.

which he counts in the history of philosophy—was to emphasise and exhibit in his systematic statement that priority or supremacy of the ' practical ' over the ' theoretical ' reason which Kant had enunciated, and to put in the very foreground that self or Ego which Kant had indicated, under the title of ' transcendental unity of apperception ', as the focus which gives coherence and objectivity to experience. But to put the final presupposition at the head and front of all, as a principle originating and governing the whole line of procedure, is really to modify in a thorough-going way the whole aspect of a doctrine and its inner constitution. Kant's way is quiet analysis : from the given, or what is supposed given, up regressively to its final presuppositions, its latent *prius*. He shows you the thing is so, apparently without effort, by judicious application of the proper re-agent, as it were. Fichte, on the contrary, pours forth a strong current of deduction : Let it be assumed that so and so is, then *must*, or then shall, something else be ; and so onwards. Instead of a glance at the secret substructure of the world, you see it, at a magician's mandate, building itself up ; stone calling to stone, and beam to beam, to fill up the gaps and bind the walls together. And you must not merely read or listen. You are summoned as a partner in the work ; a work the author feels, only half-consciously, he has not yet quite accomplished, and where therefore he complains of the bystander's dullness.

This, one may say, was a new conception, certainly a new practice, of philosophy. Kant had indeed hinted that the pupil in philosophy must ' symphilosophise ' ; but practically, even his aim had been to describe or narrate a process of thought with such quasi-historical vividness and detail that the listener was sympathetically carried through the succession of ideas which were called up before him. What had been generally given in philosophical literature was a sort of historical account of how thoughts happened : a succession of pictures presented with the interposition here and there of a little reasoning, expository of connexions. You enlisted your reader's sympathy : you set his imagination to work by translating the logical process into a historical event—the *Logos* into a *Mythos*—and blending with your narrative a little explanation as to general drift and relations, you left him to himself to enjoy the *Theôria*. The nearest approach Fichte makes to this polite and easy method is in the ' Sun-clear Statement ' where he, as he says, attempts to ' *force* the reader to understand' him. But probably these things cannot be forced. And for the rest Fichte's characteristic attitude is to request, or command, his reader (or pupil) to think with him, to put himself in the posture required, to perform the act of thought described. He has not merely to be present at the lecture, but personally to perform the experiment. It is not a mere story to be heard and admired and forgotten. *De te*, O pupil ! *fabula narratur*. If it be a play, you are the actor as well as the onlooker : and the play is not a play, but the drama—the nameless drama—of the soul transacted in the unseen sub-conscious depths which bear up its visible life.

You do not therefore begin by getting a fact put before you. Your *fact*, in philosophy, must be your own *act* : not something done and dead, passive, a thing, but something doing, alive, active : your introspection must be, let us say, an experiment in the growing, responsive, quick life, not anatomy of the mere *cadaver*. Think, therefore, and catch yourself in the act of thinking. Get something before your mind's eye, and see what it involves. It matters not what you perceive or feel : only realise it fully and penetrate its meaning and implications. It is of course the perception of something here and now. And you would be, in ordinary life, eager to get on to something else—to associate the present fact to something perceived elsewhere, to draw conclusions about things yet to come. But if you philosophise, you must check this practical-minded impatience and concede yourself leisure to ponder deeply all that the single perception involves. Be content to sit awhile with Mary, by the side of Rachel of old. Let Martha bustle about. Fichte tells you that your perception rests,— and you, you *see* that it rests, on the ' I am that I am ',— on the $I = I$, i. e. on the continuity, identity, and unity of the percipient self. Make the statement of what you perceive, believe it, that is, assert it : and you have—done what ? You have pledged your whole self—*falsus in uno*, *falsus in omnibus*—to its truth : its background is your whole and one mental life. And is that all ? You have also called the world to witness : your statement—if, as it professes, it form an item however slight in the realm of

knowledge—requests and expects every other ' I ' to acknowledge your perception. Your certainty of the fact rests on
the certainty of your self : and your self is a self certified
by its ever-postulated identity with other selves, so on *ad
infinitum*. In affirming this (whatever be your statement)
you affirm the Absolute Infinite Ego. Heaven and earth
are at stake in every jot and tittle.[1]

At which plain frankness there was much cachinnation and
even muttering among the baser sort. Even wiser heads forgot—if they ever knew—that Leibniz a century before had
startled the world of his day by a view that ' the Ego or
something like it [2] ' was, under the name of *monad*, the
presupposition of each and every detail of existence in
any organic total. It was useless for Fichte to repeat [3]
that his philosophical Ego was not the empirical or individual ego which he in this every-day world had to
provide clothes and company for. It is hard to persuade
the world that it does not know that ' I am I ', and what
that means. Later, therefore, Fichte, going along with the
movement of contemporary speculation, and willing to
avoid one source of confusion, tended to keep off the name
of Ego from the absolute basis of all knowledge and
experienced reality. But unquestionably the absolutising
of the Ego is the characteristic note of his first period in
philosophy : and it rings with the spirit of the heaven-
storming Titan. It means that the cardinal principle and
foundation of man's conscious moral and intellectual life
is identical with the principle of the Universe, even if the
Universe seem not to know it. It means that self-consciousness—the certainty that I am I and one in all my manifestations—is the highest word yet uttered. In, or under, the
surface of human knowledge and belief in reality, there is
a transcendental Ego—a self identical with all other selves,
—infinite, unlimited, unconditional, absolute. The certainty of human knowledge—and therefore of all reality in
consciousness—is the Absolute,—an absolute certainty and
knowledge—but an absolute with which I identify myself,—
which I am, and which is me. This is the absolute *thesis*—
the nerve and utter basis-laying—at the ground, or rather
under the ground, of all I know, feel, and will.

[1] Cf. notes and illustrations in vol. ii. p. 387.
[2] Leibniz, *Werke*, ed. Gerhardt, iv. p. 392.
[3] Cf. notes and illustrations in vol. ii. p. 393.

This, then, is the thesis at the very foundation of all *Wissenschaft*: and therefore figures at the head of the *Wissenschaftslehre*,—the name Fichte gives his fundamental philosophy. But alone it is powerless. A foundation is only a foundation, by being built upon. The position must be defined by counterposition : thesis by antithesis : ego by non-ego. Ego, in fact, is first made *such*, as set against *you*. In other words, the perception we assumed to start with does not merely *suppose* and indeed pre-suppose the absolute Ego ; but it sets in the absolute Ego an ego and a non-ego,—sets against the lesser ego, something limiting and limited, something defining it in one particular direction ; or, if the original consciousness we started to examine was an act of will, then, it may be said, the non-ego appears as about to be limited and defined by the Ego. Be our consciousness, therefore, practical or theoretical, of action or of knowledge, its fundamental characteristic is the conjunction (correlation with subjugation) of an ego and a non-ego. It is always a synthesis of an original antithesis ; [1] of self and not-self. But every such synthesis which brings together into one a self and a not-self, is possible only in the original thesis of a greater self—an absolute Ego— which includes the not-self and the self it contrasts within its larger self. The unity of the first principle [2] ($A=A$, or $I=I$) parting or distinguishing itself into the opposition of A versus not-A, Ego set against non-ego, re-asserts itself again in consciousness (perception of objects, and action upon them by will) as synthesis, i. e. a conjunction (not a real union). And this synthesis is either the limitation of the Ego by the non-ego or the limitation of the non-ego by the Ego. The former gives the formula of theoretical, the latter that of practical consciousness.

We begin with the absolute Ego. It is absolute activity,

---

[1] The *antithesis* has two members : the partial ego, and the non-ego, which confronts. The *synthesis* is a putting together two separate things, so as to correlate them ; but it falls short of what would be understood in some present usage by 'synthetic unity' which has a certain mystical ring. It is important for a student of Schelling or Hegel to remember this distinction of synthesis from 'absolute unity' : e.g. Schelling, *Werke*, v. 43.

[2] $A=A$ is the more purely logical formula : $I=I$ presents it as a personal and metaphysical identity. The A, which is $=A$, is to be distinguished from the A which is opposed to not-A. But it is Fichte's standpoint to insist on their being one Ego.

utter freedom. It is the source of all action, all life. Yet if thus implicitly everything, it is actually nothing. To be something, it must restrict itself, set up in itself an antithesis :—by the setting up of a not-self, at once limit and realise itself : translate itself from ideal absoluteness and unconditionality into a reality which is also limited and partial. All consciousness and action exhibit this antithesis of a limited self and an outside and adversative other-being ; but the antithesis rests upon the medium of a larger life, a thesis which transcends and includes the antithesis, and which leads to that alternating adaptation of the two sides to one another (their synthesis) which actual experience presents as its recurring phase.[1] The *Wissenschaftslehre* leaving the absolute Ego in the background deals with the play that goes on in human experience between the correlatives to which it has reduced itself ;—the antagonism, but the moderated and overruled antagonism, of Ego and non-ego.

Observe the contrast to the ordinary methods of expression. Popular language—if the popular philosophers are to be trusted as its exponents—says ' an impression is produced by an external object on the senses, and causes an idea in the mind.' The ' object ' works a series of marvellous effects on a mind, which—to begin with—is hardly describable as anything more than an imagined point of resistance, getting reality by being repeatedly impinged upon.[2] Fichte's statements are rather interpreters of the vulgar phrases, which say ' I hear, I see ' ;—as if, forsooth, the ' I ' did it all. According to Fichte, the ' I ',—the absolute ' I ', is the real (but secret) source of the position in which consciousness finds itself limited by a non-ego. But within the finite ego and its consciousness there is no reminiscence or awareness of this its great co-partner's—the absolute ego's—act. For the finite consciousness, the beginning of its activity—i. e. of all empirical consciousness, lies in an impulse or stimulus from without—a mere somewhat of which we can predicate the very minimum of attributes. It is only *felt* as opposing : and this is the first

[1] To give this interpretation of the larger Ego as Life and Blessedness is to assume that the teaching, e. g. of the *Anweisung zum Seligen Leben*, is the logical deepening of the earlier language about the Ego.

[2] Cf. the description of mind as ' a bundle of impressions '.

stage or grade of theoretical consciousness : Sensation.
But in the perpetual antithesis—in the self-opposition
which is the radical act of consciousness—the mere limitation of Ego by non-Ego is confronted by the underlying
activity of the Ego which re-asserts the limitation as its
own act. Thus while we are, as it were, impressed, we
re-act against that impression—we set it forth before us, as
ours, and free ourselves from its immediate incumbency and
oppression. Instead of mere sentiency or feeling, we have
a perception (or intuition) of it.

It would be out of place, here, to try to write the interpretation of that marvellous and difficult piece of dialectic—
the *Wissenschaftslehre* ;—a theme to which Fichte returned
again and again up to his death, ever modifying details,
selecting new modes of exposition, and gradually, perhaps,
changing the centre of gravity of his system. It will be
sufficient to note the two purposes which it keeps in view.
On the one hand it is a systematic theory of the categories.
It begins, as we have seen, with the three co-ordinates of all
reflection,—identity, difference, and reason why ; it proceeds to the co-relative principles of activity and passivity ;
to condition, quantity, &c. And its work is to show how
these forms naturally emerge in the recurrent antithesis
which arises in consciousness, and how again they are brought
together by the overmastering Absolute thesis into a
synthesis, from which the same process re-appears. How
much this corresponds in general conception to the Hegelian
Logic is obvious, and Fichte has the merit of the original
suggestion. With this however he conjoins—what Hegel
has relegated to his Psychology—an evolutional or developmental theory of the mental powers. We have already
seen how sensation is forced by the latent intelligence to
rise into perception (*Anschauung*) : the line of psychological
development is carried on by Fichte through imagination
to understanding and reason. Hegel's work is far more
complete, definite, and detailed : but that need not keep
us from giving due homage to the suggestive sketch of the
originator of the conception.[1]

---

[1] Especially given in the Grundriss des Eigenthümlichen der Wiss.
(*Werke*, i. 331). Of course Fichte goes through a corresponding
' deduction ' of the emotional or moral nature. Schelling (*System
des transcend. Idealismus*) works out the ' deduction ' still more at
length.

But the theoretical consciousness is not all ; and as we already know, the practical Ego is supreme over it. In it lies the key to the mystery of the stimulus—the shock from the unknown—which awakened the activity of the Ego. The non-ego is only a mass of resistance created by the Ego so that it may be active ; only a stepping-stone on which it may walk ; a spring-board from which it may bound. Only so much reality has the non-ego ; the reality of something which may be shaped, made, made use of. Call the something which the stimulus (*Anstoss*) pre-supposes, the thing-in-itself (after Kant) : and if you ask How are things-in-themselves constituted, you get from the *Wissenschaftslehre* the answer : ' They are as we should make them.' [1]   Or, as it is said in another place : ' My world is—object and sphere of my duties and absolutely nothing else ' : [2] if you ask whether there is really such a world, the only sound reply I can give is : ' I have certainly and truthfully these definite duties, which take the form of duties *towards* such, and *in* such, objects ; and it is only in a world such as I there represent and not elsewhere that I can perform these duties which I cannot conceive otherwise.'

This is a grand word : and yet we feel that, in the intensity of intellectual consecutiveness and moral inflexibleness, we have lost some elements to which Kant had given their place in the philosophy of life. The third of Kant's three Criticisms is conspicuous by its absence from the Fichtean field of view, and has no recognition in this scheme of the universe : and the great conception of the natural world as an organism, in which natural man is only a part, and all is controlled by an autonomous principle of life, has been for the while allowed to drop. Even more than in Kant religion tends to be an epilogue or appendix to morality : and God is identified with the moral order of the world. It is customary to speak of Fichte's idealism as ethical, or as subjective : and so long as these words are understood, no harm is done. But to call it subjective does not mean that Fichte was so far beside himself as to believe the world was only a picture or a function of his individual brain. It means that he throws the weight too much on the side of subjectivity. The Absolute is, for him in his first stage, described as an Absolute Ego—and thereby the

[1] Fichte, *Werke*, i. 286.   [2] Ibid. ii. 261.

natural world seems to be left without God : and subjective duty has too exclusively thrown on it the weight of certifying objective existence. The world, as we shall see, and have indeed indirectly gathered from Kant, is too good and worthy to be the mere block of stone out of which our duties are to be hewn. And similarly, to call Fichte an ethical idealist is only to name him right, when we add that his were idealist ethics. The world is not here merely that social decorum may be maintained, and that puritanical virtue may pronounce that all is so well, that thenceforth there shall be no cakes and ale, nor ginger be hot in the mouth. The friend of the two brothers Schlegel, and their remarkable wives, Dorothea and Caroline, touched hands with a social group,[1] which, for good and for ill, had emancipated itself from all codes except that which bids

> ' To thine own self be true :
> Thou canst not then be false to any man '.

To him, as to Kant, morality presented itself as autonomy, as the dignity and grace of human nature in freest development ; but to him, more than to Kant, there commended itself the ideal of a city of reason, a thoroughly socialised community,[2] in which the welfare of each would be an obligation on all, and the machinery of government would be so marvellously self-corrective that all would do right and all fare well.

Fichte's place in the annals of philosophy depends on his academic treatises of 1794–98, and on his more popular works from the first date down to 1808. In a study of the philosopher as a whole it would be necessary to go beyond these dates, and take account of the displacement which a development of thought, which there is no good reason to suppose other than gradual, made in the scale of his earlier views. But for our purposes that is out of the question. In justice, however, it must be added that some things

---

[1] It is perhaps hardly necessary to say that the state of affairs alluded to, which has its literary memorials in F. Schlegel's *Lucinde*, and in the warm defence of that book by Schleiermacher, was only a passing experiment in which a high-strung idealism amid a lax society sought for truth at all costs and dared a noble lie.

[2] In the *Geschlossener Handelsstaat* (of 1800), the 'classical' document of characteristic German Socialism in its earlier and idealist phase.

that seem inadequately treated, some shortcomings in catholicity of mind, would appear in another light if the later
writings—not published till after Hegel's death—were
duly taken into account. But even at the close of the
century the advancing thought of Germany was seeking
other leaders.

CHAPTER XII

THE BEGINNINGS OF SCHELLING

SCHELLING and Hegel had been fellow-students at Tübingen, where, besides the ostensible lessons of the class-room, they had drunk gladly of the springs of thought Lessing had set running, had felt the hopes and the fears of the struggle republican France waged against the German powers, and had seen that Kantian criticism contained within it a fire which would burn up the hay and stubble of old theology. Hegel, five years the elder of the two, had passed through his college career in a very creditable but by no means brilliant way. Among his fellows he had gained the reputation of a quiet, and rather reflective mind, which, however, under an old-fashioned exterior, breathed a deep impassioned zeal for that higher life of which the nobler spirits among the young then, as now, longed to accelerate the advent. Schelling, singularly gifted with speculative ability, literary art, and the receptivity of genius to catch and string together the theories that rose to the top in science and letters, had already made his mark as a philosophic writer, while his senior compatriot, leading the inconspicuous life of a private tutor, was only working up and widening his ideas. Schelling's first essays in metaphysics trod the same lines as Fichte ; but in 1797 (when he was aged 22) appeared his *Ideas towards a Philosophy of Nature.* A year later he was lecturing at Jena, in friendly association with the Schlegels, and with Fichte, who, however, soon quitted the place. In 1800 appeared the *System of Transcendental Idealism,* and in 1801 the *Exposition of my System* ; followed in 1802 by *Bruno,* and in 1803 by the *Lectures on University Studies.* Brief periods of academic teaching at Würzburg, Erlangen, and Munich, and after 1841 at Berlin, broke the silence which set in after his *Inquiries into the nature of human liberty* in 1809 ; but little certain was known to the outside public of the final standpoint till the publication of his collected works (1856–61).

An involuntary touch of sadness falls upon the historian as he surveys Schelling's career. Seldom had a thinker's life begun with better promise, and more distinguished performance; seldom had a nobler inspiration, a more liberal catholicity of mood, guided and propelled the intellectual interest; seldom had expectation of greater things yet to come followed a writer's traces than was the lot of Schelling. On one hand, a lively and active appropriation of the results of scientific discovery, at least in its more suggestive advances : on the other, a mastery of words and style which fitted him to hold his own amongst the literary leaders ; and, again, a sympathy, that seemed to be religious, with the movement which sought *lucem ex oriente*, and wisdom from the treasures of the world's purer youth. And yet—in the main—the net result, oblivion more complete than has ever befallen a great thinker. At first, one is inclined to pass on with the remark that even books and thinkers have their fates, and that some momentary forgetfulness let the tide slip unused. But it is possible to be less oracularly-obscure : and without detracting from the splendid faculty and great achievement of Schelling to note some of the causes of his lapse into a mere episode.

In the first place, though his conception is of a system, his performance is only a succession of fragments. The nearest approach to an encyclopaedic exposition of his ideas is found in his popular *Lectures on the Studies of a University*. More than once he starts on the task of exposition, but lets it break off about the middle. Again, at each new occasion, the features of his scheme of thought have slightly altered, and not merely does his philosophy profess at first to present two distinct sides, but these two sides of the shield vary. Thirdly, the interest in scientific novelties, always disposed to seek the curious, the far-reaching and suggestive, more than the sounder generalisations, tends as time goes on to fasten too greedily on the miraculous and mysterious night-side of nature, on magic powers and mystic discernments—a path which descends to the abyss of a ' positive ', i. e. a quasi-materialistic, theosophy. The matter-of-fact rationalists (both the Catholics in Bavaria, and the Protestant theologian Paulus, once a friend, but latterly his bitterest foe) regard him as a crypto-catholic, the advocate of medieval obscurantism so hateful to true enlightenment. Even his literary art renders him suspected : for there is an old quarrel between philosophy and fiction ; and grave-eyed wisdom is jealous of her gipsy rival. Ill-advised indications of a sense of lofty superiority to the average teacher increased the numbers and the venom of his opponents. Nor is it perhaps beneath the dignity of history to suggest that his first wife, Caroline, with all her wonderful attractions of intellect and character, and notwithstanding all that she had been to Schelling in encouragement and counsel, was too clever and too critical not to sow many jealousies, and to add through the female line to the ranks of those with whom he stood suspect.

But perhaps the real reason of Schelling's failure was a certain excess of objectivity. Fichte had drawn attacks down by an abnormal subjectivity which would fain reform the surroundings wherever he went. Schelling stood more apart—animated by an immense curiosity, a boundless interest in all the expanse of objective existence ; but withal he seemed not to have his heart deeply set and pledged to a distinctively human interest. His first love is the Romance in nature ; and when he turns to history it is by preference to ages far remote. His ideal of philosophy is to see it achieve its work by the instrumentality of Art. Religion seems to culminate for him in a mythology. Reflection and speculation are to him always somewhat of a disease—whence philosophy is to carry us—almost magic-ally if possible—to rest again in the primeval unity of life. It is only an instrument towards a great end—and that end a godlike, even if you like a religious, Epicurean life. From such a standpoint it would be easy, in youth, to relapse into naturalism ; it would be equally easy, in later life, to fall into supernaturalism. Philosophy—at least as Hegel understood it—is merely neither : but the life, which never can quite cease to be an effort, of idealism. And so Schelling could not earn the confidence which only goes to those who are felt to be fellow-fighters with those they lead.

With Schelling occurs the confluence, into the main current of philosophy, of streams of idea and research which had already exercised a stimulative effect on the tone and

products of the higher literature of Germany. As early as
1763 (at the very date Kant let the English and Scotch
' empiricists ' shake him out of his ' rationalist ' dogmatism)
Lessing—in a couple of pages *On the reality of things outside
God*—threw doubts on the tenability of the ordinary deistic
arrangement of his day, which set God *there* and man and
his surroundings *here*, each side, for the time at least,
undisturbedly enjoying his own. Lessing read Leibniz by
the light of Spinoza, and Spinoza by the light of Leibniz :
and, if he emphasised the absolute right to the completest
individual self-development on one hand, he no less declared
on the other that ' nothing in the world is insulated, nothing
without consequences, nothing without eternal consequences '. ' I thank the Creator that I must,—must the
best,' he adds (1774). Of his conversations on these high
topics with Jacobi, we have already spoken. While Spinoza
and Leibniz were either decried, or—what is worse—misunderstood, by the established masters of instruction, they
were welcomed by a more sympathetic and, with all its
drawbacks, more appreciative study from the non-academic
leaders of thought.

Amongst these one of the most interesting and influential
was Herder. Herder, who had been amongst Kant's
students in 1763, and who has expressed his admiration
of his then teacher, came as years passed by to consider
himself the appointed antagonist of the Kantian system.
The two men were mentally and morally of different types :
and in Herder's case, a sense of injury, in the end, positively
blinded him to the meaning no less than to the merits of
a doctrine he had decreed to be pernicious. In Herder's
opinion, the Kantian system laboured throughout from
the fault of a dead logical formalism and abstractness : it
inhabited a sort of limbo, cut off alike from the fresh
breath of nature and the growing life of history, and from
the eternal spirit of divine truth : it undermined (so his
experience at Weimar [1] indicated) the traditional faith, and
inspired its ' adepts ' with a revolutionary superciliousness
to all dogma. Its cut-and-dried logicality, its trenchant
divisions and analyses were obnoxious to his poetically-
fervid, largely-enthusiastic, and essentially-historical soul.
Man—in his concrete completeness, in his physical sur-

[1] He held posts of large general superintendence over church and
school affairs at Weimar.

roundings and his corporeal structure, in his social organisation, in his literary and artistic life, above all in his poetry
and traditions of religion—was the theme of his studies;
and he looked with distrust on every attempt to analyse and
disintegrate the total unity of humanity by a criticism first
of this, and then a criticism of that side of it, carried on
separately. Ossian had been an early favourite of his;
and the twilight that hovers with the haze of pensive myth
around the figures of that visionary world hangs with a
charm and a confusion around the ultimate horizon of
Herder's ideas.

In 1774 and 1775 Herder wrote and wrote again an
essay (published 1778) for a prize offered by the Berlin
Academy on the subject of ' Sensation and Cognition in the
human Soul'. Its fundamental points are that ' no
psychology is possible, which is not at every step a distinct
physiology': that ' cognition and volition are only *one*
energy of the soul': that ' all our thought has arisen out
of and through sensation, and in spite of all distillation still
contains copious traces of it': that there are not separate
faculties of thought, but one divine power, which unifies
all the broad stream of inflowing sensation,—' one energy,
and elasticity of the soul, which reaches its height through
the medium of language.' 'What is material, what non-
material in man, I know not,' he says; ' but I am in the
faith that nature has not fastened iron plates between them.'
' Man is a slave of mechanism (but a mechanism disguised
in the garb of a lucid celestial reason) and fancies himself
free.' 'Self-feeling and fellow-feeling (a new phase of
expansion and contraction) are the two expressions of the
elasticity of our will': they vary directly with each other:
and ' love therefore is the highest reason '—a proposition,
adds Herder, for which ' if we will not trust St. John, we
may trust the undoubtedly more divine Spinoza, whose
philosophy and ethics turn wholly upon this axis.

Herder's great work, however,—which, side by side with
Lessing's *Education of the Human Race*, and with Kant's
Idea for a Universal History, helped to constitute that conception of history, as philosophy in concrete form, which
appears in Schelling, Schlegel, and Hegel,—was the *Ideas
for a Philosophy of History*. It is the pendant and contrast to Kant's three Criticisms, with which it is nearly
contemporaneous (1784–91). Even in history Kant empha

sises the work of intelligence, of reason : and puts the intelligently-organised state—if possible, the world-commonwealth, when war shall be transformed into merely stimulating competition,—as the final triumph of the reason. To Herder, while on the one hand the nature-basis is all-essential, and must form the foundation of any genetic explanation of spiritual phenomena, the ideal of humanity presents itself rather as a free development of the many-sided individual—a development tempered by the association of the family and the claims of friendship. In Kant's view of civilisation, natural reason by its indwelling presuppositions works out the end of culture : Herder, on the contrary, allows himself to introduce—but only in and from the dim background—a supernatural aid to actualise the germs of rationality latent in man's nature. Yet, though at the first step into history the Godhead appears, and a deified humanity looms ahead as the consummation of the process of evolution, the development between these two extreme poles is homogeneous and indeed one. The same law governs it throughout : ' Ethics is only a higher physics of the mind.' Man is from the first endowed with tendencies which, through the medium of society and tradition, carry him on to the double end, so hard to combine, of ' humanity and happiness ', ' humanity and religion.' But, for this training of the spirit he is prepared by a special natural endowment of the body : and Herder can go so far as to say that ' in order to delineate the duties of man, we need only delineate his form '. Developing under the influence of cosmic and geographical conditions, and formed of the same protoplasm and on the same type as other animals, man possesses an unique organisation, a definitely proportioned mechanism, which is his distinctive and permanent specific character. General identity of plan and condition prevails for man and animals ; but Herder keeps back from the Darwinian inference which interprets the graduated diversity of type as indicating that man is the phase reached *pro tempore* in the gradual slide along which the continuous change of environment carries the unstable types which earlier environments have helped to form. For Herder's conception of nature there are fixed differences beyond which research cannot go ; and we shall see that both Schelling and Hegel accept this reservation.

Herder, finally, struck a blow in the war that was waged after Lessing's death between the friends and foes of Spinozism. His little book *God* (1787) is a vindication of Spinoza against Jacobi's attack. Antiquarian accuracy it can lay no claim to : the picture of Spinozism, one-sided at the best, is further vitiated by an interpretation of the doctrine which leavens it to indistinctness with the ideas of Leibniz and Shaftesbury. It was a grand—but it was also an audacious—vision of Spinozism which found it not inconsistent with a fundamental theism on one side and with the poetry of nature on the other. Yet Herder had the merit of being perhaps the first to pierce the hard logical shell of rationalism under which Spinoza had lain hidden, and to reveal the mystic passion for God which so quaintly called itself *amor erga rem infinitam et aeternam.* ' Spinoza,' says Herder, ' was an enthusiast for the being of God.' Even where he translates Spinoza's terms into too ample equivalents, he does service by teaching men that the vapid inanities they associate with terms like *substance, mode, cause,* are inadequate to interpret the intensity of meaning they had for the philosopher. To remove the seals which rendered both Leibniz and Spinoza a mystery for the world was to prepare the way for Schelling and Hegel.[1]

It is under the aegis of Spinoza and Leibniz that Schelling begins his first characteristic work,—the *Ideas towards a philosophy of Nature.* In these thinkers he found first proclaimed as the fundamental standpoint of philosophy the unity of the finite and the infinite, of the real and the ideal, of the absolutely active and the absolutely passive. They differed indeed in this, that whereas this unity is pre-supposed by Spinoza as infinite and absolute substance, of which all separate existence, body or mind, is only a *modus,* it is taken by Leibniz as the universal characteristic of every individual being. Every monad—and the human soul is the typical monad—is at once finite and infinite, real and ideal, active and passive. But—whether as under-lying substance, or as unity of reality—both hold the cardinal doctrine that the absolute (the ' Object ' of philo-sophy) is the unity and unification—the identity—of what outside it appears as two sides or orders of being, the real and the ideal. To philosophise, therefore—or to see things in

[1] See notes and illustrations in vol. ii. p. 420.

the absolute—is (not as Hegel's malicious joke puts it,[1] to look at them ' in the night when all cows are dark ',—but) to see them in the intense light that proceeds from the identity of the *Spirit* within us with the *Nature* without us.

Fichte had caught hold of this standpoint. He had seen that the original antithesis which confronts us, and the conjunction (synthesis) of its members, presupposed a still more fundamental and indeed absolute thesis,—an aboriginal and active unity. That antithesis is the opposition of ego and not-ego ; that synthesis is every act of knowledge and will, by which each of these powers is in turn limited by the other. Such a synthesis (volition or cognition) would be impossible unless on the fundamental thesis (or hypothesis) of a unity, or identity, which gives rise to the anti-thesis and has the power of overcoming it. Such an original unity is what he calls the absolute Ego. I am what I know and will, and what I know and will is Me. Such is the equation (briefly written, $I = I$) which identifies subject and object (of knowledge and will). But the associations clinging to the terms Fichte used gave this thought a one-sided direction. The ' *I* ' is opposed to the ' *Thee* ', and the ' *Them* ', and the ' *It* '. The ' thing '—or non-ego—is depreciated as compared with the thinker and willer. It is postulated *ad majorem gloriam* of the Ego : in order that I may work out the full fruition of my being. It is what I ought to make out of it. It *is* nothing but what it *will be*—or will be if I do what I ought to do. The identity of the two sides therefore is left as ' the object of an endless task, an absolute imperative '. The Absolute is not yet :— it is only the forecast of a postulated result.

If this be what Fichte teaches, and be called subjective idealism, then for Schelling the first thing is to quit the house of bondage. Let us leave out of view the Ego, with its misleading associations, and begin with the two fields which are known to us, the fields of Nature and Spirit. Nature—not Matter—is the one side : Mind or Spirit the other. Each of them furnishes the object of one branch of philosophy—a philosophy of Nature, on one hand, and a transcendental idealism on the other. The former is new, and more especially Schelling's own proper continuation of Kant : the other partly a continuation of Fichte's work. But as they are both philosophy, they must coincide or meet.

[1] Hegel, *Werke*, ii. 13.

The whole philosophy may therefore call itself a philosophy of Identity ; but, for the while, it will present itself under the two aspects of a philosophy of Nature, conceived as the blind and unconscious, a philosophy of Mind and history, as the free and conscious product of intelligence.[1]

---

[1] See notes and illustrations in vol. ii. p. 392.

CHAPTER XIII

THE PHILOSOPHY OF NATURE AND IDEALISM

WHAT is meant by a 'philosophy of Nature'? 'To philosophise on Nature,' says Schelling, 'means to lift it up out of the dead mechanism in which it appears immersed, —to inspire it, so to speak, with liberty, and to set it in free process of evolution: it means, in other words, to tear ourselves away from the vulgar view which sees in Nature only occurrences, or at the best sees the action *as a fact, not the action itself* in the action.'[1] There is in short a process in nature parallel in character to what Fichte had exhibited for consciousness. The natural world is no longer subordinated, but to appearance co-ordinate: and evolution or development, exhibited under the logical title of a 'deduction', is the common law of both. The real order and the ideal order of the world are equally the work of an infinite and unconditioned activity, 'which never quite exhausts itself in any finite product, and of which everything individual is only as it were a particular expression.' The nature which we see broken up in groups and masses, and individual objects, is to be explained as a series of steps in a process of development: the steps in a single continuous product which has been arrested at several stages,—which presents distinct epochs, but nevertheless all approximations, with divergences, to a single original ideal.

In Nature, as in Mind, the most typical phenomenon is an original heterogeneity, duplicity, or difference, which, however, points back to a still more fundamental homogeneity, unity, or identity. This primary unity or ground of unification does not indeed appear to sight; the 'soul of Nature', the *anima mundi*, nowhere presents itself as such in its undivided simplicity; but only as the perpetually recurring re-union of what has been divided. But though unapparent, the absolute identity is the necessary presupposition of all life and existence, as of all knowledge and action. It is the link or 'copula' which perpetually

[1] Schelling, *Werke*, iii. 13. (References always to the first series.)

reduces the antithesis to unity, and the heterogeneity to homogeneity, and the different to redintegration. To this fact of antithesis, presupposing and continually reverting to an original unity, Schelling gives the name ' Polarity '. ' It is impossible to construe the main physical phenomena without such a conflict of opposite principles. But this conflict only exists at the instant of the phenomenon itself. Each natural force *awakes* its opposite. But that force has no independent existence : it only exists in this contest, and it is only this contest which gives it for the moment a separate existence. As soon as this contest ceases, the force vanishes, by retreating into the sphere of homogeneous forces.'[1] Polarity, therefore, is a general law of the cosmos.

A ceaseless, limitless activity, therefore, as the basis or groundwork of all, for ever crossing, arresting, and limiting itself : an eternal war, which, however, is always being led back to peace,—a process of differentiation which rests upon, is the product of, and is for ever forced back to integration, is the perpetual rhythm of the natural universe. It is a process in which can be traced three grades, stages, or ' powers ' (first, second, and third, &c.). By its more generally descriptive name it is called Organisation. ' Organism,' says Schelling, ' is the principle of things. It is not a property of single natural objects ; but, on the contrary, single natural objects are so many limitations, or single modes of apprehending the universal organism.'[2] ' The world is an organisation ; and a universal organism itself is the condition (and to that extent the positive) of mechanism.'[3] ' Mechanism is to be explained from organism : not organism from mechanism.' ' The *essential* of all things is *life* : the *accidental* is only the *kind* of their life : and even the dead in Nature is not utterly dead,—it is only extinct life.'

But if the conception of an organism be thus the adequate or complete idea of Nature as a whole, that idea is only realised as a third ' power ' supervening on, and by means of two subordinate or inferior ranges or ' powers '. The first stage is that occupied by the mathematical and mechanical conception of the world,—the bare skeleton or framework which has to be clothed upon and informed with life

[1] Schelling, *Werke*, ii. 409.   [2] Ibid. ii. 500.
[3] Ibid. ii. 350.

and growth. This first ' power ' in the world-process of antithetical forces, under the control of, and on the basis supplied by, the original thetic unity which synthetises them, is Matter. In Matter we have the equilibrium and statical indifference of two opposing forces—one centrifugal, accelerating, repulsive, the other contripetal, retarding, attractive—which, working under the synthetising unity supplied by the force of universal gravitation, build up in their momentary arrests or epochs the various material forms. In this first ' power ' we have as it were the scheme or machinery through which organisation will work : the outward and ' abstract ' organism. And the essential feature of this ' construction ' or ' deduction ' of matter is that it does not take material atoms and build them into a world, but ' deduces ' the properties of matter as issuing from the play of opposing forces, and as due to the temporary syntheses resulting from the presence of unity making itself felt in the opposites.

A second and higher ' power ' is seen in the physical universe as it presents itself to the sciences of electricity, magnetism, and chemistry. If the former briefly be denominated the mechanical, this is the chemical world. The law of polarity is here especially prominent : the neutrality or indifference of parts is replaced by an intenser antithesis and affinity : and the return from heterogeneity to homogeneity takes place with more striking and even sudden effect. Here, matter, even as inorganised, has a certain *simulacrum* of life and sensibility : there is in it the trace of a spirit which emerges above the mere contiguity and juxtaposition of mechanical atoms. The atomic theory shows itself less and less adequate as an attempt to represent the whole phenomena of inanimate matter, and the material universe is already charged with sympathies and antipathies which are full of the promise and the potency of the organic world.

The mechanical theory of the universe, in the ordinary sense, which deals with the mathematical formulation of the laws of planetary movement, had been the work of the seventeenth century. The eighteenth century had seen attempts to explain the *status quo* of the planetary system as a resultant from the evolution of an elementary molecular state of the cosmic mass. With the close of the eighteenth century there appeared a group of new sciences dealing with subtler energies of matter,—with electricity, galvanism, and above all with the connexions of chemical, electric, and magnetic science. The ideas thus suggested— embraced with some generality under the title Polarity— threw light backward upon the old mechanical conceptions, and gave them a decidedly dynamic character. Even the tranquil rest of geometrical figures came to be explained as a meeting point and transition moment of opposite forces. But these ideas produced an even greater effect on biology. Here, too, the need of a special ' vital force ' to explain life and organisation disappeared : organism was but a higher stage, a completer truth of mechanism : and both found their explanation in the antithesis and synthesis of forces, or in differentiation and integration of what has recently been termed an ' idée-force '. In this direction, so far as Schelling was concerned, the obvious stimulus came from the programme sketched by Kielmeyer at Stuttgart in 1793, in a lecture ' on the proportions of organic forces '. According to Kielmeyer there are three types of force in the animal organisation, sensibility, irritability and reproduction.[1] The last of these is the basic force which builds up and propagates the animal system. With irritability, or contraction in response to external stimuli—material adaptation to environment—a higher level of animal life is reached. But the highest of all forces in the living being is sensibility. In this same order may we reasonably conceive that the ' plan of nature ' proceeds. Her first products show little beyond that reproductive power which makes broad and high the pyramid of life. But as the creature acquires increasing heterogeneity and a comparatively independent position, it plays the part of a re-agent against stimuli, and a source of movements. Lastly, it not merely responds to, but assimilates and appropriates the impression into a sensation : it internalises the external, and carries within itself by means of the sensibility an ever-increasing picture of the world around it.

The idea of Evolution or Development, thus introduced by Schelling into philosophy as a governing principle in the study of matter and of mind, is not to be confused either with the older use of these terms or with their current applications to-day.[2] By evolution (or development) and

[1] Compare vol. ii. 360 and 429.
[2] See notes and illustrations in vol. ii. p. 424.

involution (or envelopment) the earlier speculation on biology had denoted the view that the organic germ contained *in parvo* all that the matured organism showed in large. As the mature bulb of the healthy hyacinth shows, when cut open, to the naked eye, the stem and flowers that will issue from it next spring ; so in general the seed can be treated as a miniature organism needing only an increase of bulk to make it fully visible in details. Growth is thus not accretion, but explication and enlargement of a microscopic organism subsisting in the germ.

Evolution, in the present time, and especially since Darwin, means something more than this. It implies a theory of descent of the variety of existing organisms from other organisms of a previous age, less individualised in forms and functions. From comparatively simple and homogeneous creatures there have issued in the course of ages creatures of more complex, more highly differentiated structure ; and this process of gradual differentiation may be conceived as going on through an all but infinite period. At one end we may conceive matter, just endowed with the faculties of life and organisation, but in a minimal degree ; at the other end of the developmental process, creatures which have organised within themselves powers, maximal both in range and variety. The result (so far as we at present go) is a genealogy of organism which, to quote Darwin, pictures before us a ' great tree of life which fills with its dead and broken branches the crust of the earth and covers the surface with its ever branching and beautiful ramifications '.

Even Buffon, seeing how naturally he could regard ' the wolf, the fox, and the jackal ' as ' degenerate species of a single family ', concluded we could not go wrong in supposing that ' nature could have with time drawn from a single being all other organised beings '. Erasmus Darwin (1794) had insisted on the power of ' appetency ' in the organs of a living creature to create and acquire new structures which it handed down to its posterity. G. R. Treviranus [1] in his *Biology* (1802–5) had noted the influence of environment, and Jean Lamarck in his *Philosophie Zoologique* (1809) had—after

---

[1] ' Every inquiry into the influence of general nature on living beings,' says Treviranus, ' must start from the principle that all living forms are products of physical influences which still go on at the present time and are altered only in degree and direction.'

assuming that ' nature created none but the lowest organisms,
—maintained that need and use (or disuse) can so effectively
modify a creature that it may even produce new organs, and
give rise by imperceptible degrees to a variety of creatures
as widely divergent as they now appear.   E. g. ' The giraffe
owes its long neck to its continued habit of browsing upon
trees.'   And gradually it had become recognised by specu-
lators on this subject that, as Mr. H. Spencer wrote in 1852,
' by small increments of modification any amount of modification may in time be generated.'   Finally, in 1859,
Darwin, with an ample resource of illustrative examples,
enforced the doctrine that the existing fauna and flora of
the earth represent the result of a struggle for existence,
protracted during vast ages, in which those creatures have
been preserved (selected to live) which, among all the
variously-endowed offspring of any kind, were best fitted
to appropriate the means of subsistence in the circumstances
in which they for the time found themselves placed.   The
circumstances of life on the globe are perpetually varying
from place to place and time to time : progeny never exactly
reproduce their parents, and diverge widely from each other :
hence each form of life is perpetually sliding on from phase
to phase, and only those survive which are best adapted to
the new conditions of life.

So far as Darwinism is an attempt to show that the
classes of plants and animals are not a mere juxtaposition
and aggregation, but are to be explained by reference to
a single genetic principle, it is in harmony with the Evolution
taught by Schelling and Hegel.   Both alike overthrow the
hard and fast lines of division which semi-popular science
insists upon, and restore the continuity of existence.   Both
regard Nature as an organic realm, developing by action
and re-action within itself, living a common life in thorough
sympathy and solidarity, and not a mere machine in
which the several parts retain without change the features
and functions impressed upon them at creation by some
supernal architect.   But they differ in other points.
Ordinary Darwinism, at least, talks as if circumstances and
organism were independent originally, and only brought as
it were, incidentally, in contact and correlation.   It fails
to keep hold of the fact—of which it is abstractly aware—
that the two act upon and modify each other because they
are members of a larger organism.   It forgets, in short,

what Schelling so thoroughly realised, that the organic and inorganic, ordinarily so called, are both in a wider sense organic. It wants the courage of recognising its own tacit presuppositions.

But the characteristic difference between the evolution theory of to-day and that meant by the philosophers is different from this, though connected with it. ' The assertion,' says Schelling, ' that the various organisms have formed themselves by gradual development from one another, is a misconception of an Idea which really lies in reason.' [1] And Hegel no less decidedly asserts that ' Metamorphosis ' (as the term was then applied, e. g. by Goethe, to what we now call Evolution) really *exists* as a fact only in the case of the living individual,—not in the supposed or theoretical continuity of the species. ' It is an awkward way both ancient and modern speculative biology have had of presenting the development and transition of one physical form and sphere into a higher one as an outwardly-actual production,—which, however, in order to make it clearer, has been thrown back into the darkness of the past.' [2] Yet notwithstanding these and even later protests, there is a great charm for many minds in the evolutionist picture, e. g., of the horse of to-day as the literal descendant through nearly fifty great stages (called species) from some creature of the eocene age, which gradually transformed itself in consequence of innate instability or variability of construction and in obedience to changes in its environment. But whatever value there may be in these as yet hypothetical aids to the imagination in grasping and unifying the variety of organic life, they run on another line from the philosophical evolution. That evolution is in the *Idea*, the *Notion*. It is the ' fluidity ' of terms of thought that is here sought, not of the kinds of things,—except in a secondary way. And above all, philosophy does not deal with a problem in time, with a mere sequence ; if it deals with a history of nature, the agents of that history are powers and forces—and powers which are ideal no less than real.

A nearer approach to the philosophic conception is to be found in the views which modern physiology takes of the nature of organic structure and function.[3] In the simplest

---

[1] Schelling, *Werke*, iii. 63.   [2] Hegel, *Encyclopaedie*, § 249.
[3] See e. g. Professor Michael Foster's article on Physiology in the *Encyclopaedia Britannica*.

phases of protoplasm, the apparently homogeneous mass is really undergoing a series of changes, and indeed only exists as such, because it is the ever-renewed resultant of two correlated processes,—a movement up (anabolic change) by which dead matter is assimilated and built into it, and a movement down (katabolic changes) by which its composing elements are disintegrated and left behind, with accompanying liberation of energy. Protoplasm or ' living matter ' is the incessantly formed and re-formed thin line on which these two currents for the moment converge,—a temporary crest of white foam, as it were, raising itself on the Heraclitean wave of vicissitude, where all things flow on and nothing abides. But wherever protoplasm arises and maintains itself on this border-line of ascending and descending states, it exhibits the three well-known properties of assimilation, contractility, and sensitiveness. Protoplasm, placed as it were in the mean between these two processes, is or has the synthetic power which governs them and keeps them in one. It is no mere chemical substance, undergoing composition and decomposition, but rather, if looked at from the somewhat speculative standpoint of molecular physics, a kind of intricate movement or dance of particles, a shape or ' form ' instinct with the power of producing and reproducing itself, and, ultimately, in some highly differentiated phases (nerve-system), with a power of producing and reproducing a world of imagination.

A philosophy of Nature is only half a philosophy. Its purport is to set free the spirit in nature, to release intelligence from its imprisonment in material encasements which hide it from the ordinary view, and to gather together the *disiecta membra* of the divine into the outlines of one continuous organisation. It seeks to spiritualise nature, i.e. to present the inner idea, unity, and genetic interdependence of all its phenomena : to delineate *natura formaliter spectata* not as a logical skeleton of abstract categories, but in its organisation and continuous life. There remains the problem of what Schelling calls ' Transcendental Idealism ' : —called ' transcendental ' to avoid confusion with the vulgar idealism which supposes the world to be what it calls a mere ' idea ' or phantom of the mind. Schelling's is on the contrary an ' Ideal-Realism ' : it ' materialises the laws of intelligence to laws of nature '.[1]

[1] Schelling, iii. 352, 386.

We need not in details consider the genesis of Reality from the action of the Ego. Substantially it is the same as that given by Fichte. An activity, which is at once self-limiting and superior to all limit, rises through stage to stage, from sensation and intuition, to reflection and intelligence, till it becomes the consciousness of a world of objective reality. ' Give me,' says the transcendental philosopher, ' a nature with opposing activities, of which the one goes to infinity, and the other endeavours to behold itself in this infinity,—and from that I will show you intelligence arising with the whole system of its ideas.'[1] In the first phase the ' ideal-real ' world arises by the synthetic action of the ' productive intuition '. Ideas, as it were, live and move : they grow and build up : causality is neither a category nor a schema, but an intelligent ' form ' which is also a force— an ' idée-force '. They are (in the Hegelian sense) ' Ideas ', i.e. neither merely objective nor merely subjective, but both at once. But such an ideal world is outside and beyond consciousness : it belongs to the same region as that higher Ego where there is no distinction between the Ego I am and the Ego I know. To follow the movement in this region needs a combination of mental vision and visual intellect, which Schelling has called the ' Intellectual Intuition '. It is a power which rising above the materialism of sense yet retains its realism ; which, while intellectual, is free from abstractness. It is synthetic, and widely different from mere logical analysis. It is, in short, analogous to the artistic genius : it creates a quasi-objectivity, an ideal-reality, without which the mere words of the speculator are meaningless. By means of this ' organ ', philosophy can ' freely imitate and repeat the original series of actions in which the one " act " of self-consciousness is evolved '.[2]

But the ' productive intuition ' is, as Kant would say, blind : it is unconscious in its operation : and it is only after an arrest, a Sabbath when it surveys and judges its work, that it begins to realise itself through a process of analysis and reflection which elicits and fixes the categories that have been operative in it. By this abstraction intelligence rises out of mere production to intelligent and conscious production, i.e. to volition, where it has an ideal and realises it. With volition and voluntary action, objectivity is to appearance further certified and fortified. It is as active,

[1] Schelling, iii. 427.   [2] Ibid. iii. 397.

i.e. as free, and even moral, agents, that we set forward categorically the reality of the world. So, too, Fichte had declared. But, as Schelling reminds us, with this intensified assertion of a law and an ideal to which the real must and shall correspond,—with the declaration that the realm of absolute consistency and ideal truth of reason is the true and real for ever and ever—we come across the fundamental antithesis of the ' Is ' and the ' Ought ', of the objective and subjective, of unconscious necessity and self-conscious freedom. With an attempt to get a philosophy of history, —i.e. of man and mind as the culminating truth of things, we see ourselves confronted with the opposition of fatalism and chance. On one hand history is only possible for beings who have an ideal in view,—one persistent aim and principle which their work and will is the means of realising. And yet it is an ideal which only the series of generations, only the whole race, can realise. Man's license to do or to refrain rests upon a larger, latent, divine necessity which constrains it. What human agents by their free choice determine and carry out, is carried out, in the long run, by the force of an everlasting and unchanging order, to which their wills seem but a mere plaything. But that man's free agency should thus harmonise with the constrained uniformities of nature is only possible on the assumption that both are phenomena of a common ground, or basis of identity, of an ' absolute identity, in which there is no duplication, and which for that reason, because the condition of all consciousness is duplication, can never reach consciousness. This ever-Unconscious, which, as it were the everlasting Sun in the spirit-kingdom, is hidden in its own undimmed light, and which, though it is never an object, still impresses its identity on all free objects, is simultaneously the same for all intelligences, the invisible " root " of which all intelligences are only the " powers ", and the everlasting mediator between the self-determining subjective in us and the objective or percipient,—simultaneously the ground of the uniformity in freedom, and of the freedom in uniformity of the objective.' [1] To rise to the sense of this Absolute Identity, as common basis of harmony between the ' Ought ' and the ' Is ', is to recognise Providence : it is Religion.

But this ' Absolute ' is never in history completely revealed—we cannot *see* free action coincide with pre-

[1] Schelling, iii. 600.

determination. Thus if History as a whole be conceived as a ' continuous and gradual self-revelation of the Absolute ', ' God never *is*, if *is* means exhibition in the objective world : *if God were, we* should not be.' [1] Nor is the Absolute so revealed in Nature. Yet, even as the apparent contingency of human action throws us back on an everlasting necessity, which is yet freedom, so the apparent uniformity of natural order shows us in organic life the traces of a free self-regulating development. To apprehend the truth at which both seem to point we want an organ of intelligence which shall unite in itself the conscious activity of free production with the unconscious instinct of natural creation. Such an organ is found in the aesthetic power of genius, in the Artist. The artistic product is the work of two intimately-conjoined principles :—of the art (in the narrower sense) which can be taught and learned, and is exercised consciously and with reflection, and of that ' poesy in Art ', the unconscious grace of genius which can neither be handed down nor acquired, but can only be inborn by free gift of nature. In the work thus brought to birth there is something definite, precise, and capable of exposition in finite formulae : there is also something which no ' prose ' can ever explicate, something which tells us of the infinite and eternal, which ever reveals and yet conceals the Absolute and Perfect. Art, thus springing from ' imagination, the one sole power by which we can think and conjoin even the contradictory ', gives objectivity and outward shape to that ' intellectual intuition ' by which the philosopher subjectively (in his own consciousness) sought to realise to himself the unity of thought and existence.

' To the philosopher,' Schelling concludes, ' Art is supreme, because it as it were opens to him the Holy of Holies, where in everlasting and original unity there burns, as it were in one flame, what is parted asunder in nature and history, and what in life and conduct, no less than in thinking, must for ever flee apart. The view the philosopher artificially makes for himself of nature is for Art the original and natural. What we call nature is a poem which is locked up in strange and secret characters. Yet could the riddle be disclosed, we should recognise in it the Odyssey of the mind, which, strangely deceived, in seeking itself, flees from itself : for through the sense-

[1] Schelling, iii. 603.

world there is a glimpse, only as through words of the meaning, only as through half-transparent mist of the land of imagination, after which we yearn. That splendid picture emerges, as it were, by the removal of the invisible partition-wall which sunders the actual and the ideal world, and is only the opening by which those figures and regions of the world of imagination, that but imperfectly glimmer through the actual, come forward in all their fulness. Nature is to the artist no more than it is to the philosopher, viz. the ideal world as it appears under constant limitations, or only the imperfect reflex of a world which does not exist outside him, but within him.'

' If it is Art alone, then, which can succeed in making objective and universally accepted what the philosopher can only exhibit subjectively, it may also be expected that philosophy, as it was in the infancy of science born and nourished by poetry, and with it all those sciences which were by it carried on towards perfection, will after their completion flow back as so many single streams into the universal ocean of poetry from which they issued. Nor is it in general hard to say what will be the means for the return of science to poetry : for such a means has existed in mythology before this, as it now seems, irrevocable separation took place. But as to how a new mythology,— which cannot be the invention of the single poet, but of a new generation, as it were representing only a single poet,—can itself arise, is a problem, the solution of which is to be expected only from the future destinies of the world and the further course of history.' [1]

[1] Schelling, iii. 628.

CHAPTER XIV

TRANSITION TO HEGEL

Thus far Schelling (aetat. 25) had gone in 1800. Two sides of philosophy had been alternately presented as complementary to each other; and now the task lay before him to publish the System itself which formed the basis of those complementary views. To that task Schelling set himself in 1801 (in his Journal for Speculative Physics): but the *Darstellung meines Systems* remained a torso. The Absolute was abruptly ' shot from the pistol ': but little followed save a restatement in new terms of the Philosophy of Nature. Meanwhile Hegel, who had inherited some little means by his father's death, began to think that the hour had struck for his entrance into the literary and philosophical arena, and wrote in the end of 1800 to Schelling asking his aid in finding a suitable place and desirable surroundings from which to launch himself into action. What answer or advice he received is unknown: at any rate in the early days of 1801 he took up his quarters at Jena, and in the autumn he gave his first lectures at the University. Gossip suggested that Schelling, left alone (since Fichte's departure) to sustain the onset of respectability and orthodoxy upon the extravagances of the new Transcendentalism, had summoned his countryman and old friend to bear a part in the fray. And the rumour seemed to receive corroboration. The two friends issued conjointly a *Critical Journal of Philosophy*, which ran through two years. So closely were the two editors associated that in one article it seems as if the younger had supplied his more fluent pen to expound the ideas of his senior.

The influence of Hegel is to be seen in the *Bruno, or on the Divine and Natural Principle of Things*, published in 1802. It is a dialogue, in form closely modelled after the *Timaeus* of Plato, dealing with the old theme of the relation of art (poesy) and philosophy, and with the eternal creation of the universe. It presents philosophy as a higher than Art ; for while Art achieves only an individual truth and beauty, philosophy cognises truth and beauty in its essence and actuality (*an und für sich*). Philosophy itself Bruno (the chief speaker of the dialogue) does not profess to set forth, but ' only the ground and soil on which it must be built up and carried out ' : and that soil is ' the Idea of something in which all antitheses are not so much combined, as rather one, and not so much superseded, as rather not at all parted ',—' a unity, in which unity and antithesis, the self-similar with the dissimilar, are one.' [1] From such a standpoint it is not wonderful that ' in the finite understanding (*Verstand*), compared with the supreme Idea and the way in which all things are in it, everything seems reversed, and as if standing on its head, exactly like the things we see mirrored on the surface of water '.[2]

This supreme Unity is essentially a trinity : an Eternal, embracing infinite and finite ; an eternal and invisible father of all things, who, never issuing forth from his eternity, comprehends infinite and finite in one and the same act of divine knowledge. The infinite, again, is the Spirit, who is the unity of all things ; while the finite, though potentially equal to the infinite,[3] is by its own will a God suffering and made subject to the conditions of time.[4] This trinity in unity (which is the Absolute) is by logic— a mere science of understanding—rent asunder : and the one Subject-object of philosophy becomes for reflection and understanding the three independent objects which such a ' logical ' philosophy calls respectively the Soul (erewhile the infinite), the world (once the finite), and God (the eternal unity). ' Opposing and separating the world of intelligence from the world of nature, men have learned to see nature outside God, and God outside nature, and withdrawing nature from the holy necessity, have sub-

---

[1] Schelling, iv. 231, 235, 236.   [2] Ibid. 244.

[3] ' In things thou seest nought but the misplaced images of that absolute unity ; and even in knowledge, so far as it is a relative unity, thou seest nought but an image—only drawn amiss in another direction—of that absolute cognition, in which being is as little determined by thought as thought by being.'

[4] Schelling, iv. 252. See further, iv. 327 : ' The pure subject, that absolute knowledge, the absolute Ego, the form of all forms, is the only-begotten Son of the Absolute, equally eternal with him, not diverse from his Essence, but one with it.'

ordinated it to the unholy which they name mechanical, while by the same act they have made the ideal world the scene of a lawless liberty. At the same time as they defined nature as a merely passive entity, they supposed they had gained the right of defining God, whom they elevated above nature, as pure activity, utter " actuosity ", as if the one of these concepts did not stand and fall with the other, and none had truth by itself.' [1]

The problem therefore of philosophy is on one hand to ' find the expression for an activity which is as reposeful as the deepest repose, for a rest which is as active as the highest activity '.[2] On the other hand ; ' to find the point of unity is not the greatest thing, but from it also to develop its opposite, this is the proper and deepest secret of art.' [3] The world as it first presents itself labours under a radical antithesis : it offers a double face, body and soul, finite and infinite. But to an absolute philosophy, or that high idealism which sees all things in the light of the Eternal, the two sides are not so separate as they first appeared. Each is also the whole and one, but under a phase, a ' *Differenz* ', a preponderating aspect which disguises the essential identity of both. Behind mind, as it were, looms body : through body shines mind. The ideal is but a co-aspect with the real. The difference of nature and spirit presupposes and leads back to the indifference of the Absolute One. ' Wherever in a thing soul and body are equated, in that thing is an imprint of the Idea, and as the Idea in the Absolute is also itself being and essence, so in that thing, its copy, the form is also the substance and the substance the form.' [4]

' Thus,' so Bruno concludes, ' we shall, first in the absolute equality of essence and form, know how both finite and infinite stream forth from its heart, and how the one is necessarily and for ever with the other, and comprehend how that simple ray, which issues from the Absolute and is the very Absolute, appears parted into difference and indifference, finite and infinite. We shall precisely define the mode of parting and of unity for each point of the universe, and prosecute the universe to that place where that absolute point of unity appears parted into

---

[1] Schelling, iv. 306. Cp. for actuosity, notes in vol. ii. 396. Spinoza, *Cogit. Met.* ii. 11, speaks of the *actuosa essentia* of God.
[2] Ibid. iv. 305.   [3] Ibid. iv. 328.   [4] Ibid. iv. 306.

two relative unities. We shall recognise in the one the
source whence springs the real and natural world ; in the
other, of the ideal and divine world. With the former we
shall celebrate the incarnation of God from all eternity ;
with the latter the necessary deification of man. And
while we move freely and without resistance up and down
on this spiritual ladder, we shall, now, as we descend, see
the unity of the divine and natural principle parted, now,
as we ascend and again dissolve everything into one, see
nature in God and God in nature.' [1] Such was the programme which Schelling offered. Hegel accepting it,—or
perhaps helping to frame it—made two not unimportant
changes. He attempted in his *Phenomenology* to lead up
step by step to, and so warrant, that strange position of
idealism which claims to be the image of the Absolute.
He tried in his *Logic* to give for this point of view a systematic basis and a filling out of the bare Idea of a Unity,
neither objective nor subjective, neither form nor substance,
neither real nor ideal, but including and absorbing these.
He tried, in short, to trace in the Absolute itself the inherent
difference which issued in two different worlds, and to show
its unity and identity there.

A *System* of philosophy, and a philosophy of the *Absolute !*
The project to the sober judgment of common sense stands
self-condemned, palpably beyond the tether of humanity.
For if there be anything agreed upon, it is that the knowledge of finite beings like us can never be more than a
—comparatively poor—collection of fragments, and can
never reach to that which—and such is the supposed
character of the Absolute—is utterly un-related, rank non-
relativity. But in the first place, let us not be the slaves
of words, and let us not be terrified by unfamiliar terms.
After all, a System is only our old friend the unity of
knowledge, and the Absolute is not something let quite
loose, but the consummation and inter-connexion of all
ties. It is no doubt an audacious enterprise to set forth
on the quest of the unity of knowledge, and the completion
of all definition and characterisation. But, on the other
hand, it may perhaps claim to be more truly modest than
the self-complacent modesty of its critics. For ordinary
belief and knowledge rest upon presuppositions which they
dare not or will not subject to revision. They too are sure

[1] Schelling, iv. 328.

that things on the whole, or that the system of things, or
that nature and history, are a realm of uniformity, subject
to unvarying law, in thorough inter-dependence. They
are good enough, occasionally, to urge that they hold these
beliefs on the warranty of experience, and not as, what
they are pleased to call, intuitions, *a priori* ideas, and what
not. But to base a truth on experience is a loose manner
of talking : not one whit better than the alleged Indian
foundation of the earth on the elephant, and the elephant
erected on the tortoise. For by Experience it means
experiences ; and these rest one upon another, one upon
another, till at length, if this be all that holds them together,
the last hangs unsupported, (and with its superincumbent
load), ready to drop in the abyss of Nought.

This ' transcendental ', ' absolutist ', ' *a priori* ' philosophy, which stands so strange and menacing on the
threshold of the nineteenth century, is after all only, as
Kant sometimes called it, an essay to comprehend and see
the true measures and dimensions of this much-quoted
Experience. All knowledge rests *in* (not *on*) the unity of
Experience. All the several experiences rest in the totality
of one experience,—ultimate, all-embracing, absolute,
infinite, unconditioned ; universal and yet individual,
necessary and yet free,—eternal, and yet filling all the
nooks of time,—ideal, and yet the mother of all reality,—
unextended, and yet spread through the spaces of the
universe. Call it, if you like, the experience of the race,
but remember that that apparently more realistic and
scientific phrase connotes neither more nor less (if rightly
understood) than normal, ideal, universal, infinite, absolute
experience. This is the Unconditioned, which is the basis
and the builder of all conditions : the Absolute, which is
the home and the parent of all relations. Experience is no
doubt yours and mine, but it is also much more than either
yours or mine. He who builds on and in Experience,
builds on and in the Absolute, in *the* System—a system
which is not merely *his*. In his every utterance he claims
to speak as the mouth-piece of the Absolute, the Unconditioned ; his words expect and require assent, belief,
acceptance ;—they are candidates (not necessarily, or
always successful) for the rank of universal and necessary
truth : they are dogmatic assertions, and even in their
humblest tones, none the less infected with the fervour of

certainty. For, indeed, otherwise, it would be a shame and an insult to let them cross the lips.

It is the aim of the Absolute *a priori* philosophy to raise this certainty to truth : or, as one may rather say, to reduce this certainty to its kernel of truth. It seeks to determine the limits—not *of* this absolute and basic experience (for it has no external limits)—but *in* this experience : the anatomy and physiology of the Absolute,—the correlations and inclusions, the distinctions and syntheses in the unconditioned field. It examines the *foundation* of all knowledge. But—if this be the phrase—we must be on our guard against a misapprehension of its terms. The foundations are also knowledge : they are *in* all knowledge and experience, its synthetic link and its analytic distinctions. We must not shrink from paradoxes in expression. The house of knowledge, the world of experience, is as self-centred and self-sustaining, and even more so, than the planetary system. It is a totality in which each part hangs upon and helps to hold up the others, but which needs no external help, resting and yet moving, self-poised and free.

We may be spared, therefore, verbal criticism on the Absolute and Unconditioned. The Absolute, and Infinite, and Eternal is no mere negation :—the only pure negation is NOT, and even that has a flaw in its claim. It is perfectly true—and it can only be babes and sucklings that need to be reminded of the fact—that none of us realises and attains the *ne plus ultra* of knowledge and that all our systems have their day,—have their day and cease to be. ' The coasts of the Happy Isles of philosophy where we would fain arrive are covered only with fragments of shattered ships, and we behold no intact vessel in their bays.' [1] So too the whole earth is full of graves ; and yet humanity lives on, charged with the attainments of the past and full of the promise of the future. Let us by all means be critical and not dogmatic : let us never entirely forget that each utterance, each science, each system of ours falls short of what it wanted to be, and for a moment at least thought it was. But let us not carry our critical abstinence into dogmatic non-intervention : or, if so, let us silently accept the great renunciation of all utterance henceforth. System we all presuppose in our words and

[1] Hegel, *Werke*, i. 166.

deeds, and should be much hurt if our defect in it were seriously alleged : the Absolute we all rest in, though amid so many self-imposed and other distractions we feel and see it not. The philosopher proposes for his task—or rather the philosopher is one on whom this task forces itself as for him the one thing inevitable—to determine what is that system and what that Absolute, or, if the phrase be preferred, the philosopher traces to its unity, and retraces into its differences that Experience—that felt, known, and willed synthesis of Reality,—that realised ideal world—on which and in which we live and move. He does not make the system, nor does he set up the Absolute. He only tries to discover the system, and to construe the Absolute.

It may be said that the best of philosophers can do no more than give us *a* Sytsem and *an* Absolute. Undoubtedly that is so. Each philosophy is from one point of view a strictly individualist performance. It is not, in one way, *the* Absolute truth, which it promises or hopes to disclose. The truth is seen through one being's eyes ; and his ' measure ', as Protagoras might have said, is upon it. Yet it is still *the* Absolute, as seen through those eyes ; it is still in a marvellous measure that truth, that absolute truth, ' which the actual generations garble.' For both the artist and the philosopher, if they create, only re-create or imitate ; if they are makers, they are still more seers : and their power of ' imitation ' and of ' vision ' rests on their capacity to de-individualise themselves of their eccentricities and idiosyncrasies, and to bring out only that in them which is the common truth of all essential thought and vision. In proportion as they purge themselves of this *evil* subjectivity are they true artists and philosophers. They are both—and so, too is the religious genius—idealists : but the test of the value of their idealism is its power of including and synthetising reality. That is their verification : that, and not their concord with this or that opinion, this or that theory of individuals or of groups. Not that the views either of groups or individuals are unimportant. But often they are but frozen lumps in the stream, temporary islands which have lost their fluidity, and which imagine themselves continental and permanent.

Truth, then, reasoned truth, harmonious experience, absolute system, is the theme of philosophy. Or, in

Hegelian language, its theme is the Truth, and that Truth, God. Not a sum, an aggregate, or even what is ordinarily styled a system, of truths : but the one and yet diverse pulse of truth, which beats through all : the supreme point of view in which all the parts and differences, occasionally standing out as if independent, sink into their due relation and are seen in their right proportion.

BOOK II

IN THE PORCHES OF PHILOSOPHY

CHAPTER XV

THE TWO AGES OF REASON

THE eighteenth century—it has been often said—was a rationalising, unhistorical, age : and, in contrast, the nineteenth has been declared to be *par excellence* the founder and the patron of the historical method. In the one, the tendency governing the main movement of European civilisation was towards cosmopolitan and universal enlightenment. A common ideal, and, because common, necessarily rather general and abstract, perhaps even somewhat vulgarly utilitarian, pervaded Western Europe, and threw its influence for good and evil on literature and art, on religion and polity. It grew out of a revulsion, in many ways natural, from the religious extravagances of the century-and-a-half preceding, which had led prudent thinkers to reduce religion to a ' reasonable ' minimum, and to reject all things that savoured of or suggested enthusiasm, fanaticism, and superstition. In politics the same one type or system of government and laws was aimed at, more or less, in all advancing states. National peculiarities and patriotism were looked at askance, as unworthy of the free ' humanity ' which was set forward as the end of all training. To simplify, to level, to render intelligible, and self-consistent was the task of enlightenment in dealing with all institutions. To remove all anomalies and inequalities, to give security for liberty and to facilitate the right to pursue happiness,[1] was the chief

---

[1] ' We hold,' says the American Declaration of Independence (1776), ' these truths to be self-evident ; that all men are created equal : that they are endowed by their Creator with certain inalienable rights : that among these are life, liberty, and the pursuit of happiness,' &c.

watchword of this movement. Its questions were—Is religion, Is art and science, Is political organisation, a source of happiness ? Are poetry, and a belief in divine things, and abstruse knowledge, upon the whole for human advantage and benefit ? Only such civilisation can be justified as, taken all in all, is a blessing ; if not (cried some) we may as well cling to the happiness of the barbarian.

That these are important questions, and that the purposes above-mentioned are in many ways good, is clear. But before we can answer the questions, or decide as to the feasibility of the aims, there are some things to be brought and to be kept in view. And these things were not as a rule brought and kept in view. It was assumed that the standard of adjudication was found in the averagely educated and generally cultured individual among the class of more or less ' advanced thinkers ' who asked the questions and set up the aims. That class, already de-nationalised by function, forming a commonwealth or rather a friendly fraternity throughout the capitals of Europe, had cut itself off from the narrower and the deeper sympathies of the national life. Forming a sort of mean or middle stratum in the social organisation, they tended to ignore or despise equally the depths below them and the heights above. They took themselves as the types of humanity, and what *their* understandings found acceptable they dubbed rational : all else was a survival from the ages of darkness. They forgot utterly that they were only a part, a class, a member in the social body : and that they could only be and do what they were and did, because what they were not and did not do was otherwise supplied. It takes all sorts of people to make a world : but each class—and the order of literature and intelligence is no exception—tends to set itself up as the corner-stone (if not something more) of the social edifice. What is more : in such a loose aggregate as the intelligent upper-middle class, the individual tends more and more to count as something, detached and by himself, to be an equal and free unit of judgment and choice, to be emancipated from all the bonds which hold in close affinity members of a group whose functions are unlike each other's, and yet decidedly complementary. Such a class, again—though there are of course conspicuous exceptions—is, by the stress of special interests, removed from direct contact with nature and reality, and lives what in the main may be styled an artificial life.

When such a class asked what were the benefits of art or religion, it thought first of itself ; and it looked upon art and religion—and the same would be true of philosophy and science, or of political sanctions—as *merely* objective and outward entities, foreign to the individual, yet by some mechanical influences brought into connexion with him,— as one might apply to him a drug or a viand. But clearly to a person of practical aims, bent on conveying information and enlightenment, bent on making all men as like each other as possible in the medium range of cultivation which he thinks desirable, the utility of some of these things is questionable and limited. It is only a little modicum of religion, of art and of science, which can be justified by its obvious pleasure-giving power ; and it is easy to point the thesis against enthusiasm in these regions, by reference to the disastrous wars fanned by religion, to the license that has followed the steps of art, and to the lives wasted in the zeal for increasing knowledge. In his ideal of human life such a practical reformer will tend to suppress all that bears too clear a trace of natural, infra-rational, non-intelligent kindred,—all that ties us too closely to mother earth and universal nature.

But if this was the dominant tone of the literary teachers who had chief audience from the public ear, there was no lack of dissentient voices who appealed to nature, who loved the past, who set sentiment and imagination above intellect, and who never bowed the knee to the great idols of en- lightened middle-class utilitarianism. Even in the leaders of the enlightening host—amongst the chiefs of the *Auf- klärung*—there is a breadth and a depth of human interest which sets them far above their average followers, and which should prevent us from joining without discrimina- tion in the depreciatory judgments so often passed on the eighteenth century. The pioneers in the great emanci- patory movement of modern times should not be allowed to suffer from the exaggerations and haste of their more vulgar imitators—still less refused the meed of gratitude we owe them. But when their ideas were violently trans- lated into reality, when the levelling, unshackling process was set at work by vulgar hands, the shortcomings of their theories were made to show even greater than they were :

and inevitable reaction set in. Even the revolutionist himself has come to admit that fraternity at that time came
badly off in comparison with liberty and equality.[1] But
these drawbacks were accentuated when the cosmopolitan
reform-movement, by its haste and intolerance, awakened
the spirit of national jealousy. The deeper instincts of life
rose in protest against the supposed superiority of intellect :
the heart claimed its rights against the head : the man of
nature and feeling was roused up to meet the man of
reasoning and criticism. The spirit of war evoked those
energies of human nature—some of them not its least
valuable—which had slumbered in times of easy-going
peace. The days of adversity and humiliation taught men
that the march of literary culture is not the all-in-all of
life and history.

It was made apparent, practically at least, that intelligence, with its hard and fast formulae, its logical principles,
its keen analysis, was not deep enough or wide enough to
justify its claim to the august title of reason. To be
reasonable implies a more comprehensive, patient, many-
sided observation than is necessary to prove the claim to
mere intelligence. To be intelligent is to seize the right
means to execute a given or accepted end—it is to be quick
and correct in the practice of life, to carry out in detail
what has been determined on in general. Understanding
plays upon the surface of life and deals with the momentary
case : and its greatest praise is to be fleet in the application
of principles, apt to detect the point on which to direct
action, correct in its estimate of means to ends. Clear-
sighted, prudent, and direct, it is the supreme virtue in
a given sphere : but the sphere must be given, and its end
constituted in the measured round of practical life, its
system complete : or, understanding is bewildered before
a hopeless puzzle. Understanding is—the improvident
cynic might say—a certain animal-like sagacity—(such
cynical philosophers were perhaps Hobbes and Schopenhauer[2])—a mere power of carrying out a given rule in a new
but similar case, and of doing so, perhaps, through a long
chain of intermediate links and means.

But there are more things in heaven and earth than are

[1] Louis Blanc, *History of the Revolution*, vol. i.
[2] Hobbes, *Leviathan*, Part I. chaps. 2 and 3 ; and elsewhere.
Schopenhauer, *Welt als Wille*, Book I. § 6.

heard of in the philosophy of the logical intellect. The *subtilitas naturae*[1] far surpasses the refinements of the practical intellect : and if the latter is ever to overcome or be equal to the former, it must, so to speak, wait patiently upon it, as a handmaiden upon the hands of her mistress. Such a trained and disciplined intellect which has conquered nature by obedience is what the philosophers at the beginning of this century called *reason*.[2] It is in life as much as in our mind. It comes not by self-assertion, by the attempt to force our ends and views on nature, but by feeling and thinking ourselves in and along with nature. Or, briefly, it breaks down the middle wall of partition by which man had treated nature as a mere world of *objects*—things to be used and to minister to his pleasure—but always alien to him, always mere matter to be manipulated *ab extra*. Yet even to get full use and enjoyment out of a thing it is well to be in closer community with it, and on terms of friendly acquaintance. The function of this fuller reason cannot be performed without something analogous to sympathy and imagination. Sympathy, which realises the inner unity of the so-called ' thing ' with ourselves : imagination, which sets it in the full circumstances of those relationships which the practical intelligence is inclined to abstract from and to neglect. Yet only something *analogous* to sympathy and imagination : if, as may well be the case, we attach to these terms any association of irregular or mere emotional operation. The imagination in question is the ' scientific ' imagination—the power of wide large vision which sets the object fully in reality, and is not content with a mere name or abstract face of a fact—a name which represents a fact no doubt, but represents it, as many such ' agents ' or deputies do, in a hard and wooden spirit. The sympathy in question is the transcending of the antithesis between subjective and objective ; not a fantastic or fortuitous choice of one or a few out of many on whom to lavish locked-up stores of affection, but the full recognition of unity as pervading differences, and reducing them to no more than aspects in correlation.

What has been said of sympathy and imagination, as the allies and ministers of reason, might be extended and applied to humour, to wit, to irony. These also it may

---

[1] Bacon, *Novum Organum*, i. 10.
[2] See notes and illustrations in vol. ii. p. 400.

be said—and with the same qualifications—are essential to a philosopher in the highest sense. The humour, viz., which strides over the barriers set up by institution and convention between the high and the humble, and sees man's superficial distinctions overpowered by a half-grim, half-jubilant *Ananke*,—which notes how human proposal is overcome, not without grace, by divine and natural disposal, how the deep inner identity in all estates breaks triumphantly through the fences of custom and deliberate intention. The wit, which upsets the hardened fixity of classes and groups, flits from one to another, shows glimpses of affinity between remote provinces of idea, and all this, without laboured and artificial search for analogies, though to the slower-following practical mind, hampered by its solid limits, these leaps from province to province seem paradoxical and whimsical. The irony, which notes the tragi-comedy of life under its apparent regularity of prose, which detects the vanity of all efforts to check the flux of vitality and make the volatile permanent ; which contrasts the apparent with the real, the obviously and officiously meant with the truly desired and willed, and shows how diplomatically-close design is dissipated in a jest, or the soul bent on many years of enjoyment is plunged into torment. Thus, in a way, imagination, sympathy, wit, humour, irony and paradox are elements that go to the making of a philosopher : but in the serenity of reasoned wisdom they lose their frolicsome and fantastic mood, and fill their minor place with sober cheer. Wedded to the lord of wisdom, the Muse of poesy and wit loses her sprightly laugh and her dancing step, becoming a subdued, yet gracious matron, who, with her offspring, sheds gleams of brightness and warmth and colour in the somewhat austere household. Yet still the free maiden of poesy, in the open fields where the shadow of reflective thought has not yet fallen, has the greater charm ; and a certain jealousy not unfrequently reigns between the married sister and the virgin yet untamed.

But though poetry and the allied arts of words were very helpful to philosophy—witness the services which, though in widely different ways, Goethe and Schiller rendered to the higher thinking of Germany—even more stimulative and fruitful was the research into nature and history. Nature *and* history : but they lie closer together than the conjunction suggests. It is true that in recent times we have been forcibly taught to separate civil from natural history, if we have not even been further taught that the latter is an improper application of the term. But when Aristotle said that ' Poetry is more philosophical than History ' he was probably not restricting his remark to the story of nations and states ; even as when Bacon set history as the field of memory beside the fields of imagination and reasoning, he was not solely referring to the records of the human past. The distinction between natural and civil history is no doubt for practical education a distinction of supreme importance. But it is so, because in this scholastic phase the conception of both, under these comprehensive names, was superficial and abstract. Natural history meant only the classificatory description of animals, plants, and minerals : civil history the tale composed to string together the succession of human actions on the public and national field of life.

We have seen in an earlier chapter the advances which Lessing, Kant, and above all Herder, made in this direction.[1] Emphasising in their several ways the great dictum of Spinoza that human passions, and the whole scheme of human life, are *res naturales, quae communes naturae leges sequuntur*, they gave to history a higher, more philosophical, more scientific scope than what the name used to connote. Neither in Spinoza himself, nor in these his followers, did this insistence on the unity of nature at all lead them to neglect the difference—almost equivalent, it may be said, in the end to an *imperium in imperio*—by which rational man marks himself off to a special kindred with the divine.[2] We have seen too what Schelling did to show that history, if in one aspect it be the product of free human volitions, is, in another and as he thought a superior aspect, the realm subject to a divine or natural necessity. The whole tendency of this epoch of thought—the tendency which entitles it above all to the name of speculative—is its impulse to over-ride this distinction between Nature and History ; to over-ride it, however, not in the sense of simply ignoring or denying it, but of carrying it up into a unity which would do justice to both, without exclusively favouring either,

[1] See Chapter XII.
[2] Cf. *Ethica*, iv. 37, Schol. I, contrasting *rerum externarum communis constitutio* with *ipsa hominis natura, in se sola considerata*.

and hardly without clipping both of any extravagant claims.
The distinction remains,—no longer an abrupt division, but
now tempered and mellowed by the presence of a paramount
unity. Nature now has a real history : no longer a mere
factitious aggregate of classified facts, it is the phenomenon
of a ' latent process ', due to a ' latent schematism ', and
a ' form ' or principle of organisation. Classification does
not cease : but it ceases to be an end in itself, and becomes
only subordinate or auxiliary to a higher scientific end.
The main theme is to construe the complete cycle of life-
change and the complete organisation of life-state from the
evidence pieced out and put together from the various
orders, classes, and species of living creatures. And on the
other side the mere tale or narrative of history, with its
gossip of personalities, and its accidents of war and intrigue,
tends to become insignificant in the presence of the great
popular life, in its deep and subtle connexion with agencies
of nature hitherto unsurmised, in its dependence upon
necessities and uniformities which envelope or rather permeate and constitute the human will. It is not indeed that
the force of great personalities has come to be treated as
a quantity we may neglect. The force of the great leader,
of the genius, of the hero, is not less admirable to the wise
philosophical historian to-day than it ever was to his story-
telling predecessor. But he flatters himself that he understands better, and can better take account of, the conditions
which make the genius and the hero possible. Achilles
still counts for more than a thousand common soldiers, and
Homer himself is not merely the composite image by which
a long tradition has fused into a dim pictorial unity the
countless bards who sang for ages on the isles of Greece and
the coasts of Ionia. Yet we feel sure that Achilles did
what he did, because of the race he sprang from, the inspiration he felt around him, the companionship in body and
spirit of his peers. We feel that the hero derives his strength
from earth and air, from the spiritual and material substance in which he draws his breath. True, we cannot
explain him, as if he and his heroisms were a mere product
of mathematical and mechanical forces. But where we
once recognise that behind the single visible deed and agent
there is a spiritual nature—an underlying agency—which,
unperceived, keeps the hearth-fire of public life burning
in the celestial temple of Vesta, we can at least see that

though genius is a marvel and a mystery, yet it is according to law, and no mere will-o'-the-wisp.

But when we say that the actions and sayings even of the foremost individuals are to be comprehended only in the light of universal forces and laws, there is an error which is only too ready to substitute itself for the truth. It soon appears for example that, among the general causes which control the development of civilisation and the acts of individuals, the economical condition is of great and prominent effect. And, above all, it is easily measurable, and subject to palpable standards (such as statistics of exports and imports, &c.). It was natural therefore that a school of historico-social philosophers should arise who maintained that the economical state of a given society was the fundamental principle or form of its life, of which all other phases of its civilisation, religious, aesthetic, &c., were only variable dependent functions. This view, which comes out in the socialist theory of Marx, is clearly the exaggeration or abstract statement of a partial truth into a pseudo-complete theory. The truth is one which found expression as early as Plato. It is this : that in the economical system of a society we find the first and somewhat external or mechanical suggestion of the organism to which the state is yet to grow. In the economic law of reciprocity there is a ' certain faint image ' of the principle of social organisation or political life. But when we go beyond, and interpret this first phase to mean the original foundation, we are stating a figment which has a plausibility only when by the economic state we mean a great deal more than abstractly economic facts include. And this again arises because it is really impossible to carry out thoroughly the abstraction of one aspect of social life from the others. There are no purely economic facts which are independent of other social influences,—of ideals, e. g. moral or aesthetic,—ideals which nobody would call economic, though they never quite part company from economical conditions.

So again there is occasionally a tendency to magnify the influence of what in the narrowest sense may be termed political systems. Forms of government, and titles of sovereignty are regarded as forces to which individuals— even the highest—must bow. But here again the exaggeration of a principle need not tempt us to rush with Tom Paine into the opposite extravagance that govern-

ment and state-power are superfluities, or quasi-ornamental
additions to a social fabric, which can do without them
and, like other beasts of low organisation, can, when shorn
of them, reproduce them with ease.   And thus though we
may dissent from the view that laws and constitutions are
omnipotent, we may admit that in them the central unity
and controlling principle of social life finds its dominant
expression in great outlines.   We shall not agree with him
who said ' Let who will make the laws of a nation if I may
make its ballads ': because we know that the nation
will in the end have the chief voice in determining what
are to be its ballads no less than its laws.   We shall not
quite accept the dictum that the intellectual class which
formulates ideas and sets up programmes of ideals gives the
real lead to the process of civilisation ; for we shall remember
that real ideas are not formed by individuals, but are the
slow work of concrete experience in the so-called inorganic
masses, finding at length utterance through the lips of
those appointed to that end by the natural and divine order.
Yet we shall, on the other hand, see that the high things of
the world are dependent on the lowly : that a song-maker
is sometimes not less potent than a legislature : that
pecuniary conditions are effective in the sanctuaries of
religion and the high places of art : and that the noblest
ideas of great thinkers draw their strength and life through
roots that run unseen through very humble ground.

   La Raison, says Leibniz, *est l'enchainement des verités*.[1]
Truth linked into truth, and so made truer : truth, with
which all things harmonise and nothing cries dissent :
truth, which is neither the prerogative of the mere *demos*,
nor of the intellectual aristocracy, but of that rarer unity
which, when they can exercise several and mutually-
tendered self-abnegation, is the real spirit of both : truth,
thus conceived, is that king of life, that sun of Reason which
lighteth every man.   Truth—to use again the language of
Leibniz,—which is not merely the aggregate of monads,—
but the monad of monads, their mutual penetration and
corrective completion, in that Idea-reality where they retain
their individuality, but retain it in the fullness and fruition
of the absolute which each essentially or implicitly is.   This
kingdom of suffering and yet triumphant truth is the true
age of Reason—not outwardly-critical, individualistically-

   [1] See the *Discours préliminaire* to the *Théodicée*.

reforming, mere intellectual and abstract intelligence,—
but intelligence, charged with emotion, full of reverence,
reverent above all to the majesty of that divinity which,
much disguised, and weather-beaten, like Glaucus of the
sea, resides in common and natural humanity. This is the
Reason of German idealism at the commencement of the
century. To the clear-cut dogmas of the abstract intellect
it savours of mysticism. If it is friendly to distinctions
and constantly makes them, it is the pronounced enemy of
hard and fast separations. Begin where you like, the reason
of things, if you allow it to work, carries you round till you
also see identity where you only saw difference, or effects
where you only looked for causes. You begin, as the
inductive logician, with the belief that the process is from
the known to the unknown. You start with your basis
of fact, as you called it. The nemesis of things forces
you to admit that your facts were partly fictions which
waited for the unknown to give them a truer and fuller
reality. You talk at first of induction, as if it were a single
and simple process, which out of facts builds up generalities
and uniformities. You learn as you go on that the only
induction that operates, except in cases which have been
artificially simplified by supposing half the task done
before you apply your experimental methods, is an induction
of which the major part is deductive, and where your conclusion will be recurrently made your premiss. Your
induction only works on the basis of a hypothesis, and must
itself be linked in the ' concatenation of truths,'—a concatenation which is also a criticism and a correction.

CHAPTER XVI

THE NEW IDEALISM

THIS new idealism which conjures by the name of Reason is a different thing from the pseudo-idealism of Jacobi, as it is from the ' rationalism ', so-called, of the mere intellectualist. Its ideal is not a desperate refuge from the hard and bitter reality, only to be reached by the plunge of faith,—which seems rather the leap of despair : not a *mere* other-world,—always *other*, longed for, presaged, beheld in dreamy vision, but unperceived by the clear light of intelligence : clutched at, but elusive of every effort. It is not won by turning the back on reality and flying on the wings of morning faith to the better land and the presence of the divine : but by persistence in unfolding, expanding, adjusting, re-combining, and fortifying those partial glimpses of the unseen which occur in every vision of the seen. It is true the ideal is, in a way, always an other world : but not a *mere* other world ; it is another, and yet not another, but the same, seen, if you like to say, transfigured, idealised. But idealisation, if so applied, means not an addition here and a subtraction there made in reality, from some source outside—from some indeterminable Whence (Whence indeed should such additions come ?). It does not mean a correction of faults and failures in the real, at the will of an artist who is dissatisfied with his subject-model and would mend it out of other faces and forms stored up in memory or sketch-book. This idealism does not in that sense idealise (so as to falsify). It means complete reality ; absolute, systematic, unconditioned reality : nowhere fragmentary, nowhere referring outside, but completing itself in all its members. It means—to quote the Hegelian term—seeing all things in the Idea—their notion (or ideality) i. e. their unifying ' grip ', reflecting itself in their objectivity, and their reality completing itself in art, religion, and philosophy to that ideal which to the non-artistic, non-religious, non-philosophic mood is only dimly suggested and partially supposed. Still less is it an idealism which, as popularly understood, turns reality and historic fact into *mere* ideas.

But, as perhaps may have been apparent, to call this way of thought idealism need not keep us from acknowledging that the same philosophy is also realism. If it insists, so to say, on the idealism of—what we sometimes call material —nature, it no less insists on the realism of—what is supposed immaterial—mind. The mental or spiritual world loses its unsubstantial intangibleness, its mere supposedness, its ' ideal ' or *merely*-ideal character. To the older, and we may say vulgar, view the mind or soul was a mere ' thought ', something of which all that could be seen were certain acts or phenomena. It was a *mere idea*, which one could pretty well get on without—so long as he kept, as the phrase was, to the phenomena—phenomena without reality. How vague and aëry again was the subject-matter of morals ! A few virtues and vices, confessedly general descriptive titles, a talk about will and conscience,—all of them merely several predicates of an unknown, spoken of, postulated, but unproducible. Compared with this mere supposedness the spiritual world in Schelling and Hegel acquires the reality of a quasi-organism (really supra-organic), growing and constituting itself, and making room in it for a host of human relationships. The abstract faculties of mind get reality (not indeed sensible) : the intangible notions of morals become almost palpable : the kingdom of mind becomes a real pendant to the kingdom of nature. And, on the other hand, the kingdom of nature gets its ideality recognised : its unity and continuity made effective in an Idea which embraces, co-ordinated and systematised, its disparate and unconnected portions.

This new Idealism, if it led men back from the historical world to nature, was yet hardly in all respects a pupil of Rousseau. Not ' Back from civilisation and artificiality to nature and the freedom of the woodland ', was its cry : but rather ' Remember that man always rests on and grows out of nature, always has his ideals made directly or indirectly visible in physical (sensible) structures ; and that, when culture turns away from sense and nature to some supposed higher, it is really entering on a path which leads to abysses '. Its voice, in fact, was much like the longing expressed in Schiller's *Gods of Greece ;* it wished man more godlike and the divine more human. But instead of backward,—its motto was forward : or back to nature, only to resume the true starting-point, and retreat from a path of civilisation whose end is perdition. Man also was nature [1]—if he is never *mere* nature, i. e. the nature unexalted to its truth— but he brought to expression, and might bring to ever clearer and fuller expression, a something which was in infra-human nature, but which nature elsewhere had failed adequately to present. Thus the relation of Man to Nature was apparently two-fold. On one hand, the physical world was essentially a world of reason and intelligence—though of intelligence petrified.[2] So far Hegel agreed with Schelling. But, on the other hand (and here Hegel took up the great paradox of Fichte), man's place in the universe is to fulfil the promise and implication of Nature to the full reality of Spirit, to fulfil it by law and morality ; but (here he completes Fichte by the help of Schelling) also in higher measure, by art, religion, and science. The world of intelligence and reason which man constructs as an ethical, artistic, and religious being, is the full truth of the natural world,—the higher meaning, and fuller, more consistent, and complete reality of the sensible : and it is so, because the lord of Nature is one with the lord of the human soul. The new way of philosophy therefore, if it could be ever charged with saying that the so-called real things of ordinary life were only ideas, or mental images, meant that, as taken by the unthinking or imperfectly thinking perception, they were something of which all that could be said was to describe their relations to something else, of which in turn the same remark might be made ; so that—as far as they went—reality was never with us, but only an assurance (soon to be proved vain) that it was next door.[3] On the contrary—in *its* use of the term Idea—what this idealism asserted rather was that the objects of Nature in their *prima facie* apprehension were not yet an Idea: if, i. e., an Idea is a mental or spiritual reality which explains and completes itself, instead of sending us on endless fool's errands elsewhere,—is a concept which

[1] Cf. Spinoza's remark on Body, *Eth.* iii. pr. 2 Schol. ' Etenim quod corpus possit, nemo hucusque determinavit ; hoc est neminem hucusque experientia docuit quid corpus ex solis legibus naturae quatenus corporea tantum consideratur possit agere,' &c.

[2] See vol. ii, notes and illustrations, p. 392.

[3] Schopenhauer's well-known description of this recurrent throwing back of the responsibility of reality on something else is here suggested (' World as Will and Idea,' § 17).

is exactly adequate to reality, and has gathered in it the power of reality.

The new idealism is not subversive of realism, but includes it and makes it the reality it professed to be. It may therefore, as Schelling proposed,[1] be called an ideal-realism, or a real-idealism. If any body likes, he may even, if he is no Greek scholar, call it Monism ; but in that case he had better begin by admitting to himself that any Monism, which can stand its ground and serve for an explanation of the universe, will not exclude Dualism. All is indeed one life, one being, one thought ; but a life, a being, a thought, which only exists as it opposes itself within itself, sets itself apart from itself, projects its meaning and relations outwards and upwards, and yet retains and carries out the power of reuniting itself.   The Absolute may be called One : but it is also the All ; it is a One which makes and overcomes difference : it is, and it essentially is, in the antithesis of Nature and Spirit, Object and Subject, Matter and Mind ; but under and over the antithesis it is fundamental and completed unity. Monism, literally understood, is absurd—for it ignores, what cannot be ignored, the many : and Dualism, which is offered sometimes as a competitive scheme, is not much better ; unless we understand the Dualism to be no fixed bisection, but an ever-appearing and ever-superseded antithesis which is the witness to the power and the freedom of the One,— which is not alone, but One and All, One in All, and All in One.

The central or cardinal point of Idealism is its refusal to be kept standing at a fixed disruption between Subject and Object, between Spirit and Nature. Its *Idea* is the identity or unity (not without the difference) of both. In its purely logical or epistemological aspect one can easily see that, as Schopenhauer was so fond of repeating, There is no Object without a Subject and no Subject without an Object.[2] The difficulty arises in remembering these excellent truisms when one of the correlatives is out of sight, and the other seems to be independent and to come before us with a title to recognition apparently all its own. When the Subject figures as the individual

---

[1] See p. 121 (chap. xiii).

[2] *Satz vom Grunde*, § 16 : *Welt als Wille und Vorstellung :* Ergän-zungen.   Cap. 1.

consciousness, encased, it may perhaps be added, in an individual body, and the Object as a thing apparently out there in a world beyond all by itself, then the lapse from this rudimentary idealism becomes easy. In the practice of life and business, each of us, self-conscious and auto-nomous *subject* as he may be, comes to rank in the estimate of others, and ere long to some extent in his own, as also a part of the aggregate of objects. All reality and substance seem as it were to slide over into the object-side. The conscious subject counts as a mere onlooker or the passive spectator of a performance that goes on in an outside field of event,—yet that outside is his own object-mind ; his mind counts as a mere idea, or rather as a succession of ideas, i. e. of mental pictures with a certain meaning in them. A little step more and the very subject-mind itself is turned into an object. There stands indeed—according to the ordinary introspective psychology—as it were in one corner, or at one loophole of vision, a mind looking on, observing and criticising another thing which is also called a mind ; but the mind observing can only reflect or register, and the mind which is observed is very much thing-like, apparently acted upon by other things, and acting upon them in turn. This object-mind, a real among other reals, in relations of cause and effect with them, does not, if we can trust the *words* of those who tell about it, see itself, but lies open to the inspection of this other mind, repre-sented by the psychological observer, who is good enough to report to us something of its blind and dark estate. Its re-actions, he informs us, exhibit a remarkable pecu-liarity. They are equivalent to states of consciousness : and even to acts of will and knowledge. As when a violin is touched in certain ways by the bow, you get a musical note, so when certain agents come in contact with this peculiar real, they elicit a re-action, termed sense or idea.

To distinguish in this manner between mental passivity and activity is natural and right. The basis of all con-sciousness and mental activity is an original division, a ' judgment ' or dijudication of self from self. But, once the dijudication made for such ends, it is a mistake to forget its initiation and lose sight entirely of the fact that the observing mind is also the active, and that the object-self is not merely in relation to the subject-self, but in a higher unity is identifiable therewith. Still the thing is done, habitually done.   We all profess this faith of ordinary realism in our first reflections upon ourselves.   And the effect of the oblivion is that we seek elsewhere for the initial activity, which we have abstracted from and lost sight of.   The receptive passive mind,—called subject still, but now become a subject in the sense of the anatomist,— has to be set in motion, to be impinged upon or impressed. The psychical event which you *call* knowledge, and which no doubt *means* knowledge,—the mental ' state ' which you observe—or, it may even, if your authority is a particularly obstinate and *intransigeant* realist, be the molecular change in brain cells,—requires an antecedent event to account for it.   The origin of the movement which issued in the given psychical or molecular change is sought in a self-subsistent thing which *out there* gives rise to a series of movements which *in here* result in a sensation.   Or, a thing somehow produces an attenuated image of itself in the brain, or in the mind ; for, in this mythological tale of psychical occurrence, accuracy is unattainable, and one must not seek to be too precise.   In any case the relationship between thing and idea is conceived after the analogy of the nexus of cause and effect, or original and copy ; and the verbal imagination of the analogical reasoner is satisfied.   What Hegel, after Schelling, teaches, on the other side, is that the process of sense-impression and the manipulations to which it is subjected by intellect pre-suppose, for their existence and their objective truth, a Reason which is the unity of subject and object, an original identity uniting knowledge to being.

But the same defect of unphilosophic consciousness has another phase which philosophy has to remember.   Popular language speaks of *things*,—of things here and things there, which act upon each other and upon the so-called mind : i. e. on this imagined and supposed passive mind.   For things, a more ' scientific ' conception has been substituted —that of *forces* ;   which, whether attached to atoms or not, are asserted to be the real sources of the change and event which fill the world of our experience.   And as, according to some psychologists, the mind is only a vacant ground or space with more or less narrow limits of room, on which the entities called ideas are for that reason forced into more or less close relationships, without any nearer or more essential tie ; so, too, the mind is apt to be treated

by others only as a battle-field or wrestling-ground of
opposing forces. Here the atom-forces, as in the other
case the atom-ideas, are, it is assumed, merely and purely
independent : and yet such is the force of a limited environment—shall we say, in more popular language, the force of
space and time ?—that they must meet with one another,
must, as it were, form associations, connexions, relationships. Great, verily, is the force of juxtaposition. Space
and time, because they are essentially limiting, correlating,
defining, weld links which the great prophet of this empirical school has not scrupled to call insoluble, ineradicable,
inseparable. Space and time, says his great successor, are
infinite. But they are infinite only in the sense that they
can never be exhausted : they are everywhere, and for
ever : but as real they are only here and now. Time can
precede time, and space fade away into remoter space :
but every space and every time is finite, defining, limiting,
relative, and synthetic. And, if we look closer, space and
time may come to seem the visible, ghostly, abstract
outline—on one hand stiffening and bodying-out the ideal
synthesis of thought and intelligence, on the other, faintly
reproducing or fore-casting the real synthesis of organisation and living nature.

In saying this we give the reasonable interpretation of
' association ' : —so far at least as association is supposed
to be brought about by juxtaposition in time and space.
Time and space, as Kant might say, give the schema—the
sensible and visible reflex of the eternal and universal
thought-relation : they are *a priori* because they are in the
physical world the *primitive*, the first phase and the lowest
manifestation of that unity which as we know it in nature
and mind always blends with sense, or displays itself in
sensible forms. They are the first stamp of reality, of
real Nature : with them we are in Nature, but it is an
abstract shadowy nature. They mark the ascent (which
only from the mere logician's standpoint shall we call the
descent) of the abstract (pure) idea into the element of
multiplicity, of opposition, of life and consciousness. In
the psychical and intellectual world, again, as it rises to
more perfect ideality (as it elicits more *meaning* from
crude *fact*) they lose their prominence ; they sink into the
powers of memory and imagination, which build up past
and future into the unity of the ever present, until in their

consummation they leave as their residual product the abstract element of pure thought : a thought which claims the attributes of universality and eternity, which claims, i.e., to merge or submerge in it all space and all time.[1]

It is evident therefore that if an associationist theory, like that of Hume, proposes to explain the actual field of mental life by elements given in it, and by no other, it can only do so on certain assumptions, which may be summed up in the proposition that the mind—the real mental space and time even (and not its supposed ' image ')—is at once subjective and objective, at once real and ideal, at once the field of operation, the force which directs operations, and the mind which is aware of itself and its acts. To say, as Hume appears to do, that an unintermittent long-established custom breeds *in us* certain irresistible and essential habits of thought, can only refer to an unexplained and unnoticed duplication of the self. There is here one self, which is only a bundle of fragments, of ideas intrin-sically separate and only incidentally connected by outside pressure, which enter into ties, peradventure necessary or indissoluble, though not due to inner affinity. And there is another self which is a self-same unity, dividing and growing, or assimilating, acted upon but only because it solicits action, and in a way controlling the process going on within it. The difficulty for the investigator is to realise that these two selves are one. No amount of ingenuity will ever succeed in honestly showing unity to be the mere resultant—even should it be a fictitious or phenomenal unity—of the collisions and fortuitous attachments or detachments of different and independent reals. The reals which behave in such a way as to engender unities, to cause syntheses, are reals in a mind ; and the mind must not merely, as it were, flow around them, but have them fluid members of itself. If they are reals, they are ideal-reals. You must begin with an ideal-unity which is also a real-unity, in which variety can play and by which it is controlled.

' Forces,' no less than ' things ', are terms of thought, names of reality indeed, but inadequate because due to an abstraction and leaving their correlatives out of sight— names of momentary elements seized in the flux, and made with more or less success to indicate ' moments ' and

[1] See later, chapter xxvi.

'factors' or 'aspects' in the total sum and power of reality. Explanation by permanent and separate forces labours under the same disadvantages as that by things. Science, grown more self-critical, begins to see that in forces, &c., it has names and formulae which are not the full reality, but only useful (*if* useful) abstractions. Neither things nor forces, though called real, are so in the full sense. Hume said,—and said not untruly, though with some relish of paradox,—that we never had any real impression or idea of power and force. The statement should be taken along with another that what we mistake for power in things is only our own want of power to over-come a suggested association, or to break a customary train of ideas. Lotze, again, has remarked that the supposed consciousness of power exerted in voluntary movement is confused with a feeling of work done, or inertia over-come. Whatever may be the truth about the psychological experience, there can be no doubt for the epistemologist that the so-called perception of force is an interpreta-tion of one aspect of experience which, with a certain amount of arbitrary arrest and simplification, renders it intelligible and real by means of an antithesis and corre-lation. Force in fact only exists, or arises, in relation or opposition to a counter-force : action and re-action are always equal and opposite, says the mathematical formula. Two forces are as little independent as an up and a down, or as a west and a north ; force solicits force, and force only *is* in so far as it is solicited. The soliciting can only solicit because it is solicited. In other words, it is not enough to say that the forces which thus confront each other are correlatives. The relationship must be carried up a stage higher : the forces themselves get their pseudo-real character, only so long as they are kept apart forcibly or by inertia. Carry out their implications : and they re-unite (not however to the loss of all distinction) in a higher idea, an intelligible unity which, by its division and return to unity, makes possible and real their con-tention. It is this carrying-out of implications to their explicit truth which is at the root of Schopenhauer's playing fast and loose with the distinction between force and will. But with him the two terms are taken up vague and indefinite, in the haze of popular conception or want of conception, and are without effort or justification identified: whereas in Hegel, there is, on the lowest estimate, an *attempt* made to trace the somewhat intricate steps which mediate the metamorphosis.

The new idealism thus maintains the organic and even supra-organic nature of thought and being. The world of experience, when taken in its reality and fullness, is an organism which lives and knows and wills, and which is life, action, knowledge ; its own means and its own end. The subject acting, living, knowing is action, knowledge, life. In the ordinary organism there is a subject of functions, a being in relation to an inorganic world. In the world-organism (if the inadequate name is still to be retained) there is no outside world, no inorganic or extra-organic thing. In the world-organism the organ and its environment is combined in one, re-united : the plant or animal is not without its place, and its place is not without plant or animal. They are not merely in correlation, but essentially and actually one. *Quid prosunt leges sine moribus ?* asks the moralist : but in the Absolute or the supra-organic Idea, law and morality are not apart : the necessity is also freedom : the law is not severed from its phenomenon. Such an organism which is life, thinking, will, is what Hegel calls the Idea : an organism which is completely organic, with no mere matter : and that Idea is the foundation of his Idealism. Conceived under its conditions, the forces which are sometimes represented as struggling with each other on the field of man's life, are no longer independent ; still less completely separable forces. They are the inner division by which the spirit re-establishes and makes secure its unity : their antagonisms are the breath of life. And they have their relations in their common service, building up one life. They form a certain hierarchy of organisation ; in which however the higher or more developed does not merely supervene upon the cruder, but in a way supersedes it, and yet contrives to retain its worth and its real truth.

CHAPTER XVII

METHODS, ARTIFICIAL AND NATURAL

WHEN modern philosophy took its first steps, it was disdainful and depreciatory to the past, both Medieval and Old-Greek. Bacon and Hobbes, Descartes and Spinoza,—be their other differences what they may—all echo the same disparagement. Like Wordsworth's *Rob Roy*, they cry—

> ' What need of books ?
> Burn all the statutes and their shelves.
>
> We'll show that we can help to frame
> A world of other stuff.'

On this iconoclastic age supervenes the attempt of Leibniz to combine in one all that was good in the new corpuscular philosophy with all that was precious in the old Platonic idealism as expanded by Aristotle. So, at the later philosophic crisis towards the close of the eighteenth century, the somewhat destructive and revolutionary tendencies of Kant and Fichte lead up by a natural revulsion and complement to the reconstructive systems of Schelling and Hegel. In them the conservative instinct comes to supplement the defects of the radical go-ahead. Instead of tossing the past away to the winds, and crying out *Écrasez l'infâme,*—instead of throwing medievalism behind, breaking all the restrictions on individual liberty which feudal Europe had created to secure and safeguard the communities that housed its early freedom, the new spirit of the time saw that the problems of modern life were not solved by merely throwing overboard as encumbrances and refuse all checks and forms. On the contrary, the reflective mind saw that forms and checks so-called there must be, and that the art of statesmanship, though it could not entirely consist in copying the old, had still to work in some way after the analogy of the old methods : i. e. to do under new circumstances what would solve the same requisites, as the old constitution had done for its time.

The change is well illustrated by the attitude towards state organisation shown by William von Humboldt at different epochs of his life.

People talk glibly of the Historical Method, and what it has done for us. To hear what is sometimes said it might be supposed that this was the method that had been always habitual in history, but which in these latter days had been applied to other topics, and had proved its value on the new ground by achieving results that had hitherto been mere desiderata. This however is pretty nearly to reverse the true state of the case. It was long till history came to have any method worthy of the name. In most of those who figure as great historians the object had been to tell a good tale, to keep the thread of events distinct, to subordinate incidents to the main issue, to portray personal and public character and its influence on events. History was practised—we may even say—more as an art than as a science. If it dealt with causes, it dealt with individual, concrete, living causes, not with cold, dead abstractions of forces, laws, or tendencies. If it did not altogether ignore the suggestions of a quest for principles to be found in Thucydides and Polybius, it was much more enamoured of the art of Livy and Tacitus, or even of the naïveté of Herodotus. Of such history who has not felt the power ; who has not admired the genius that reconstructs the men and circumstances of the past, and makes them live over again their deeds, and again in the end yield the palm to inevitable fate ! But it was not from such history that the historical method arose.

The historical method was the product of the new conception of nature and mind in their mutual relations which has been already noted. To estimate the labours of thinkers towards this view of history would be an interesting but complex inquiry. Leibniz in particular by his principles of development, of continuity, of general analogy, should have made two things for ever clear. And these two results that might have been supposed secure were, first, that the present existence (which at first seems to be alone real) is only a narrow transition line between a past and a future,—a line of points intersecting a complex movement or development ; and secondly, that all development is of something which is essentially infinite, which requires nothing external, no fillip from circum-

stances or from an external providence, to set it going, but
is in itself a synthesis of active and passive force in a something at least analogous to an Ego. The first principle is
embalmed in Leibniz's maxim : ' The present is laden with
the past, and full of the future ' : and the second, in the
maxim ' the Monads have no doors or windows '. In
virtue of the first, the existent (of this instant) is only
a stage or grade, rooted in what has been, and insignificant
unless in reference to what is to come. In virtue of the
second, all development is from within, and presupposes
therefore that the developing individual includes within
it a great deal which a cursory view would at first sight
assume to be without it, and only accidentally in contact
with it. It might indeed be well to add a third principle—
what Leibniz has sometimes called the Law of Continuity—
the law that, as he says, distinct and noticeable perceptions
are the resultants of an infinite number of insensible or
little perceptions. But continuity proper is not this :
continuity proper or identity is a pure idea. The visible
or sensible discontinuity reposes on, and is to be explained
by, an invisible or ideal continuity. Each body, for
instance, in nature, appearing to have a separate existence
of its own, is only a stage isolated or insulated in a continuing process : and that process, binding, as it does,
past to future, is the process of a Mind. *Omne Corpus*,
wrote Leibniz in 1671, *est mens momentanea seu carens
recordatione*. Every physical and material object is an
intelligence, but an intelligence which neither looks before
nor after, but is limited *for itself* to the mere instant : an
intelligence which has no history. Yet to the intelligent
observer it has a past,—it has a memory, it bears in it
the traces of its antecedent. Yet to read that book of
memory, to decipher the ' insensible perceptions ' which
are buried beneath the momentary present, beneath its
unspiritual reality, and to knit present with past and
future, is the work of an intelligence, in and to whom the
material discloses its store of meaning, or in whom it is
re-spiritualised. In other words, the presupposition of
this historial method is the ideal continuity of being, transcending and absorbing the differences of time.

But the teaching of Leibniz—even more perhaps than
that of Spinoza—fell on an evil age : if it was not actually
choked with thorns, it found a soil with little depth, and

its brief verdure was soon followed by a fearful withering. Anxious as Leibniz was to commend his theories to all men,—and not least perhaps to win the suffrages of some illustrious and intelligent women—he was led to present them under forms and phrases which were to each correspondent specially familiar. And the natural consequence was not absent. The forms of accommodation were what told : they stuck, and the truth they were meant to convey slipped away : the Leibnitian theory was re-interpreted into the doctrines it had been meant to supersede. As with Spinoza, so with Leibniz, a keen apprehension of his meaning came first to the thinkers on the border-land of literature and philosophy, to Lessing and Herder, and found an appreciative welcome in the more academic systems first from Schelling and Hegel. Above all, this theory of ' petites perceptions ' so closely bound up (as was to be expected) with his mathematical discoveries in the Calculus, is what marks him as having a finer ear for the secret harmonies and principles of existence than the coarser organs of popular philosophy could catch up or appreciate.

'In order,' says Leibniz, ' to get a clearer idea of the little perceptions which we cannot distinguish in the crowd, I am accustomed to employ the example of the roar or noise of the sea which strikes us upon the shore. To hear this sound, as we do hear it, we must hear the parts which compose this total, i. e. the sounds of each wave, though each of these little sounds only makes itself perceptible in the confused assemblage of all the others together, (that is to say, in that same roar,) and would not be noticed if this wave which causes it were alone. For we must be a little affected by the movement of that wave, and we must have some perception of each of these sounds, however small they may be ; otherwise we thould never have the perception of a hundred thousand waves, since a hundred thousand zeros would never make anything. . . . These little perceptions are of greater efficiency by their consequences than we suppose. It is they which form that *Je ne sais quoi*, those tastes, those images of sensible qualities, clear in the assemblage, but confused in the parts ; those impressions made upon us by surrounding bodies which envelop the infinite, that *nexus* which each being has with all the rest of the universe. It may even be said

that in virtue of these little perceptions the present is big
with the future and laden with the past, that everything
conspires together : and that in the least of substances,
eyes as piercing as those of God could read the whole
sequel of the things of the universe.

' These insensible perceptions, further, mark and constitute the same individual, who is characterised by the
traces or expressions which they preserve of the preceding
states of that individual, thus forming the connexion with
his present state. These may be known by a superior
spirit, though that individual himself should not feel them,
i. e. though express memory should no longer be there.
But these perceptions also supply the means of rediscover-
ing that memory, at need, by periodic developments, which
may one day happen. . . . It is also by these insensible
perceptions that I explain that admirable pre-established
harmony of mind and body, and even of all monads or
simple substances,—which takes the place of the impossible
influence of one upon another. . . . After this, I should
add but little if I said that it is these small perceptions
which *determine* us in many conjunctures without our
thinking of it, and which deceive the vulgar by the appearance of an *indifference of equilibrium*, as if we were entirely
indifferent whether we turned, e. g., to right or to left.

' I have remarked also that in virtue of insensible variations two individual things could never be perfectly alike,
and that they ought always to differ more than *numero*.
And with this we have done once for all with the empty
tablets of the mind, a soul without thought, a substance
without action, the void of space, the atoms, and even
parcels not actually divided in matter ; we have done
with pure repose, entire uniformity in a portion of time,
of place or of matter, . . . and a thousand other fictions of
philosophers which come from their incomplete notions,
fictions which the nature of things does not suffer, and
which our ignorance and the little attention we have for
the insensible lets pass, but which could never be rendered
tolerable, unless we confine them to abstractions of the
mind which protests that it does not deny what it puts
aside and considers out of place in any present considera-
tion. Otherwise, if we took it quite in earnest, to mean
that things which we do not perceive do not exist in the
soul or body, we should fail in philosophy as in politics by

neglecting τὸ μικρόν, insensible steps of progress :—whereas an abstraction is not an error provided we know that what we put out of sight is still there.'

This was the conception which Bacon had shadowed out, which Leibniz had presented under many names and with many applications, as the olive-branch between Plato and Democritus ; it now became through philosophical and extra-philosophic acceptance a current maxim in the general field of knowledge. Nature assimilated to history, and history assimilated to nature : freedom built upon necessity, and efficient causes rounded off, though not entirely merged, in final. It is the recognition of law, order, causality in the psychical world, yet not of *mere* so-called natural law ; and therefore without reducing it to a merely physical and material world. It is in fact the new method which is inevitable and necessary, as soon as it is manifest that life, organisation, development is the underlying truth and central notion of things. You look at the world at first, let us say, as a mere collection of separate things in varying degrees of juxtaposition : and all that you think of doing to them, either by way of theory or practice, is to put them together, to link them closer, or separate them more widely. You do so from outside by an arranging force ; for they are assumed to be purely passive, waiting to be touched, each set in its place—from which it can only be moved by a push or a pull. This is the method of mathematics or mechanics. It shows the dexterity of the agent or of the expositor : but you feel that it is artificial, and arbitrary. It is analytic or synthetic—but not auto-analysis or auto-synthesis. The director of the movement (we may call it ' construction ') may no doubt have the real secret : he may work the things well and fairly, and unite or divide them according to inner affinities ; but we cannot, as matters stand, be sure of this. The things, in fact, he deals with have been already emptied of all life and peculiarity of their own : they are alike in quality, only differing by a more or less,— a difference which at any moment may be altered by an act of subtraction or addition. No doubt you can build up what are *called* systems—compounds of a kind—in this way : but they do not really hang and grow together ; they are only prevented from breaking up by the absence of any empty place to which the parts may withdraw.

Bit holds up bit ; but how all the bits have found themselves so caged up without exit is a mystery. Absolute neutrality or indifference of each part to others, and yet absolute equilibrium [1] in the total composite,—such is the situation.

The chemical method (taking chemistry as a type of the sciences like optics, electricity, &c.) is a revelation of a different state of affairs. The elements of things are here seen to be unique and incomparable ; yet in each there is a latent sympathy ready to break out when the proper occasion arrives. Bring two things together, and their affinity suddenly, in the proper circumstances, leads to their complete fusion : a product arises which, when formed, hardly betrays its origin and composition. In a way this is the converse of the mechanical or mathematical method. In it was no fusion, no inner mixture : each part after composition lay beside the other, and their union was only in the ideas of the onlooker. It was mere juxtaposition still,—though now closer : an abnormally keen eye would still have been able to descry the dividing lines and measure the gaps. At least mere mechanical physics tends so to conceive it. Here, on the contrary, there is union—but only at the moment of fusion : once that is accomplished, the result is apparently simple, and bears no suggestion of being a compound. In the mechanical union the result is exactly equal to the sum of the elements which go to make it : in the chemical there is something positively new, something, i. e., of which the premises gave no indication and made no promise.

Either of these methods,—of these conceptions of existence—works well in a certain region. But both of them only do their work on a certain hypothesis, or with a certain abstraction. The mechanical method supposes that objects are all qualitatively alike, differing only in quantity or weight : all therefore entirely comparable with each other, and capable of being substituted for each other in an equation. Where this assumption holds good, the method of addition and division, the method of the calculus does its work.[2] The chemical method works on another

[1] Of course the term ' equilibrium ' may be used loosely to mean a great deal more than this,—how much will depend on the context. These quasi-mathematical analyses have great fascination : their apparent simplicity imposes upon us.

[2] The distinction, it will be observed, lies between the method of mathematical physics and that of physics which has learned some-

assumption,—the assumption of a number of qualitatively-differenced elements, of elements which also are, so to speak, set on edge against some, and ready to leap into the arms of others. If the observer in the first case had the game entirely in his own hand,—could build up and separate at his pleasure, could determine results *a priori* : he is here baffled by the unexpected, and can only wait and watch to learn *a posteriori* the behaviour of the bodies possessed of this occult and non-predictable affinity. At the best he can only formulate what he observes, try to classify it, ascertain any common principles running through it, any serial recurrences, or the like : and that is all that chemical philosophy can achieve. Chemical affinity—the fact that certain elements combine in certain ways, and refuse to enter into certain alliances—is a great fact : but to *a priori* reasoning or abstract syllogising it is an entire inexplicability, one of the accidents in the universe which must be reckoned with, but cannot be understood.

It is probably evident that, if we want to get a comprehension of the life and concrete reality of things, neither of these methods will quite answer the purpose. With the first alone, if it could be universally carried out, the universe would be thoroughly explained : everything would be exactly equivalent to some sum or multiple of every other : there would be no mystery, nothing unique, and strictly individual. Given time, we could find a formula for every reality, and a predicate exactly fitted to any subject. Yet even mathematics has to confess the existence of irrationals, surds, infinite series, and the like. For our unities and standards are always arbitrary, artificial, and one-sided, and fall short of the subtlety of nature. Even our simpler types of surfaces—the circle and the square—remain irreducible to each other : and we only avoid the collision by the remark that practically and with any required amount of exactness the discrepancy between the two can be adjusted. If we turn to the chemical method, again, there is a nearer approach to actuality in the recognition of the presence of

thing from the researches of electricity or chemistry. If the method or principles of chemistry are thus said to be reduced to those of physics, this is because the conceptions of physics have been revolutionised from the side of chemistry, &c., and even of biology. This tendency of modern science is precisely in the line indicated by Schelling and Hegel.

something more than mere composition and juxtaposition.
It is not that there is something which is *not* juxtaposition :
but rather it is much *more than mere* juxtaposition.   There
may be degrees of this something more : but it is only to
a gross or abstract view that it is not present at all.   Mere
cohesion even shows a unity in things juxta-posed.   Mere
contact is contagious : it infects. ' When a violin has been
played on frequently by a tyro,' says G. H. Lewes, ' its tone
deteriorates, its molecules become re-arranged, so that one
mode of vibration is more ready than another.'[1] ' Toute
impression,' he quotes from Delbœuf, ' laisse une certaine
trace ineffaçable.'   So-called chemical composition is only
a conspicuous instance, with peculiarities, of this alteration
in state produced by what, from the mechanical standpoint,
are called inner molecular displacements.   But to recognise
a fact is one thing : to give its explanation is another.
Yet, on the other hand, to recognise the fact is to note
an important point which had been omitted by the mechanical construction of things.   There the result could hardly
be called new : it was exactly equal to its constituent
elements : and the equation was transparent.   And it was
transparent because the whole process, analysis and
synthesis, was not a work or process of the observed thing,
but the work of the observing mind : it makes the (artificial)
unities, numbers them, and adds them or subtracts.   But
with the chemical result, though it also is equal to its
elements, there is something new.   Water, no doubt, is
oxygen and hydrogen, but here, at least, there is no doubt
that the *plus* sign unduly simplifies the relationship, and
rather indicates or represents a nexus than accurately defines
it.   And yet, there is nothing in water which was not, in
some—shall we say mysterious ?—way, in the oxygen and
the hydrogen.   Chemical physics, therefore, brings out
clearly, or comparatively clearly, something which the
ordinary and coarser simplicity-loving theory is obliged
and is able to neglect : it realises the virtue that lies in
juxtaposition, and shows that the mere outer change of
quantity goes with a deeper inward and qualitative one.
The result does more than sum up and condense what was
spread out in extension and dispersed in parts before : it
brings out or reveals something which previously was
unsurmised.   Always, in a liberal interpretation of the

[1] *Problems of Life and Mind*, iii. p. 58.

maxim, it is true that *Ex nihilo nihil fit :* but here, especially, the effect actually discloses what was—but was latent or unperceived—in the premises. The maxim, to be fairly treated, must be read backwards as well as forwards.

But we must go a step further if we wish the full explanation. If the premises are to be adequate to support the conclusion, they must be restated in terms which hint at the conclusion—which in a way contain it, but contain it in potentiality and promise, not in act. This is the method of development, which is the method that is applicable to full concrete reality, not like the others to parts abstracted from or insulated in reality. So long as you deal with these selected bits of fact—abstracted from their surroundings, subject to strict observation or strict experiment, you can apply a comparatively simple and straightforward method. You are dealing with abstracted, mutilated, prepared fact. You are guided in these cases by the canons of identity and difference : you add and subtract, or subtract and add ; and that is all. You use what are called the rules of experimental method. But these canons do not directly apply—except by happy accident—to the real world, where antecedent and consequents are not separate and tabulated, as the logical canons, the rules of formal logic, require. In dealing with this concrete reality, a much more complex method is needed, a method which has to blend induction with deduction, and to start from both ends in the series of causation at once. You can apply observation or experiment, only when the issues have already been extremely simplified and narrowed down : when the question has been rendered so definite that it is next-door to the answer, and the removal of a slight partition-wall will as it were make the two one clear space. Where observation and experiment are available, indeed, is where the general outlines and principles of the subject are settled, where the scheme of reality is defined in large, but a variety of minor issues still remains to be settled. Unless this general framework is fixed, neither observation nor experiment, with their canon of identity and difference, are of any avail. These methods, therefore, only apply in sciences which are in principle or substantially complete, though admitting of possibly infinite extension in details and particulars. Where the science is yet to constitute, i. e. in dealing with the kinds of real things in their completeness,

and not as viewed in some definite aspect, induction and
deduction must go hand in hand and help each other at
every step : and if they, as they must, have recourse to
experiment and observation, it will be at first in a very
unsatisfactory and tentative way.

Such is the way the contrast between the simplicity
belonging to an artificial method dealing with picked
instances, and the complexity that real concrete organic
nature demands, presented itself to J. S. Mill as he advanced
in his inquiry.   The only complete method for the investigation of unsophisticated nature, not yet mapped out and
defined in general departments, is the deductive-inductive
method in which induction and deduction separately have
a subordinate place,—using induction in the narrow sense
the term has been hitherto allowed to bear.   And that
sense, it may be added, is, as in some passages of Aristotle,
little else than a reverse of syllogism, or to speak more
accurately, it is a syllogism which goes up to generals
instead of descending from them.   It is like the syllogistic
deduction formal and abstract in character.   The (deductive)
syllogism assumes the existence of major premises—of
general propositions which in the last resort, if they are real
bases, must be primary and true, or self-evident facts.   But
a critic, like Mill, had little difficulty in showing that a
general truth rests upon and presupposes the very particular
conclusions which it is used to establish.   Unless every
singular is true, the universal which embraces or unifies them
cannot really be true.   Therefore the conclusion is really
implied and presupposed in the principles of its premises.
But, unfortunately for the application and supposed
sequel of this not unjust remark, a similar remark may be
made on the ordinary exposition of the inductive method.
Induction, it is said, infers from or on a basis of single facts.
But if a single truth is really, i.e. unconditionally true, it is
indistinguishable from the universal.   If it is really true
once, it is true for ever.   The assertion of the individual
proposition as true, if it can be supported—(and unless it
be true, what basis can it afford for the general conclusion ?)
—implies the truth of the universal it is sometimes used to
establish.   The inductive logician tells us to build on singular and definite facts, on truths of definite and individual
experience : but a definite or determinate truth rests upon
universality (indeed is a universal), and cannot be found

unless we have already found the special total or organism of truth in which it forms a part. Individuals and universals presuppose each other, and do not, as the first impression leads us to think, stand apart as two unconnected termini, from either of which, if we happen to be so located, we can without road or railway make a legitimate passage to the other.

If it be urged, as it may naturally be, that on this showing there is no solid or ' absolute ' starting-point at all, the contention may be conceded. The only fixed and steady points in knowledge are points hypothetically fixed,—certified, that is, for the time and in the circumstances we employ them. But in the open field—or rather in the wilderness—of knowledge, where the ground of fact is not staked off, and the unexpected may always turn up, the only test of truth is the corroboration given by the consilience of paths initiated from different points : it is only by an undesigned coincidence in the results of independent operations that you can succeed in orienting yourself. You begin your road at two ends, and you meet : you locate or fix your point by drawing its co-ordinates to two direction-lines taken anyhow at first, and only in formed science diverging at a fixed angle. And in the absolute your direction-lines cannot be supposed fixed : you can only gradually adjust them to each other as you proceed. Intelligence, says Aristotle, is a principle, a beginning ; and intelligence, he says again, supplies beginnings.[1] Science, in the technical sense, only comes into operation,—or, in other words, deduction and (in the narrower sense used by Mill, and proceeding by *pure* observation and experiment) induction only find a way,—where beginnings and principles have been set up, where an approximate order or provisional system has been established. And if logic, in its stricter sense, is the method of sciences already made and in their essentials constituted, then logic can be asked to do no more than to provide a theory of such formal processes. If it traces the path which leads ' from the known to the unknown ', if it always proceeds on the hypothesis of a given knowledge, then such induction or deduction (from certain and approved singular facts, or from certain and approved general truths) fully satisfies the practical need of the scientific reasoner. But if Logic be, as it sometimes is, and

[1] *Eth.* vii. 7 ὁ νοῦς ἀρχή : vi. 6 νοῦς ἐστι τῶν ἀρχῶν.

may very reasonably be, taken in the wider sense of an epistemology,—a theory of the nature and origin of knowledge as a whole, and not of mere inference or syllogism ;—if it does not merely ask how we can satisfactorily get from one piece of knowledge (we are supposed to have) to another (not yet supposed to be), but how we come to have knowledge at all ; then its problem must go behind the rudiments of vulgar induction and deduction. It must ask—what, so far as one can see, Mill and his mere followers have never seriously asked at all—what induction is, what are its relations with deduction, and what is the place of either in the process of knowledge. And as the process of knowledge is the path to reality, it must also ask about the nature of this goal,—reality and truth. It is all very well for the narrower Logic to formulate in terms the methods actually employed in sciences : to state in abstract canons what is there seen in life and action. But a *Science of Logic*—an epistemology—(and a genuine epistemology cannot claim to be anything short of an ontology) must face the fact of science itself—must ask how the ideas of the knower must·-- or otherwise they are not knowledge—embrace and contain the reality of the known. The other and narrower Logic is and will remain a theory of forms of reasoning—a transcript in fainter terms of the procedure of science in any given step it takes upward to generals or downward to particulars : but the logic which deals with knowledge as such, in its systematic entirety,—the transcendental Logic, in short, must have a real value, an invincible relation to reality. The formal Logic—the logic of Mill and Hamilton—must be carried back to its principles, to its first step : and that first step which will also be the last step, and the inspiring principle of every intermediate step, is that of Intelligence (Aristotle's Νοῦς), of which the products or manifestations are λόγοι, i.e. definite conceptions, categories, formulations of rules and principles of definite range,—determinations or special types of unity.

Mill really faced the problem of method to better effect when he came to deal with a class of questions in which he was really interested, and which moreover have for epistemological purposes the advantage of being as yet unreduced into the rank and file of disciplined science. These questions are those dealing with man, his mental and moral nature, and history. Even its advocates or patrons occasionally admit that there is no accepted idea of what Sociology is or does. Its name at least expresses a longing towards a unity, or a presentiment that there is some underlying unity and common method in the group of what are loosely called the moral, or the historical, or the social and political sciences. But sociology is, as most people will allow, the name of a science unrealised—the felt and consciously-apprehended need of a science, and the dissatisfaction with the existing state of knowledge in certain departments. And undoubtedly it was with problems of social science,—problems of politico-economic and socio-ethical or socio-religious matters, that Mill's interests were mainly engaged. Like his master in this department, Auguste Comte, he wanted to carry into the topics which he was chiefly bent upon that ' scientific ' precision which they by pretty general admission lacked, and which revolutionary movements had shown they greatly needed. But he could not help seeing that the ' induction ' of dynamics and physics was not exactly the instrument he was in search of. Theory and hypothesis here demanded a much larger share in the process than in the more mathematical sciences. Causes and effects in reality here rolled round into each other, instead of remaining calmly fixed, one set here, and the other there. Of course even here—i.e. in organic and concrete sciences—it is possible to introduce observation and experiment,—no doubt, with greater effort and constraint, but still not altogether impracticable. But the artificial and mutilative character of such experimentation is felt here in a way different from its pressure in other cases. And what is more important, to institute an experiment or set on foot a scientific observation (and to observe means to *watch* a definitely restricted natural process with a view to answer some question about it), presupposes—as we have already seen—a tolerably definite provisional theory as to the general lie of the country to be investigated. Only when the country has been reasonably well mapped out in provinces and provided with some system of roads, can these problems of detail—questions to be answered Yes or No—be profitably put. And it is—in some parts of the historical sciences at least—somewhat premature to put questions requiring a categorical reply. There is only the vague *malaise* of felt difficulty to guide us. We do not, in many cases, know what it is that we want to know ; for, it demands a good deal of wisdom and trained art to put the proper or reasonable question,—so much so, indeed, that to succeed in formulating your question fully is equivalent or nearly equivalent to being able to answer it.   The value of observations and experiments—which are ways of putting nature to the question and it may be to the torture—depends entirely upon the knowledge and the command of general ideas possessed by the observer and experimenter.   And the same may be said of the reduced and tabulated conspectuses of the results of many observations and experiments which are called Statistics.   Their value depends on the truth and breadth of view which presided at their collection and arrangement.[1]

The historical or genetic method is the method of Science in general, but considered and employed under a limited aspect.   And under its more comprehensive aspect it may be called—though no name is unimpeachable—the method of development.   Now the essence of the idea of development—as was clearly shown by Leibniz—is the refusal to admit external interference, and the resolve to let a thing explain itself by itself.   It does not, like the mechanical method, manipulate the thing from outside—try to add it up out of factors or items fashioned and fabricated after some external standard.   Nor does it, like the chemical, look at the result as an inexplicable alteration, due apparently to a mere stroke of combination or disintegration—yet not obviously reducible to a mere equivalent of its elements. On the contrary, it recognises in the object a certain independence or originality, yet also the presence of an immanent law which does not wait for the outsider to put it together, but constructs itself, as it were, after a plan of its own.   There is in the so-called object, though we do not at first sight recognise it, the same originative principle both analytic and synthetic, as we own in thought.   The

---

[1] Statistics only define—and primarily for the imagination—the general laws and principles on which they rest.   The clear-cut mathematical form strikes and ' catches on ', where a more universal statement sounds vague and glides off.   Hence, as one says, they may prove *anything*.   The fact is, they prove *nothing*.   They only illustrate in diagrammatic form the theory which presided at their collection.   To emphasise the fundamental nature of ethics for human development you need only say that conduct is three-fourths or (as to some minds the precision rises with the denominator of the fraction) $\frac{17}{20}$ of human life.

object is—in a true logic—a process, a self-completing process, and not merely an object, mechanical, or other object.
It changes, grows or decays, while we observe, unless for
brief instants we cut it off from its connexions and arrest
its development. And our observation, if truly scientific,
must be sympathetic with its process of change. It is
neither a mere thing to be explained and construed *ab
extra* : nor a mystery of sudden transformation to be
passively accepted ; but a growth, a history, to be sympathetically watched and understood,—understood, because
it follows the same order as the movement of our own
thought in the process of knowledge. *Similia similibus
cognoscuntur.*[1]

One sometimes hears it asked by paradoxical critics at
which end a history should begin. And to ordinary
dogmatic recklessness, paradoxical the question may well
seem. Begin at the beginning, no doubt, is the vulgar
reply ; which in this case is understood to mean from the
earliest point in date (that, of course, being easily ascertained, and a thing known to all men). But,—so Plato
long ago well raised the difficulty which will always confront
us,—are we to go from the beginnings, or towards the
beginnings ? And it does not quite solve the question to say
that we are to begin with what is known : for under that
word the same difficulty re-appears. Can you really know
one end without the other ? To the vulgar partisan of
historical method, its precept means Go to the earlier, if
you wish to understand the meaning, the value, and the
elements constitutive of the later and subsequent. Begin
with origins, with the earliest elements, the phases that first
appear ; and thus you will get light to see the later as
they really stand. That this is a common interpretation
of the historical method is notorious. To explain *Homo
sapiens*, one is told to study the ape,—the nearest analogue
of his lost or missing progenitor : to understand the con-

---

[1] The resolute misinterpretation—as it often seems—of the maxim
that like is known by like,—is a curious chapter in the history of
Logic. All knowledge is based upon,—or, to speak more simply, *is*
—the identity of differents : of differents, which in knowledge are
identified,—of identity which in knowledge is put under difference.
And yet the ordinary meaningless talk on this matter seems to
assimilate knower and known to two separate things (or persons),
who casually and, we may add, inexplicably know each other :
which is mythology, perhaps, but not epistemology.

temporary horse, go to eohippus, or hipparion, or however his early prototype may be at present named and recognised. And in all this there is a truth—or at least a half-truth. But let us equally recognise the other half of the truth. If past throws light on present, present throws not less light on past. You propose, let us say, to write a history of Greece. A wordy philosophy, wise in its own conceit and in fine phrases, will advise you to approach the subject without prepossession or prejudice. So far, good. But what is meant by the absence of prepossession or prejudice ? Not a blank openness to impression, not a mere passivity ; but if passivity at all, a wise passivity : if openness, the openness of the trained judge.

The advice, so often associated with Francis Bacon, to get rid of all false pre-conceptions, of all *idola*, is one which it is easy to mistake in an over-zeal to follow it. That mere negation of prejudices which we call childish innocence is no match for the craft by which Nature seeks to keep or disguise her secrets. The free consciousness, the unbiassed mind, is not the easy result of one great act of renunciation, but the work of continued self-discipline, self-conquest, self-realisation. If you are not to impose upon the thing a pre-conception alien to it, neither must you rashly give yourself away to the thing, or to the first whims which accident puts upon you as the thing. What seems a fact or thing is only a candidate for the post of thing or fact : and its credentials need to be examined, and compared with other evidences. To detect a fact, therefore, is only possible for a tried and tested consciousness which by patience and self-mastery has won the key of interpretation. What Bacon apparently meant—though, as often happens, in his eagerness to combat a prevailing folly, he sometimes over-shot himself in statement—was to insist on the eternal wedlock of the mind and things, of things and the mind, as the sole and sufficient condition for the reality of knowledge and truth. The mind may not presume to do without things, or things to domineer the mind ;—or the result is a windy and frothy vanity. And the wedlock is eternal : in his own eloquent words, ' the mind itself is but an accident to knowledge,' [1] and he might have added, so also are things :

---

[1] Bacon : ' In Praise of Knowledge ' (a mere leaflet of much significance towards estimating his true grandeur). On the *Conjugium* of *Mens* and *Universus* see *Novum Organum*, distrib. op.

for, as he says, ' the truth of being and the truth of knowing is all one ' : only in the bond of knowledge are things true and real,—being otherwise only ' permanent possibilities ', or possibilities barely even permanent—or not even possibilities. Yet he scarcely realised that his ' due rejections and exclusions ' and negations were a fundamental *constitutive* element in those facts of which he habitually emphasises only the positive side.

He therefore who would understand—or would write— the history of Greece must really in his studies begin at both ends—both at the Greece of to-day, and at the Greece of Solon, or what earlier period may be taken as the start of Greek history. With perhaps the least qualified dogmatism, one may assert that he will begin with the Greece of to-day ; or if he deals solely with Ancient Greece he will begin with the full blaze of Hellenic civilisation which still has a pale reflection in the modern world, and gradually work back to the beginnings. It is no doubt customary to begin Greek history, say, with the Homeric Age, and work downwards, as it is customary to begin a formal treatise on geography with the general features of the earth's shape and surface. But that beginning represents really the temporarily accredited and accepted result of a process which, starting from the other end, has worked backwards to commencements or origins. And the teacher, in particular, will do well not to imitate too slavishly the method of the formal treatise. A day may come—or may have come—for example, for Greek history to start from periods long anterior to the supposed or traditional date of the wars around the wall of Troy. But when it does so, it will have done so by more thoroughly ransacking the Greece of to-day: and so disclosing the secrets of what is termed pre-historic Greece. Then, conversely, when modern diggings on Greek soil reveal the features of an earlier than what was erewhile to older historians its earliest past, the reconstruction of that early people's life reflects a new light on the directions and the limitations of its subsequent civilisation. We see better into the reality of Homer, and even of Demosthenes—into their ideal glory and their historical limitations, when we explore the cradle in which their race's life was erst fostered, and the rock out of which they and nature hewed them. And this is no peculiarity of Greece. The deepest research into the social institutions

which control the England of to-day is the best propaedeutic
for the study of Anglo-Saxon times ; and the same is true
vice versa.

Nor, again, is the truth of the proposition confined to
what we ordinarily mean by history.   The Greek poet has
said ' Art had to wait on and welcome chance, and chance
to wait on Art ' : or as we may paraphrase it, if every invention and discovery is in a measure a lucky chance, it is a luck
that only falls to the wisely prepared head and hand.   The
casual event falls as a germ of new construction or theory
only on an intelligence ready to welcome it,—prepared
with its complement in the spirit of an idea, eager to take
shape.   The means again, in the arts and crafts, is not only
a means to something else ; it is also a means to its own
end, to realise or perfect itself.   The rude tool of the
savage, for instance, is not merely a means to supply his
wants : it is also a means towards completing and im-
proving itself, and towards perfecting itself by constructing
an ampler tool, which supersedes it, because it can do all
and more than all the work of the earlier, or can do it more
economically.   All progress that deserves the name is an
incessant and continuous revision of a first step : a re-
adaptation of an old instrument : a repeated and unending
self-correction.   It is only a partially-true symbol of human
advance to speak of it as a line : unless we add, by another
piece of symbolism, that the line is only the protracted or
extended phase in which the form of time drags out for us
the magnified and organised point-nucleus.   It is a truth—
which we are only too ready to forget or discount—that the
savage (and he bears with justice both epithets, ' the noble
savage,' and ' the brute barbarian ') is not something left
happily behind us, in the onward march of civilisation ;
but that he is, however much we may fancy him suppressed
and superseded, still present, at least ' ideally ' in the finest
products of humanity, and may hap only too likely—as the
Russian is said, when scratched, to betray his original
Tartar breed—to burst out on provocation into a grim
reality.   The Pullman car of to-day retains within it for
the archaeologically-trained eye the rudiments of the
primitive wain of the primitive nomade : and the careful
study of either end of the scale will not merely throw a
marvellous light on the excellences or the defects of the
other, but will probably also tend in the impartial observer

to moderate the self-gratulations of modern advance. For it is only those whose view ranges within narrow limits that are over-impressed by the magnitude of the advance made in the ' last new thing '.

If progress were but the addition of bit to bit, of new bits to what is already there, or if we could change *this*, and leave *that* unchanged,—as the word perhaps verbally means, and as many people at any rate seem to understand it, progress might indeed seem an easy thing, and to be undertaken with a light heart. For, it would appear as if we could lose nothing, and might probably (indeed, as enthusiasm and forgetfulness of the merits of the past are in certain periods ready to urge, must certainly) gain. But it is a more serious matter when we realise that we must move altogether, if we really are to move at all ; i.e. really are to make progress, and not merely change, so to speak, from one foot to rest on another. For progress,—if it be what it is expected to be, and what it must be if it does what it is expected to do—is an organic, and not merely a mechanical or chemical change. A mechanical change is only a nominal or formal change : a chemical is more than change ; but in organic change, that which changes also abides, and the new is not merely other than the old, and not merely a re-arrangement of the old, but the old transmuted,—the same yet not the *mere* same.[1] Progress in short is always the unity of differentiation and integration. It must not be an externality, nor a mere dead product of a transformation scene, but a continuous growth, inwardly digested, made part and parcel of the collective life, which it has thereby rendered more full, real, and not merely made less intense at the cost of some extension. In true progress, which is only another name for true growth, nothing is quite lost, but only changed, retained in a richer shape and a fuller reality. How far such progress is possible, except in limited and finite spheres : how far progress in one involves necessarily deterioration in another : and how, therefore, progress is not attributable to the Absolute, are questions we need not here discuss. But so far at least we may go as to say that a progress which does not follow the natural law of development and carry on into the future

---

[1] The said *mere* same is not really the same at all. Nobody in his senses predicates sameness except where he also sees differences : or, the term always implies relation.

the worth and substance of the past, is not a progress which any general enthusiasm ought to be spent upon.

Development then has two faces, one to the future and another to the past. And what is called the historical method is apt to emphasise only one of the two aspects, just as, it may be added, practical considerations are often likely to produce an opposite but equally partial bias in favour of the future. The historical method in incapable hands is liable to lead to unprofitable sighs,—not unaccompanied by a certain luxury of tears—over the lowly hole of the pit—it may even be the filth and brutishness, out of which so much of noble humanity (for thither the interest of development always reverts) has been dug ; and in empty heads the practical, the vulgarly-utilitarian satisfaction is liable to equally vain fits of self-applause on our magnificent progress. But both the self-depreciation of him who loiters regretfully round the beggarly rudiments, and the self-laudation of glorious ' improvements ' looking derisively on less glorious days, are unworthy of the reasonable and scientific spirit. The philosophical method does not allow itself to be imposed upon by the lapse of time, and insists that in a sense the past contained the present—that, as the poet says, the child is father of the man. Not indeed contained in any grosser or more delicate mechanical way. The coming development does not necessarily lie prefigured—if we had the proper microscope to see it—as a germ in the first and original state. That may be, or may not be. Yet prefigured it is by the law of its structure, or in the intelligible unity by which only can its existence be understood and construed.

But if this be the method of real development, in the growth of nature, and the progress of history, it is also the method of that supreme product of historical progress, the spirit and system of philosophy. Thought, also, the culminating stage in which the spirit of man becomes conscious of itself and of its universe, will move or grow on the same lines as that of which it is the comprehension and theory. It will begin at the two ends, and each beginning will complete and presuppose the other. Nature will suppose and yet lead up to Spirit or Mind : Spirit or Mind will throw light on the mystery of Nature : Being will point to knowledge or Idea ; and Idea show itself the basis of Being. Or, if we consider the triple division of the philosophic system, as it runs in Hegel's *Encyclopaedia*, we can see how misleading it may be to take that one order as absolute. To understand it thoroughly we must begin with each of the three in turn : so as thus to realise that each does not except figuratively succeed the other, but that in each an aspect of the whole truth is presented which had been put by the other parts somewhat in the background. In each part there is a definition and a revelation of the Absolute. But each is also, as it were, a projection, a perspective view, a condensed or expanded image of the other. In each the Absolute is one and whole, in some more veiled, more restricted, and more meagre than in others ; but the veil, and the restriction, and the emptying, are self-imposed : and for that reason the veil is really transparent, the restriction is negatived, and the emptying is not only a self-humiliating but a self-ennobling irony— the irony of the Absolute.

CHAPTER XVIII

THE RANGE OF PERSONALITY

THE difference between the conceptions of reality held by Aristotle and Plato respectively is that where Plato said Being, Essence or Substance (οὐσία), Aristotle said Activity (ἐνέργεια). To be is to act, to be active. To the outsider —the plain man of philosophic legend, it seems at first that a thing must *be* before it can *do* : that you must have an agent before you get an action. And, in a way, Aristotle admits this not quite satisfactory criticism. Every activity presupposes, he allows, a power to act, a potentiality : every actual presupposes an implicit or a mere possibility. Existence seems, as it were, to be doubled ; or the mere surface-being is turned into a subject which has a predicate. But if the existence is to be real, it has to include both elements, and with the latter or the actuality, as its crown. Nor is this all. The possibility which issues forth in action may be fairly called self-realisation. That is to say : A— the hypothetical agent—acts, does something : and in so doing, seems to go forth and beyond itself, to externalise itself. Or, A is acted upon, and thus seems to be diminished. But what it externalises, or puts forth, is after all what it *is* : it puts forth itself : and, on the other hand, if it be a patient, it is no less an agent and self-limitative. What a thing really is, is what it *makes* itself be : what it allows itself to be made, that it really is. Yet further, if the word self-realisation be taken in its fullness of meaning,—if there be really a *self*, and it be realised, then this self-realisation, which is the truth or more developed conception of being, seems to imply or postulate in it a self-consciousness, an awareness of the process of completed being,—completed in its return from utterance of possibility to self-fruition or in its re-assumption of itself.

To us, of course, as beings aware of what we do and achieve, this is simple enough : but it is also true of *things*, that we only understand them, in so far as we put into them, or invest them with, the same activity and apperception of activity as we are familiar with in our own experience. The veriest materialist cannot help speaking of things as agents, as behaving, as having a function. He would, no doubt, if he were to be cross-examined, refuse to identify himself with the primitive anthropomorphism, or at least zoömorphism of the natural man who sees the river run and the clouds sweep the sky ; and he would probably mutter something referring to people who cannot see when they ride a metaphor to death. Still less, perhaps, would he be inclined to adopt the spiritualistic or animistic hypothesis of philosophising physicists, like Fechner, who would accredit even the plants at our feet, and the stars in the sky, with souls, or soul-like centres of their life. But, however he may shrink from what we may call the ontological consequences of his language, there is no doubt that for him the meaning of the world, its reality and truth, is obtained by an interpretation in terms which, rigidly employed, imply their environment by a self-consciousness to which they are relative. Take from him the tacit assumption (which he often finds it difficult to realise just because it is the foundation of all his language) that reality is in the last resort a self-conscious reality, and his words become meaningless, or what he might think worse, metaphorical.

To Bacon, who, though not without a strong speculative impulse, approached philosophic dicta from the standpoint of an average intelligent Englishman (and it is on that account that his remarks are often so instructive), it seemed a grave fault of the Stagirite to define the soul, that ' most noble substance ', by words of the second intention. Without substance—a solid something as basis of act and event— the reality of the soul seemed likely to fare badly. Behind consciousness he, like many others, felt there must be a something of which consciousness is the state, act, or predicate and attribute. The thinking must come from a thinker. There must be a permanent subject of thought— a persistent substance which does not disappear when thinking for the nonce stops. And thinking is according to common experience very liable to stops and interruptions. Both Bacon and Locke felt that without this refuge to fall back upon, personal identity was in a bad way, or personality itself little better than a delusion. And therefore when

Aristotle, and his modern followers, treated soul and mind as essentially definable by the terms activity, self-realisation, it has been freely urged against them that they are tampering with the pearl of great price which all our hopes and aspirations fondly guard.

And this is a subject on which there is inevitably a good deal of misunderstanding. And the misunderstanding will probably last so long as one set of writers flaunts over it that blessed word Personality as a holy, a sacrosanct thing, like the visionary cross with its inscription *In hoc signo vinces* : and as another set treats it as a mere fetish, under which is hidden nothing better than stock or stone, or a heap of old bones. Perhaps some concessions might well be made on both sides. And the first of them would be to try to come to some clearer understanding what the term in question means. And, on that point, if we follow the example of Aristotle and examine popular usage, to see if it can help us to any consistent use of the term, we shall find that by personal as opposed to real we mean something peculiarly attached to the individual, of which he cannot divest himself as of other outward things, though it also is an outward thing.[1] The person in this narrowest sense means the body ; and if the epithet is further extended it still expresses what is directly manipulated through the members of the living agent, and is more or less closely attached to it. Yet if it means the body, we must be careful to add that it is the body, regarded not as such but as the representative, the outward manifestation, the inseparable sign or symbol of a spirit, an intelligence and a will. The person is the visible or tangible phenomenon of something inward,—the phase or function by which an individual agent takes his place in the common world of human intercourse and interaction—his peculiar and definite part in the general or universal world and field.

Personality thus mingles or unifies in it a universal and an individual aspect or element : it hints that the universal work always has in reality an individually-determinate tone,—that nothing in the world, even if it be called the same, is really and actively the same. *Si duo*

---

[1] The legal use of the distinction between ' real ' and ' personal ' is only partly ' logical ', and largely retains traces of the larger logic of life and history. Yet, roughly speaking, personal property is what we can, so to speak, carry on our backs or in our pockets.

idem faciunt, non est idem quod faciunt. Thus, what separates personality from individuality is simply that in the narrower or abstracter use of the latter term there is an absence of the due subordination of all individuality to universality, and of all universality to individuality. Personality, in short, is an individuality which is not a mere freak, not merely different from other things, but also [in itself charged with a universal meaning or function. Yet even this is not enough to describe it. It is the individuality of an intelligence : the flesh and blood, and, in a secondary degree, the outward things, stamped with intelligence. Every member of a kind, every natural existence, has this double character ; this convergence or union of universal and individual. In being this individual object, it is at the same time a universal, and *vice versa.* But in the attribution of personality there is involved something beyond what is common to all creatures. And that something, we may first of all say, is this. Whereas in the case of other *things* the individuality is distinctly subordinate, and each is reckoned primarily by its kind, in the case of *persons* we can almost declare that the universality is subordinate to the individuality. This union of individuality and universality in a single manifestation, with the implication that the individuality is the essential and permanent element to which the universality is almost in the nature of an accident, is what forms the cardinal point in Personality. And one can understand, when the distinction is thus put, the obvious and palpable antagonism in which the view stands to the central principles of Spinoza.[1]

We speak of a man as a Personality when we wish to note the fact that he is no mere manufactured article, the representative of a common type, with nothing to choose

---

[1] See Spinoza, *Cogitata Metaph.*, Pars II. cap. 8 ' Nec fugit nos vocabulum (*Personalitatis* scilicet) quod theologi passim usurpant ad rem explicandam : verum quamvis vocabulum non ignoremus eius tamen significationem ignoramus : quamvis constanter credamus, in visione Dei beatissima Deum hoc suis revelaturum.' For Hegel, it may be noted, Person, so far as he uses the term at all, bears its restricted legal and juridical sense. A person is a free intelligence, which realises that independence by appropriating an external thing as its sign and property. It probably belongs therefore to a world in which people count rather by what they *have* than by what they *are* ; the world of law where rights and duties tend to oppose each other. This is not the highest kind of world for human beings.

between him and a thousand others, but that he is, as it were, one of a thousand, one ' Whom nature printed and then broke the type ', that he has in the highest sense ' distinction ', the nobility of nature's own patent. Other things exist, so to speak, for the sake of their kind, and for the sake of other things ; a person, in the strictest sense, is never a mere means to something beyond, but always at the same time an end in itself or himself. Other things are mere examples in illustration of a law that rides superior to them and overrules them : the person is a law unto himself. He has the royal and divine right of creating law—of starting by his exception a new law which shall henceforth be a canon and a standard. For in such a personality when he claims his full rights there is the visible immanence of the divine and universal—or there is the visible unity of the eternal and the temporal. He rules as the natural king, the great ruler whose judgment and authority are better than the complex code of common laws : he guides as the artistic genius who sees truth steadily in a single intuition and in that single picture sees it whole.[1]

But when we ask if such a personality is found in the field of actual experience and history, there arises a divergence of opinions. It is at any rate matter of common experience that there is a good deal of unjustified identification of the self with the universal—identification in which the universal suffers violence and is taken by force. There are only too often cases where the personal interest is allowed to disguise itself under a semblance of zeal for the common good, and that even without conscious intent or act of deception. No good and noble deed, Hegel has said, can ever be done without faith in its goodness, and zeal for its attainment : without a holy passion and fervour of devotion, which exceeds the cold service of duty rendered for duty's sake.[2] But it is equally true and equally to be remembered that this interference of personal passion and disinterested interest has defaced the noblest causes and made flow endless torrents of fanaticism and persecution. A personality in

[1] This one may call the Platonic ideal of the State, where Equity rules supreme in the incarnate spirit of wisdom,—a guide adapting its measures to circumstances, not tied down to the inflexible letter of one law in an incoherent and imperfect code. See the *Politicus*, p. 294 ; *Phaedrus*, p. 275 ; and compare Aristotle's Wise man whose conduct is not κατὰ λόγον, but μετὰ λόγου.

[2] See e. g. *Encyclopaedia*, § 475.

which the universal was perfectly incarnated in the individual would be in truth a God amongst men.   And it is probably a more likely occurrence that where the individual as such arrogates to himself the privilege of the universal, there should be seen not the deeds of the god, but the ebullitions of the beast that is in man.

A personality, then, in popular language, and perhaps also in popular philosophy, is the living and conscious individual in whom general forces, truths, or ideas become real, active, efficient forces, truths, and ideas.   And the importance of the conception resides in the safeguard thus supposed to arise, which will prevent the realities of the world from being dissipated away into the endless and restless flux of the terms of thought,

'La bufera infernal che mai non resta.'

To such a common frame of mind ideas, truths, forces are vacant, ghostly forms, devoid of true life and reality : to get such they need blood and flesh to clothe them, to give them substance and power.   Now Hegel, no less than those who offer this criticism, regards ideas (in the ordinary sense of that term), truths and forces, also as abstractions which need something to make them powers in the real world of nature and the ideal world of mind.   Hegel, like Schelling, has a sublime contempt for mere universals.   But as to the something else, there is a divergence of view.   Two well-known answers are given by the popular philosophy known as materialism or spiritualism : two systems which are probably not so wide apart as the contrast of their names might imply.   According to the former, thinking, ideas, truths, goodness and beauty are special functions (the grosser materialists say secretions) of a special kind of matter—of something which is accessible to ordinary mechanical and chemical tests, but which exhibits also, in certain cases, the exceptional phenomena of consciousness.   Here the essential reality is a something, permanent and essentially indestructible,—something which no man has seen, nor indeed can see,—but which is called Matter.   The spiritualistic philosopher (as distinguished from the *idealist*) regards as the essential realities in the universe what he calls spirits.   What these are, also, nobody has as yet (any more than in Kant's time [1])

[1] See his ' Dreams of a Spirit-seer, illustrated by Dreams of Metaphysics '.   (*Werke*, ed. Ros. und Schub. Bd. VII. p. 38 sqq.)

given any very authoritative account, but so far as the quasi-scientific expositions in regard to them throw any general light on the subject, we may say that they suggest only a differently-constituted matter, a matter e. g. of less or more dimensions than that we are most familiar with.

Now the advocate of spiritual reality, who protests most strongly against the injury done to personality by reducing it to something fluid and not fixed, something in process and not in persistent substance, seems mostly to lean to a quasi-spiritualistic hypothesis, or to the—so-called—higher materialism. He is an advocate of what we may describe as the soul-thing, of a permanent, (he would even hold, an absolutely permanent) substance or substratum of psychical reality which, no doubt, exhibits certain properties, but is always more than any one, or any mere series of its phenomena. It has been said, indeed, by one who spoke with authority that he that will save his soul shall lose it, and he that will lose it shall find it. But this has always been a hard saying, which has been as far as possible explained away by exegesis. Yet its moral import is not so very far removed from its philosophical equivalent. The true life is not that of self-seeking pleasure, but the life spent in the service of truth and love, the life dedicated to impersonal interests, and ideal good. So also the reality of the human soul as we first know it lies not in itself, but in its transfiguration, its purification, and liberation to higher forms of being. The Soul, in its first avatar in each of us, is after all of the earth, earthy, unless it continue on that path of growth and development on which it has entered. It is as Aristotle said, and said well, the first actualisation [1]—the proximate ideality of an organic body. In soul organic body carries out its promise : in soul we, the observers, or untrained psychologists, note our first awareness of mental life in its organic environment. But there are other grades, other heights of achievement, yet set before the principle of life, which is more than mere life and mere soul : or soul contains a germ which must bear

[1] It is perilous and misleading (said the ancient Graiae, who dwell on the way to the Hesperides of philosophy) to interpret an old system by the language of modern (and especially German) idealism. It is much worse, replied Perseus, not to interpret it at all, but to repeat its magic *ipsissima verba*,—carefully Latinised, as if they belonged to a cabinet of fossils.

higher fruit. To be itself, or to become all that it in promise and potency contains, it must dispossess itself of what clings to it and possess itself of what is its own ; and so transmute its first phase into one more adequate. The soul is, as Hegel has said, the awakening of mind from the sleep of nature : [1] it is nature gathering itself out of its absorption in its dispersion, the breath of life and feeling striving through the scattered members of the material world, and finding itself at first half-asleep, a pervading, unifying current that flows through and makes continuous the various portions of the universe. It is the earliest real, felt unity in which the logical or synthetic pulse—as yet purely potential in Nature, and only surmised by science—re-appears in the actual concrete world. And as the earliest, it is, like first loves, what one clings to hardest as our prime and fundamental *differentia*. Here at least we are something—a centre of being, and not a mere centreless expanse of extension : something emerging from the world of silence and of night—something in which each feels

> ' I am not what I see,
> And other than the things I touch.'

And that something we would not lose, at any cost.—But the only way not to lose it, is to use it as a stepping-stone to higher things. The metaphor, indeed, like metaphors in general, must not be pressed too far. For it is more than a stepping-stone and it is never left behind as a mere dead self : there is

> ' Nothing of it that doth fade
> But doth suffer a sea-change
> Into something rich and strange.'

And that richer result into which it is transformed is the consciousness of a self, and the intelligence which wills and knows.

If it be asked in what respects the result is richer, the answer is as follows. The soul,—this ' first entelechy '— is exclusive, and it is immersed in its natural limits of organic life. It has yet to go through the school of self-detachment, the process of ' erecting itself above itself ' ; and of thus extending its view and its range of control over a wider field of objects. Gradually it attains to the rank of a consciousness before which is unrolled the spectacle of a world of

[1] *Encyclopaedia*, §§ 387, 389.

objects set over against it, and even of a world within it;
itself as an object deposed to the rank of something to be
surveyed. As such, it seems almost to have left all immersion in corporeity completely behind, and to have completely divested itself of any limitation. It floats freely
above the real psychical life out of which it emerged—
a detached but somewhat shadowy self, not burdened by
any restrictions of nature or circumstance. As such a mere
Ego, or logical self—as the mere theatre on which the play of
ideas takes place, it surveys its real psychical self far below;
it finds itself as a strange sort of thing, and says *This was
me* (which however is not exactly the same as *I am I*, $I = I$).
Yet it was a great step to have thus ceased to be absorbed
in its qualities, to be the mere breath of life and feeling,
stirring in its several affections and modifications. In
order to get forward, it was necessary to recoil a little : to
save itself—and that must mean to get itself in fuller and
richer being—the mind had, as it were, to measure and
realise the full depth of its nonentity, and to surrender all
that it had hitherto clung to as its own. In an attitude
of reflection upon itself it fancies that it is the empty room,
the *tabula rasa*, on which experience is to write itself : but
in its secret heart it retains the faith and acts upon it, that
it is the power of intelligent and intelligible unity which
makes the writing intelligible, if it does not even itself play
the writer. What it now seems to find—what fills up its
consciousness, presumed empty and merely receptive,—it
gradually recognises to be its very and original own. Through
labour and experiment it fills up the vacant form (the passive half of itself to which it deposed itself) of consciousness ;
and thus, as an intelligent self, a true mind, it has for itself
and realises as in itself all the life and reality which in its
earlier stage of soul it only was and felt itself naturally to
be. But on this stage of free intelligence it is no longer
bound up with its natural being in such a way as to feel
itself a fixed and restricted centre, sunk in the living
environment so as to see no further, and to deem itself in
its seclusion the permanent reality, the exclusive fact. It
is no longer exclusive and self-concentrated, but inclusive
and all-embracing. It is no longer a mere consciousness—
a mere receptive and synthetic unity of apperception—but
a reason and a mind. And a reason and a mind already
refuse to be narrowed and confined by the same limits as

seem appropriate to the soul. In the province of free self-realised intelligence we at least seem to occupy a ground on which others can equally come,—to have nothing peculiar or merely individual. In Knowledge, which is reasoned perception, and in Will, which is reasoned impulse, there is a king's highway, a public forum, where souls meet and converse and perform a collective work ;—and in both *mere*, i. e. essentially restricted, individuality is at a discount.[1]

Such would be the course of development if we looked at it only in the inwardness or subjectivity of psychical, conscious, and intelligent life. But an analogous or parallel development may be observed if we look at man as an active, i. e. a practical and moral being, a being who makes Nature his own, stamps it with his title of possession, and who gives to his fellowship with other souls an objective, outward existence in the forms and institutions of social life. Here too his first achievement is the affirmation of his individuality, the distinction in outward and tangible shape of the Mine from the Thine : the creation of property, and the projection of himself in a world of mutually-recognised personalities. As the individual soul in the inner life, so the personal being with its property is the solid, insoluble basis of the life in public—the field of social ethics. The same instinct, which in its dread of dissolution clings to the perpetuity of the inner nucleus of soul, upholds the other as containing the stable and eternal security of all social well-being. The immortality of soul in the inner world : the sacro-sanctity of property in the outer. But if these postulates are to be permitted, if individuality and personality are to abide, they must, in the one case as in the other, bow to the law of development, the law of history and of life. They must correct themselves, re-adjust themselves,—include what they excluded, and re-combine their elements, transmute themselves into what we have, after Hegel, called their *truth* : must redintegrate themselves with suppressed correlatives, and carry out their implications of larger unity. The soul, exclusive and fast-clad in its mere organic vestment, in which it is as yet only the name and form of intellectual life, has first of all to retract itself into the bare abstract consciousness, or mere self, on which the masses of reality stream,

[1] The above is an attempt to give a very condensed synopsis of Hegel's Philosophy of Mind (*Encyclopaedia*).

to fill its vacant rooms and empty forms up with ideas.
So too the person—that close concretion or coalescence of
mind with material—that identification of self with its
' clothes ', its property and all it can vulgarly be said to
own, is only an aspect of truth which tends to be over-
estimated when it is reflected upon, and must notwithstanding be over-ridden and merged. Withdrawing itself
from its clothing of earth and water, and even perhaps
from its inner mansion of flesh and bone, personality floats
in the free air as the impersonal personality of conscience,—
the ethereal realm where pure practical reason rules. In
that ether where morals reign absolutely is the home of
the categorical imperative, of the Stoical law of duty, of
the conscience which, here at least, has might as it has
right. It too, like its parallel, consciousness, in the inner
mental life, has, or seems to have, all its fulfilment from
without. As even Kant admits, it is itself a vacant form ;
yet a form of such influence as to impress on whatever
comes within its range an obligation to be universal and
to be uniform. Here too, as in the parallel stage, it was
of inestimable importance that mind should, in the socio-
ethical sphere, see itself supreme in its innermost dignity
and personality,—the personality which lies within,—even
though that supremacy were at first no better than as
a law, a form, a category, recognised as authoritative and
imperative. For conscience, like the field of consciousness,
is after all only a quasi-passive self—a remarkable property
or endowment, a sort of innate principle or idea by which
the mind was seen to be distinguished in a unique way
from all things else. To realise once for all the fact that
consciousness and conscience form an absolute tribunal
from which there can be no appeal : that the ' synthetic
unity of apperception ' in the theoretical, and the ' autonomy of the rational will ' in the practical sphere, are the
ultimate and final *a priori* : this is a great thing to do,—
even though it only expands and defines the Cartesian
principle of clear and distinct ideas, and will remain as
Kant's title of honour in the history of philosophy. He
thus fenced off or consecrated the sanctuary of the mental
and moral life.

But it was not enough to set apart the sacred principle,
the central hearth-fire of truth and goodness. If at an
earlier stage,—earlier, i.e. in this logical analysis,—the

formal was wholly sunk in the material, if i. e. the mere
series of legal formulae in their hard and brittle outlines
were absolutely identified—without doubt or hesitation—
with the morally and socially good ; the formal side, or
mere spirit and will of good, the abstract principle of
morality, is now invested with an equally undue prominence. The actual or concrete ethical community—be
it family or state, or other social organisation—is animated
and maintained by a spirit which transcends and includes
alike the outward shell of civil law and the inward law of
conscience. For, curiously enough, as it may seem at
first, both conscience and civil legislation assume the form
of imperative and definite commands—laws political or
civil, and laws moral. Both fall therefore into an inflexi-
bility, a rigorous and mechanical hardness in their enounce-
ments. Both worship the idol of what men call logic,
i. e. of formal consistency and formal uniformity, to an
excess which sometimes issues in fantastic irregularities.
Their several maxims of legal conformity and of duty for
duty's sake are in first appearance excellent : but a further
reflection shows that the Law covers a good many inconsistent or at least unrelated laws within its code, and Duty
is often sadly to seek in presence of the collisions between
what offer themselves as *prima facie* duties in any given
case. The amplest code of laws that ever existed will
always leave lots of loop-holes for negligence and villainy,
and would never work for an instant, were it not for ever
supplemented by the spirit of faith and love, by social
piety and political loyalty, by the thousand ties of sentiment and feeling which really vivify its dry bones. So
too the abstractions of the conscientious imperative, of
the law of duty, of the moral tribunal, of the man within
the breast, and of the dignity and beauty of human nature,
would effect nothing unless they could always tacitly
count on the support of recognised and authoritative social
law and usage. Outward rests upon inward ; and rules
direct feelings.

Here, again, as in the purely intellectual or cognitive
sphere, it is evident that the spirit of man has its source
of life neither in its abstract self-hood (in consciousness
and conscience) nor in its mere natural environment and
organic endowment (in sense-affections, and social law and
usage), but in the unity of both,—a unity which transcends

either. Both individual and society live and grow, because
they are continuous and one : because they presuppose an
ideal unity or a living Idea at the root of their being, as
their inner and essential guiding-principle, at once constitutive and regulative of their action. The machinery
of language supplies to the intellectual sphere a sort of
sensible meeting-ground and common field in which the
development of knowledge becomes possible : and the
same purpose is subserved in the social sphere by the
machinery of ethical and political forms and institutions.
These are the field, the home of freedom, as the other are
of knowledge. It is in these collective and objective
structures that we get the expression of the law of human
development : the visible sign, viz. of the essentially
universal nature of the individual. The individual in
these attains his relative truth : for they show the weakness
of the individuality of the mere individual. They show
that his exclusiveness, his quasi-originality, is only an
appearance :—confronted, no doubt, by an appearance
of an opposite character, as if the originality and the
reality lay in the environment and the collective body.
They point therefore beyond and behind both foci to a
common centre or inclusive unity of life.

But they do not destroy personality and individuality :
they only transform it and made it a more adequate and
consistent representation of reality, by giving in it a place
to factors or ' moments ' which, though always effective,
were not recognised as constitutive elements, and treated
only as externally interfering agencies. It may be a
question, of course, how far it is wise to retain the term
after its meaning has thus been altered by expansion and
redistribution of elements. On the whole it seems impracticable—and it would be undesirable, perhaps, even if it
were more feasible—to be too hard and fast in our use of
denotations. It is hardly the province of philosophy to
coin new terms in which to deposit the results of her
researches. A term no doubt—particularly if, as the
phrase runs, it be luckily discovered, or judiciously selected
—may save the expenditure of thought. But it is hardly
the business of philosophy to encourage economy in this
direction. Much more is it the perpetual task of philosophy
to counteract the ossification that sets in in terms,—to re-
interpret the meaning which is absorbed in these ' counters

of thought', and make them once more sterling money
for the market of life. What, for instance, is the work of
Aristotle's Ethics, but to set free the genii which the black
magic of every-day intercourse has incarcerated in the
non-significant Greek term Εὐδαιμονία? Like our own
Happiness, it flits from lip to lip, little better than a mere
name, which is still prized, but—except for a few synonyms
that are equally vague with itself—is attached to things
which a little reflection shows it cannot truly denote.
Aristotle seeks—we may say—to define it. But the phrase
' definition ' seems barely applicable to the complex process
thus implied,—a process of which definition, as ordinarily
understood, is only one small portion. For to define
happiness, is to reconstruct the conception. Or, to be
more accurate, it is really to construct it or reproduce in
consciousness its construction. As it stands, the thing
to be defined is a name and a thing, of which certain
relations to other things soon begin to show themselves,
which is more or less similar to one thing, and more or
less to be distinguished from another. To mark it off
from these co-terminous things, and to show how they are
related to it on different sides,—this would be what we
may perhaps call strict, or formal, or nominal, or *mere*
definition.

Now whatever be the other uses of such definitions—
and they are serviceable at the outgoing in any branch
of enquiry,—they are not precisely the work we expect
a philosopher to do for us. And assuredly it is not Aristotle
who would stop short at that sort of definitions. We find
accordingly that for the purpose of realising what happiness
—the common name for human good—means, he is obliged
to bring into the field the whole system of his thought in
its cardinal notions of Energy, Soul, &c. Aristotle here
as elsewhere retraces the path of thought which carries us
from mere, vulgar, inadequately-apprehended happiness
(he follows the same process in his treatment of pleasure,
friendship &c.—to take only ethical examples) to true,
essential and completely-apprehended happiness,—or, to
use Hegel's technical phrases, from happiness as it is
an-sich (in or at itself) or as it is *für-sich* (for or to itself),
to happiness as it is *an-und-für-sich*. In so ' defining '
happiness Aristotle is thus obliged to bring in his conceptions of man and of society, of human life and its powers,

of natural and acquired faculty, of mind in its relations to
nature ; and if not to expound, at least to employ, his
fundamental categories of philosophical thought. Such
a machinery can hardly be called less than a construction,
i. e. a re-construction by conscious effort of the latent but
actual concatenation of the elements in the fact.

In this case we traverse the distance which separates
mere happiness from true happiness, from happiness imperfectly or abstractly conceived to happiness adequately and
concretely conceived. Of course when we say real or true
happiness, we use these terms as they are used within the
ordinary range of human speech. An ultimate and absolute in truth and reality is for us at any given time only
a comparatively or relatively ultimate and absolute. It is
that which, so far as we can see and think (all philosophising
presumably goes on under this stipulation, tacit or express),
gives an expression, an interpretation, a meaning and
a construction to reality which leaves no feature unrecognised, no contradiction unsolved, no discord unreconciled,
which leaves nothing outside and alien to it, and suppresses
without acknowledgment nothing that has ever been
recognised within it. It is, if you like so to call it, the completest, or (if you are really in earnest with your philosophising and have carried it on to what for you is the
end) the complete formula of the Absolute—of that which
in a transcendent sense *is*, is *all*, is the infinite and eternal
one. Yet, after all, it is a formula. But here that undying
adversary of all thought steps in and says A *mere* formula.
And to that we must here as elsewhere rejoin : No, not
a mere formula. A mere formula would be not even
a formula,—a formula only in name—and with no reality
which it served to formulate. It is a real and true formula,
if it be a formula at all, and not something which merely
swaggers about under that title. Nay more, if it be a true
and real formula, it is the truth and the reality in its day
and generation, until at least a truer truth and a more
real reality shall have been discovered. Let us by all
means be modest : but there is a false humility which
becomes no man and is the guise of hypocrisy or insincere
sincerity. Let us—in other words—never assume that
' we are the men, and that wisdom will die with us ' :
but equally let us hold fast the faith of reason that what
we know as true and real can never be false, i. e. utterly

false, however much it may turn out one day to be sur-
mounted. And, on the other hand, let us equally remember that in the mere and abstract commencement—the
unreal and the untrue, as we must perforce style it by
contrast with the (*pro tempore*) truth and reality—there
is no utter and sheer error or unreality. It has always
been felt to be one of the most loveable sides of Aristotelianism—this recognition of the reasonableness of all
actual fact, or of the truth latent in the honest, though
narrow and ill-defined judgments of the mass.

Thus, coming back to personality, let us admit that the
mere personality which at first sight seemed only worth
rejecting, is an element, at least, in true personality,—or
is a part which, because an organic member and no mere
mechanical part, is full of traces and indications which
involve and postulate the whole. The true personality
and the true individuality of being is something which
presupposes for its completeness the social state—the
organic community. It is no doubt familiar to us that,
according to an old but never quite dormant view, the
collective community is but the aggregate or congeries of
individuals. But the individuals whose aggregation makes
the community are themselves products of the social
union. Complete, all-round, harmonious personality, it is
sometimes said, is the highest fruit to be yielded by social
development. Or, as the last century would have preferred to put it, the main or sole aim of the State is further-
ance towards Humanity—to the stature of the perfect man.
And these are true sayings,—but perhaps only half true.
If all must grow so that one and each may grow, so and
not less must each one grow so that the all—the commonwealth of reason and the kingdom of God—may be more
and more present, 'may come'. And that kingdom only
comes when All is in Each, and Each is in All : and when,
without loss or diminution, each is each and all is all.
Then and not till then does personality become true and
infinite, free and harmonious individuality, which is in the
same instant universality. The monad—to use the language of the great Idealist who did not find individuality
at all incompatible with universality—never ceases to be
a monad : it is eternal and indestructible, an absolute
centre of being. The monad in its individual measure
' expresses ' or ' envelopes ' the Infinite or Absolute : it is,

i. e. under a subjective limitation, identical with the absolute,
a concentration or condensation of it into an impenetrable,
i. e. literally an individual, point,—but a point which is in
the psychical or intellectual world never entirely *carens recordatione*, or oblivious of its essential totality. But if the
monad ' expresses ' the Absolute, it no less concords or
sympathises in harmonious development with all its
congeners, the other monads : so that while it neither
interferes with them, nor suffers violence from them, it
yet exists and acts in an ideal identity, that is, in a real
fellowship, with them. Again, the monad has what may
be called its side of passivity, but passivity here does not
mean *mere* passivity, but rather the essential limitation
due to its special and peculiar stand-point—a limitation
which in the higher orders of being becomes transparent
or is transcended. How far Leibniz succeeds in reconciling this apparent contradiction—how far even any one
can reveal the mystic indwelling of universal and individual in each other, this is a serious question in its place :
but it is only bare justice to Leibniz to say that he at least
never failed to emphasise both aspects of reality, and that
if one ' moment ' is predominant and fundamental in his
work it is not the monad, but the Monad of Monads. If
necessity be the right word to express the relation of the
Universal Law to the individual being and to affirm that
the individual is not a loose self-supporting unit (and
Leibniz, far from thinking so, always uses in its stead the
phrase *inclinat, non necessitat*,[1] to emphasise the immanence
of law, or the autonomy of every completed being), then
Leibniz is not less, but more necessitarian than Spinoza.
His difference from Spinoza, in fact, lies mainly, if not
solely, in his clearer recognition of the transcendence, no
less than the immanence, of the Absolute, which Spinoza
has somewhat veiled under the apparent insignificance of
the difference between *natura naturans* and *natura naturata*.
Yet the Monad of Monads is no supramundane, or *merely*
transcendent God.

But if we further ask whether such personality is attainable in the world of experience and describable in terms of
thought—whether there be any actual and visible agent

---

[1] See especially in the *Théodicée*, part I. § 43 seqq. Cf. Nouv.
Ess. II. § 9, *incline sans nécessiter :* I. § 13, *La nécessité ne doit pas
être confondue avec la détermination.*

possessed of this true personality, as we have agreed to call it, we are in face with a higher stage of the problem of personality. And that question in other words brings us back to where we began. A true and real personality, a complete individuality is something which so transmutes all that we are most accustomed to call by that name that it is hardly any use clinging to it, unless to protest against the danger of mistaking such expansion and trans-mutation to be only a blank negation. Yet to cling to it too much involves a danger for the true recognition of that transcendent's universality. All human personality, all natural individuality is, as Lotze has eloquently pointed out,[1] something which falls far short of what it professes to be. But in the general failure to unite the universal with the particular, or the fact with the idea, there are degrees ; and we can at least affirm so much as this that the truest individuality and the most real personality is not that which is least permeated by thought, but that in which thought has had the largest share. Individuality is some-thing more than a mere sum of general qualities ;—that is certainly the fact ; but it is not less the fact, that for us an individuality and personality is more perfect and true in proportion as more general function and universal character coalesce into harmony and power in it. Assert then the initial presence and virtue of individuality and personality in the human soul : but remember that it has this virtue, not for what it is, but for what it promises and may reasonably be expected to be, and that, to realise the promise, it has to behave inclusively, rather than exclusively, gather up into itself and make its own all content, rather than set itself up in reserve and isolation.

We have seen that the social organisation, animated as it is by the moral idea, is rather the arena on which the true union of mind and matter, of idea and nature, of thought and fact may be worked for, than itself the fruition of such an effort. All-important is the State ; all-important the ethical idea which pervades it. But the world of freedom—the ideal world so far made actual—is not what it promised to be. ' Is it not,' said Plato, ' the nature of things that the actual should always lack the perfection of theory ? ' In the visible world the State, indeed, rules supreme : ' it is,' as Hegel might say in the words of his

---

[1] *Microcosmus*, Book IX. chap. 4.

great predecessor in political theory, ' that Leviathan or
mortal God to whom under the immortal God we owe our
welfare and safety.'   But there is something in the State
which the State in its palpable reality cannot adequately
express. If it is highest in the hierarchy of this world, the
lowest in the ideal kingdom of the Absolute is higher than
it.   Above the State as the embodiment and the guarantee
of the moral life, there is the realm of Art, Religion, and
Philosophy.   In them man's craving for individuality and
personality finds a satisfaction it could never hope for
below them : they at least restore the truth and reality of
man's life and of the universe in a measure far exceeding
what even morality could do.

   If we ask then what Art, Religion, and Science have
to show of Personality or true realised individuality, the
answer is briefly as follows.   Had it not been that august
names have spoken of imitation as the essence of Art-work,
we should hardly have deemed it possible that men should
speak of Realistic Art.   Yet here, as in Religion and in
Science, the epithet is introduced to guard against a misconception of the province of Idealism.   All Art, all
Religion, all Science, are and must be idealistic : but they
can never be—as the familiar phrase puts it—merely
idealistic, i. e. visionary, fantastic, unreal.   All of them,
in other words, may be said to show us ' the light that
never was on sea or land '—the heavenly city—the eternal
truth of things.   But they must, on their peril, show it
here and now, and not in a pretended or other world.
They must—no less than law and morality—work in
terrestrial materials, and not with superfine celestialities.
Mentem mortalia tangunt.   It is out of the oldest and
commonest realities of life and death that the poet and the
painter make the melodies of heaven sound in our ears,
and gladden us with the rays of the empyrean.   It is out
of the hard rock of the real that the artist's rod must strike
the well-spring of the ideal.   So too, in like manner, a
religion must show the Divine, but show Him immanent :
an immanence which, on one hand, shall not drag Godhead
down to the level of casual reality, nor on the other set
Him far off in lonely transcendence.

   The aesthetic faculty, awakened as it is by the natural
response of man's perceptions to the harmonies of existence,
to the spontaneous coherency of its many parts in a united

whole, and stimulated by the creative work of human art, which moulds even the naturally discordant or unconnected into a concordant expression (sometimes it may be, as in handicraft, only to satisfy human needs), lifts us above the imperfections and fragmentariness of things, above our selfish interest in them, into a frame of mind where they are seen whole and perfect, and yet one and veritably individual. In its supreme or comprehensive phase it does not deal merely with the beautiful, nor merely with the beautiful and sublime. All true art, whether it awakes awe or admiration, laughter or tears, whether it melts the soul, or steels it to endurance, has a common characteristic ; and that is to raise the single instance, the prosaic or commonplace fact, into its universal, eternal, infinite significance. It frees the fact from the limitations which our distractions, our practicality, our temporary hopes and fears, have deeply stamped upon it. It is still, after art has dealt with it, to all appearance a single fact : but it now has the universe behind it and within it. It carries us away from the incompleteness, the pressure of externals, the solicitude for the future and the regrets for the past, into a self-contained, self-satisfying totality, into freedom and leisure, rest which is not stolid, and action which involves no toil. Such a result is partly, as was said, the gift of common nature, which speaks peace, comfort, joy, self-possessed fruition for all her children when their sense is open and free : partly it comes through those select ones among these children who have a larger perception of the meaning and inner truth of her works, and who can by a sensible reconstruction, which if it is fair and successful will only bring out more clearly the unity and harmony which deeper insight detects, help others to see and enjoy what they have felt and rejoiced over. Such are the poets—in the widest sense—the makers, the seers, who in verse, in music, in picture and sculpture—who, in human lives, it may be even in the conduct of their own, show us how divine a thing is nature and humanity : show us the secret and unheard harmonies that to the full-opened ear absorb and transmute the lower discords of life and vulgar reality. It is they who give immortality and divinity, who make heroes and demigods.[1]   Or, if they

---

[1] See the well-known passage in *Wilhelm Meisters Lehrjahre*, Book II. chap. 2.

may not be said to make them, they half-reveal and half-construct the ideal figures which stand high and beneficent in the history of the world. And by those who thus half-construct, and half-reveal, are meant not merely the single artists in whom the process culminates to final outline and publicity, but the many-voiced poesy of the collective human heart which out of its myriad elemental springs constitutes the total figure, the august image of the hero, and the saint, lending him from its plenitude all that his abstract self seemed to want. It is on the tide of national and human enthusiasm that the individual artist is lifted up to realise the full significance of his ideal figure, and his imaginative craft can only be inspired by the vigour and warmth of the collective passion for noble ends and high action.

Nowhere it would seem is the ideal of personality and many-sided individuality more adequately realised. Here, at last, the whole truth of life, the indwelling of individual and universal in one body, seems to be realised. But it is realised in an ideal. It is—if we analyse it—a synthesis of three elements ; partly in the material reality which serves as bodily vehicle ; partly in the conception and technique of the artist ; partly in the general mind which inspires both the material and the form with its own larger life. It is—as its name implies—an artificial product—a synthesis of elements which tend to fall apart. Technique varies, conceptions lose their interest, the tone of general culture alters, and materials are dependent on locality. When that happens, the work of art is left high and dry : no longer a living God, but a dead idol, still wondrous, but speaking no more its human language.

So it is with the heroic figures who rise into the purer air of universal history. They also—so far as they live with a personal power—are works of art : works of real-idealism. For all history which deserves the name, and is not mere abstract dry-as-dust chronicle (as to the possibility of which utter aridity there may be legitimate doubts), is a work of fiction or invention, of reconstruction. It seeks to understand its characters. But to understand them it is not (and as historical art cannot be) content with a mere reference to motives acting on them from outside. It seeks to understand them with and in their times—to see in them the full measure of contemporary life and thought which elsewhere has found so meagre expression. Such is the artistic completion of personality in the ideal,—whether in what is called history, or what is called art. It exaggerates a truth, because it loses sight of the background. And that background, which helps to constitute such ideal personality, is no constant element. The centuries and generations as they roll contribute their varying quota to set, as they say, the historical character in its true light, in its fulness and truth of reality. And thus this personality of the great leaders of human life is only an image and a sign—a fruit of development, no bare fact which remains unchanged and always the same. It is rather a personification than a personality. It incarnates the living spirit who is universal and eternal in the limits of a sensuously-defined individual, and indeed incarnates there only so much as the generation it speaks to can see of complete truth. It is only after all a vehicle of truth ; though a nobler vehicle than social and personal ethics can afford.

As it is felt that the treasure of the idea—that the full power of spiritual life—cannot be adequately stored in the earthen vessels of mortality, the consummation of personality is forced to recede into the invisible if it would be still conceived as attainable. ' True personality,' says Lotze, ' is with the Infinite.' What here is fragmentary, is there a rounded total, a perfect unity : He alone is absolutely self-determining, self-explaining : is all that He means to be, and means all that He is. In a sense, philosophy does not hesitate to countersign all this. But, in adopting it, philosophy must reserve the right of noting the danger and the ambiguity of such language. Religion does well, philosophy may say, in thus insisting upon the dependence of all appearance on one Absolute reality ; but it is well also not to forget that all appearance is also the appearance of that reality or Absolute. And in so saying, be it added, philosophy assumes no essential superiority to religion. Religion in its fulness, and apart from any theories that may grow up under its wing, is more than theory, more than mere philosophy : it is the consummating unity of life—the enthusiasm and supreme power of life, its consecration and divinisation by its assured immanence in the eternal and universal. It is, in short, as was long ago said of it, the true life, the light which is the light and life of men ;

and its inspiring principles are faith, hope, and love. But
when unassisted religion proceeds to set before itself the
meaning and lesson of its life, when it proceeds to formulate
a theory of the world and set out a scheme of world-history,
it trespasses on the field of knowledge, and is amenable to
the criticisms of the reflective spirit—the spirit of philosophy.
And that criticism briefly is to the effect that the religious
theory in its ordinary form is an imperfect interpretation
of the religious experience. Nor is this to derogate from
the prerogative of the friends of God. It is only to criticise
the formulae and phrases of dogmatic theology—a theology,
however, which is as old as religion itself, and which takes
different forms from age to age, and from one level of
thought to another, always in its measure translating
religious reality, truth, or experience into the categories,
naïve or artificial, simple or complex, of the science (it may
be the pseudo-science) of the time. Philosophy, therefore,
is the criticism of the science of God—that is of theology—
as it is the criticism of other sciences. For criticism philosophy always is : always the reflection upon fixed dogma,
and the discussion of it till it becomes sensible of its defects,
and stands upon another and higher plane. And to some
it may seem that this is the sole function which philosophy
can legitimately undertake. ' Yet,' as Aristotle remarked,
' the good critic must know what he criticises.' He must
not merely reflect upon it from outside, but deal with it
from the plenitude of experience, from the abundance of
the heart. If he be a critic then, he cannot be a mere critic,
but also an agent in the work of reconstruction. Or, if we
put the thing otherwise ; though, as Fichte said (p. 19),
philosophy is a different thing from life, the true philosopher
can never be a mere philosopher, but must, if he is to reach
the height of his vocation, have also entered into the full
experience of reality, into the whole truth of life. His
philosophy will then not be outside of religion and aesthetic
perception. In its comprehension of all grades and forms
of reality and truth, goodness, holiness, beauty, will have
their place. He also will be among the theologians.

And when the philosopher deals with personality in this
high, this supreme sphere, he will submit that the truth of
personality is subordinate to the truth of spirituality. He
will argue that by sticking too closely and fixedly to personality we are running a risk of bringing down the divine

to the level of the human. If, with Dante, he can say that in its very heart the Light Eternal

> ' Mi parve pinta della nostra effige ' ;

he will undoubtedly add with Dante

> ' Oh quanto è corto 'l dire e come fioco
> Al mio concetto ' ;

or, with the first philosophical theologian who interpreted the experience of Christian life, he will rise from the historical Jesus to the inward witness of the Spirit.

CHAPTER XIX

GENESIS IN MENTAL LIFE

ARISTOTLE, who saw into the nature of abstract entities, remarked that the mind was nothing before it exercised itself.[1] The mind,—and the same will turn out true of many things else where it is at first unsurmised,—is not a fixed thing, a sort of exceedingly refined substance, which we can lay hold of without further trouble. It is what it has become, or what it makes itself to be. This point, that ' To be ' = ' To have become ', or rather to have made itself, is an axiom never to be lost sight of in dealing with the mind. It is easy to talk of and about conscience and freewill, as if these were existing things in a sort of mental space, as hard to miss or mistake as a stone and an orange, or as if they were palpable organs of mind, as separately observable as the eye or ear. One asks if the will is free or not, as glibly as one might ask whether an orange is sweet ; and the answer can be given with equal ease, affirmatively or negatively, in both cases. Everything in these cases depends on whether the will has made itself free or not, whether indeed we are speaking of the will at all, and on what we mean by freedom. To ask the question in an abstract way, taking no account of circumstances, is one of those temptations which lead the intellect astray and produce only confusion and wordy war—as a good deal of so-called popular metaphysics has done. The mind and its phenomena, as they are called, cannot be dissected with the same calmness of analysis as other substances which adapt themselves to the scalpel : nor is dissection after all more than a part of the scientific process, subject to the control of the synthesis in physiology.

The ordinary metaphysician makes his own task easy and his thoughtful reader's a burden, by plunging too lightly *in medias res*. He wants patience—often, perhaps,

---

[1] *De Anima*, iii. 4.

because he thinks too much of his reader's impatience at analysis—to unravel the tangled mass which human experience, when first looked at, presents. He is apt to catch at any end which promises to effect a temporary clearance. True philosophy, on the contrary, must show that it has got hold of what it means to discuss : it has to construct its subject-matter : and it constructs it by tracing every step and movement in its construction shown in actual history. The mind is what it has been made and has made itself ; and to see what it is we must consider it not as an Alpha and Omega of research, as popular conception and language tend to represent it, but in the stages constituting its process, in the fluidity of its development, in the elements out of which it results. We must penetrate the apparent fixity and simplicity under which it comes forward, and see through it into the process which bears it into being. For, otherwise, the object of our investigation is taken, as if it were the most unmistakable thing of sense and fancy,—as if everybody were agreed that this and no other were the point in question.

But in this matter of stability and the reverse, there is a broad distinction between the natural and the spiritual world. In Nature every step in the organisation, by which the Cosmos is developed, has an independent existence of its own : and the lowest formation confronts the highest, each standing by itself beside the other. Matter and motion, for example, are not merely found as subordinate elements entering into the making of a plant or an animal. They have a free existence of their own : and the free existence of matter in motion is seen in the shape of the planetary system. So, too, chemical or electrical phenomena can be observed by themselves, operating in spheres where they are untrammeled by the influence of biological conditions. It seems, at least at first sight, to be different in the case of mind. There the specific types or several stages in the integrating process of mental development seem to have no substantive existence in the earlier part of the range, and to appear only as states or factors entering into, and merged in, the higher grades of development. This causes a peculiar difficulty in the study of mind. We cannot seize a formation in an independent shape of its own : we must trace it in the growth of the whole. Mental fusion and coalescence of elements is peculiarly close, and hardly leaves any traces of its constituent factors.[1] Sensation, for instance, in its purity, as mere sensation, is apparently something which we can never study in isolation. All the sensation which we can, in the strictly psychological (as opposed to the physiological) mode of study, examine, i. e. which we can reproduce in ourselves, is more than mere sensation : it includes elements of thought, and probably of desire and will. This, of course, makes the difficulties of so-called introspection : difficulties so great and real that they have provoked in natural reaction a set against introspection altogether, and the adoption of the external observation (physiological or so-called psycho-physical) employed in the ' objective ' sciences. And hence when we accept the name, such as intellect, conscience, will, &c., as if it expressed something specially existent in a detached shape of its own, we make an assumption which it is impossible to justify. We are reckoning with paper-money which belongs to no recognised currency, and may be stamped as the dealer wills. The consequence is that the thing with which we begin our examination is an opaque point,— a mere *terminus a quo*, from which we start on our journey of explication, leaving the *terminus* itself behind us unexplained.

The constituents of mind do not lie side by side tranquilly co-existent, like the sheep beside the herbage on which it browses. Their existence is maintained in an inward movement, by which, while they differentiate themselves, they still keep up an identity. In our investigations we cannot begin with what is to be defined. The botanist, if he is to give us a science of the plant, must begin with

---

[1] A philological parallel may make this clearer. ' The Indo-German,' says Misteli (*Typen des Sprachbaues*, p. 363), ' embraces or condenses several categories in a single idea in a way which though less logical is more fruitful ; for in this way he procures graspable totals with which he can work further, and not patchwork which would crumble away in his hands. Our *He* includes four grammatical categories, which work not separately, but as a whole :—third person, masculine gender, singular, nominative ; whereas the Magyar ö is the vehicle only of one category, the third person, which is either determined as singular by the context, or as plural by the addition of *k* : gender in these languages does not exist : and as subject again ö is specially interpreted from the context. The unification of the four categories makes *He* an individual and a word ; the generality and isolation of one category makes ö an abstract and a stem.'

something whose indwelling aim it is to be itself and to realise its own possibility. He must begin with what is not the plant, and end with what is ; begin, let us say, with the germ which has the tendency to pass into the plant. The speculative science of biology begins with a cell, and builds these cells up into the tissues and structures out of which vegetables and animals are constituted. The object of the science appears as the result of the scientific process : or, *a science is the ideal construction of its object*. As in these cases, so in the case of thought. We must see it grow up from its simplest element, from the bare point of being, the mere speck of being which, if actually no better than nothing, is yet a germ which in the air of thought will grow and spread ; and see it appear as a result due to the ingrowing and outgrowing union of many elements, none of which satisfies by itself, but leads onward from abstractions to the meeting of abstractions in what is more and more concrete. The will and conscience, understanding and reason, of man are not matter-of-fact units to be picked up and examined. You must, first of all, make sure what you have in hand : and to be sure of that is to see that the mind is the necessary outcome of a course of development. The mind is not an immediate *datum*, with nothing behind it, coming upon the field of mental vision with a divinely-bestowed array of faculties ; but a mediated unity, i. e. a unity which has grown up through a complex interaction of forces, and which lives in differences through comprehending and reconciling antagonisms.

If the mind be not thus exhibited in its process, in the sum and context of its relations, we may mean what we like with each mental object that comes under our observation : but with as much right another observer may mean something else. We may, of course, define as we please : we may build up successive definitions into a consistent total : but such a successful arrangement is not a real science. Unless we show how this special form of mind is constituted, we are dealing with abstractions, with names which we may analyse, but which remain as they were when *our* analysis is over, and which seem like unsubstantial ghosts defying our coarse engines of dissection. They are not destroyed : like immaterial and aëry beings they elude the sword which smites them, and part but to re-unite. The name, and the conception bodied forth in it, is indeed

stagnant, and will to all appearance become the ready prey
of analysis : but there is something behind this materialised
and solidified conception, this worn-out counter or sign,
which mere analysis cannot even reach. And that underlying nature is a process or movement, a meeting of
elements, which it is the business of philosophy to unfold.
The analyst in this case has dealt with ideas as if they were
a finer sort of material product, a fixed and assailable
point : and this is perhaps the character of the generalised
images, which take the place of thoughts in our customary
habits of mind. But ideas, when they have real force and
life, are not hard and solid, but, as it were, fluid and transparent, and can easily escape the divisions and lines which
the analytical intellect would impose. Perhaps some may
think that it is unwise to fight with ghosts like these, and
that the best plan would be to disregard this war of words
altogether. But, on the other hand, it may be urged that
such unsubstantial forms have a decided reality in life :
that men will talk of them and conjure by their means,
with or without intelligence ; and that the best course is
to understand them. It will then be seen that it is our
proper work as philosophers to watch the process, by which
the spiritual unity divides and yet retains its divided
members in unity.

Even in the first steps we take to get a real hold of an
object we see this. To understand it, we must deprive it
of its seeming independence. Every individual object is
declared by the logician to be the meeting of two currents,
the coincidence of two movements. It concentrates into
an undecompounded unit,—at least such it appears to
representative or material thought,—two elements, each
of which it is in turn identifiable with. The one of these
elements has been called the self-same (or identity), the
universal, the genus, the whole : while the second is called
the difference, the particular, the part. And by these two
points of reference it is fixed,—by two points which are for
the moment accepted as stationary. What has thus been
stated in the technical language of Logic is often repeated
in the scientific parlance of the day, but with more
materialised conceptions and in more concrete cases. The
dynamic theory of matter represents it as a unity of attraction and repulsion. A distinguished Darwinian remarks
that ' all the various forms of organisms are the necessary

products of the unconscious action and reaction between the two properties of adaptability and heredity, reducible as these are to the functions of nutrition and reproduction '.[1] The terms ' action and reaction ' are hardly sufficient, it may be, to express the sort of unity which is called for : but the statement at least shows the reduction of an actual fact to the interaction of two forces, the meeting of two currents. The one of these is the power of the kind, or universal, which tends to keep things always the same : the other the power of localised circumstances and particular conditions, which tends to render things more and more diversified. The one may be called a centripetal, the other a centrifugal force. If the one be synthetic, the other is analytic. But such names are of little value, save for temporary distinction, and must never be treated as permanent differences which explain themselves. The centre is relative and so is the totality.

Thus it is that the so-called Evolutionist explains the origin of natural kinds. They are what they severally are by reason of a process, a struggle, by alliances and divisions, by re-unions and selections. They are not independent of the inorganic world around them : it has entered into their blood and structure, and made them what they are. To understand them we must learn all we can of the simpler and earlier forms, which have left traces in their structure : traces which, without the existence of such more primitive forms, we might have misunderstood, or have passed by unperceived. And, again, we learn that our hard and fast distinctions are barely justified by Nature. There, kind in its extreme examples seems to run into kind, and we do not find the logically-exact type accurately embodied anywhere. Our classifications into genera and species turn out to be in the first instance prompted by a practical need to embrace the variety in a simple shape. But though perfectly valid, so far as we use them for such ends, they tend to lead us false, if we press them too far.

And when we have seen so much, we may learn the further lesson that the variety of organisation, animal and vegetable, is only the exhibition in an endless detail by single pictures, more or less complementary, more or less inclusive of each other, of that one vital organisation in

[1] Häckel, *Natürliche Schöpfungs-Geschichte*, p. 157.

principle and construction which we could not otherwise have had presented to us. In a million lessons from the vast ranges of contemporary and of extinct life there is impressed upon the biological observer the idea of that system of life-function and life-structure which is the goal of biological science. The interest in the mere variety whether of modern or of primeval forms of life is as such merely historical ; its truer use is to enable the scientific imagination to rise above local or temporary limitations. And thus in the end the records and guesses of evolution in time and place serve to build up a theory of the timeless universal nature of life and organisation.

And what is true of Nature is equally true of the Mind. For these two, as we have already seen, are not isolable from each other. Neither the mind nor the so-called external world are either of them self-subsistent existences, issuing at once and ready-made out of nothing. The mind does not come forth, either equipped or un-equipped, to conquer the world : the world is not a prey prepared for the spider, waiting for the mind to comprehend and appropriate it. The mind and the world, the so-called 'subject' and so-called 'object', are equally the results of a process : and it is only when we isolate the terminal aspects of that process, and in the practical business of life forget the higher theoretical point of view, that we lose sight of their origin, and have two worlds facing each other. As the one side or aspect of the process gathers feature and form, so does the other. As the depth and intensity of the intellect increases, the limits of the external world extend also. For the psychical life is just the power which maintains a continuing correlation between the body and its environment, and between the various elements in that environment. It is the unity in which that correlation lives and is aware of itself. It is the subject-object, which sets one element against another, and gives it quasi-independence. The mind of the savage is exactly measured by the world he has around him. The dull, almost animal, sensation and feeling, which is what we may call his mental action, is just the obverse of the narrow circumference that girdles his external world. The beauty and interest of the grander phenomena of terrestrial nature, and of the celestial movements, are ideally non-existent for a being, whose whole soul is swallowed up in the craving for food, the fear of attack, and the

lower enjoyments of sense. In the course of history we can
see the intellect growing deeper and broader, and the limits
of the world recede simultaneously with the advance of the
mind. This process or movement of culture takes place in
the sequence of generations, and in the variety of races and
civilisations spread over the face of the world. But here too,
the higher science, not resting in the merely historical
inquiry, takes no interest in the medium of time, and merely
uses it to supply material for the rational sequence of ideas.[1]

The objective world of knowledge is really at one with
the subjective world : they spring from a common source,
what Kant called the ' original synthetic unity of apperception '. The distinction between them flows from abstraction, from failure to keep in view the whole round of life
and experience. The subjective world—the mind of man—
is really constituted by the same force as the objective
world of nature : the latter has been translated from the
world of extension, with its externality of parts in time and
space, into an inner world of thought where unity, the
fusion or coalescence of all types and forms, is the leading
feature. The difficulty of passing from the world of being
to the world of thoughts, from notion to thing, from subject
to object, from Ego to Non-ego, is a difficulty which men
have unduly allowed to grow upon them. It grows by
talking of and analysing *mere* being, *mere* thought, *mere*
notion, or *mere* thing. And it will be dispelled when it is
seen that there is no *mere* being, and no *mere* thought : that
these two halves of the unity of experience—the unity we
divide and the division we unify in every judgment we make
—are continually leaning out of themselves, each towards
the other. But men, beginning as they must from themselves, and failing to revise and correct their stand-point
till it became an ἀρχὴ ἀνυπόθετος, argued from a belief
that the individual mind was a fixed and absolute centre,
from which the universe had to be evaluated. In Hegel's
words, they made man and not God the object of their
philosophy.[2] So that Kant really showed the outcome of
a system which acted on the hypothesis that man in his
individual capacity was all in all. Hegel, on his own
showing, came to prove that the real scope of philosophy
was God ;—that the Absolute is the ' original synthetic

[1] See above, pp. 120, 152.
[2] Hegel's *Werke*, vol. i. p. 15.

unity' from which the external world and the Ego have issued by differentiation, and in which they return to unity.

If this be so, then there is behind the external world and behind the mind an organism of pure types or forms of thought,—an organism which presents itself, in a long array of fragments, to the senses in the world of nature, where all things lie outside of one another, and which then is, as it were, reflected back into itself so as to constitute the mind, or spiritual world, where all parts tend to coalesce in a more than organic unity. The deepest craving of thought, and the fundamental problem of philosophy, will accordingly be to discover the nature and law of that totality or primeval unity,—the totality which we see appearing in the double aspect of nature and mind, and which we first become acquainted with as it is manifested in this state of disunion. To satisfy this want is what the Logic of Hegel seeks. It lays bare the kingdom of those potent shades,—the phases of the Idea—which embodies itself more concretely in the external world of body, and the inward world of mind. The psychological or individualist conditions, which even in the Kantian criticism sometimes seem to set up mind as an entity parallel to the objects of nature, and antithetic to nature as a whole, have fallen away. Reason has to be taken in the whole of its actualisation as a world of reason, not in its bare possibility, not in the narrow ground of an individual's level of development, but in the realised formations of reasonable knowledge and action, as shown in Art and Life, Science and Religion. In this way we come to a reason which might be in us or in the world, but which, being to a certain extent different from either, was the focus of two orders of manifestations.

To ascertain that ultimate basis of the world and mind was the chief thing philosophy had to see to. But in order to do this, a good deal of preliminary work was necessary. The work of Logic, as understood by Hegel, involves a stand-point which is not that of every-day life or reflection on experience. It presupposes the whole process from the provisional starting-point which seems at first sight simplest and universally acceptable, upwards to the un-hypothetical principle which—though at a long distance—it involves and leads up to, or presupposes. We all know Aristotle's dictum Ἐν τοῖς αἰσθητοῖς τὰ νοητά ἐστιν : *Nihil in intellectu quod non prius in sensu.* The fact of sense and

feeling *is* the fact of experience : or rather the fact and
reality of experience is the underlying truth which the
expression of it in terms of sense and perception inadequately
interprets. Even in the principles of sensation there is
judgment, thought, reasoning : but it needs eliciting, re-
statement, opening up, and explanation. The Phenomenology of Mind is, as Hegel himself has said, his voyage of
discovery. It traces the path, and justifies the work of
traversing it, from the ill-founded and imperfect certainties
of sense and common-sense, up through various scientific,
moral, and religious modes of interpreting experience and
expressing its net sum of reality, till it culminates in the
stand-point of ' pure thought ', of supreme or ' absolute '
consciousness. It is certainly not a history of the individual
mind : and equally little is it a history of the process of the
intellectual development of the race. In a way it mixes up
both. For its main interest is not on the purely historical
side. It indulges in bold transitions, in sudden changes
of scene from ancient Greece and Rome to modern Germany,
from public facts and phases of national life to works of
fiction (compare its use of Goethe's *Faust* and his version of
Rameau's Nephew). It lingers—for historical accuracy and
proportion unduly—over the period of Kant and Fichte,
and reads Seneca by the light of the *Sorrows of Werther*.
For its aim is to gather from the inspection of all ways in
which men have attempted to reach reality the indication
of their several content of truth, and of the several defects
from it, so as to show the one necessary path on which even
all their errors converge and which they serve to set out in
clearer light.

Hegel's philosophy is undoubtedly the outcome of a vast
amount of historical experience, particularly in the ancient
world, and implies a somewhat exhaustive study of the products of art, science, politics, and religion. By experience
he was led to his philosophy, not by what is called *a priori*
reasoning. It is curious indeed to observe the prevalent
delusion that German philosophy is the ' high *priori* road ',
—to hear its profundity admired, but its audacity and
neglect of obvious facts deplored. The fact is that without
experience neither Hegel nor anybody else will come to
anything. But, on the other hand, experience is in one
sense only the yet undeciphered mass of feeling and reality,
the yet unexpounded psychical content of his life ; or,

taken in another acceptation, it is only a form which in one
man's case means a certain power of vision, and in another
a different degree.   One man sees the idea which explains
and unifies experience as actuality : to the other man it is
only a subjective notion.   And even when it is seen, there
are differences in the subsequent development.   One man
sees it, asserts it on all hands, and then closes. ·Another
sees it, and asks if this is all, or if it is only part of a system.
An appeal to ' my experience ' is very much like an appeal
to ' my sentiments ' or ' my feelings ' : it may prove as
much or as little as can be imagined : in other words, it
can prove nothing.   The same is true of the appeal to
consciousness, that oracle on whose dicta it has sometimes
been proposed to found a system of philosophy.   By that
name seems meant the deliverances of some primal and
unerring nucleus of mind, some real and central self, whose
voice can be clearly distinguished from the mere divergent
cries of self-interest and casual opinion.   That such discernment is possible no philosophy will seek to deny : but it is
a discernment which involves comparison, examination, and
reasoning.   And in that case the appeal to consciousness
is the exhortation to clear and deliberate thinking.   While,
on another side, it hints that philosophy does not—in the
end—deal with mere abstractions, but with the real concrete life of mind.   And if an appeal to other people's
experience is meant, that is only an argument from authority.
What other people experience is their business, not mine.
Experience *means* a great deal for which it is not the right
name : and to give an explanation of what it is, and what
it does, would render a great service to English methodo-
logists.
    There are, however, two modes in which these studies
to discover the truth may appear.   In the one case they
are reproduced in all their fragmentary and patch-work
character.   They are supposed to possess a value of their
own, and are enunciated with all the detail of historic incident.   The common-place books of a man are, as it were,
published to instruct the world and give some hint of the
extent of his reading.   But, in the other case, the scaffolding
of incident and externality may be removed.   The single
facts, which gave the persuasion of the idea, are dismissed,
as interesting only for the individual student on his way to
truth : or, if the historical vehicle of truth be retained at

all, it is translated into another and intellectual medium.
Such a history, the quintessence of extensive and deep
research, is presented in the Phenomenology. The names
of persons and places have faded from the record, as if they
had been written in evanescent inks,—dates are wanting,—
individualities and their biographies yield up their place to
universal and timeless principles. Such typical forms are
the concentrated essence of endless histories. They remind
one of the descriptions which Plato in his Republic gives of
the several forms of temporal government. Or, to take
a modern instance, the Hegelian panorama of thought
which presents only the universal evolution of thought,—
that evolution in which the whole mind of the world takes
the place of all his children, whether they belong to the
common level, or stand amongst representative heroes,—
may be paralleled to English readers by Browning's poem
of *Sordello*. There can be no question that such a method
is exposed to criticism, and likely to excite misconception.
If it tend to give artistic completeness to the work, it also
tantalises the outsider who has a desire to reach his familiar
standing-ground. He wishes a background of time and
space, where the forms of the abstract ideas may be embodied to his mind's eye. In most ages, and with good
ground, the world has been sceptical, when it perceived no
reference to authorities, no foot-notes, no details of experiments made : nor is it better disposed to accept provisorily,
and find, as the process goes on, that it verifies itself to
intelligence.

CHAPTER XX

GENERAL LAW OF THE PHILOSOPHY OF HISTORY

' THE order and concatenation of ideas,' says Spinoza,
' is the same as the order and concatenation of things '.[1]
The objective world at least of acts and institutions develops
parallel with the growth and system of men's ideas. In
the tangled skein which human life and reality present to
the observer, the only promising clue is to be found in the
process by which in history the past throws light on the
present and gets light in return. There in the stream of
time and in the expanses of space the condensed results, the
hard knots, which present life offers for explanation, are
broken up into a vast number of problems, each presenting
a different aspect, and one helping towards a fairer and
clearer appreciation of another.

The present medium of general intelligence and theory
in which we live embraces in a way the results of all that
has preceded it, of all the steps of culture through which the
world has risen. But in this body of intellectual beliefs and
ideas with which our single soul is clad,—in this common
soil of thought,—the several contributions of the past have
been half or even wholly obliterated, and are only the shadows
of their old selves. What in a former day was a question of
all-engrossing interest has left but a trace : the complete
and detailed formations of ancient thought have lost their
distinctness of outline, and have shrunk into mere shadings
in the contour of our intellectual world. Questions, from
which the ancient philosophers could never shake themselves loose, are now only a barely perceptible *nuance* in
the complex questions of the present day. Discussions
about the bearings of the ' one ' and the ' many ', puzzles
like those of Zeno, and the casuistry of statesmanship such
as is found in the Politics of Aristotle, have for most people
little else than an antiquarian interest. We scarcely detect

[1] *Eth.* ii. 7.

the faint traces they have left in the ' burning questions '
of our own age.   We are too ready to forget that the past
is never altogether annihilated, and that every step, however slight it may seem, which has once been taken in the
movement of intellect, must be traversed again in order to
understand the constitution of our present intellectual
world.   To outward appearance the life and work of past
generations have so completely lost their organic nature,
with its unified and vital variety, that in their present phase
they have turned into hard and opaque atoms of thought.
The living forces of growth, as geologists tell us, which pulsed
through the vegetables of one period are suspended and put
in abeyance :   and these vegetables turn into what we call
the inorganic and inanimate strata of the earth.   Similarly,
when all vitality has been quenched or rendered torpid in
the structures of thought, they sink into the material from
which individuals draw their means of intellectual support.
This inorganic material of thought stands to the mind, almost
in the same way as the earth and its products stand to the
body of a man.   If the one is our material, the other is our
spiritual *substance*.   In the one our mind, as in the other
our body, lives, moves, and has its being.

But in each case besides the practical need, which bids
us consume the substance as dead matter, and apply it to
use, there is the theoretical bent which seeks to reproduce
ideally the past as a living and fully developed organism.
' This past,' says Hegel, ' is traversed by the individual, in
the same way as one who begins to study a more advanced
science repeats the preliminary lessons with which he had
long been acquainted, in order to bring their information
once more before his mind.   He recalls them :   but his interest and study are devoted to other things.   In the same
way the individual must go through all that is contained
in the several stages in the growth of the universal mind :
but all the while he feels that they are forms of which the
mind has divested itself,—that they are steps on a road
which has been long ago completed and levelled.   Thus,
points of learning, which in former times tasked the mature
intellects of men, are now reduced to the level of exercises,
lessons, and even games of boyhood :   and in the progress of
the schoolroom we may recognise the course of the education
of the world, drawn, as it were, in shadowy outline.' [1]

[1] *Phenomenologie des Geistes*, p. 22.

The scope of historical investigation therefore is this.   It shows how every shading in the present world of thought, which makes our spiritual environment, has been once living and actual with an independent being of its own.   But it also reveals the presence of shades and elements in the present which if our eyes had looked on the present alone we should scarcely have suspected : and it thus enables us to interpolate stages in development of which the result preserves only rudimentary traces.   And, when carried out in a philosophical spirit, it shows further, that in those formations, which are produced in each period of the structural development of reason, the universe of thought, or the Idea, is always whole and complete, but characterised in some special mode which for that period seems absolute and final.   Each form or ' dimension ' of thought, in which the totality is grasped and unified, is therefore not so simple or elementary as it may seem to casual observers regarding only the simplicity of language :   it is a total, embracing more or less of simpler elements, each of which was once an inferior total, though in this larger sphere they are reduced to unity.   Thus each term or period in the process is really an individualised whole, with a complex interconnexion and contrast included in it :   it is *concrete*.   No single word or phrase explains it :   yet it is one totality,—a rounded life, from which its several spheres of life must be explained. But when that period is passing away, the form of its idea is separated, and retained, apart from the life and mass of the elements which constituted it a real totality ;   and then the mere shading or shell, with only part of its context of thought, is left *abstract*.   When that time has come, a special form, a whole act in the drama, of humanity has been transformed into an empty husk, and is only a name.

The sensuous reality of life, as it is limited in space and time, and made palpable in matter and motion, is however the earliest cradle of humanity.   The environment of sense is prior in the order of time to the environment of thought. Who, it may be asked, first wrought their way out of that atmosphere of sense into an ether of pure thought ?   Who first saw that in sense there was yet present something more than sensation,—that the deliverances of sense-perception rest upon and involve relations, ties, distinctions, which contradict its self-confidence and carry us beyond its simple

indications ? Who laid the first foundations of that world
of reason in which the civilised nations of the modern
period live and move ? The answer is, the Greek philosophers : and in the first place the philosophers of Elea.
For Hegel the history of thought begins with Greece.   All
that preceded the beginnings of Greek speculation, and
most that lies outside it, has only a secondary interest for
the culture of the West.

But ' many heroes lived before the days of Agamemnon '.
The records of culture no longer begin with Greece.   Even
in Hegel's own day, voices, like those of the poet Rückert
(in his ' habilitation '-exercise), were heard declaring that
the true fountain of European thought, the real philosophy,
was to be sought in the remoter East.   Since the time of
Hegel, the study of primitive life, and of the rise of primitive
ideas in morals and religion, has enabled us to some extent
to trace the early gropings of barbarian fancy and reason.
The comparative study of languages has, on the other
hand, partly revealed the contrivances by which human
reason has risen from one grade of consciousness to another.
The sciences of language and of primitive culture have revealed new depths in the development of thought, where
thought is still enveloped in nature and sense and symbols,—
depths which were scarcely dreamed of in the earlier part of
the present century.   Here and there, investigators have
even supposed that they had found the cradle of some
elements in art, religion, and society, or, it may be, of
humanity itself.

These researches have accomplished much, and they
promise to accomplish more.   They help us perhaps to
take a juster view of the early Greek thinkers, and show
how much they still laboured under conditions of thought
and speech from which their struggles have partly freed us.
But for the present, and with certain explanations to be
given later, it may still be said that the birthday of our
modern world is the moment when the Greek sages began
to construe the facts of the universe.   Before their time the
world lay, as it were, in a dream-life.   Unconsciously in the
womb of time the spirit of the world was growing,—its
faculties forming in secresy and silence,—until the day of
birth when the preparations were completed, and the young
spirit drew its first breath in the air of thought.   A new
and to us all-important epoch in the history of thought

begins with the Greeks : and the utterances of Parmenides
mark the first hard, and still somewhat material, outlines
of the spiritual world in which we live.   Other nations of
an older day had gathered the materials : in their languages, customs, religions, &c., there was an unconscious
deposit of reason.   It was reserved for the Greeks to
recognise that reason : and thus in them reason became
conscious.

For us, then, it was the Greek philosophers who distinctly
drew the distinction between sense and thought, and who
first translated the actual forms of our natural life into their
abbreviated equivalents in terms of logic.   The struggle to
carry through this transition, this elevation into pure
thought, is what gives the dramatic interest to the Dialogues
of Plato and keeps the sympathy of his readers always
fresh.   Socrates, we are told, first taught men to seek a
general definition : not to be content with having—like
Pythagoreans—their meaning wrapped up inseparably in
psychical images and quasi-material symbols.   He taught
them to refer word to fellow word, to elicit the underlying
idea by the collision and comparison of instances, to get at
the ' content ' which was identical in all the multiplicity of
forms.   He taught them, in brief, to think : and Plato
carried out widely and deeply the lesson.   The endeavour
to create an ideal world, which, at its very creation, seems
often to be transformed into a refined and attenuated copy
of the sense-world, meets us in almost every page of his
Dialogues.   In Aristotle this effort, with its concomitant
tendency to give ' sensible ' form to the ideal, is so far
over and past ; and some sort of intellectual world, perhaps
narrow and inadequate, is reached,—the logical scheme in
which immediate experience was expressed and codified.
What these thinkers began, succeeding ages have inherited
and promoted.

In the environment of reason, therefore, which encompasses the consciousness of our age, are contained under
a generalised form and with elimination of all the particular
circumstances, the results won in the development of mind
and morals.   These results now constitute the familiar
joints and supports in the framework of ordinary thought :
around and upon them cluster our beliefs and imaginations.
During each epoch of history, the consciousness of the
world, at first by the mouth of its great men, its illustrious

statesmen, artists, and philosophers, has explicitly recognised, and translated into terms of thought,—into logical language,—that synthesis of the world which the period had practically secured by the action of its children. That activity went on, as is the way of natural activities, spontaneously, through the pressure of need, by an immanent adaptation of means to ends, not in conscious straining after a result. For the conscious or reflective effort of large bodies of men is often in a direction contrary to the Spirit of the Time. This Spirit of the Time, the absolute mind, which is neither religious nor irreligious, but infinite and absolute in its season, is the real motive principle of the world. But that Spirit of the Time is not always the voice that is most effective at the poll, or rings loudest in public rhetoric. It is often a still small voice, which only the wise, the self-restrained, the unselfish hear. And he who hears it and obeys it, not he who follows the blatant crowd, is the hero. It is only to a mistaken or an exaggerated hero-worship, therefore, that Hegel can be said to be a foe. Great men are great : but the Spirit of the Time is greater : their greatness lies in understanding it and bringing it to consciousness. The man, who would act independently of his time and in antagonism to it, is only the exponent of its latent tendencies. Nor need the synthesis be always formulated by a philosopher in order to leaven the minds of the next generation. The whole system of thought,—the theory of the time,—its world, in short, influences minds, although it is not explicitly formulated and stated : it becomes the nursery of future thought and speculation. Philosophy in its articulate utterances only gives expression to the silent and half-conscious grasp of reason over its objects. But when the adaptation is not merely reached but seen and felt, when the synthesis or world of that time is made an object of self-consciousness, the exposition has made an advance upon the period which preceded. For that period started in its growth from the last exposition, the preceding system of philosophy, after it had become the common property of the age, and taken its place in their mental equipment.

Each exposition or perception of the synthesis by the philosopher restores or re-affirms the unity which in the divided energies of the period, in its progressive, reforming, and reactionary aspects, in its differentiating time, had to a great extent been lost. By the reforming, progressive, and scientific movement of which each period is full, the unity or totality with which it began is shown to be defective. The value of the initial synthesis is impaired ; its formula is found inadequate to comprehend the totality : and the differences which that unity involved, or which were implicitly in it, are now explicitly affirmed. But the bent towards unity is a natural law making itself felt even in the period of differentiation. And it makes itself felt in the pain of contradiction, of discord, of broken harmony. And that pain—which is the sign of an ever-present life that refuses to succumb to the encroaching elements—is the stimulus to re-construction. Only so far as pain ceases to be pain, as it benumbs, and deadens, does it involve stagnation : as pain proper, felt as resistance to an inner implicitly victorious principle, it stimulates and quickens to efforts to make life whole again. The integrating principle is present and active. There is then an effort, a re-action ; the feeling has to do something to make itself outwardly felt : the implicit has to be actually put in its place, forced as it were into action and set forth :[1] and the existing contrasts and differences which the re-forming agency has called into vigorous life are lifted from their isolation and show of independence, and kept, as it were, suspended in the unity.[2] The differences are not lost or annihilated : but they come back to a centre, they find themselves, as it were, at home : they lose their unfair prominence and self-assertion, and sink into their places as constituents in the embracing organism.[3] The unity which comes is not however the same as the unity which disappeared, however much it may seem so. The mere *notion*—the inner sense and inner unity—has put itself forward into the real world : it is no longer a mere subjective principle, but as moulded into actuality, into the objective world, it has become an Idea. (*Begriff* is now *Idee*.) For the Idea is always more than a notion : it is a notion translated into objectivity, and yet in objectivity not sinking into a mere congeries of independent parts, but retaining them ' ideally '—united by links of thought and service—in its larger ideal-reality. It is all that the object ought to be (and which in a sense it must be, if it is at all), and all that the subject sought to be and looked forward to.

[1] Gesetzt.   [2] Aufgehoben.   [3] Idee : Ideeller Weise.

The mind of the world moves, as it were, in cycles, but with each new cycle a difference supervenes, a new tone is perceptible. History, which reflects the changing aspects of reality, does and does not repeat itself. The distinctions and the unity are neither of them the same after each step as they were before it : they have both suffered a change : it is a new scene that comes above the horizon, however like the last it may seem to the casual observer. Thus when the process of differentiation is repeated anew, it is repeated in higher terms, multiplied, and with a higher power or wider range of meaning.[1] Each unification however is a perfect world, a complete whole : it is the same sum of being ; but in each successive level of advance it receives a fuller expression, and a more complexly-grouped type of features.[2] Such is the rhythmic movement,—the ebb and flow of the world, always recurring with the same burden but, as we cannot but hope, with richer variety of tones, and fuller sense of itself. The sum of actuality, the Absolute, is neither increased nor diminished. The world, the ultimate reality of experience and life, was as much a rounded total to the Hebrew Patriarchs as it is to us : without advancing, it has been, we may say, in its expression deepened, developed, and organised. In one part of the sway of thought, however, there is a harder, narrower, insistance (by practical and business minds) on the sufficiency of a definite principle to satisfy all wants and to make all mysteries plain, and a disposition to ignore all other elements of life : at another, there is a fuller recognition of the differences, gaps, and contradictions, involved in the last synthesis,—which recognition it is the tendency of scientific inquiry, of reforming efforts, of innovation, to produce : and in the last period of the sway, there is a stronger and more extended grasp taken by the unity pervading these differences,—which is the work appointed to philosophy gathering up the results of science and practical amendments.

To this rhythmical movement Hegel has appropriated the name of Dialectic. The name came in the first instance

[1] Potenz.

[2] ' Nicht nur die Einsicht in die Abhängigkeit des Einzelnen vom Ganzen ist allein das Wesentliche ; ebenso dass jedes Moment selbst unabhängig vom Ganzen das Ganze ist, und dies ist das Vertiefen in die Sache.' (Hegel's *Leben*, p. 548.)

from Kant, but ultimately from Plato, where it denotes the
process which brings the ' many ' under the ' one ', and
divides the ' one ' into the ' many '. But how, it may be
asked, does difference spring up, if we begin with unity, and
how do the differences return into the unity ? In other
words, given a universal, how are we ever to get at particulars, and how will these particulars ever give rise to
a real individual ? Such is the problem, in the technical
language of the Logic of the ' Notion '. And we may
answer, that the unity or universal in question is either
a true and adequate or an imperfect unity. In the latter
case it is a mere unit, amid other units, bound to them and
serving to recall them by relations of contrast, complement,
similarity. It is one of many,—a subordinate member in
a congeries, and not *the One*. If, on the contrary, it be
a true Unity, it is a concrete universal,—the parent of
perpetual variety. The unity, if it be its genuine shape
which is formulated by philosophers, is not mere monotony
without differences. If it is a living and real Idea, containing a complex inter-action of principles : it is not a
single line of action, but the organic confluence of several.
No one single principle by itself is enough to state a life,
a character, or a period. But as the unity comes before
the eye of the single thinker, it is seldom or never grasped
with all its fulness of life and difference. The whole
synthesis, although it is implicitly present and underlies
experience and life as its essential basis, is not consciously
apprehended, but for the most part taken on one side only,
one emphatic aspect into which it has concentrated itself.
And even if the master could grasp the whole, could see the
unity of actuality in all its differences, (and we may doubt
whether any man or any philosopher can thus incarnate
the prerogative of reason,) his followers and the popular
mind would not imitate him. While his grasp of comprehension may possibly have been thorough, though he may
have seen life whole through all its differences, inequalities,
and schisms, and with all these reduced or idealised to their
due proportions, into the unity beyond, the crowd who
follow him are soon compelled to lay exclusive stress on
some one side of his theory. Some of them see the totality
from one aspect, some from another. It is indeed the whole
which in a certain sense they see : but it is the whole
narrowed down to a point. While *his* theory was a compre-

hensive and concrete grasp, including and harmonising many things which seem otherwise wide apart, theirs is abstract and inadequate : it fixes on a single point, which is thus withdrawn from its living and meaning-giving context, and left as an empty name. Now it is the very nature of popular reasoning to tend to abstractions, in this sense of the word. Popular thought wants the time and perseverance necessary to retain a whole truth, and so is contented with a partial image. It seeks for simple and sharp precision : it likes to have something distinctly before it, visible to the eye of imagination, and capable of being stated in a clear and unambiguous formula for the intellect. And popular thought—the dogmatic insistence on one-sided truth—is not confined to the so-called non-philosophic world : just as, on the other hand, the inclusive and comprehensive unity of life and reality is seen and felt and recognised by many—and felt by them first—who have no claim to the technical rank of philosophers. Popular thought is the thought which skims the surface of reality, which addresses itself to the level of opinion prevalent in all members of the mass as such, and does not go beyond that into the ultimate and complex depths of experience.

Thus it comes about that the concrete or adequate synthesis which should have appeared in the self-conscious thought of the period, when it reflected upon what it was, has been replaced by a narrow and one-sided formula, an abstract and formal universal, a universal which does not express all the particulars. One predominant side of the synthesis steals the place of the total : what should have been a comprehensive universal has lowered itself into a particular. Not indeed the same particular as existed before the union : because it has been influenced by the synthesis, so as to issue with a new colouring, as if it had been steeped in a fresh liquid. But still it is really a particular : and as such, it evokes a new particular in antagonism to it and exhibiting an element latent in the synthesis. If the first side of the antithesis which claims unduly to be the total, or universal, be called Conservative, the second must be called Reforming or Progressive. If the first step is Dogmatic, the second is Sceptical. If the one side assumes to be the whole, the other practically refutes the assumption. If the one agency clings blindly to the

unity,—as when pious men rally round the central idea
of religion, the other as tenaciously and narrowly holds to
the difference,—as when science displays the struggle for
existence and the empire of chance among the myriads of
aimless organisms. They are two warring abstractions,
each in a different direction. But as they are the offspring
of one parent,—as they have each in their own way
narrowed the whole down to a point, it cannot but be that
when they evolve or develop all that is in them, they will
ultimately coincide, and complete each other. The contradiction will not disappear until it has been persistently
worked out,—when each opposing member which was
potentially a total has become what it was by its own
nature destined to be. And this disappearance of the
antithesis is the reappearance of the unity in all its strength,
reinforced with all the wealth of new distinctions.

Thus on a large scale we have seen the law of growth, of
development, of life. It may be called growth by antagonism. But the antagonism here is over-ruled, and
subject to the guidance of an indwelling unity. *Mere*
antagonism—if there be such a thing—would lead to
nothing. A mere positive or affirmative point of being
would lead to no antithesis, were it not, so to speak, a point
floating in an ether of larger life and being, whence it
draws an outside element which it overcomes, assimilates
and absorbs. A bare national mind only grows to richer
culture, because it lives in a universal human life, and can
say *Nihil humani a me alienum puto*. So too the mere
unit is always tainted with a dependence on outside : or
it is always implicitly more than a mere unit : and what
seems to come upon it from outside, is really an enemy
from within, and it falls because there is treason within
its walls. The revolution succeeds because the party of
conservative order is not so hard and homogeneous as it
appears. So, too, it is the immanent presence of the
complete thought, of the Idea, which is the heart and
moving spring that sets going the pulse of the universal
movement of thought, and which reappears in every one
of these categories to which the actualised thought of an
age has been reduced. In every term of thought there are
three stages or elements : the original narrow definiteness,
claiming to be self-sufficient,—the antagonism and criticism
to which this gives rise,—and the union which results when

the two supplement and modify each other. In the full life and organic unity of every notion there is a definite kernel, with rigid outlines as if it were immovable : there is a revulsion against such exclusiveness, a questioning and critical attitude : and there is the complete notion, where the two first stages interpenetrate.

CHAPTER XXI

ABSTRACT AND CONCRETE : AND THE ORDINARY LOGIC

THE ordinary logic-books have made us all familiar with the popular distinction between Abstract and Concrete. By a concrete term they mean the name of an existence or reality which is obvious to the senses, and is found in time and place ;—or they mean the name of an attribute when we expressly or tacitly recognise its dependence upon such a thing of the senses. When, on the contrary, the attribute is forcibly withdrawn from its context and made an independent entity in the mind, the term expressing it becomes in the usual phraseology abstract. Any term therefore which denotes a non-sensible or intelligible object would probably be called abstract. And there is something to be said for the distinction, which, though unsuccessful in its expression, has some feeling of the radical antithesis between mere being and mere thought. It is true, that in the totality of sense and feeling, in the full sense-experience, there is a concrete fulness, as it were, an infinite store of features and phases waiting for subsequent analysis to detect. In the real kind of actual nature there is an inexhaustible mine of properties, which no artificial classification and description can ever come to the end of. Every quality which we state, every relation which we predicate, is a partial and incomplete element in this presupposed reality, this implicit concrete ; and as such is abstract, and comparatively unreal. It is something forcibly torn out of and held apart from its context. But on the other hand the concrete reality is not at first real, but implicit : it becomes really concrete only as it re-embraces, and re-constitutes in its totality the elements detected by analysis. But the popular distinction forgets this, and gives the title and rank of concrete to what very poorly deserves the name, viz. to the yet undiscerned reality denoted by a substantive name. Yet there can be little doubt that the popular use of these terms, or the popular apprehension of what constitutes reality,—for that is what it comes to,—is sufficiently represented by the ordinary logic-books. So that, if the whole business of the logician lies in formulating the distinctions prevalent in popular thought, the ordinary logic is correct.

Now the popular logic of the day,—the logic which has long been taught in our schools and universities—has three sources.—In the first place, but in a slight degree, it trenches upon the province of psychology, and gives some account of the operation by which concepts or general ideas are supposed to be formed, and of the errors or fallacies which naturally creep into the process of reasoning. This is the more strictly modern, the descriptive part of our logic-books.—But, secondly, the logic of our youth rests in a much higher degree upon the venerable authority of Aristotle. That logic, within its own compass, was a masterpiece of analysis, and for many centuries maintained an ascendency over the minds of men, which it well deserved. But it was not an analysis of thought or knowledge as a whole, and it treated its subject in fragments. It gave in one place an analysis of science and in another an analysis of certain methods, which could be observed in popular discussions and practical oratory. As Lord Bacon remarked, it did little else than state and, it may be, exaggerate the *rationale* of argumentation. A high level of popular thought it unquestionably was, which Aristotle had to investigate,—a level which many generations of less favoured races were unable to reach. But there were defects in this Logic which fatally marred its general usefulness, when the limited scope of its original intention had been lost sight of. The thoughts of Greece, it has been said, were greatest and most active in the line of popular action for the city and the public interest, in the discussions, the quibbles, the fallacies, and rhetorical arts of the barber's shop and the ' agora '. The aim of such exercises was to convince, to demonstrate, to persuade, to overcome ;—it might be for good and truth, but also it might not. And accordingly the Logic of Aristotle has been said to have for its end and canon the power to convince and to give demonstrative certainty. There is some ground, it may be, for this charge. The ancient logician seems to luxuriate in a rank growth of forms of sophism, and in an almost childlike fondness for variety of argumentative method. He seems resolved to trace the wayward tricks of thought and its phases through every nook and cranny, to exhaust all the permutations and complications of its elements. But let us be just, and remember that all this was in the main a speculative inquiry—for the sake of theory. It developed the powers of judgment and inference, just as the modern research for new metals, new plants, or new planets, develops the powers of observation. Both have some value in the material results they discover : but, after all, the mental culture they give is the main thing. And the talents quickened by deductive research are no whit less valuable than those owed to the other. Forms are essential, even if it be possible to make the terrible mistake of regarding them as all-important to the exclusion of matter.

And then, this is not the whole truth. There is a perfectly serious Greek science—Mathematics—a science of many branches : a science which, from Plato downwards, always stood in alliance with the studies of philosophy. Now, it might be said, perhaps with ground, that the conception of mathematical method too much dominated all attempts to get at the rationale of science, and led to the supremacy of syllogism. It would be fairer perhaps to put this objection in another shape. We should then say that the logic of Aristotle, —the *Analytics*—is too much restricted to dealing with the most general and elementary principles of reasoning. But this is not in itself a fault. It becomes a fault only where there is no growth in philosophy—when it is merely handed on from master to pupil; and where there is a tendency to put philosophic doctrine to immediate use. To expend the whole energy of intellect in laying bare the general principles, the fundamental method, of knowledge and inference, is precisely what the founder of a science has a duty to do. But the beginning thus made requires development—and development which is fruitful must proceed by correction and antithesis, no less than by positive additions. It was not given to Aristotle's logic to be so carried on. His logic, like his system in general, had no real successor to carry it on in the following generation : and when in the less original ages of early Byzantine rule it again found students, it had become a quasi-sacred text which could only be commented on, not modified and developed. From the great *Exēgētai* of Greece it passed westward to Boëthius and eastward to the Syrian and Persian commentators in the early centuries of the Caliphate. From these, and from other intermediaries, it may be, it finally culminated in the work of the Latin Schoolmen of the later Middle Ages. But the very reverence which all these expositors felt for the text of *the* Philosopher rendered true development impossible.

Then, on the other hand, the lust of practical utility caused a grave misconception of what logic can do. For Aristotle, logic is a scientific analysis of the modes of inference ; its uses are those which follow intrinsically from all noble activity freely and zealously prosecuted. But with the death of Aristotle the great days of knowledge for the sake of knowledge and divine wisdom were over. The Stoics into whose hands the chief sceptre of philosophy, directly or indirectly, passed never rose above the conception of life as a task and a duty, and of all other things, literature, science, and art, as subservient to the performance of that task. The conception is an ennobling one : but only with a relative or comparative nobility. It ennobles, if it is set beside and against the view that life is a frivolous play, a sport of caprice and selfishness. But it darkens and narrows the outlook of humanity, when it loses sight of life as a joy, a self-enlarging and self-realising freedom, of life as in its supreme phase Θεωρία—or the enjoyment of God. To the Stoic, therefore,—and to the dominant Christian theory which entered to some extent on the Stoic inheritance—logic, like the rest of philosophy, was something only valuable because ultimately it helped to save the soul.

It thus sunk into the position of an Organon or instrument. To the Stoic,—for instance to Epictetus—its value was its use to establish the doctrines of the Stoic faith, by confuting the ill-arranged and futile inferences on which were founded the aims and approvals of ordinary worldly life. To the Christian, again, it served as a method for putting into systematic shape (under the guidance of certain supreme categories or principles also borrowed from Greek thought) the variety of fundamental and derivative aspects which successive minds, pondering on the power and mystery of the Christian faith, had set forward as its essential dogmas. It thus helped to build up (out of the leading ideas of Greek metaphysics, and the principles emerging in the earliest attempts to formulate the law of Christ) that amalgam of the power of a divine life with the reflective thought of the teachers of successive generations, which constitutes the dogmatic creed of Christendom. Such a reconstruction in thought of the reality which underlies experience—(in this case the experience of the Christian life), is inevitable if man is to be man, a free intelligence, and not a mere animal-like feeling. But its success is largely, if not entirely, dependent on the value of the logic and metaphysics which it employs : and it would be a bold thing to say that the subtle, abstract, and unreal system of Neo-Platonist and Neo-Aristotelian thought was an organon adequate to cope with the breadth and depth, latent if not very explicit, in the fulness and reality of the religious life.

Yet even as an Organon, Logic had to sink to a lower rank. As traditionalism grew supreme, and religion ossified into a stereotyped form of belief and practice, logic had less to do as an organiser of dogma. It sank, or seemed to sink (for it would be rash to speak too categorically of an epoch of thought so far removed from modern sympathy and understanding as the age of the Schoolmen), into a futile (and as it seems occasionally almost a viciously-despairing) play with *pro* and *contra*,— into a lust of argumentation which in masters like Ockam comes perilously close to scepticism or agnosticism. More and more, Scholastic thought, which, at one time, had been in the centre of such intellectual life as there was, came to be stranded on the shore, while the onward-flowing tide spread in other directions. These were the great days of logical sway, when it seemed as if logic could create new truth : as if forms could beget matter. So at least ran an outside rumour, which was probably based on some amount of real folly. But the more important point was that the old logic had lost touch with reality. New problems were arising, which it was—without a profound reconstruction—quite incapable of solving. Of these there were obviously two—not unconnected perhaps, but arising in different spheres of life. There was the revival of religious experience, growing especially since the thirteenth century with an ever-swelling stream in the souls of men and women, till it burst through all bounds of outward organisation in the catastrophe of the Reformation. Luther may have been historically unjust (as Bacon afterwards was) to the ' blind heathen master ', as he called Aristotle : but he was governed by a true instinct when (unlike the compromise-loving Melanchthon) he found the traditional system of logic and metaphysics no proper organon for the new phase of faith and theory. So, too, the new attempts at an inception and instauration of the sciences grew up outside the walls of old tradition, and were at first perhaps discouraged and persecuted as infidel and heretical, and were, even without that burden, pursued at much hap-hazard and with much ignorance both in aims and methods. Intelligent onlookers,— especially if inspired by an enthusiasm for the signs of an age happier for human welfare—could not but see how needful it was to come to some understanding on the aims and methods of the rising sciences.

This want, which he keenly felt, Francis Bacon tried to satisfy. He pointed out, vaguely, but zealously and in a noble spirit, the end which that new logic had to accomplish. Bacon, however, could not do more than state these bold suggestions : he had not the power to execute them. He imagined indeed that he could display a method, by which science would make incredible advances, and the kingdom of truth in a few years come into the world. But this is a sort of thing which no man can do. Plato, if we take his *Republic* for a political pamphlet, had tried to do it for the social life of Athens. What Plato could not do for the political world of Greece, Bacon could not do for the intellectual world in his time : for as the Athenian worked under the shadow of his own state, over-mastered even without his knowledge by the ordinances of Athens, so the Englishman was evidently enthralled by the medieval conceptions and by the logic which he condemned. What Aristotle had for ages been supposed to do, no philosopher could do for the new spirit of inquiry which had risen in and before the days of Bacon. That spirit, as exhibited in his great contemporaries, Bacon, as he has himself shown, could not rightly understand or appreciate. He failed, above all, to recognise the self-corrective, tentative, and hypothetical nature, of all open inquiry. But one need not for this disparage his work.

It showed a new sense of the magnitude of the modern
problem : it set prominently forward the comprehensive
aim of human welfare : and by its conception of the ' forma'
it kept science pledged to a high ideal. But Bacon could
only play the part of the guide-post : he could not himself
lay down the road. And negatively he could warn against
the belief that mathematics could *generate* or do more
indeed than *define* the sciences. The spirit of free science,
of critical investigation, of inductive inquiry, must and
did constitute its forms, legislation, and methods for itself.
For no philosopher can lay down laws or methods before-
hand which the sciences must follow. The logician only
comes after, and, appreciating and discovering the not
always conspicuous methods of knowledge, endeavours to
gather them up and give them their proper place in the
grand total of human thought, correcting its inadequacies
by their aid, and completing their divisions by its larger
unities. Or rather this is a picture of what English logic
might have done. But it does not do so in the ordinary
and accepted text-books on the subject. What it does
do, is rather as follows. To the second and fundamental
part which it subjects to a few unimportant alterations,—
i. e. to the doctrine of terms, propositions, and reasonings,—
it subjoins an enumeration of the methods used in the
sciences.

To the rude minds of the Teutonic peoples the logical
system of Aristotle had seemed almost a divine revelation.
From the brilliant intellect of Greece a hand was stretched
to help them in the arrangement of their religious beliefs.
The Church accepted the aid of logic, foreign though logic
was to its natural bent, as eagerly as the young society
tried for a while to draw support from the ancient forms
of the Roman Empire. So with the advance of the Sciences
in modern times some hopeful spirits looked upon the
Inductive Logic of Mill in the light of a new revelation.
The vigorous action of the sciences hailed a systematic
account of its methods almost as eagerly as the strong,
but untaught intellect of the barbarian world welcomed
the lessons of ancient philosophy. For the first time the
sciences, which had been working blindly or instinctively,
but with excellent success, found their procedure stated
clearly and definitely, yet without any attempt to reduce
their varied life to the Procrustean bed of mathematics,

which had once been held to possess a monopoly of method. The enormous influence of the physical sciences saw itself reflected in a distinct logical outline : and the new logic became the dominant philosophy. Such for a while was the proud position of the Inductive Logic. Enthusiastic students of science in all countries, who were not inaccessible to wider culture, used quotations from Mill to adorn and authorise their attempts at generalisation and theory. A period of speculation in the scientific world succeeded the period of experiment, in which facts had been collected and registered. A chapter on Method became a necessary introduction to all higher scientific treatises. In our universities methodology was prodigally applied to the study of ancient philosophy. And so long as the scientific epoch lasts in its one-sided prominence, so long the theory of inductive and experimental methods may dominate the intellectual world.

But the Inductive Logic hardly rose to the due sense of its situation. It has not held to the same high ideal as Bacon set before it. It has planted itself beside what it was good enough to call the Deductive Logic, and given the latter a certain toleration as a harmless lunatic, or an old pauper who had seen better days. Retaining the latter with certain modifications, although it has now lost its meaning in the changed outlines of the intellectual world, Inductive Logic adds a methodology of the sciences, without however founding this methodology upon a comprehensive analysis of knowledge as a whole, when enlarged and enlightened by the work of the sciences. Hence the two portions,—the old logic, mutilated and severed from the Greek world it grew out of, and the new Inductive or specially-scientific logic, not going beyond a mere classification of methods,—can never combine, any more than oil and water. And the little psychology, which is some times added, does not facilitate the harmony.

But Inductive Logic should have adopted a more thorough policy. There can only be one Logic, which must be both inductive and deductive, but exclusively, and in parts, neither. To achieve that task however Logic must not turn its back indifferently on what it calls metaphysics, and it must rise to a higher conception of the problems of what it calls psychology.

In these circumstances the ordinary logic, in its fundamental terms, is more on the level of popular thought, than in a strictly scientific region, and does not attempt to unite the two regions, and examine the fundamental basis of thought on which scientific methods rest. The case of Concrete and Abstract will illustrate what has been said. To popular thought the sense-world is concrete : the intellectual world abstract. And so it is in the ordinary logic. To Hegel, on the contrary, the intellectual interpretation of the world of reality and experience is a truer and thus a more concrete description of it than that contained in a series of sense-terms. Now the difference between the two uses of the term is not a mere arbitrary change of names. When the philosopher denies the concreteness of the sense-world, and declares that it, as merely sensible, is only a mass of excluding elements, a ' manifold ', and in the second instance a series of abstractions, drawn out of this *congeries* by perception, the change of language marks the total change of position between the philosophic and the popular consciousness. Reality and concreteness as estimated by the one line of thought are the very reverse of those of the other. A mere sense-world to the philosopher is a world which wants unity, which is made up of bits imperfectly adjusted to each other, and always leading us to look for an explanation of them in sources outside them. The single things we say we perceive,—the here and the now we perceive them in—are found, upon reflection and analysis, to depend upon general laws, on relations that go beyond the single,— on what is neither here nor now, but everywhere and timeless. The reality of the thing is found to imply a general system of relations which make it what it is. Sense-perception in short is the beginning of knowledge : and it begins by taking up its task piecemeal. It rests upon a felt totality : and to raise this to an intelligible totality, it must at first only isolate one attribute at a time.

The apprehension of a thing from one side or aspect,— the apprehension of one thing apart from its connexions, —the retention of a term or formula apart from its context,—is what Hegel terms ' abstract '. Ordinary terms are essentially abstract. They spring from the analysis of something which would, in the first stage of the process, in strictness be described not as concrete, but as chaos :— as the indefinite or ' manifold ' of sensation. But the first conceptions, which spring from this group when it is analysed, are abstract : they are each severed from the continuity of their reality. To interpret our feeling, our experience as felt, we must break it up. But the first face that presents itself is apt to impress us unduly, and seems more real, because nearer feeling : on the other it is more unreal, because less adequate as a total expression of the felt unity. In the same sense we call Political Economy an abstract science, because it looks upon man as a money-making and money-distributing creature, and keeps out of sight his other qualities. Our notions in this way are more abstract or more concrete, according as our grasp of thought extends to less or more of the relations which are necessarily pre-supposed by them. On the other hand, when a term of thought owns and emphasises its solidarity with others, when it is not circumscribed to a single relation, but becomes a focus in which a variety of relations converge, when it is placed in its right post in the organism of thought, its limits and qualifications as it were recognised and its degree ascertained,—then that thought is rendered ' concrete '. A concrete notion is a notion in its totality, looking before and after, connected indissolubly with others : a unity of elements, a meeting-point of opposites. An abstract notion is one withdrawn from everything that naturally goes along with it, and enters into its constitution. All this is no disparagement of abstraction. To abstract is a necessary stage in the process of knowledge. But it is equally necessary to insist on the danger of clinging, as to an ultimate truth, to the pseudo-simplicity of abstraction, which forgets altogether what it is in certain situations desirable for a time to overlook.

In a short essay, with much grim humour and quaint illustrations, Hegel tried to show what was meant by the name ' abstract ', which in his use of it denotes the cardinal vice of the ' practical ' habit of mind. From this essay, entitled ' Who is the Abstract Thinker ? ' [1] it may be interesting to quote a few lines. ' A murderer is, we may suppose, led to the scaffold. In the eyes of the multitude he is a murderer and nothing more. The ladies perhaps may make the remark that he is a strong, handsome, and interesting man. At such a remark the populace is horri-

[1] ' Wer denkt abstrakt ? ' (*Vermischte Schriften*, vol. ii. p. 402.)

fied. ' What ! a murderer handsome ? Can anybody's
mind be so low as to call a murderer handsome ? You
must be little better yourselves.' And perhaps a priest
who sees into the heart, and knows the reasons of things,
will point to this remark, as evidence of the corruption of
morals prevailing among the upper classes. A student of
character, again, inquires into the antecedents of the
criminal's up-bringing : he finds that he owes his existence
to ill-assorted parents ; or he discovers that this man has
suffered severely for some trifling offence, and that under
the bitter feelings thus produced he has spurned the rules
of society, and cannot support himself otherwise than by
crime. No doubt there will be people who when they
hear this explanation will say "Does this person then
mean to excuse the murderer ? ' In my youth I remember
hearing a city magistrate complain that book-writers were
going too far, and trying to root out Christianity and good
morals altogether. Some one, it appeared, had written
a defence of suicide. It was horrible ! too horrible ! On
further inquiry it turned out that the book in question
was the *Sorrows of Werther*.

' By abstract thinking, then, is meant that in the murderer we see nothing but the simple fact that he is a murderer,
and by this single quality annihilate all the human nature
which is in him. The polished and sentimental world of
Leipsic thought otherwise. They threw their bouquets,
and twined their flowers round the wheel and the criminal
who was fastened to it.—But this also is the opposite pole of
abstraction.—It was in a different strain that I once heard
a poor old woman, an inmate of the workhouse, rise above
the abstraction of the murderer. The sun shone, as the
severed head was laid upon the scaffold. " How finely,"
said the woman, " does God's gracious sun lighten up
Binder's head ! " We often say of a poor creature who
excites our anger that he is not worth the sun shining on
him. That woman saw that the murderer's head was in
the sunlight, and that it had not become quite worthless.
She raised him from the punishment of the scaffold into
the sunlit grace of God. It was not by wreaths of violets or
by sentimental fancies that she brought about the reconciliation : she saw him in the sun above received into grace.

CHAPTER XXII

FROM SENSE TO THOUGHT

INDUCTION and Experience are names to which is often assigned the honour of being the source of all our knowledge. But what induction and experience consist in, is what we are supposed to be already aware of ; and that is—it may be briefly said—the concentration of the felt and sense-given fragments into an intimate unity. The accidents and fortunes that have befallen us in lapses of time, the scenes that have been set before and around us in breadths of space, are condensed into a mood of mind, a habitual shading of judgment, or frame of thought. The details of fact re-arrange themselves into a general concept ; their essence gets distilled into a concentrated form. Their meaning disengages itself from its embodiment, and floats as a self-sustaining form in an ideal world. Thus if we look at the larger process of history, we see every period trying to translate the sensuous fact of its life into a formula of thought, and to fix it in definite characters. The various parts of existence, and existence as a whole, are stripped of their sensible or factual nature, in which we originally feel and come into contact with them, and are reduced to their simple equivalents in terms of thought. From sense and immediate feeling there is, in the first place, generated an image or idea which at least represents and stands for reality ; and from that, in the second place, comes a thought or notion proper, which holds the facts in unity.

The phenomenon may, perhaps, be illustrated by the case of numbers. To the adult European, numbers and numbering are an obvious and essential part of our scheme of things that seems to need no special explanation. But the experience of children suggests its artificiality, and the evidence from the history of language corroborates that surmise. If number be in a way describable as part of the sense-experience, or total impression, it certainly does not come upon us with the same passivity on our part as the

perception of taste or colour, or even of shape. It postulates
a higher grade of activity. As Plato says, it ' awakes the
intelligence ' : it implies a question and looks forward to
an answer : it is thus the first appearance of what in its
later fulness will be called ' Dialectic '. To put it otherwise : Numbering can only proceed where there is a unit,
and an identity : it implies a one, and it implies an infinite
repetibility of that one.[1] It thus postulates the double
mental act, first of reducing the various to its basis of
identity, and, secondly, of performing a synthesis of the
identical units thus created. In the highly artificial world
in which we live all this seems simple enough. The products
of machinery, articles of furniture, dress, &c., &c., are
already uniform items : and the strokes of a clock seem
almost to invite summation. But in free nature this
similarity is much less obviously stamped on things : and
the products of primitive art—of literal *manu*-facture—
display an individuality, an element of personal taste, even,
which is necessarily lacking in things turned out by machinery. Thus it was necessary, before we could number, to
reduce the qualitatively different to a quantitative equality
or comparability. There are indeed some instances, in
that nearest of things to us, the human body, which might
help. There is the obvious similarity of organs and limbs
which go in pairs, and which might easily suggest a dual,
as, so to speak, a sensuous fact amongst other facts. Again,
there is the hand and its five fingers, or the two hands and
the ten fingers. The five or ten, as a whole naturally given,
suggest a grouping of numbers in natural aggregates. The
fingers, again, (and here we may keep at first to the fingers
proper, minus the thumb,) may be without much ingenuity
said to give us a set of four, naturally distinct, yet naturally
alike, and needing, so to speak, the minimum of intelligence
to create the numerical scale from one to four. It is by
them, indeed, that Plato, it may be unconsciously, illustrates the genesis of number. Here in short you have the
natural abacus of the nations, but one restricted, first,
perhaps to the group 1–4, secondly to the group 1–10.

We have seen how the dual was, in certain instances,
almost a natural perceptive fact. But when it is so en-
visaged, it is hardly recognised as number strictly so called.
It is only a fresh and peculiar sensuous attribute of things :

[1] See vol. ii. p. 190 (*Logic*, § 102).

a thing which has the quality of duplication, not a thought which is the synthesis of two identical units. It is a sort of accident, not part of a regular system or series. So again with the plural, which may appear in several shapes before it is assigned to its proper place as a systematic function of the singular. If the Malay, in order to say ' the king of all apes ' has to enumerate one after another the several sub-species of ape, or if to express ' houses ' he has to reduplicate the singular, to insert a word meaning ' all ' or ' many ', we can see that the conception of number is for him still in the bonds of sense. It is not a synthetic category, but only a material multitude. But in other cases the plural proper is almost confounded with the so-called ' collective '. It is not an unfamiliar fact in Greek and Latin that the plural has acquired a meaning of its own, —not the mere multiple of its singular ; as also that the collective term is occasionally used as an abstract, occasion-ally as the more or less indeterminate collection of the individuals. Such plurals and such collectives represent a stage of language and conception when the aggregate of singulars form a uniquely-qualified case of the object. And the peculiarity of them is seen in the way the plurality is immersed in and restricted to the special class of objects : as e. g. when in English the plurality of a number of ships is verbally stereotyped as against the plurality of a number of sheep, or of partridges (fleet, flock, covey). In such instances the category of number is completely pervaded and modified by the quality of the objects it is applied to. So, in the Semitic languages, the so-called ' broken plural ' is a quasi-collective, which grammatically counts as a feminine singular (like so many Latin and Greek collectives) : and whereas the more regular plural is generally shown by separable affix, this quasi-collective plural enters the very body of the word by vowel-change, indicating as it were by this absorption the constitution of a specifically new view of things. On the other hand, it may be said, there is in this collective a trace of the emergence of the universal and identical element through the generalisation due to the conjunction of several similars all acting as one.[1]

In a true plural, on the contrary, it is required that the sign of number be clearly eliminated from any peculiarities of its special object, and be distinctly separated from the

[1] See Max Müller in *Mind*, vol. i. 345.

collective. And similarly the true numeral has to be realised in its abstractness, as a category *per se*. And to do this requires some amount of abstraction. In Greek, for example, we meet the distinction between numbers in the abstract, pure numbers (such as four and six), and bodily or physical numbers (such as four men, six trees).[1] The geometrical aspect under which numbers were regarded by the Greeks, e. g. as oblong or square numbers, bears in the same direction. But another phenomenon in language tells the tale more distinctly.[2] Abundantly in Sanscrit and Greek, more rarely in Zend and Teutonic, and here and there in the Semitic languages, we meet with what is known as the dual number, a special grammatical form intended to express a pair of objects. The witty remark of Du Ponceau [3] concerning the Greek dual, that it had apparently been invented only for lovers and married people, may illustrate its uses, but hardly suffices to explain its existence in language. But a comparison of barbarian dialects serves to show that the dual is, as it were, a prelude to the plural,—a first attempt to grasp the notion of plurality in a definite way, which served its turn in primitive society, but afterwards disappeared, when the plural had been developed, and the numerals had attained a form of their own. If this be so, the dual is what physiologists call a rudimentary organ, and tells the same story as these organs do of the processes of nature.

The language of the Melanesian island of Annatom, one of the New Hebrides, may be taken as an instance of a state of speech in which the dual is natural. That language possesses a fourfold distinction of number in its personal pronouns, a different form to mark the singular, dual, trial, and plural : and the pronoun of the first person plural distinguishes in addition whether the person addressed is or

---

[1] Pure number is ἀριθμὸς μοναδικός : applied number is ἀριθμὸς φυσικός or σωματικός. Aristotle, *Metaph.* N. 5, speaks of ἀριθμὸς πύρινος ἢ γήϊνος. But this is only Greek idiom : as we say ' Greek history ' instead of ' History of Greece ', or vice versa, when we translate *Populus Romanus* by ' people of Rome '. Aristotle is speaking of ' proportions ' or ' amounts ' of fire or earth in the compounds of these elements.

[2] See L. Geiger, *Ursprung und Entwickelung der menschlichen Sprache und Vernunft* (vol. i. p. 380). And Gabelenz (' Die melanesischen Sprachen ') in the *Abhandlungen der Sächsischen Gesellschaft der Wissenschaften* (VIII), 1861, pp. 89–91.

[3] *Mémoire sur le système grammatical*, &c. p. 155.

is not included in the ' we-two ', ' we-three,' or ' we-many '
of the speaker.[1]   The same language however possesses only
the first three numerals, and in the translation of the Bible
into this dialect it was necessary to introduce the English
words, four, five, &c.   The two facts must be taken together :
the luxuriance of the personal pronouns and the scanty
development of numerals in such languages are two phenomena of the same law.   The numeral ' four ' to these tribes
is said to bear the meaning of ' many ' or ' several '.   Another
fact points in the same direction.   In many languages, such
as those of China, Further India and Mexico, it is customary
in numbering to use what W. von Humboldt has called
class-words.   Here it is felt that an artificial unity has to be
created, a common denominator found, and all reduced to
it, before any summation can be carried out.   Scholars and
officials, in Chinese, can only be classed under the rubric of
' jewel ' or dignity :   and animals or fish by ' tails ', as if
thereby only could one get a handle to hold them and
count them.   (The idiom still lingers in western languages :
as in English, heads of cabbage, or of cattle : or German,
sechs Mann Soldaten.)   So in Malay, instead of ' five boys '
the phrase used is ' boy five-man ' : in other words, the
numerals are supposed to inhere as yet in objects of a special
kind or common occurrence.[2]   And among the South Sea
Islanders the consciousness of number is decidedly personal :
that is to say, the distinction between one and two is first
conceived as a distinction between ' I ' and ' we two '.
Even this amount of simplification surpasses what is found
amongst some Australian tribes.   There we find four duals :
one for brothers and sisters : one for parents and children :
one for husbands and wives : and one between brothers-in-
law.[3]   Each pair has a different form.   We thus seem to see
to what early language is applied : not to designate the
objects of nature, but the members of the primitive family
and their interests.   The consciousness of numbers was

[1] Cf. *nous* and *nous autres*.   The same distinction is found in
some American languages.   There is a dual in the language of the
Greenlanders ; but it is not, however, used when a natural duality
seems to call for it, but in cases when, though there might have
been several things, only two are actually found.

[2] W. von Humboldt, *Verschiedenheit des menschlichen Sprachbaues*,
p. 423 (ed. 1841) ; Misteli, *Typen des Sprachbaues* (1893).

[3] Capt. Grey, *Vocabulary of the dialects of S. W. Australia*, pp. xxi
and 104 (1840).

first awakened by the need of distinguishing and combining
the things that belonged to and specially interested men and
women in the narrow circle of barbarian life.[1] It is not
altogether imaginative in principle, though it may be
occasionally surmise in details, to connect the rise of grammatical forms with the temperament and character of the
people, and therefore with its social organisation. If the
Bantoo or Caffir languages of Southern Africa instead of
a single third personal pronoun and third personal termina-
tion to the verb use the separate forms corresponding to the
ten class-prefixes of the nouns, it must be in accordance
with the general spirit and system of these tribes. The
various plural forms, if they persist, will reflect contemporary modes of life.

Numbers were at first immersed in the persons, and then,
as things came to be considered also, in the things numbered.
The mind seems to have proceeded slowly from the vague
one to definite numbers. And the first decided step was
taken towards an apprehension of numbers when two was
distinguished from one, and the distinction was made part
of the personal terminations. The plural was a further
step in the same direction : the real value of which, however,
did not become apparent until the numerals had been
separately established in forms of their own. When that
was accomplished, the special form of the dual became
useless : it had outlived its purpose, and henceforth it
ceased to have any but that poetical beauty of old association which often adorns the once natural, but now obsolete
growths of the past. When the numerals were thus
emancipated from their material and sensuous environment,
quantity was translated from outward being in its embodi-
ments into a form of thought. At first, indeed, it was
placed in an ethereal or imaginative space, the counterpart
as it were of the sensuous space in which it had been
previously immersed. It became a denizen of the mental
region, as it had been before a habitant of the sense-world.

The mind was informed with quantity in the shape of
number : but it does not follow from this, that the new
product was comprehended, or the process of its production

---

[1] The sharp distinction between the first and second personal
pronouns and the third : the want of any apparent connexion in
the Indo-Germanic languages between the first and second persons
singular and the plural form seems to point in the same direction.

kept in view. Like all new inventions (and numeration may fairly be classed under that head), it was laid hold of, and all its consequences, results, and uses estimated and realised by the practical and defining intellect. In one direction, it became, like many new inventions in the early days of society, a magic charm, and was invested with mystery, sacredness, and marvellous powers. But the intelligent mind,—the understanding,—resolved to make better use of the new instrument : and that in two ways, in practical work and in theory. On the one hand it was applied practically in the dealings of life,—in commerce, contracts, legislation, and religion. On the other hand, the new conception of number, which common sense and the instinctive action of men had evolved, was carried out in all its theory : it was analysed in all directions, and its elements combined in all possible ways. The result was the science of arithmetic, and mathematics in general. Such consequences did the reflective understanding derive from the analysis of its datum,—the fact of quantity freed from its sensuous envelope.

The general action of understanding, and of practical thought, is of this kind. It accepts the representative images which have emerged from sensation, as they occur : and tries to appreciate them, to give them precision, to carry them into details, and to analyse them until their utmost limits of meaning are explored. Where they have come from, and where they lead to,—the process out of which they spring, and which fixes the extent of their validity,—are questions of no interest to the understanding.[1] It takes its objects, as given in popular conception, as fixed and ultimate entities to be expounded in detail.

We have taken number as one example of the transference of a sensible or sense-immersed fact into a form of thought : but a form which is still placed in a superior or mental space. One advantage of taking number as illustration, is that numbered things are distinguished from numbers in an emphatic and recognised way. Nobody will dispute that the abstraction, as it is called, has an existence of its own, and can be made a legitimate object of independent investigation. But if the process be more obvious in the case of the numerals, there must have been a similar course of development leading to the pronouns,

[1] Cf. vol. ii. *Notes and Illustrations*, p. 400.

the prepositions, and the auxiliary verbs—to what has been called the ' formal ' or ' pronominal ' or ' demonstrative ' element, the connective and constructive tissue of language. Whether these pronominal 'roots' form a special and originally-distinct class of their own, or are derived from a transmutation of more material or substantial elements, is a question on which linguistic research casts as yet no very certain light.   It is true that on the one hand etymology is mainly silent on the origin of pronouns, numerals, and the more fundamental prepositions (i. e. cannot refer them to roots significant of qualitative being) : and one need not lay much stress on remarks, like that of Gabelenz,[1] that in the Indo-Chinese languages the words for *I, five, fish* have a like sound, as do those for *thou, two, ear,* or that *I am,* originally means *I breathe.*   In all languages—though with immense diversities of degree, this formal element has attained a certain independence.   And in many instances we can more or less trace the process by which there grew up in language an independent world of thought : we can see the natural existence passing out of the range of the senses into spiritual relations.   Before our eyes a world of reason is slowly constituting itself in the history of culture : and we, who live now, enter upon the inheritance which past ages have laid up for us.

There is, however, a difference between the way in which these results look to us now, and the way in which they originally organised themselves.   The child who begins to learn a language in the lesson-books and the grammars finds the members of it all, as it were, upon one level : adjectives, adverbs, prepositions, and verbs confront him with the same authority and rank.   This appearance is deceptive : it may easily suggest that the words are not members in an organism, in and out of which they have developed.   And this organism of thought has its individual types, expressed in the great families of human speech. Its generic form (as drawn out in a logical system) appears in different grades, with different degrees of fulness, in Altaic and Dravidian from what it does in Malay, or in Chinese, and these again have their own predominant categories as compared with those used in the American or African languages, or in Indo-Germanic and Semitic.   If the Altaic languages e. g. are wanting in the verb proper,

[1] *Die Sprachwissenschaft*, p. 168.

and manage with possessive suffixes and nouns ; if the Semitic tenses display a poverty which contrasts with their wealth in Greek ; and yet each group performs its function, we may infer that each speech has a complete organism, though it does not bring all its parts to adequate expression. All this distinction of ' parts of speech ', of forms, prefixes and suffixes, &c., is part of the life of language, embodying in more or less distinct organs the organisation of thought in the individual form it reached in that speech-type.   Thus in Chinese there are strictly speaking no isolated words, nouns, or verbs : there are only abstract parts of a concrete sentence ; and grammar in Chinese therefore has no acci-dence (no declensions, conjugations, &c.) but only syntax. Yet it is these abstract fragments which exist and seem to have independence and inherent meaning : whereas the unity in which they cohere to form a concrete context is the fleeting sentence of the moment.   At the opposite extreme, again, the Mexican family of languages tend to incorporate relations to subject and object with the verb, in such a degree that the word almost becomes a sentence. Facts like these suggest that a science of the forms of language, in proportion as it generalises, tends to approach logic ; and that logic will have a converse tendency to elevate to an unduly typical position the grammatical form of the languages with which the logician is best acquainted.

If these points were remembered, there would be less absurd employment of the grammatical categories of one group of languages to systematise another. Greek and Sanscrit grammar plays sad havoc with the organism of a Semitic tongue, and it is not less out of place as a schema for delineating e. g. South African dialect.   Isolated words even in an Indo-Germanic language—even, we may say, in such a language as English—are still fractional, and do not get life and individuality except in their context.   And it needs but a little experience to show how various that individuality may be.   It needs perhaps still more medita-tion to realise that it is in this individuality that the real life of language lies : in the words said and written to express the thought of a personality.   But, first, because language has its material and mechanical side, and secondly, because in civilised countries it further acquires a more stereotyped mechanism in written and printed language, its parts tend to gain a pseudo-independence.   It is one aim of a philosophical dictionary to restore the organic interconnexion which in the mere sequence of vocables in juxtaposition is apt to be lost. What we call the meaning of a word is something which carries us beyond that mere word,—which restores the connexions which have been broken off and forgotten. In the form of a dictionary, of course, this can only be done piece-meal: but if each piece is done thoroughly, it can hardly fail to bring out certain comprehensive connexions. The mere word seems a simple thing; and one is at first disposed to get rid of its difficulty by substituting a so-called synonym. But a deeper study reveals the fact that an exact synonym is a thing one can no more find than two peas which are absolutely indistinguishable. A synonym is only a practical *pis aller*. But every word is really as it were a point in an infinitely complex organic life, with its essence or meaning determined by the currents to and fro which meet in it.

Words as we see them *prima facie* in a printed page do look separate entities. They stand, one here and another there, in a quasi-extension, with marks of direction and connexion pointing from one to another, but of connexion apparently extraneous to the more solid points which are represented by nouns and verbs, or names of substances, actions, and attributes. Results, as they are, of that practical analysis which the need of writing down language has led to, they are treated as complete wholes, which by the speaker are forced into certain temporary connexions. But this is an illusion which, because a thing changes its relationships, assumes that it can exist out of all relationships whatever. Every word of Language is such an abstraction, isolated from its context. But amid these contexts there are certain similarities: identical elements are detected: and these identical elements are the common names of language, the terms of general significance. In all cases, however, what an utterance of language describes or expresses is a definite individual event or scene, conceived as a concrete of several parts. Each separate vocable is a contribution to the total: a step towards the real redintegration of the whole out of its several parts. But the total itself—the content of fact in any single sentence—is only an abstraction,—a part of the universe which human interest and need have isolated from the comprehensive scope of things. Thus, in two degrees, we may say, the picture produced in the sentence falls short of the truth of things. Each statement is an arbitrary or accidental cutting out of the totality : each element of the cutting is dependent on that abstraction, and relative to it. But—as in a given group of speech, the same sets of circumstances will naturally be selected, and tend to recur again and again, —the terms which describe them will acquire a certain association with the objects, and will come to be called the common names of these agents, acts, and qualities. They denote or ' represent ' the things and acts, conceived how- ever in certain aspects and relations, and not in their entirety and totality of nature.

In this product of intellectual movement above the limits of sensation we have the ' representation ' [1] as Hegel calls it, on which the Understanding turns its forces. We have one product of the organic whole of thought taken by itself as if it were independent, set forth as a settled nucleus for further acquaintance : and this one point discussed fully and with precision, elaborated in all detail and conse- quence, to the neglect of its context, and the necessary limitations involved in the notion. The process of name- giving may illustrate this tendency in human thought to touch its objects only in one point. The names given to objects do not embrace the whole nature of these objects, but give expression only to one striking feature in them. Thus the name of the horse points it out as ' the strong ' or ' the swift ' : the moon is ' the measurer ' or ' the shining one ' ; and so in all cases. The object as expressed in these names is viewed from one aspect, or in one point : and the name, which originally at least corresponds to the concep- tion, meets the object, properly speaking, on that side only, or in that relation. The object is not studied in its own nature, and in its total world, but as it specially enters the range of human interest, and serves human utilities. One can at least guess why it should be so : why a name should, in logical language, express an ' accidens ' and not the ' essentia ' of the object. For the investigation of primitive language seems to show that words, as we know them in separate existence, are a secondary formation : and that the first significant speech was an utterance intended to describe a scene, an action, a phenomenon, or complex of event. In point of time, the primary fact of language is

[1] ' Vorstellung,' as distinguished from ' Begriff '

an agglomeration or aggregate,—we may call it either word
or clause (λόγος, in short)—which describes in one breath
a highly individualised action or phenomenon.   The spirit
or unifying principle in this group might be the accent.
Such a word-group denotes a highly specialised form of
being : and if we call it a word, we may say that the
earliest words, and the words of barbarous tribes, are
ingeniously special.[1]   But it would be more correct to say,
that in such a group the elements of the scene enter only
from a single aspect or in a single relation.   Accordingly
when disintegration begins, the result is as follows.   The
elements of the group, having now become independent
words held together by the syntax of the sentence, are adopted
to denote the several objects which entered into the total
phenomenon.   But these words, or fragments of the word-
group, ' represent ' the objects in question from a certain
point of view, and not in their integrity.   The names of
things therefore touch them only in one point, and express
only one aspect.   And thus, although different names will
arise for the same thing, as it enters into different groups,
in each case the name will connote only a general attribute
and not the nature of the thing.   These names are in the
Hegelian sense of the term ' abstract '.   In popular phraseology, they are only ' signs ' of things : i. e. not ' symbols '
(though they may have been in some cases symbolic in
origin), for in a symbol there is a *natural* correspondence or
sensible analogy to the thing symbolised, but something
' instituted ', due to an ' understanding ' or convention.

  [1] Thus in Malay, there are about twenty words for *strike*, according
as it is done with thick or thin wood, downwards, horizontally, or
upwards, with the hand, with the fist, with the flat hand, with
a club, with the sharp edge, with a hammer, &c. (See Misteli,
Typen des Sprachbaues, p. 265.)

CHAPTER XXIII

FIGURATE OR REPRESENTATIVE THOUGHT

THE compensating dialectic whereby reason, under the guise of imagination, overthrows the narrowness of popular estimates, makes itself observed even in the popular use of the terms abstract and concrete. Terms like state, mind, wealth, may from one point of view be called abstract, from another concrete. At a certain pitch these abstractions cease to be abstract, and become even to popular sense very concrete realities. In the tendency to personification in language we see the same change from abstract to concrete : as when Virtue is called a goddess, or Fashion surnamed the despot of womankind. In such instances, imagination, more or less in the service of art and religion, upsets the narrow vulgar estimates of reality. But it upsets them, so to speak, by giving to the abstraction (through its creative power) that sensuous concreteness which the mere abstract lacks and which the ordinary mind alone recognises as real. It ' stoops to conquer '. Such a representation is, as Hegel says,[1] ' the synthetic combination of the Universal and Individual : ' ' synthetic,' because not their free, spontaneous, and essential unity, but the supreme product of the artistic will and hand, which, rather than let the universal perish by neglect, build for it, the eternal and omnipresent, ' a temple made with hands.' In mythology we can see the same process : by which, as it is phrased, an abstract term becomes concrete : by which, as we may more correctly say, a thought is transformed into, or rather stops short at, a representative picture. The many gods of polytheism are the fixed and solidified shapes in which the several degrees of religious growth have taken ' a local habitation and a name ' : or they bear witness to the failure of the greater part of the world to grasp the idea of Deity in its unity and totality apart from certain local and temporary conditions. So, too, terms like force, law, matter,—the abstractions of

[1] *Werke*, ii. 529, 555.

the mere popular mind—are by certain periods reduced to the level of sensuous things, and spoken of as real entities, somewhere and somehow existent, apart from the thinking medium to which they belong. Such terms, again, as property, wealth, truth, are popularly identified with the objects in which they are for the time and place manifested or embodied.

In these ways the abstract, in the ordinary meaning, becomes in the ordinary meaning concrete. The distinction between abstract and concrete is turned into a distinction between understanding and sense, instead of, as Hegel makes it, a distinction in the adequacy and completeness of thought itself. Thought (the Idea), as has been more than once pointed out, is the principle of unification or unification itself : it is organisation plus the consciousness of organisation : it is the unifier, the unity, and the unified, —subject as well as object, and eternal copula of both. An attempt is at first made in two degrees to represent the thought in terms of the senses as a sort of superior or higher-class sensible. When the impossibility of that attempt is seen, common sense ends by denying what it has learned to call the super-sensible altogether. These three plans may be called respectively the mythological, the metaphysical, and the positive or nominalist fallacies of thought. In the mythological, or strictly anthropomorphic fallacy, thought is conceived under the bodily shape and the physical qualities of humanity, as a separate unifying, controlling, synthetic agent, through whose interference the several things, otherwise dead and motionless, acquire a semblance of life and action, though in reality but puppets or marionettes : that is to say, it is identified with a subject of like passions with ourselves, a repetition of the particular human personality, with its narrowness and weakness. The action of the Idea is here replaced by the agency of supposed living beings, invested with superhuman powers. In the metaphysical or realist fallacy we have a feeble ghostly reproduction of the mythological. The living personal deity is replaced by a faint scare-crow of abstract deity. The cause of the changes that go on in nature is now attributed to indwelling sympathies and animosities, to the abhorrence of a vacuum, to selection, affinity, and the like : to essences and laws conceived of as somehow existent in a mystic space and

time. In the positive or nominalist fallacy, the failure
of these two theories begins to be felt : and the mind,
which had only heard of unifying reason under these two
phases and is meanwhile sure of its sense-perceptions,
treats the objective synthesis as a dream and a delusion.
Or, at best, it regards the synthesis as essentially subjective—as a complementary idealising activity of ours
which ekes out the defects of reality, and brings continuity
into the discontinuous. Our thought—(it is only *our*
thought)—is but an instrument, distinct from us and from
the reality : yet acting as a bridge to connect these two
opposing shores—a bridge, however, which does not really
reach the other side, but only an artificial image, which
simulates to us, and will for ever simulate, the inaccessible
reality. This last view is the utterance of the popular
matter-of-fact reason, when in weariness and tedium it
turns from the attempt to grasp thought pure and simple,
and instead of reducing the metaphysical antitheses to the
transparent unity of comprehension, relapses into mere
acceptance of a given reality.

In some of these cases the full step into pure thought
is never made. The creations of mythology, for example,
display an unfinished and baffled attempt to rise from
the separation of sense to the unity and organisation of
thought. The gods of heathenism are only individuals—
and individuals only *meant to be,* and by the act of faith
and devotion set forth as reality before the worshipper :
but they are individuals in which imagination embodies
a unified and centralised system of forces or principles.
They *mean* the powers of nature and of mind, but the
sceptre in their hands is only a sign of power attributed
by the believer ; and far away, encompassing alike them
and him, is the great relentless necessity. In other cases
there is a relapse : when the higher stage of thought has
been attained, it is instantaneously lost. Terms which are
really thoughts are again reduced to the level of the things
of sense, individualised in some object, which, though it is
only a representation or sign, is allowed to usurp the place
of the thought which it but partially and by extraneous
institution embodies. The intuition of the sensuous
imagination at every step throws its spells on the products
of thought, and turns them into a representative picture,
which in popular use and wont occupies the place of the

notion.   Instead of being retained in their native timeless-
ness, the terms of the Idea are brought under the laws of
Sense-perception, under the conditions of space and time.

The term 'representation', which Hegel employs to
name these picture-thoughts or figurate conceptions,
corresponds to the facts of their nature.   A 'representation' is one of two things : either a particular thing sent
out accredited with general functions, or a universal
narrowed down into a particular thing.   Thus, as it has
been seen, a general name implies or connotes a universal
relation or attribute, but confines it to denote a particular
object or class.   'Swift,' for example, was an epithet tied
down to express the horse.   In the first instance we may
suppose the name to be a sort of metaphor : differing only
by its simplicity and frequency of suggestion from those
endless epithets, which in Norse or Arabic poetry veil and
adorn the object which they are meant to designate.
That is, we conceive the object as an embodiment or representation of the quality, as an eagle is the emblem of
strength : only in the latter case we distinguish between
the object and its metaphorical signification.   In the
second place, however, the object of experience is allowed
completely to coincide with the aspect discriminated by the
selective epithet, and we can no longer in ordinary thought
separate the imaging object from the general relation
which it images forth.   This is the level of thought to
which Hegel appropriates the term 'representation'.   It
includes under it the three fallacies of thought already
noted :—and saves the trouble of comprehending the
reality.   In the Hegelian sense, a representation is abstract ;
because it solidifies, hardens, and isolates the term of
thought, makes it a particular, and never rises above the
single case to the general notion embodied in it.

The world of representative thought is a world of independent points in juxtaposition, which we arrange as
seems best to us.   It lies in an undefinable borderland
between us and things.   It is a would-be, but not an
actual, reality.   It is not like a true Idea—the unity of
subjective and objective : but only a make-believe.   We
have put it there, and yet we credit it with an effective
existence.   When our mind moves amongst these picture-
thoughts, it can only institute external relations between
the terms.   A judgment, in that case, is interpreted to

mean the conjunction of two terms, which at once step
into the rank of subject and predicate by means of the
copula. A sentence is an arrangement of words *ab extra*
in conscious or unconscious conformity with the rules of
grammar. The world of knowledge, or the Idea, as a whole
is turned into a plane surface with its typical terms,—the
members of the organism of reason,—like dots put in
co-ordination and juxtaposition, not spontaneously affected
towards each other. Even if they are not embodied and
reduced to a sensuous level of existence, they are held to
be originally separate and unconnected. How they all
came into being, and whether they do not all by gradations
and differentiation proceed from one root, are questions
neither asked nor answered.

The level of representative thinking—thinking i. e.
which is not the grasp (*Begriff*) of the reality, but only
the apprehension of something which stands for and
represents it—is the level on which we all come, more or
less, to stand in our non-philosophic moments. It is, in
essentials, the realm of what Plato called δόξα,—the level
of consciousness which fails to rise to see the unity of
essence in the many single goods and beauties, which holds
its knowledge (such as it is) at the mercy of accidents, not
bound by the conclusions of reasoning,—the realm which
is not without reality, but an immature and uncertain
reality. It is, in essentials, the same as what, as opposed
to *intellectus*, Spinoza styled *imaginatio*. Imagination, to
Spinoza, is an understanding under the bondage of particular passions and temporary interests, which loses sight
of the great bond of being or *Substantia*, and fixes its
glance on the parts in subordinate and infra-essential
relationships : which is always finite, i. e. never really
comprehensive and self-sustaining in its view, but always
limited by a tacit reference to something outside itself.
The ' Representation ' is the idea, in the loose and inexact
use of that word, which goes with the phrase *mere idea*,—
i. e. a mere mental image, which is not the reality, though
it is believed to do duty for and to represent it.[1] Yet it is
not a mere thought : rather its whole aim and meaning
is to refer to reality, to suggest it, to bring it nearer us.

---

[1] Hegel's *Werke*, ii. 431 : '*Wobei das Selbst nur repräsentirt* und
vorgestellt ist, da ist es nicht wirklich : wo es vertreten ist, ist es
nicht.' Cf. *ib.* 416.

Its fault is that it is an imperfect, partial, one-sided, or
even one-pointed idea. It is really an instance and phase
of the *ignava ratio*, to which a date or name serves as a
ποῦ στῶ of explanation.

> ' At Kilne there was no weathercock,
> And that 's the reason why.'

Such ' representation ', according to Hegel, is, e. g., the
mode of intelligence accessible to those who cling to the
mere, or abstractly, religious mood, and who cannot or will
not rise to the comprehension of their creed. Its facts
or dogmas present themselves to such a restricted conception as the parts of a picture or the stages of a history,
in visible or imaginatively-construable space, and in a
succession of times. The essence of religion, of course, for
Hegel as for other exponents of its inmost nature, is a feeling
of certitude or faith which transcends the gulfs and separations of the secular consciousness, which sees with the
believing soul the inner peace, the absolute harmony of
the true reality. *Pectus facit theologum.* The sense of
utter dependence on God, in complete identity with the
sense of absolute independence in God—that strength of
faith is the very life of religion. But when religion seeks
to give an intelligent expression of her faith, when she
tries to give a reason acceptable to the outside world, she
is apt, unless specially trained in the high things of the
spirit, to base her creed not on the rock of ages, but on
the signs and miracles of the times. She has tried to
theorise the faith : but, although her faith may be sound
and true, the religious spirit, unless it be also the spirit
of wisdom and reasoned truth, runs a risk of falling into
the fallacy of *Post hoc, ergo propter hoc.* She descends
therefore to the region of representation : she uses the
language of sense and analogy ; she presents the spiritual
under the guise of the natural. Yet in her heart of hearts
these things are only a parable,—they are but

> ' Flesh and blood
> To which she links a truth divine '.

Hegel—in the introduction to his lectures on the Philosophy of Religion—is reported to have given the following
characteristics of ' representation '. (*a*) It is still tram-
meled by the senses. Thought and sensation strive for
the mastery in it. Thought is bound fast to an illustration :

and of this illustration it cannot as representative thought divest itself :—the eternally living idea is chained to the transient and perishable form of sense. It is metaphorical and material thinking, which is helpless without the metaphor and the matter. (b) Representative thought envisages what is timeless and infinite under the conditions of time and space. It loses sight of the moral and spirit of historical development under the semblance of the names, incidents, and forms in which it is displayed. The historical and philosophical sense is lost under the antiquarian. Representative thought keeps the shell, and throws away the kernel. (c) The terms by which such a materialised thought describes its objects are not internally connected : each is independent of the other ; and we only bring them together for the occasion by an act of subjective arrangement.[1]

The thing—the so-called *subject* of the properties, of which it is really no more than the *substratum*—affords no sufficient ground for the unity of the properties attached to it. The substratum or subject of the proposition is given, and we then look around to see what other properties accompany the primary characteristic for which the name was applied. But the term of popular language is not a real unity capable of supporting differences ; it is only one aspect of a thing, a single point fixed and isolated in the process of language by the action of natural selection. And so, to ask how the properties are related to the thing, is to ask how one aspect, taken out of its setting, is related to another isolated aspect : which is evidently an unanswerable question. Science is right in rejecting the ' thing ' of popular conception. If *a* is *a*, and nothing more, as the law of Identity informs us, then it is for ever impossible to get on to *b, c, d*, and the rest. The union between the thing divided or defined, and its divided or defining members, is what is termed extralogical ; in other words, it is not evident from what is given or stated in the popular conception. That union must be sought elsewhere, and deeper.

And when *we* step in to overcome the repugnance which the point of conception, or what is supposed the subject, shows against admitting a diversity of predicates,—when *we* force it into union with these properties : or when we try to remove the separation which leaves the cause and

[1] *Philosophie der Religion*, i. p. 137 seqq.

effect as two independent things to fall apart ; our action, by which we effect a unification of differences, may, from another and a universal point of view, be said to be the notion, or grasp of thought, coming to the consciousness of itself. Thought, as it were, recognises itself and its image in those objects of representative conception, which seem to be given and imposed upon the intellect. The two worlds, which the understanding accepts as each solid and independent,—the world of external objects or conceptions, and the world of self,—meet and coincide in the free agency of thought, developing itself under a double aspect. It is the ' original synthetical unity of apperception ' (to quote Kant's words), from which the Ego or thinking subject, and the ' manifold ' or body and world, are simultaneously differentiated. Thus, on the one hand, we ourselves no longer remain a rigid unity, existing in antithesis to the objects presupposed or referred to by representative thought : and on the other hand the so-called thing loses its hardness and fragmentary independence, as distinguished from our apprehension of it. *Our* action, as we incline to call it, which mends the inadequacies of terms, is from a philosophic point of view, the notion itself coming to the front and claiming recognition. The process of thought is then seen to be a totality, of which our faculties, on the one hand, and the existing thing, on the other, are isolated abstractions, supposed habitually to exist on their own account. To view either of these systems, the mental, on the one hand, and the objective world, on the other, as self-subsistent, has been the error in much of our metaphysics, and in the popular conceptions of what constitutes reality. The idealism of metaphysicians has been often as narrow and insufficient as the realism of common sense. An adequate philosophy, on the contrary, recognises the presence of both elements, in a subordinate and formative position. Representations may be compared to the little pools left here and there by the sea amongst the rocks and sand : the notion, or grasp of thought, is the tidal wave, which left them there to stagnate, but comes back again to restore their continuity with the great sea. In our thinking we are only the ministers and interpreters of the Idea,—of the organic and self-developing system of thought.

The difference between a representative conception and

a thought proper may be illustrated by the case of the
term 'Money'. Money may be either a materialised
thought, i.e. a Representative Conception, or a Notion
Proper. In the former case, money is identified with
a piece of money. It is probably, in the first instance,
embodied in coins of gold, silver, and bronze. In the
second place, a wide gulf is placed between it and the
other articles for which it is given in exchange. If other
things are regarded as money, they are generally treated
on the assumption that they can in case of need be reduced
to coinage. The conception of money by the unscientific
vulgar considers it separately from other commodities :
and the laws which forbade its exportation gave a vigorous
expression to the belief that it was something *sui generis*,
and subject to conditions of its own. The scientific notion
of money modifies this belief in the peculiarity and fixity of
money. Science does so historically, when it can point
to a time and a race where money in our sense of the
word does not exist, and where barter takes the place
of buying and selling. Science does so philosophically,
when it expounds what may be called the *process* of money,
—the inter-action or meeting of conditions to which the
existence of money is due. The notion of money, as given
in the *Ethics* of Aristotle, says that it is the common
measure of utility or demand. When we leave out of sight
the specific quality of an object, and consider only its
capacity of satisfying human wants, we have what is called
its worth or value. This value of the thing,—the psychological fact which is left, when all the qualities marking the
objective thing are reduced to their social efficiency—is
the notion, of which the currency is the representation,
reducing thought to the level of the senses, and embodying
the ' ideality ' of value in a tangible and visible object.
So long as this ' idea ' of value is kept in view, the currency
is comprehended : but when the perception of the notion
disappears, money is left a mere piece of currency, the
general notion being narrowed down to the coinage. Thus
the notion of money, like other notions in their ideal truth,
is not in us, nor in the things merely : it is what from
a minor point of view, when we and the things are regarded
under the head of want or need, may be called the *truth* of
both, the unity of the two sides. Thus considered, money
falls into its proper place in the order of things.

CHAPTER XXIV

FROM SUBSTANCE TO SUBJECT

'It is, in my view, all important,' says Hegel,[1] 'to apprehend and express the True not as *Substance*, but equally much as *Subject*.' Substance, as Spinoza defines it, is that which is in itself and which is conceived through itself, something which does not need the conception of something else by which its concept may be formed.[2] Substance, in other words, is something which serves to explain itself, which is *causa sui*. The mind, looking out on the wide world of mutable and manifold objects, finds its rest in the great calm of a something at their base, the eternal nature which, itself unmoved, is the one foundation, complete and sufficient, of all things,—a *res aeterna et infinita*, which can feed the mind with joy alone.[3] These words suggest only an object—a transcendent object— the basis of an objective order. They seem to leave little for the contemplating subject to do save to discern it and, so discerning, to rest in it and to love. They seem to leave substance a mere datum, a far-off all-embracing end in which the variety of human effort can find a central object and a final close. Yet, in the end it appears [4] that this *Res aeterna* loves himself with an intellectual love, and this love is identified with the love of man to God, so far at least as man's mind, considered *sub specie aeternitatis*, can be said to 'explicate' Deity. From this conclusion it might be said that Spinoza rises above the mere category of substance : God is no longer the mere foundation of things—the absolute object of all objects. He rises in human spirit (regarded in its eternal significance) to the rank of a true subject. He is not merely known as the True ; but He himself, living and moving in the essential spirit of man, knows himself and acquiesces in his infinite beatitude. But if this be the legitimate infer-

---

[1] Hegel, *Werke*, ii. 14. [2] Spinoza, *Eth.* Def. 3.
[3] Spin. *De intell. Em.* i. 10. [4] Spin. *Eth.* v. 35

ence to be drawn from the closing sections of the *Ethics*, it is not the view ordinarily suggested by the mention of Spinoza's doctrine. That doctrine, on the contrary, seems, as it first confronts us, and as it has taken its place in history, to omit the subjectivity which had found so decided a recognition in the commencement of Cartesianism. In the *cogito ergo sum* so much at least is clearly stated : true being—the true—is not merely known, but itself knows ; not a mere object, but a subject : a subject-object, or, an Idea. It is to be admitted, indeed, that Descartes hardly remains at this altitude, but he touches it for a moment. Even when he finds in the conception of God a security for truth and reality, and thus seems to base these on a one-sidedly objective standard, he regards God as, on the other hand, the truth and reality postulated and presupposed by the structural system of our ideas. God—such seems the tendency of his so-called ' proof '—is the inevitable prius and presupposition of our thought and being : He makes us know, as much as He is ultimately the object known : He is the unity and the creator of subject and object.

But it is hardly possible to get in philosophy the full recognition of the antithesis between subject and substance and the inclusion of both in the fuller Idea, till after the time of Kant. Kant himself is, in essentials, the antithesis of Spinoza, but it is not till Fichte that the full force of that antithesis is expressly recognised. With Hegel, the two opposite points of view are equally insisted on : the immanence and the transcendence of the True, the Real, the Absolute : or, in other words, the unity in it of subject and object, or of thought and existence. Or, in the words of the religious spirit, though heaven and the heaven of heavens cannot contain Him, He dwells in the spirit of the righteous, and is not far from any one of us. The truth is not the correspondence or agreement of an idea with a further reality which it represents. Such an idea or ' representation ' is a projection which has escaped from our hands, which has slipped from our grip, and which, while owning its mere vicarious character, at the same time beckons us on to seek a reality we can never find. The ' representation ' is in a way objective—it is set over against us : but yet it is not truly objective, not self-subsistent and self-possessed. Its objectivity is the objectivity of a name : a quasi-objectivity, which requires to be dipped in the living waters of intelligence before it can really exist and act. It seems, to the untrained observer, to point only outwards to the real object which it copies or designates : to a deeper reflection, it is seen to point equally inward to the mind which informed it and projected it. Thus the knowing subject, and the known object, with the representation which acts as a perpetual mediator to connect and yet not unify the one of these terms with the other,—all at last take their place, reduced and transfigured, in the unity of the Idea.

According to the Spinozist point of view, thought, it might seem by a sort of miracle, dispels the mists that envelop and bewilder it, sees through the multeity of modes, and the isolated pictures of imagination, to the true reality, one, infinite and eternal. Before that august vision of absolute wholeness the only attitude of a finite mind would seem to be resignation, worship, reverence,—deeply shading into the submission of absorption. For in it intellect and will are declared to have no place.[1] With such a statement, we get that first aspect of religion which has found its most imposing representative in the faith of Islam. In every religion there must, however, be more than this : or it would fail to do what all religion essentially does. Sheer dependence—*Schlechthinnige Abhängigkeit* (as Schleiermacher has named it)—can never be the whole burden of a religious teacher's message. Always—at least in the background—there is a contradictory element—in apparent discrepancy with the first—the deification of the worshipper. And as the Ethics of Spinoza—like every complete system of speculative truth—deals with a problem parallel to, if not even identical with, that of religion, its initial definitions and main programme must never let us forget the tacit presuppositions worked out to explicitness, as they are partly, in its conclusion. When Intellect and Will are denied to the *Deus=Natura=Substantia*, it is meant that the Absolute is and has more than intellect and will can well name, and that in Him (or Her, or It, for the pronominal distinctions of gender matter nothing here), the separation of will from intellect is a fallacy which can have no place. What Spinoza casts out are the lower

[1] *Eth.* i. 17 schol.

passions, the affections of weakness ; these *as such*, i.e. as elements of weakness, can have no place in Him. But in God, as in the free man who most resembles God, and in whose love He loves himself, there is—but that also in terms we cannot fathom—abundance of joy—the joy of infinite self-realisation.

Partly by the complementary theory of Leibniz, partly by the antagonist theories of Kant, the way had been prepared for setting forth, and in fuller outline, the implications so tardily admitted by Spinoza. It was only by a misuse or mal-extension of a word that Herder's God—a God who is Force—and the Force of Forces—could be supposed an advance upon Spinoza. There is in Force an analogue of Life ; but it is life in dependence, life not self-centred, always going forth, and when it goes forth dissipated. It is as it were pushed from behind, and is lost in what comes after it. If a Force of Forces means anything, it means something more than Force : it means a master of force, a force-controller, and force-adjuster, a unity and principle of forces. And Substance, as Spinoza understood it, is more than this variability, this deification of instability. It is the unity in which the variety and disparity of existence, the multiplicity of vicissitude, is merged and lost, only again to issue from it, and yet not leave it behind, in the infinitely-various modes of its two great and conspicuous attributes of consciousness and extensionality. If Hegel then sought to go beyond Spinoza, he sought to find a formula which would lose nothing that Spinoza had reached, but would at the same time bring out what Spinoza had left an implication, or noted in a partial rectification. As in religion, besides the utter dependence on God (so that, God failing, I perish), there must be also an absolute union, complete reconciliation—complete as culminating in unity and identity (so that God shall not be God, unless I am I) : so it is in philosophy. The Absolute cannot merely *be*, and be far away—the last goal in which the variety of life is made one, and the turmoil of the passionate existences laid to rest. The Soul which is (as some of the medieval Christians would say) still *in itinere*, a wayfarer, is such because its glance is turned on outward circumstances : but country is no accident : the soul even here carries with it that *patria*, ' which is the heavenly,' in its longings, and has it, even while yet on pilgrimage, in that strong possession of all

things by itself, which the theologian styles Faith.   This
goal determines the pilgrimage, fixes its direction, gives
progress to its steps.

In the myth-loving language of Plato (and of Wordsworth in his Platonic ode) the Soul has in other spheres
of being dwelt with the gods and seen the secret of the
world : it is itself one of the immortals, and as it is here
and now, is in a land of exile.   At the morning of birth,
the living sample of humanity has left his original glory
behind ; and a deep forgetfulness—only short of absolute—
cuts it off from his every-day consciousness.   In his present
reality he finds himself in a land of darkness, fast bound in
a hollow of the rock, looking out only on the ghostly images
that flit across his prison wall, cast there by the objects
that move between his back and the light of a mysterious
fire behind him and them.   Such is his natural estate, as it
meets the bodily eye : the estate of the lowly savage, whom
superstition and ignorance seem to hold as their captive
for ever.   But, though his high home and his glory of other
days have left no conscious memory in the soul, asleep and
imbruted in its fleshly house, they have not departed
without leaving a trace behind.   For forgetfulness is not
blank non-existence.   The sample of humanity inherits the
birthright of his fathers—he has hopes and fears, duties
and rights, which are his, if he can mature himself to take
possession of them.   He suffers from the pains of growth,
from the sense of disparity between what he is and what he
may and should be—from the noble uneasiness and dissatisfaction of a being who feels—if he does not know—his
infinite potentialities.   For these potentialities—otherwise
they have no title even to that name—are also actualities,
yet actualities which protest their own incompleteness, and
crave imperiously for what they lack.   What he has is his
right, but his right only in so far as it is also his duty.   It is
as such, and only as such, that he still retains the soul in all
its prerogatives : as the right, which is the duty, of knowledge.   Such a pre-figured and promised, but yet to be
realised, possession is what Plato has called *Erôs*, or Love.
But it is a Love whose wings are at first invisible, and who
often seems rather to crawl among ignoble things than to
soar in the free fresh air.

The process of experience has been by Plato called
Anamnêsis or Recollection.   But Recollection is not

always an easy, and never a merely passive, process ; and sometimes the forgetfulness seems so deep that no extraneous stimulus can at all move it. We have seen already one of these stimuli which rouse the sleeping sense—the mystery of numbers : and there are many others. But, we have also learned, that in the psychical sphere items of memory are not, as reckless fancy puts it, stored up in compartments, sorted and arranged, ready to be pulled out. The process of recollection is a complicated affair : an affair of give and take, of comparison and selection and rejection, of construction and reconstruction. You cannot haul up ready-made memories from the mine. And this perhaps was sometimes forgotten by Plato ; it certainly has been by more than one of his commentators. You may, no doubt, call up ideas from the vasty deep : but they come by laws and principles of their own. Even when they come, which they sometimes do unexpectedly, they come as an echo of the calling mind. Recollection involves intellectual process : as Kant said, the synthesis of imagination reposes upon the synthesis in the concept. Yet—and this is the point which Plato's title of *Anamnêsis* accentuates—unless ' the soul had been such as to be affected in this way ' (the words are those of Aristotle), unless the soul had been implicitly intellectual in tone and faculty, it would not have grasped the presented universe under the categories which it uses. There is, says Aristotle, in the barest act of sensation a congenital power of judgment ; there is, says Plato, an eye of the soul—a natural virtue of intelligence, which can never be put into it, and must always be presupposed in any theory of its processes.

There are, therefore, no innate ideas, says Cudworth in explanation of Plato, if these ideas mean formed and completed products of knowledge. All ideas in this sense begin and grow within the range of experience, and the history of their growth or development in literature and art can be at least approximately traced. We can trace, that is, the successions and connexions of the various types of beauty, or goodness : can show how the idea at one time dwelt in one of its aspects, at another in a different one. We can observe the variation, and it may be the progress, in men's conception of God. But it is another matter when we seek to explain these ideas themselves out of other elements, heterogeneous to them. When that question is asked, then with Plato we seem, in the absence of any theory of origins, obliged to own that it is by the Beautiful that beautiful things come to be beautiful. The μετάβασις εἰς ἄλλο γένος —the crossing of essential boundaries—which Aristotle forbids to science, still raises its eternal barrier in the logical, if it cease to hold good (as has been suggested) in the physical sphere. In the totality which we call the world and experience of reality there are, so to say, ultimate and irreducible provinces. The utmost that philosophy, i.e. science, can do with these is to co-ordinate them,—to show their mutual filiations, adaptations, and harmonies,— to note their inadequacies and discrepancies. They are not all of equal rank, perhaps ; they have to yield to each other, it may be in turn : but none of them can be arbitrarily expunged from the totality, and none of them shown to be a mere phase of others. To do that is to strip the universe of its variety and—it may be added—of its beauty and its interest. If it be a false philosophy that does it, there is a good deal of false philosophy abroad. There is a lust of explanation which is never content till it has found an equation for everything, till it has expressed everything in terms of the common-place, till it has emptied everything of all that made it individual and real, and turned it into an abstract, identical (as only abstracts can be) with some other abstract. Such abstractions are of course useful, and therefore need no excuse, when restricted to a special sphere. So long, that is, as we remember that it is an abstraction we are making, and that we are arbitrarily simplifying the real natural problem, no harm is done by these artificial constructions ; and they are important steps in a larger process. But what is correct and useful within a range whose limits we can define, becomes dangerous when carried beyond all bounds. Its approximate truth then becomes misleading error.

It is these irreducible elements—these great provinces in human experience, in reality, in the system of reason—that correspond to the more important of what are known as Platonic ideas. As ultimate constituents of the actual world they are in the narrower sense inexplicable. One does not amount to an exact sum of some others, nor is one got from another by the simple process of subtraction. But if they cannot be explained, by being reduced to multiples of some one basis, they can be comprehended in the respective implication and explication they exhibit with their co-realities. They can be correlated, reduced, and unified : we may even say, they can be identified ; but if we use such a term, we must mean that there is some totality beyond and above them in which they all find a place and all are harmonious ; in which all when brought to their Truth are really one and the same. This birthright of human nature in all ages and countries—this central essence of man's spirit—is the realm of Platonic ideas. They are the great elements, or constituent members, of humanity and of reality : the framework of his mind and of the world. How in each case they may be wrought out in detail, to what degree they may here be evolved, and there stunted, is a matter of historical research. And, in a sense, even it is not wrong to try to trace them one to another : to explain them, as the phrase is, one by another. For they are essentially connected : they are members of one system : they are unified and harmonised in a way for which even the word ' organism ' is wholly insufficient. They are the poles and lines on which the tent of human life, of intelligent life, is stretched : but they are also the invisible ties which bind together the earth and heavens, and all that is therein.

These ideas therefore are immanent in man : for they are the basis of human nature. But to name, to disentangle them, to measure out their bounds and describe their connexions—that is no easy work. And that is the work of Platonic recollection. That is the process of historical experience. But it is a small thing for Plato to say that these ideas are innate in man. What he is more concerned to make clear is that in the possession or vision of these eternal forms, the human soul is a partner of the gods, a citizen of the heavens. In less mythical language, man, as an intelligent, artistic, moral, and religious being, is not a mere accidental on-looker on the surface of things, but near their central and abiding truth. The forms of his mind, to speak after the manner of Kant, are the objective essences of the real world of experience. Degrees there may be in the reality which they possess—less or larger measures of truth to full experience—but true and real they are : never mere falsity or emptiness. To estimate the amounts of that reality is a problem Plato often tried. At one time it seems as if the Good were in his estimate the

form of forms, the real of reals : but when we look closely,
we see that it is a goodness which is synonymous with real
reality or perfect being. At another time truth, i.e. reality,
seems to be lord of all : at another, beauty : and again he
seems to confess his inability to lay down the order of
precedence in this hierarchy. Of one thing only he is
perfectly clear : and that is the unreality, the non-entity of
the sense-world as merely perceived, and the true being of
the world of reason. But he has no doubts as to the central
truth that in the good, the true, and the beautiful, there is
a higher reality—a more far-reaching and deep-piercing
influence than in all the mere variety of sensation, the mere
multitude of sensible fact.

What Plato has sometimes called the art of reminiscence,
what he has sometimes called the instinct of Love, is also
known to him as the process of Dialectic. For reminiscence
has to watch and wrestle with the inertia of oblivion, has to
set the imagined beside the real, and to correct percepts by
concepts, concepts by percepts, has to brace up its energies,
and to advance not by mere pressing onward, but by tacking
and zigzagging through contrary difficulties finally realise
itself. And love too is a battle, where the craving for
union has to measure its force with the instinct of independence, where selfishness and self-surrender seek a reconciliation, and where in the close, if the close be love, each is
self-retained only as self-abandoned, and each rises to a
higher union in which lower selfhoods are absorbed. Even
so in the course of Dialectic. It is the art which divides and
conjoins, which unifies and distinguishes : the art of asking
and answering. To Plato it appears in the main as an action
of the intelligent subject : but an action which, as he hints,
is almost a natural instinct, which through discipline has
become an art. In the hands of its typical artist, it proceeds,
or seems to proceed, as if unconscious of its principle and
end. Socrates has, as he professes, no overt conception of
the result : he has no knowledge of the positive conclusion
to be reached. It is the Logos—the logic of reality—which
sustains the movement. Abandoning any subjective
humour of carrying the argument to a preconceived end,
one is swept on by the current of real logic—the reason in
things. The dogma we have set up and seemed to see
before us, will, if we are dispassionate, carry us on beyond
itself, and suggest aspects calling for recognition and

acceptance. If only we refrain from arresting the movement of criticism,—a course to which prudence, ease, custom, and every form of the *ignava ratio* counsel us,—truth will reveal itself in us, and by us. It is because other aims, personal and particular, are so ever-present with us, that speculative free inquiry seems so hard. It is we who insist on closing up the door, not the truth that is reluctant to show itself.

Truth, then, is self-revelation or development. Not a result which is to be accepted, bowed to, and reverenced : but the result issuing (and only valuable as issuing) from a process in which we and objectivity are fellow-workers. The truth may no doubt be presented—as Spinoza does present it—in definitions, stating the net result as fundamental fact. Fundamental fact it is ; but as so stated, as Substance, it comes as a stranger, almost as an enemy : the great vision, suddenly offered to untrained eyes, overwhelms and alarms the living sense of self, of personality. Hegel wishes to show it as a friend, as our very own,—as Subject (but not merely subject). It is for this that philosophy runs through its cycle and returns into itself. Man points to nature and nature to man : universal to individual : thought to things : the self to God, and God to the human soul.

CHAPTER XXV

REASON AND THE DIALECTIC OF UNDERSTANDING

REPRESENTATIVE conceptions, besides being the burden of our ordinary materialising consciousness, are also the data of science, accepted and developed in their consequences. Because they are so accepted, as given into our hand, scientific reasoning can only institute relations between them. Its business as thus conceived is progressive unification, comparing objects with one another, demonstrating the similarities which exist between them, and combining them with each other. The exercise of thought which deals with such objects is limited by their existence : it is only formal. It is finite thought, because it is only subjective : it begins at a given point and stops somewhere, and never gets quite round its materials so as to call them truly its own. Each of the objects on which it is turned seems to be outside of it, and independent of it. Each point of fact, again, when it is carried out to its utmost, meets with other thoughts which limit it, and claim to be equally self-centred. Such knowledge creeps on from point to point. To this thinking German philosophy from the time of Kant and Jacobi applied a name, which since the days of Coleridge has been translated by ' Understanding '.[1] This degree or mode of thinking—not a faculty of thought—is the systematised and thorough exercise of what in England is called ' Common Sense '. In the first place, it is synonymous with practical intelligence. It takes what it calls facts, or things, as given, and aims only at arranging and combining them and drawing from them counsels of prudence or rules of art. Seeing things on a superficies, as it were so many unconnected points, here itself and there the various things of the world, it tries to bring them into connexion. It accepts existing distinctions, and seeks to render them more precise by pointing out and sifting the elements of sameness. Its greatest merit is an abhor-

[1] ' Verstand.'

rence of vagueness, inconsistency, and what it stigmatises
as mysticism : it wishes to be clear, distinct, and practical.
In its proper sphere,—and it has an indispensable function
to perform even in philosophy : wherever, that is, it is
unnecessary to go into the essential truth of things, and one
has only to do good work in a clearly defined sphere,—the
understanding has an independent value of its own.[1] Nor
is this true merely of practical life, where a man must
accommodate himself to facts : it is equally applicable in
the higher theoretic life,—in art, religion, and philosophy.
If intelligent definiteness does not make itself apparent in
these, there is something wrong about them.

It is only when this exercise of thought is regarded
as a *ne plus ultra*, and its mandates to restrict investigation
by the limits of foregone conclusions find obedience, that
understanding deserves the reproachful language which
was lavished upon it by the German philosophers at the
close of the last century. The understanding is abstract :
this sums up its offences in one word. Its objects, that is
the things it deals with and believes utterly real, are only
partly so, and when that incompleteness is unrecognised,
are only abstractions. Both in its contracted forms, such
as faith and common sense, and in its systematic form, the
logical or narrowly-consistent intellect, it is partial and
liable to be tenacious of half-truths. Only that whereas in
feeling and common-sense there is often a great deal which
they cannot express,—whereas the heart is often more
liberal than its interpreting mind will allow—the reverse is
true of the logically-consistent intellect. The narrowness
of the latter is, in its own opinion, exactly equal to the truth
of things : and whatever it expresses is asserted without
qualification to be the absolute fact. Its business is, given
the initial point (which is assumed to be certain and per-
spicuous), to see all which that point will necessarily
involve or lead to. For example, Order may be supposed
to be the chief end of the State. Let us consider, says the
intelligent arguer (without wasting time on abstruse inquiries
as to what Order is or means, and what sort of Order we
want), to what consequences and institutions this conception will lead us. Or, again, the chief end of the State
is assumed to be Liberty. To what special forms of organi-

---

[1] 'Die Vernunft ohne Verstand ist Nichts ; der Verstand doch
Etwas ohne Vernunft.' Hegel's *Leben*, p. 546.

sation will this hypothesis (also assumed a self-evident conception) lead ? Or we may go a step further. It is evident, some will say, that in a State there must be a certain admixture of Order and Liberty. How are we to proceed—what laws and ordinances will be necessary, to secure the proper equilibrium of these two principles ? The two must be blended, and each have its legitimate influence.

These are examples of the operation of Understanding. It can only reach a synthesis (or conjunction), never a real unity, because it believes in the omnipotence of the abstractions with which it began : but must either carry out one partial principle to its consequences, or allow an alternate and combined force to two opposite principles. Its canon is identity : given something, let us see what follows when we keep the same point always in view, and compare other points with the one which we are supposed to know. Its method is analytic : given a conception in which popular thought supposes itself at home, and let us see all the elements of truth which can be deduced from it. Its statements are abstract and narrow : or, in the words of Anaxagoras, one thing is cut off from another with a hatchet.[1] In its excess it degenerates into dogmatism, whether that dogmatism be theological or naturalistic.

The fact is that the Understanding, as this analytic, abstract, and finite action of mind is called,—the thought which holds objective ideas distinct from one another, and from the subjective faculties of thought as a whole,—that this Understanding is, when it claims to be heard and obeyed in science, not sufficiently thorough-going. It begins at a point which is not so isolated as it seems, but is a member of a body of thought : nor is it aware that the whole of this body of thought is in organic, and even more than organic, union. It errs in taking too much for granted : and in not seeing how this given point is the result of a process,—that in it, in any thought or idea, several tendencies or elements converge and are held in union, but with the possibility of working their way into a new independence. In other words, the Understanding requires, as the organon and method of philosophy, to be replaced by the Reason,[2]—

---

[1] Ὅτι οὐ κεχώρισται ἀλλήλων τὰ ἐν τῷ ἑνὶ κόσμῳ οὐδὲ ἀποκέκοπται πελέκει. Simplic. Phys. fol. 38 a (ed. Diels, p. 176).

[2] ' Vernunft.'

by infinite thought, concrete, at once analytic and synthetic. How then, it may be asked, can we make the passage from the inadequate to the adequate ? To that question the answer may be given that it is our act of arbitrary arrest which halts at the inadequate : that in complete Reason, which is the constituent nature both of us and of things, the Understanding is only a grade which points beyond itself, and therefore presupposes and struggles up to the adequate thought. In other words, it is Reason which creates or lays down for behoof of its own organisation the aims, conditions, and fixed entities,—the objects, by which it is bound and limited in its analytic exercise as understanding. Reason, therefore, is the implicit tendency to correct its own inadequacy : and we have only to check self-will and prejudice so far that the process may be accomplished.

The movement is not at one step : it has a middle term or mean which often seems as if it were a step backward. Progress in knowledge is usually described as produced by the mode of demonstration or the mode of experience. Formal Logic prefers the first mode of describing it : Applied Logic prefers the second. Either mode may serve, if we properly comprehend what demonstration and experience mean. And that will not be done unless we keep equally before us the affirmative and the negative element in the process. The law of rational progress in knowledge, of the dialectical movement of consciousness, or in one word of experience, is not simple movement in a straight line, but movement by negation and absorption of the premisses. The conclusion or the new object of knowledge is a product into which the preceding object is reduced or absorbed. Thus the movement from faith (which is concentrated and wholly personal knowledge) to open and universal knowledge, which is capable of becoming the possession of a community, —truth and not merely conviction, must pass through doubt. The premisses from which we start, and the original object with which we begin, are not left *in statu quo* : they are destroyed in their own shape, and become only materials to build up a new object and a conclusion. It is on the stepping-stones of discarded ideas that we rise to higher truth : and it is on the abrogation of the old objects of knowledge that the new objects are founded. Not merely does a new object come in to supplement the old, and correct its inadequacies by the new presence : not merely do *we* add new ranges to *our* powers of vision, retaining the old faculties and subjoining others. The whole world—alike inward and outward,—the consciousness and its object—is subjected to a thorough renovation : every feature is modified, and the system re-created. The old perishes : but in perishing contributes to constitute the new. Thus the new is at once the affirmation and negation of the old. And such is the invariable nature of intelligent progress, of which the old and not a few modern logicians failed to render a right account, because they missed the negative element, and did not see that the immediate premisses must be abolished in order to secure a conclusion,—even as the grapes must be crushed before the wine can be obtained.

This is the real meaning of Experience, when it is called the teacher of humanity : and it was for this reason that Bacon described it as ' far the best demonstration '.[1] Experience is that absolute process, embracing both us and things, which displays the nullity of what is immediately given, or baldly and nakedly accepted, and completes it by the rough remedy of contradiction. The change comes over both us and the things : neither the one side nor the other is left as it was before. And it is here that the advantage of Experience over demonstration consists. Demonstration tends to be looked upon as subjective only (*constringit assensum, non res*) : whereas Experience is also objective. But Experience is more than merely objective : it is the absolute process of thought pure and entire ; and as such it is described by Hegel as Dialectic, or Dialectical movement. This Dialectic covers the ground of demonstration,—a fragment of it especially described and emphasised in the Formal Logic,— and of Experience,—under which name it is better known in actual life, and in the philosophy of the sciences.[2]

Dialectic is the negative or destructive aspect of reason, as preparatory to its affirmative or constructive aspect. It is the spirit of dissent and criticism : the outgoing as opposed to the indwelling : the restless as distinguished from the quiet : the reproductive as opposed to the nutritive instinct : the centrifugal as opposed to the centripetal

---

[1] *Novum Organum*, Book I. 70.
[2] *Phenomenologie des Geistes*, p. 67.

force : the radical and progressive tendency as opposed to the conservative. But no one of these examples sufficiently or accurately describes it. For it is the utterance of an implicit contradiction,—the recognition of an existing and felt, but hitherto unrecognised and unformulated want. Dialectic does not supervene from without upon the fixed ideas of understanding : it is the evidence of the higher nature which lies behind them, of the dependence on a larger unity which understanding implicitly or explicitly denies. That higher nature, the notion or grasp of reasonable thought, comes forward, and has at first, in opposition to the one-sided products of understanding, the look of a destructive agent. If we regard the understanding and its object, as ultimate and final,—and they are so regarded in the ordinary estimation of the world,— then this negative action of reason seems utterly pernicious, and tends to end in the subversion of all fixity whatever, of everything definite. In this light Dialectic is what is commonly known as Scepticism ; just as the understanding in its excess is known as Dogmatism. But in the total grasp of the rational or speculative notion, Dialectic ceases to be Scepticism, and Understanding ceases to be Dogmatism.

Still there can be no doubt that the Dialectic of reason is dangerous, if taken abstractly and as if it were a whole truth. For the thoughts of ordinary men tend to be more abstract than their materials warrant. Men seek to formulate their feelings, faith, and conduct : but the *rationale* of their inmost belief,—their creed,—is generally narrower than it might be. Out of the undecomposed and massive ' substance ', on which their life and conduct is founded, they extract one or two ingredients : they emphasise with undue stress one or two features in their world, and attach to these partial formulae a value which would be deserved only if they really represented the whole facts. Hence when the narrow outlines of their creed are submitted to dialectic,—when the inlying contradictions are exposed, men feel as if the system of the world had sunk beneath them. But it is not the massive structure of their world, the organic unity in which they live, that is struck by dialectic : it is only those luminous points, the representative terms of material thought, which float before their consciousness, and which have been formulated in hard and fast outlines by the understanding. These points, as so defined and exaggerated, are what dialectic shakes. Not an alien force, but the inherent power of thought, destroys the temporary constructions of the understanding. The infinite comes to show the inadequacy of the finite which it has made.

In philosophy this second stage is as essential as the first. The one-sidedness of the first abstraction is corrected by the one-sidedness of the other. In the Philosophy of Plato, as has been noted, the dialectical energy of thought is sometimes spoken of under the analogy of sexual passion —the Love which, in the words of Sophocles, ' falls upon possessions ' and makes all fixed ordinance of no account, and finds no obstacles insuperable to its strong desire. But Love, as the speaker explains, is a child of Wealth and Want : he is never poor, and never rich : he is in a mean between ignorance and knowledge.[1] Thus is described the active unrest of growth, the ' *inquiétude poussante* ', as Leibniz called it,—the quickening force of the negative and of contradiction.

At the word ' contradiction' there is heard a murmur of objection, partly on technical, partly on material grounds. There are, it is said, other ways of getting from one idea to another than by contradiction : and it is not right to give the title to mere cases of contrast and correlation. Now it may be the case that the relations of ideas are many and various. In particular there is to many people a decided pleasure in the mere accumulation of bits of knowledge,—in their mental stock there are only aggregates,—conjunctions due to accidents of time and place,—associations and fusions which do not reach organised unity. In all of us, perhaps, there are more or less miscellaneous collections of beliefs, perceptions, hopes, and wishes, in no very obvious connexion with one another. An united self, one, harmonious, and complete, is probably rather an ideal of development than a fact realised. There are in each two or three discordant selves,—among which it might sometimes be difficult to select the right and true one (for that will depend on the momentary point of view). The deeper consciousness may go on entirely independent of the train of the more superficial ideas : the world of reality may glide past without touching the

[1] Plato, *Symposion*, 203.

world of dream or of fiction : our business part may live
in a region parted off from our religion by gulfs inscrutable.
In all these cases there cannot be said to be any contradiction.

But Hegel speaks of the essential progress of knowledge,
and of that true self or real mind which has attained complete harmony—the self and mind that is implicitly or
explicitly Absolute. In such a mind where the finite has
passed or is passing into the infinite, in a mind that is
really becoming one and total, its parts must meet and
modify each other. At each phase, if that phase is earnest,
self-certain, and real, it claims to be complete, and can
brook no rival. The bringer of new things must appear
as an enemy : for the old system, however imperfect as
a mere form, has behind it the strength of an infinite and
perfect content : it is more than it has explicated : but as
it (from its imperfection and honesty) identifies itself with
its form, it is resolved to resist change. Progress then
must be by antagonism : it cannot be real progress otherwise, but only the mere shifting of dilettante doubt and
dilettante toleration. Both new and old are worth something, and they must prove their value by neither being
lost, but both recognised, in a completer scheme of
things.

Yet there is a difference in the measure of contradiction
at different stages of thought. It is always greatest when
there is least to be opposed about. The more meagre an
idea, a creed, a term of thought, the more violent the
antitheses to it. The more abstractly we hold a doctrine,
the more readily are we disposed to sniff opposition. And
as in more concrete belief, so in the more abstract terms
of thought. They seem so wide apart—like ' Is ' and
' Is not '—and yet, taken alone, they are really so ready
to recoil into one another. As thought deepens, contradiction takes a more modified form. The relativity of
things becomes apparent : and what were erewhile opposed
as contradictory, turn out as pairs of correlatives, neither
of which is fully what it professed to be, unless it also is
all that seemed reserved for the other. Lastly, and in
the full truth of development, progress is seen to be not
merely a sudden recoil from one abstraction to another,
nor merely a continual reference to an underlying correlative, but the movement of one totality which advances

by self-opposition, self-reconciliation, and self-reconstruc-
tion. In this stage, the weight and bulk of unity keeps the
contradiction in its place of due subordination. But both
elements are equally essential, and if the unity is less palpable in the abstract beginnings, and the divergence less
wide at the close, at neither beginning nor close can either
be absent.

But if we merely look at the differentiation or negation
involved in the action of reason, we miss the half of its
meaning : and the new statement is as one-sided as the
old. We have not grasped the full meaning until we see
that what, as understanding, affirmed a finite, denies, as
dialectic, the absoluteness or adequacy of that finite.
Both the partial views have a right to exist, because each
gives its contribution to the science of truth.[1] If we
penetrate behind the surface,—if we do not look at the
two steps in the process abstractly and in separation,—it
will be seen that these two elements coincide and unite.
But we must be careful here. This coincidence or identification of opposites has not annihilated their opposition
or difference. That difference subsists, but in abeyance,
reduced to an element or ' moment ' in the unity. Each
of the two elements has been modified by the union : and
thus when each issues from the unity it has a richer significance than it had before. This unity, in which difference
is lost and found, is the rational notion,—the speculative
grasp of thought. It is the product of experience,—the
ampler affirmative which is founded upon an inclusion of
negatives.

We began with the bare unit, or simple and unanalysed
point, which satisfied popular language and popular
imagination as its *nucleus* :—the representation which had
caught and half-idealised a point, moment, or aspect in
the range of feeling and sensation. In this stage the
notion or thought proper is yet latent. In the first place,
the *nucleus* of imagination was analysed, defined, and, as
we may surmise, narrowed in the Intellect. And this
grade of thought is known as the Understanding. In the
second place, the definite and precise term, as understanding supposes it, was subjected to criticism : its contradictions displayed ; and the very opposite of the first
definition established in its place. This is the action of

[1] Cf. Dante, *Parad.* iv. 130.

Dialectic. In the third place, by means of this second stage, the real nature or truth was seen to lie in a union where the opposites interpenetrate and mould each other. Thus we have as a conscious unity,—conscious because it, as unity, yet embraces a difference as difference—what we started with as an unconscious unity, the truth of feeling, faith, and inspiration. The first was an immediate unity : —that is to say, we were in the midst of the unity, sunk in it, and making a part of it : the second is a mediated unity, which has been reached by a process of reflection, and which as a conscious unity involves that process.

Reason, then, is infinite, as opposed to understanding, which is finite thinking. The limits which are found and accepted by the analytic intellect, are limits which reason has imposed, and which it can take away : the limits are in it, and not over it. The larger reason has been laying down those limits, which our little minds at first tend to suppose absolute. Let us put the same law in more concrete terms. It is reason,—the Idea,—or, to give it an inadequate and abstract name, Natural Selection—which has created the several forms of the animal and vegetable world : it is reason, again, which in the struggle for existence contradicts the very inadequacies which it has brought into being : and it is reason, finally, which affirms both these actions,—the hereditary descent, and the adaptation —in the provisionally permanent and adequate forms which result from the struggle.

The three stages thus enumerated are therefore not merely stages in our human reason as subjective. They state the law of rational development in pure thought, in Nature, and in the world of Mind—the world of Art, Morals, and Science. They represent the law of thought or reason in its most general or abstract terms. They state, mainly in reference to the method or form of thought, that Triplicity, which will be seen in those real formations or phases to which thought moulds itself,—the typical species of reason. They reappear hundreds of times, in different multiples, in the system of philosophy. The abstract point of the Notion which parts asunder in the Judgment, and returns to a unity including difference in the Syllogism :—the mere generality of the Universal, which, by a disruption into Particulars and detail, gives

rise to the real and actual Individual :—the Identity which
has to be combined with Difference in order to furnish
a possible Ground for Existence :—the baldness and
nakedness of an Immediate belief, which comes to the
full and direct certainty of itself, to true immediacy, only
by gathering up the full sense of the antithesis which can
separate conviction from truth, or by realising the Mediation connecting them :—all these are illustrations of the
same law really applied which has been formally stated
as the necessity for a defining, a dialectical, and a speculative element in thought. The three parts of Logic are
an instance of the same thing : and when the Idea, or
organism of thought, appears developed in the series of
Natural forms, it is only to prepare the kingdom of reason
actualised in the world of Mind. The Understanding, on
the field of the world, corresponds, says Hegel,[1] to the
conception of Divine Goodness. The life of nature goes on
in the independence and self-possession of all its parts,
each as fixed and proud of its own, as if its share of earth
were for ever assured. The finite being then has his
season of self-satisfied ease : while the gods live in quiet,
away from the sight of man's doings. The dialectical
stage, again, corresponds to the conception of God as an
omnipotent Lord : when the Power of the universe waxes
terrific, destroying the complacency of the creatures and
making them feel their insufficiency,—when the once
beneficent appears jealous and cruel, and the joyous
equanimity of human life is oppressed by the terrors of
the inscrutable hand of fate. The easy-minded Greek
lived for the most part in the former world : the uneasy
Hebrew to a great extent in the latter. But the truth lay
neither in the placid wisdom of Zeus, leaving the world to
its own devices, nor in the jealous Jehovah of Mount
Sinai : the true speculative union is found in the mystical
unity of Godhead with human nature. In this comprehensive spirit did Hegel treat Logic.

This Triplicity runs through Hegel's works. If you
open one, the main divisions are marked with the capitals
A, B, C. One of these, it may be, is broken up into chapters
headed by the Roman numerals I, II, III. Under one or
more of these probably come severally the Arabic numerals
1, 2, 3. Any one of these again may be subdivided, and

[1] See in the *Logic* (vol. ii. p. 145).

gives rise to sections, headed by the small letters a, b, c.
And, lastly, any one of these may be treated to a distri-
bution under the three titles a, β, γ.   Of course the division
is not in each case carried equally far : nor does the subject
always permit it : nor is Hegel's knowledge alike vigorous,
or his interest in all directions the same.

BOOK III

LOGICAL OUTLINES

CHAPTER XXVI

THOUGHT PURE AND ENTIRE

THE English reader may probably be taken to be familiar with the conception of Logic as the Science of the *Form* of Thought. He may also have heard this explained as equivalent to the Science of Thought as Thought, or of Thought as Form, or of Formal Thought. But, probably, also, he brings to the lesson no very high estimate of *form* as such. In the old language of Greek philosophy, transmitted through the Schoolmen of the West, and still lingering in the phraseology of Bacon and Shakespeare,[1] Forms and substantial forms were powers in the world of reality. But a generation arose which knew them not: to which they were only belated survivals of the past. The forms had lost connexion with matter and content, and had come to seem something occult, transcendent, and therefore, to a practical and realistic age, something fantastic and superfluous. Yet it may be well to recall that the same author who has put on record his view that forms are only mental figments, unless they be fully ' determinate in matter ', has equally laid it down that the so-called ' causes ' of vulgar philosophy—the matter and the agent—are only ' vehicles of the form '. Thus spontaneously did Bacon reconstruct the Aristotelian theory of the interdependence of form and matter, that form is always form *of* (or *in*) matter, and that matter is always *for* form.

The relativity of form and matter, or of form and content,

---

[1] E. g. 'formal' in *Hamlet*, iv. 5. 215; 'informal' in *Measure for Measure*, v. 236.

is indeed almost a commonplace of popular discussion on logical subjects. But like other uncritical applications of great truths, this is both carried beyond its proper bounds, and is not carried out with sufficient thoroughness. There cannot—it is said—be a formal logic, because every exercise of thought is internally affected or modified by the material—the subject-matter—with which it deals. It is implied in such an argument that the ' subject-matter ' finds no difficulty in existing by itself, but that the ' thought ' is a mere vacuity or un-characterised something which owes its every character to the said matter. But a subject-matter which has content and character has therefore form : it is already known, already thought. And as to this thought, which is said to approach its matter with a self so blank, so impartial, so neutral—what is it ? It is a thought or a thinking which has never as yet thought,— which is only named ' thought ' by right of expectation, but is itself nothing actual. Of such—fictitious—thought there can hardly be a science.

On the other hand, that may be easily called a formal logic, which is much more than formal : and that may be called material, which is only a species of formal. Great indeed is the virtue of names, to suppress and to replace thought. When forms hang on as mysterious names after their day is passed—when they are retained in a certain honour, while the real working methods have assumed other titles ; then these forms become purely formal and antiquated. Thus the Logic of Aristotle seemed in its unfamiliar language to a later generation to be purely formal and superfluous. It was only another side of the same mistake when the new forms—the forms efficient and active in matter,—were not recognised as formal, but were boldly styled material : and the Logic which discussed such matter-marked forms was called a material Logic.

The phrase Matter of Thought, like its many congeners, is a fruitful mother of misconceptions. Caught up by the pictorial imagination, which is always at hand to anticipate thought, it suggests a matter, which is not thought, but is *there*, all the same, lying in expectation of it. It suggests two things—(for are there not two words, and a preposition or term of relation between them ?). But there are not two things. This *matter* is just as much a nonentity as the aforesaid *thought* : a matter of thought is a thought matter,—matter, thought once, and possibly to be thought again.

All this talk about the Relativity of form and matter is insincere, and semi-conventional. It is (like the well-known antithesis between Matter and Mind, of which indeed it is only a variation) a halting between two views. That which it chiefly leans to, is that there can be no form without matter, though there may well be matter which is not yet formed. At the best it goes no further than to admit or assert that *besides* the one there is *also* the other. It establishes a see-saw, and is proud of it. This is Dualism. Its maxim is, Don't forget that there is an Other. You have explored the One : you have perhaps done well. But there is also and always the Other. The second view is not the mere negation of this dualism. That there is a dualism is a fact which it acknow-ledges.[1] All life and reality is manifested in dualism—in antithesis : but the life and the reality is one. Mind—*Geist*—actualised and intelligent experience—is the one ultimate and essential reality.[2] In the face of its unity, mere matter is only a half-truth, and mere thought is only another. The reality, the unity, and the truth, is matter as formed, nature as reflected in mind. In the reality of experience there is always the presence of thought : and thought is only real when it is wedded with nature in the truth of man's mind. So far Bacon and Hegel coincide. Man—in so far as he is Mind—and of course Mind in its fullness is not merely subjective nor merely objective, but absolute—is the measure of all things, the central and comprehensive reality. Such a man—and such a mind—is, we need hardly add, not the man in the street, nor the man in the study : but the infinite, universal, eternal mind in whom these and all others essentially have their being. Such truth of man—such Mind—is the Absolute : it is sometimes named God : it is the ideal of all aspiration, and the fountain of all truth.

' Logic,' says Hegel,[3] ' is the science of the Idea in the medium of mere thought.' It exhibits the truth in one partial aspect, or shows one appearance of the total unity of the world,—the aspect it would wear if we could for a moment suppose the reality of Nature to vanish out of

---

[1] *Encycl.* § 574 (*Philosophy of Mind*, p. 196).
[2] *Encycl.* § 377.   [3] *Logic*, vol. ii. p. 30.

sight, and the ideality of Mind reduced to a ghost. It dissects the underlying organisation—the scheme of unification—which the world of mental or spiritual experience presents in all its concreteness. And it does so because it exhibits the last result of the ever clearer and clearer experience which Mind achieves as it comes to see and realise itself. The logical skeleton is the sublimated product of a rich concrete experience. It has been a curious delusion of some who were probably satisfied by a casual glance at Hegel's *Logic*, especially in its earlier chapters, to suppose that the Logic was meant to be the absolute beginning : and that pure or mere thought was the congenital endowment of the heaven-born philosopher.[1] To Hegel, on the contrary, Logic was an abstraction from a fuller, more concrete reality. He did not indeed suppose that the symbolical conception of Movement—in its popular pictorialness—would be an adequate substitute or representative for thought ; but he knew that the energy of mental development was the fact, and the truth, of which ' becoming ' is a meagre, abstract phase.

Logic, then, is not the Science of mere or pure thought, but of the Idea (which is co-terminous with reality)—of the Mind's synthetic unity of experience—looked at, however, abstractly, in the medium of pure thought. Just so, Nature-philosophy is the same Idea, as it turns up bit after bit distracted, fragmentary, and more or less mutilated, in the multiplication, the time and space division, of physical phenomena. But as science requires us to go from the simple to the more complex, as the truth has to prove itself true, by serving in its conclusion as the corroboration of all its premises or presuppositions ; so the system of philosophy begins with the Logic. Yet it can only begin there, because it has already apprehended itself in its completeness : and it can only move onward because it is the concentrated essence—the implicit being—of all that it actually and explicitly is. It may appear to emerge from a point : but that point has at its back the intellectual unity of a philosophy which embraces the world. It presupposes the complete philosopher who shall be the complete organ of absolute intelligence, of universal and eternal Spirit.

[1] The criticisms of A. Trendelenburg, in his *Logische Untersuchungen*, rest on such assumptions. ' Trendelenburg,' says Hartmann, ' means low-water mark in German philosophy.'

A satisfactory Logic then presupposes or implies a complete system of philosophy. No doubt, for a logic which deals with the minor problems of ratiocination or formal induction, all that is needed is a certain general acquaintance with popular conceptions, and with the results or methods of physical science. But if logic takes its business seriously, it must go behind these presuppositions. It must trace back reasoning to its roots, fibres, and first principles. And to do that it is not enough to put at the front a psychological chapter. Far from helping, psychology in these matters is much more in need of being helped itself. Till it has learned a little of the puzzle of the one and the many, the same and the diverse, being, quality, and essence, psychology will be as little use to Logic as blind guides generally are. Nor need this prevent us from saying that when psychology has thoroughly learned these mysteries, it will give fresh life and reality to the logic which it touches upon. The principles of Logic lie in another field,[1] and are deeper in the ground, than obvious psychological gossip.

If Logic then deals with form, it deals with a form of forms—the form of the world, of life, and of reality. It is a form, which is a unity in diversity, an organism,— a form which is infinitely manifold, and yet in all its multiplicity one. Logic is the morphology of thought,— of that thought which in Nature is concealed under the variety and divisions of things, and which in the theory of mental and spiritual life is resumed into a complete biology of the world-organism. The problem of Logic then demands an abstraction—an effort of self-concentration—an effort by which the whole machinery of the sensible universe shall be left behind, and the accustomed clothing of our thoughts be removed. To move in this ether of pure thought is clearly one of the hardest of problems.

Like Plato, we may occasionally feel that we have caught a glimpse of the super-sensible world unveiled ; but it disappears as the senses regain their hold. We can probably fix a firm eye on one term of reason, and criticise its value : but it is less easy to survey the Bacchic dance from term to term,[2] and allow them to criticise

[1] See above all Bradley's *Principles of Logic*, and Bosanquet's *Logic*, &c.

[2] 'Das Wahre ist der bacchantische Taumel, an dem kein Glied

themselves. The distracting influence of our associations, or of outside things, is always leading us astray. Either we incline to treat thoughts as psychological products or species, the outcome of a mental process, which are (a) given to us from the beginning, and so *a priori* or innate, or which (b) spring up in the course of experience by mutual friction between our mind and the outside world, and so are *a posteriori* or derivative. Or disregarding the subjective side of thoughts, we act as if they were more correctly called things : we speak of relations between phenomena : we suppose things, and causes, and quantities to form part of the so-called external universe, which science explores. The one estimate of thought, like the other, keeps in view, though at some distance, and so as not to interfere with their practical discussions, the separate and equal existence of thoughts and things. The psychologists or subjectivists of logic scrutinise the world within us first of all, and purpose to accomplish what can be done for the mind as possessing a faculty of thought, before they turn to the world of things. The realists or objectivists of logic think it better for practical work to allow thought only the formal or outside labour of surveying and analysing the laws of phenomena out of the phenomena which contain them. Neither of them examines thought— ' the original synthetic unity '—in its own integrity as a movement in its own self, an inner organisation, of which subject and object, the mind and the things called external, are the vehicles, or, in logical language, the accidents.

If it is possible to treat the history of the English Constitution as an object of inquiry in itself and for its own sake, without reference to the individuals who in course of time marred and mended it, or to the setting of events in which its advance is exhibited, why not treat the thought, which is the universal element of all things, of English Constitution, and Italian Art, and Greek Philosophy, in the same way,—absolutely, i.e. in itself and for its own sake ? When that is done, distinctions rigidly sustained between *a priori* and *a posteriori* become meaningless because now seen to belong to a distinction of earlier and later in the history of the individual consciousness. There

nicht trunken ist ; und weil jedes, indem es sich absondert, ebenso unmittelbar sich aufföst,—ist es ebenso die durchsichtige und einfache Ruhe.' *Phenom. des Geistes*, p. 35.

is at best only a modified justification for such mottoes
and cries, as ' Art for Art's sake ', or ' Science must be left
free and unchecked ', or ' The rights of the religious conscience ought always to be respected ' : but there can be
no demur or limitation to the cry that Thought must be
studied in Thought by Thought and for the sake of Thought.
For Art, and Science, and Religion are specialised modes
in which the totality or truth of things presents itself to
mankind, and none of them can claim an unconditioned
sway : their claims clash, and each must be admitted to be
after all a partial interpretation, a more or less one-sided
interpretation of the true reality of the world. Thought
on the other hand is unlimited : for it exists not merely
in its own abstract modes, but interpenetrates and rules
all the other concrete forms of experience, manifesting
itself in Art and Religion, not less than in Science. And
thus when we study Thought, we study that which is in
itself and for itself,—we study Absolute Being. On the
other side it must be noted that in Logic it is Absolute
Being, only when and as it is *thought*, which we study.
The two sides, Being and Thought, must both come forward : and come in unity, although in some phases of the
Idea the thought-element, in others the being-element is
more pronounced.

Thought, too, is Being. An old distinction of the
Stoics, which not inaptly represents popular views on
this matter, set on one side ὄντα, existences (which were
always corporeal, whether they were the things we touch
and feel, or the words and breathings by which we utter
them), and on the other side the meanings or thoughts
proper or σημαινόμενα (which were incorporeal). These
λεκτά, as they were otherwise called, were to the Stoics the
proper sphere of Logic. In the sense therefore which the
Stoics and popular consciousness give to being, the object
of logic does not possess being. It is not corporeal. It
cannot however be said to be in the sphere of non-being.
It is rather a part of reality—of concrete being—which
can be considered apart, as if it stood alone. Alone it does
not stand. And yet it holds a position so fundamental,—
is the same theme again and again repeated under endless
variations,—is so obviously the universal of things—that it
may properly form the subject of independent study.

It is, moreover, a part of Reality, which may well claim

to stand for the whole. It is, so to say, the score of the musical composition, rolled up in its bare, silent, unadorned lineaments ; the articulated theme, besides, and not the mere germinal concept, of all the variety of melody. But it is only laid up there *in abstracto*, because in the soul of the composer it had already taken concrete form, due to his capacity and training, his mental force, his art and science. It is there that the score has its source. But secondly, the musical work exists in the performance of the orchestra : in the manipulations of the several instruments, in the notes of the singers, in all the diversity of parts which make up the mechanism for unfolding the meaning or theme—that unreality, that mere thought, which to the stricter Stoic might be said to have no ὕπαρξις, or bodily subsistence. And there are still people who will be disposed to assert that it is only in the multitude of notes of violin, trombone, flute, &c., that the music is real :— though perhaps these hardy realists do not quite mean what they say. For what they probably mean, and what is the fact, is that the music exists as a complete reality in those who have ears and minds capable of comprehending and enjoying it : in those who can re-unite meaning and theme to execution and orchestration : and we may even add that it is more and more real, in proportion to the greater power with which they can bring these two into one.

We shall rather say then that thought points to reality, and that mere nature seeks for interpretation : that mere thought and mere being both seek for re-union. Yet if in the complete reality we thus distinguish two elements, we may follow Hegel in setting the pure Idea first. It is no doubt in a way true that, as has been said, Hegel may be often read most easily if we first begin with his concluding paragraphs. In psychology and ethics the fundamental principles have assumed a more imposing, a larger, a more humanly-interesting shape, than they bear in the intangible outlines of Logic. There they are written in blacker ink and broader lines than in the grey on grey. But after all, it is only for those who have grasped the faint—yet fixed—outlines that the full-contoured figure speaks its amplest truth. The true sculptor must begin with a thorough study of anatomy. For those therefore who do not care merely for results, it is indispensable to begin—

or at least to turn back to the beginning—to the Logic.
No doubt the full tones of the heard and sounded harmony
are the true and adequate presentation of the composer's
purpose : but they will be best comprehended and appreciated by those who have thoroughly grasped the score.

In Logic, so regarded, thought is no longer merely our
thought. It is the constructive, relational, unifying element of reality. Without it reality would not articulately
be anything for us : and such thoughts seem to be its net
extract, its quintessence, its concentrated meaning. But
really they are only the potent *form* of reality. Or, more
exactly, in its limits, under its phases, must come all
reality if it is to be part and parcel of our intelligent possession, our certified property. Such a thought is the framework, the shape-giver of our world, of our communicable
experience. It is the formative principle of our intelligent
life, as it is the principle through which things have meaning for us, and we have meaning for and fellowship with
others. It is not so rich as religion and art, perhaps it
does not have the intensity of feeling and faith : but it is
at the very basis of all of these, or it is the concentrated
essence of what in them is explicated and developed.
Humanity in these its highest energies is more than mere
thought—more than mere logic : but it is still at the root
thought, and it is still governed by the laws and movement
of this higher logic. For this is a logic which is no mere
instrument of technical reasoning, for proof or disproof :
no mere code of rules for the evaluation of testimony.
It is a logic which deals with a thought—or an Idea in
thought-form—which is the principle of all life and reality :
the way of self-criticism which leads to truth : a thought
which is at home in all the phases and provinces of experience.

Under the same name, Logic, therefore, we find something quite different from what the example of Aristotle
and his ancient and modern followers had accustomed us
to.[1] Under the auspices of Kant and his ' Transcendental
logic ' there has emerged the need of something more
corresponding to the title. For the word itself was not
used either by Aristotle or the Stoics. Neither the Analytics
and Topics of the one, nor the Dialectic of the other,
exhaust the conception of the science, or, to put it more

[1] Prantl, *Geschichte der Logik*, i. 87.

accurately, they are only inceptions of a science, the fulfilment of which was reserved for a later time. Bacon and Locke, Descartes and Spinoza, all the thinkers of modern Europe call for a deeper probing of the logical problem : for a grasp of it which shall be more worthy of its conventional name, Logic, the theory of Reason. And we may even say that what is wanted is a unification of the problem of the Organon with that of the first philosophy, a unification of Logic with Metaphysics : a recognition that the problem of reason is not merely the method of reasoning, but the whole theory as to the correlations of perception and conception, of thinking and reality.

This conception of Logic as the self-developing system of Thought pure and entire, is the distinctive achievement of Hegel. ' I cannot imagine,' he says, ' that the method which I have followed in this system of Logic, or rather the method which this system follows in its own self, is otherwise than susceptible of much improvement, and many completions of detail : but I know at the same time that it is the only genuine method. This is evident from the circumstance that it is nothing distinct from its object and subject-matter : for it is the subject-matter within itself, or its inherent dialectic, which moves it along.' [1]

But how is this universe of thought to be discovered, and its law of movement to be described ? From times beyond the reach of history, from nations and tribes of which we know only by tradition and vague conjectures, in all levels of social life and action, the synthetic energy of thought has been productive, and its evolution in the field of time has been going on. For thousands of years the intellectual city has been rearing its walls : and much of the process of its formation lies beyond the scope of observation. But fortunately there is a help at hand, which will enable us to discover at least the main outlines in the system of thought.

The key to the solution was found somewhat in the same way as led to the Darwinian theory concerning the Origin of Species. When the question touching the causes of variation and persistence in the natural kinds of plants and animals seemed so complex as to baffle all attempts at an answer, Darwin found what seemed a clue likely to lead to a theory of descent. The methods adopted in

[1] *Wissenschaft der Logik*, i. p. 39.

order to keep up, or to vary, a species under domestication
were open to anybody's inspection : and those principles,
which were consciously pursued in artificial selection by
the breeder, suggested a theory of similar selection in free
nature.   In studying the phenomena of thought, of which
the species or types were no less numerous and interesting
than those in organic nature, it was perhaps impossible to
survey the whole history of humanity.   But it was comparatively easy to observe the process of thought in those
cases where its growth had been fostered consciously and
distinctly.   The history of philosophy records the steps
in the conscious and artificial manipulation of what for the
far greater part is transacted in the silent workshops of
nature.   Philosophy, in short, is to the general growth
of intelligence what artificial breeding is to the variation
of species under natural conditions.   In the successive
systems of philosophy, the order and concatenation of
ideas was, as it were, clarified out of the perturbed medium
of real life, and expressed in its bare equivalents in terms
of thought, and thus first really acquired.   Half of his
task was already performed for the logician, and there
remained the work, certainly no slight one—of showing
the unity and organic development which marked the
conscious reasoning, and of connecting it with the general
movement of human thought.   The logician had to break
down the rigid lines which separated one system of philosophy from another,—to see what was really involved
in the contradiction of one system by its successor,—and
to show that the negation thus given to an antecedent
principle was a definite negation, ending not in mere zero
or vacuity, but in a distinct result, and making an advance
upon the previous height of intelligence.

    To say this was to give a new value to the history of
philosophy.   For it followed that each system was no
mere opinion or personal view, but was in the main a
genuine attempt of the thinker to give expression to the
tacit or struggling consciousness of his age.   Behind the
individual—who is often unduly regardless of his contemporaries and predecessors, and who writes or thinks
with little knowledge or sympathy for them, there is the
general bearing and interest of the age, its powerful solidarity of purpose and conception.   The philosopher is the
prophet, because he is in a large part the product of his

age. He is an organ of the mind of his age and nation ; and both he and it play a part in the general work of humanity.

On the other hand, it is dangerous to insist too forcibly on the rationality of the history of philosophy. For it may be taken to mean—probably only by blinded or wooden commentators—that each step in the evolution and concatenation of the logical idea is to be identified with some historical system, and that these systems must have appeared in this precise order. And this would be to expect too much from the ' impotence of nature ' which plays its part in the historical world also : as that on one side forms part of the Natural. There is Reason in the world—and in the world of history ; but not in the pellucid brightness and distinct outlines proper to the Idea in the abstract element of thought. It may take several philosophers to make one step in thought ; and sometimes one philosopher of genius may take several steps at once. There may even be co-eval philosophies : and there may be philosophies which appear to run on in independent or parallel lines of development. It may well be that Hegel has underestimated these divergencies, and that he has been too apt to see in all history the co-operation to one dominant purpose. But these errors in the execution of a philosophy of history, and especially of the history of philosophy, should not diminish our estimate of its principle.[1]

At first this process was seen in the medium of time. But the conditions of time are of practical and particular interest only. The day when the first leaves appear, and the season when the fruit ripens on a tree, are questions of importance to practical arboriculture. But botany deals only with the general theory of the plant's development, in which such considerations have to be generalised. So logic leaves out of account those points of time and chance which the interests of individuals and nations find all-important. And when this element of time has been removed, there is left a system of the types of thought pure

---

[1] See *Encyclop.* § 549 (*Philosophy of Mind*, pp. 148 seqq.). It is, of course, quite another question—to be answered by intelligent research—how far in particular cases Hegel has accurately studied a thinker, and faithfully interpreted him. Some of his critics in this line appear to mistake philology—which is a highly important authority in its own field—for philosophy : and will no doubt go on doing so.

and entire,—embalming the life of generations in mere words. The same self-identical thought is set forth from its initial narrowness and poverty on to its final amplitude and wealth of differences. At each stage it is the Absolute : outside of it there is nothing. It is the whole, pure and entire : always the whole. But in its first totality it is all but a void : in its last a fully-formed and articulated world,—because it holds all that it ever threw out of itself resumed into its grasp.

In these circumstances nothing can sound higher and nobler than the Theory of Logic. It presents the Truth unveiled in its proper form and absolute nature. If the philosopher may call this absolute totality of thought ever staying the same in its eternal development,—this adequacy of thought to its own requirements—by the name of God, then we may say with Hegel that Logic exhibits God as He is in His eternal Being before the creation of Nature and a finite Mind.[1] But the logical Idea is only a phantom Deity—the bare possibility of a God or of absolute reality in all the development of its details.

The first acquaintance with the abstract theory is likely to dash cold water on the enthusiasm thus awakened, and may sober our views of the magic efficacy of Logic. ' The student on his first approach to the Science,' says Hegel, ' sees in Logic at first only one system of abstractions apart and limited to itself, not extending so as to include other facts and sciences. On the contrary, when it is contrasted with the variety abounding in our generalised picture of the world, and with the tangible realities embraced in the other sciences,—when it is compared with the promise of the Absolute Science to lay bare the essence of that variety, the inner nature of the mind and the world, or, in one word, the Truth,—this science of Logic in its abstract outline, in the colourless cold simplicity of its mere terms of thought, seems as if it would perform anything sooner than this promise, and in the face of that variety seems very empty indeed. A first introduction to the study of Logic leads us to suppose that its significance is restricted to itself. Its doctrines are not believed to be more than one separate branch of study engaged with the terms or dimensions of thought, besides which the other scientific occupations have a proper material and body

[1] Hegel's *Werke*, iii. 33.

of their own. Upon these occupations, it is assumed, Logic may exert a formal influence, but it is the influence of a natural and spontaneous logic for which the scientific form and its study may be in case of need dispensed with. The other sciences have upon the whole rejected the regulation-method, which made them a series of definitions, axioms, and theorems, with the demonstration of these theorems. What is called Natural Logic rules in the sciences with fall sway, and gets along without any special investigation in the direction of thought itself. The entire materials and facts of these sciences have detached themselves completely from Logic. Besides they are more attractive for sense, feeling, or imagination, and for practical interests of every description.

' And so it comes about that Logic has to be learned at first, as something which is perhaps understood and seen into, but of which the compass, the depth, and further import are in the earliest stages unperceived. It is only after a deeper study of the other sciences that logical theory rises before the mind of the student into a universal, which is not merely abstract, but embraces within it the variety of particulars.—The same moral truth on the lips of a youth, who understands it quite correctly, does not possess the significance or the burden of meaning which it has in the mind of the veteran, in whom the experience of a lifetime has made it express the whole force of its import. In the same way, Logic is not appreciated at its right value until it has grown to be the result of scientific experience. It is then seen to be the universal truth,—not a special study beside other matters and other realities, but the essence of all these other facts together.' [1]

[1] *Wissenschaft der Logik*, i. p. 43.

CHAPTER XXVII

ABSOLUTE AND RELATIVE : OR THE CATEGORIES

ACCORDING to the strict reasonings of Kant in his *Criticism of Pure Reason,* and the somewhat looser discussions of Mr. Spencer in his *First Principles* a science of Metaphysics or theory of the Infinite, Absolute, or Unconditioned is impossible. As a result of the criticism by Kant, Jacobi claimed the Absolute for Faith : and Spencer banishes the Absolute or Unknowable to the sphere of Religion to be worshipped or ignored, but in either case blindly. As we have already seen, Hegel does not accept this distribution of provinces between religion and philosophy. There is only one world, one reality : but it is known more or less fully, more or less truly and adequately. It is presented in one way to the sensuous imagination : in another to the scientific analyst : in a third to the philosopher. To the first it is a mere succession or expanse of pictures, facts, appearances : and outside it—somewhere, but not here,—there is a land, a being of perfect wholeness and harmony. To the second it is an unending chain of causes and effects, of one thing simplified by being referred to another till at last a mighty all-explaining nullity, called an ' Ultimate Cause ', is presumed to linger, eternally unperceived at the infinitely-distant end of the series. To the third everything is seen in connexion, but not a mere unilinear connexion : each, when studied, more and more completes itself by including those relations which seemed to stand outside : each fully realised, or completely invested with its ideal implications, is seen no longer to be an incident or isolated fact, but an implicit infinite, and a vice-gerent of the eternal. Philosophy thus releases both ordinary and scientific knowledge from their limitations ; it shows the finite passing into the infinite. And Hegel, accordingly, purposes to show that this unfathomable Absolute is very near us, and at our very door : in our hands, as it were, and especially present in our every-day language. If we are ever to gain the Absolute, we must be careful not to lose one jot or tittle of the Relative.[1] The Absolute—this term, which is to some so offensive and to others so precious—always presents itself to us in Relatives : and when we have persistently traced the Proteus through all its manifestations,—when we have, so to speak, seen the Absolute Relativity of Relation, there is very little more needed in order to apprehend the Absolute pure and entire. One may say of the Absolute what Goethe[2] says of Nature : ' She lives entirely in her children : and the mother, where is she ? '

It is a great step, when we have detected the Relativity of what had hitherto seemed Absolute,—when a new aspect of the infinite fullness of the world, the truth of things, dawns upon us. But it is even a greater step when we see that the Relativity which we have thus discovered is itself Relative. And this is one advantage of first studying the value of the categories of ethics and physics on Logical ground. On the concreter region of Nature and Mind, the several grades and species into which reality is divided have a portentous firmness and grandeur about them, and the intrinsic dialectic seems scarcely adequate to shaking the foundations of their stability. They severally stand as independent self-sustaining entities, separate from each other, and stereotyped in their several formations. But in the ether of abstract Idea, in the fluid and transparent form of mere thoughts, the several stages in the development of the Absolute, the various grades of category, clearly betray their Relativity, and by the negation of this Relativity lead on to a higher Absolute.

To the practical man,—so long as his reflection does not go deep,—the concepts on which his knowledge and faith are built seem eternal, unshifting rock, parts of the inmost fabric of things. He accepts them as ultimate validities. To him matter and force, cause and effect, distinctions between form and content, whole and part,

---

[1] Cf. Herbart's maxim, ' Wie viel Schein, so viel Hindeutung auf Sein.' (*Hauptpunkte der Metaphysik.*)

[2] *Die Natur* (1780) : ' Sie lebt in lauter Kindern : und die Mutter, wo ist sie ? . . . . Sie ist ganz und doch immer unvollendet. . . . Sie verbirgt sich in tausend Namen und Termen, und ist immer dieselbe.'

quantity and quality, belong to the final constitution of the world. (And so, in a sense, they do.) If he ever overcome the absoluteness which popular thought attributes to the individual things of sense and imagination, and show their relativity, he does so only to fall under the glamour of a new deception. Causes and matters, forces and atoms, become new ultimates, new absolutes, of another order. Fictions or postulates of the understanding take the place of the figments of imagination. The ordinary scientific man labours especially under the ' metaphysical ' fallacy : he realises abstractions in their abstractness. As against this it is the business of the logician to show how such terms are to be interpreted as steps in a process of interpretation—containing so much that others of simpler structure have handed on, and themselves presupposing by implication a great deal they fail properly to explicate. Thus, the logician evinces at one blow the relativity of each term in its mereness, abstractness, or false absoluteness, and the ideal absoluteness which always carries it beyond itself, and makes it mean more than it says.

The natural mind always hastens to substantiate the terms it employs. It makes them a fixed, solid foundation, an hypostasis, on which further building may be raised. If such pseudo-absolutising of concepts is to be called metaphysics, then logic has to free us from the illusions of metaphysics, to de-absolutise them, to disabuse us of a false Absolute. The false Absolute is what Hegel calls the Abstract : it is the part which, because it succeeded in losing sight of its dependence, had believed itself to be a whole. Logic shows—in the phrase of Hegel—that each such term or concept is only an attempt to express, explicate, or define the Absolute :[1] a predicate of the Absolute, but falling short of its subject, or only uttering part of the whole truth of reality. But while Logic shows it only to be an attempt, and therefore in an aspect relative, it equally shows its ingrained tendency to complete itself, to carry out to realisation its ideal implication,—shows, in short, that e. g. force is more than *mere* force, that thing-in-itself is not properly even a thing ; that a veritable notion (*Begriff*) or grasp of a thing is more than a *mere* (subjective) notion, &c. Thus the true Absolute is not

[1] *Logic (Encyclop.)* §§ 85, 87, 112, 194, &c.

the emptiest and most meagre of abstractions,—what is
left as a residual after the relative in all its breadth and
length has been cut out of it ; it is the concretest of all
being, the whole which includes without destroying all
partial aspects.   Yet as it includes them, it shows itself
their master and more than master : making each lose
and win in the other, till all are satisfied in unity, and no
shade of individuality is utterly lost in the totality of the
Universal.

Accordingly, Metaphysics and Logic tend to form one
body.   For the distant and transcendent Absolute, which
was the object of older Metaphysics, was substituted an
Absolute, self-revealing in the terms of thought.   Being
is deposed from its absoluteness, and made the first postulate of thought.   Former Metaphysics had dashed itself
in vain against the reefs that girdle the island of the super-
sensible and noümenal, the supposed world of true Being :
and the struggle at last grew so disastrous that Kant gave
the signal to retreat, and to leave the world of true Being,
the impregnable Thing-in-itself, to its repose.   His advice
to metaphysicians [1] was that, while scientific research
continued to concentrate the attack of analysis upon single
experiences conforming to certain conditions, they should
investigate these conditions of possible experience or
foundations of objectivity.   In other words, he turned
observation to what he called Transcendental Logic.   It
was by means of this suggestion, understood in the widest
sense, that Hegel was led to treat Logic as the science of
ultimate reality.   He had to show how these conditions
when carried out in full gave the Unconditioned.   He
attacked the Absolute, if we may say so, in detail.   The
Absolute, as the totality, universe or system of Relativity,
lays itself open to observation by deposing itself to a
Relative.   It possesses the differentiating power of separating itself as an object in passivity, from itself as a subject
in action,—of deposing itself to appearance, of being *for*
itself, and also *in* and *for* itself.   And thus Thought is the
active universal,—which actualises itself more and more
out of abstraction into concreteness.

---

[1] Metaphysic is, in Kant's usage, ambiguous.   It means (*a*) a supposed science of the supersensible or unconditioned reality ; (*b*) a
study of the conditions or presuppositions—the Kantian *a priori*—
of some aspect of Experience, e. g. a Metaphysic of Moral rules.

Hegel, then, solved the problem of Metaphysics by turning it into Logic. The same principle, Thought, appeared in both : in the former as a fixed and passive result, showing no traces of spontaneity,—in the latter as an activity, with a mere power of passing from object to object, discovering and establishing connexions and relations. The two sciences were fragments, unintelligible and untenable, when taken in abstract isolation. This is the justification, if justification be required, for Hegel's unification of Logic and Metaphysics. The Hegelian Logic falls into three parts : the theory of Transitory Being : the theory of Relative Being : and the theory of the Notion. The first and second of these in his Science of Logic are called Objective Logic ; they also might be described as Metaphysics. The third part is more strictly on Logical ground. Or perhaps it is best to describe the whole as the Metaphysics of Logic.

The Logic of Hegel is the Science of Thought as an organic system of its characteristic forms, which in their entirety constitute the Idea. These forms or types of thought, the moulds in which the Idea confines itself in its evolution, are not unlike what have been otherwise called the Categories. (Of course the foreign word ' Categories ' does not commend itself to Hegel).[1] They are the modifications or definite forms, the articulated and distinct shapes, in which the process of Thought ever and anon culminates in the course of its movement. The Infinite and Absolute at these points conditions itself, and as so conditioned or differentiated is apprehended and stamped with a name. They specify the unspecified, and give utterance to the ineffable. They are the names by which reason grasps the totality of things,—the names by which the truth (or God) reveals itself, however inadequately. From one point of view they constitute a series,

---

[1] His usual term is *Denkbestimmungen*, the several expressions or specific forms of the unification which thought is. The term Categories has been identified by Kant with his list of *Stammbegriffe*, and by Mill with his classes of nameable things,—with some critical remarks on Aristotle's use of the word. That use—to denote the elements of predicable reality, what Grote called *ens*—is probably not so ' rhapsodical ' as Kant, with his new-born zeal for the contrast of sensibility and intellect, was inclined to suppose. A real history of the Category-theory would be almost a history of philosophy. Perhaps the name might be more sparingly used.

each evolved from the other, a more completely detailed
term or utterance of thought resulting by innate contradiction from a less detailed. From another point of view
the total remains perpetually the same ; and the change
seems only on the surface. The one aspect of the movement conceals the Absolute : the other puts the Relative
into the background.

What then are the Categories ? We may answer : They
are the ways in which expression is given to the unifying
influence of thought : and we have to consider them as
points or stations in the progress of this unification, and
in the light of this influence. These Categories are the
typical structures marking the definite grades in the
growth of thought,—the moulds or forms which thought
assumes and places itself in,—those instants when the
process of thought takes a determinate form, and admits
of being grasped. The growth of thought, like other
growths, is often imperceptible and impalpable. And
then, unexpectedly, a condensation takes place, a form is
precipitated out of the transparent medium. A new
concept, a new grasp of reality, emerges from the solution
of elements : and a name is created to realise the new
shade of the Idea. These thought-terms are the world of
Platonic forms, if we consider his ' form of Good ' as
corresponding to the ' Idea ' of Hegel. For if we look
carefully into this mystic word ' Good ' which plays so
brilliant a part in ancient philosophy, we shall see that it
only expresses in a more concrete and less analytic form,
as ancient thought often does, the same thing as so many
moderns love to speak of as Relativity, and which is also
implied in Aristotle's conception of an End. To see things
sub specie boni—which Plato describes as the supreme
quality of the truth-seeker who is to guide men into up-
rightness, or into conformity with the true nature of things,
—is to see them elevated above their partial self-subsistence
into the harmony and totality of that which is always and
unvaryingly its real self. The Good is the sun-light in
which things lose their earlier character (which they had
in the days of our bondage and ignorance) of mysterious
and perplexing spectres of the night. In the light of the
Good, things are shorn of their false pretence of self-
subsistence and substantiality, deposed by comparison
with the perfect and unspotted, and as it were stung into

seeking a higher form of being by struggle. And this is the abstract moral way of looking. But to see them in the form of Good means also that they are seen to be more and better than we thought, that they are not condemned to inadequacy, but bear in them the witness and revelation of infinity and absoluteness. And this is rather the faith of religion and the vision of art. And the ' form of Good ' is only a brief and undeveloped vision of an Absolute, which is the ' form of Relativity ',—Relativity elevated into an Absolute.

A Category is often spoken of as if it were the highest extreme of generalisation, the most abstract and most widely applicable term possible. If we climb sufficiently far and high up the Porphyry's tree of thought, we may expect, thought the old logicians, to reach the ' *summa genera* ' or highest species of human thought. Nor have modern logicians always refrained from this byway. But these quantitative distinctions of greater and less, in which the Formal Logic revels, are not very suitable to any of the terms or processes of thought, and they certainly give an imperfect description of the Categories. The essential function which the Categories perform in the fabric of thought and language is, in the first place, to combine, affirm, demonstrate, relate, and unify,—and *not* to generalise.[1] Their action may be better compared to that fulfilled by those symbols in an algebraical expression, which like *plus* and *minus* denote an operation to be performed in the way of combining or relating, than to the office of the symbols which in these expressions denote the magnitudes themselves.

To the student of language the Categories sometimes present themselves as pronominal, or formal roots,—those roots which, as it is said, do not denote things, but relations between things. He meets them in the inflections of nouns and verbs ; in the signs of number, gender, case, and person : but, as thus presented, their influence is subordinate to the things of which they are, as it were, the accidents. He meets them in a more independent and tangible shape in the articles, pronouns, prepositions, conjunctions, and numerals, and in what are called the

---

[1] Generalisation is only one small aspect of thought, with specialisation as its, at least as important, pendant. To read certain logics, one might think the all-comprehensive virtue of truths were to be general,—not to be true.

auxiliary verbs. In these apparently trifling, and in some languages almost non-existent words or parts of words, we have the symbols of relations,—the means of connexion between single words,—the cement which binds significant speech together. There are languages, such as the older and classical forms of Chinese, where these categorising terms are, as it were, in the air : where they are only felt in accent and position, and have no separate existence of their own. But in the languages of the Indo-European family they gradually appear, at first in combination, perhaps, with the more material roots, and only in the course of time asserting an independent form. Originally they appear to denote the relations of space and time,—the generalised or typical links between the parts of our sense-perceptions : but from there they are afterwards, and in a little while, transferred into the service of intellect. These little words are the very life-blood of a language, —its spirit and force. It is in these categories, as they show themselves in the different linguistic families, that a nation betrays its mode and tone of thought. The language of the Altaic races, e. g., expresses activity only as a piece of property, an appropriation of a substance, and knows no true distinction of noun and verb : the Semitic Tongues in their tense-system perhaps betray the intense inwardness of the race : whereas the immense inflectionalism of the Indo-European seems not unconnected with his greater versatility and energy. Complete mastery in the manipulation of these particles and forms is what makes an idiomatic knowledge of a language, as distinct from a mere remembrance of the vocabulary. And philosophy is the recognition of their import and significance. Thus in Greek philosophy the central questions turn upon such words as Being and not-Being : Becoming : that out of which : that for the sake of which : the what-was-being : the what is : the other : the one : the great and small : that which is upon the whole : what is according to each : this somewhat : &c.[1] And again in Modern Philosophy, how often has the battle raged about the meaning of such words as I : will : can : must : because : same and different : self : &c. !

---

[1] ὄν and μὴ ὄν : τὸ γιγνόμενον : τὸ ἐξ οὗ : τὸ οὗ ἕνεκα : τὸ τί ἦν εἶναι : τὸ τί ἐστι : θάτερον : ἕν : τὸ μέγα καὶ τὸ μικρόν : τὸ καθ᾽ ὅλου : τὸ καθ᾽ ἕκαστον : τόδε τί.

CHAPTER XXVIII

THE THREE PARTS OF LOGIC

LOGIC, as it is understood in these pages, is the critical history of the terms of thought by which reality, the sum of experience, the world, is described or expressed. It is the philosophical criticism of the concepts, or elements of conception, by which we define or develop the Totality, the Absolute. It describes the constitution of the intellectual realm, by and in which we give body, coherence, unity, and system to reality. It is the self-developing organisation of the thoughts by which we think things, and by which things are what they are. It is the ripe fruit of the experience of the ages of humanity, and it therefore bears in itself a principle of growth. But if it be a fruit, it is a fruit which can watch its own growth, which reflects upon its own life. Its three parts show the main stages of its development, beginning with the least adequate and most abstract or general description of reality.

The first part of Logic, the theory of Being,[1] may be

---

[1] Being (*das Seyn*) probably conveys much more to an English reader than is here meant or wanted. It is Being, where the distinction between essence and appearance has not yet emerged or been thought of. If being = τὸ ὄν, then essence (*Wesen*) = τὸ ὄντως ὄν, the being which underlies and yet includes appearance. *Wesen* has more right to the substantival vocable of Being: *Seyn* is little better than an ' Is ' or ' Be '.

In writers of Locke's time, ' Being ' seems to mean a reality, an actually existing object, e. g. Clarke : ' There has existed from eternity some one unchangeable and independent Being.' ' What the substance or *essence* of that Being is, we have no idea.' ' Essence,' says Locke, ' may be taken for the very being of anything, whereby it is what it is.' Of course Aristotle long ago noted Being as one of the terms with variety of implication ; and his own fluctuation about οὐσία is an obvious illustration of this.

In the translation of the *Logic*, *Wesen* is occasionally rendered by Being (e. g. Supreme Being) ; *Seyn*, by existence. *Seyn* here means so little that one can hardly find any word of sufficiently minimal content for it.

called the theory of unsupported and freely-floating Being.
We do not mean something which *is*, but the mere ' is ',
the bare fact of Being, without any substratum. The
degree of condensation or development, where substantive
and attribute, or noun and verb, co-exist, has not yet
come. The terms or forms of Being float as it were freely
in the air, and we go from one to another, or—to put it
more correctly—one passes into another. The terms in
question are Is and Not : Become : There is : Some and
Other : Each : One : Many : and so on through the
terms of number to degree and numerical specificality.
This Being is immediate : i. e. it contains no reference
binding it with anything beyond itself, but stands forward
baldly and nakedly, as if alone ; and, if hard pressed, it
turns over into something else. It includes the three
stages of Quality, Quantity, and Measure. The ether of
' Is ' presumes no substratum, or further connexion with
anything : and we only meet a series of points as we
travel along the surface of thought. To *name*, to *number*,
to *measure*, are the three grades of our ordinary and natural
thought : so simple, that one is scarcely disposed to look
upon them as grades of thought at all. And yet if thought
is self-specification, what more obvious forms of specifying
it are there than to name (so pointing it out, or qualifying
it), to number (so quantifying it, or stating its dimensions),
and to measure it ? These are the three primary speci-
ficates by which we think,—the three primary dimensions
of thought. Thought, in so determining, plays upon the
surface, and has no sense of the interdependence of its
terms. And if we could imagine a natural state of consciousness in which sensations had not yet hardened into
permanent things, and into connexions between things, we
should have something like the range of Immediate Being.
Colours and sounds, a series of floating qualities, pass
before the eye and the ear : these colours and sounds are
in course of time counted : and then, by applying the
numbers to these qualities, we get the proportions or limits
ascertained. When this process in actual life,—the
advance from the vague feelings which tell us of sweet,
cold, &c., by means of a definite enumeration of their
phenomena, to the rules guiding their operation,—is
reduced to its most abstract terms, we have the process
of Being. It would be the period when a distinction

between things and their actions or properties has not arisen. The demonstrative pronouns and the numerals are among the linguistic expressions of Being in its several stages. Perhaps too we may illustrate it by the so-called ' impersonal ' verb—which has hardly reached the stage of verb proper, having no subject : or by the name which still fluctuates between the stage of substantive or adjective.

The first sphere was that of Being directly confronting us, and using the demonstrative pronouns first of all. The second is Relative or Reflective Being : and in this we have to deal with the relative pronouns. The surface of Being is now seen to exhibit a secondary formation, to involve a sort of permanent standard in itself, and to be essentially relative. The mere quality, when reduced to number, is seen to be subjected to a certain measure, rule, sort, or standard : and this reflex of itself always haunts it, modifying and determining it. Thus instead of qualities, we begin to speak of the properties of a thing : we have, as it were, two levels of Being, in intimate and necessary connexion, where there was only one before. At first it was but a mere surface-picture, one thing here and another there : a this and a that ; one, *now*, and another, *then*. *This*, it might be, was round, and *that* square : *now*, it was bright, and *then*, it was dull : *here* was a head, and *there* was a limb. But the comparison of quality with quantity, measuring one by the other, gave rise to the conception of something permanent, a true nucleus amid the changes. The fact, previously single, is now become double : the mere event is now a phenomenon, a temporary and outward manifestation of something inner. We now see each that *is*, in the halo of what it *has been*, or will be : the passing modification in the light of the permanent type. But as yet the permanent and the passing are separate, and only throw light on each other : A explaining itself by B and B by A. We have apparently two facts ; neither of which can however stand by itself and therefore refers us to the other. But to get a real rest in this incessant round of mutual reference of one to another we must take a higher stand-point.

In this sphere of Relativity the terms expressive of things come in pairs : such as Same and Different, Like and Unlike : True Being and Show or Semblance : Cause and Effect : Substance and Accident : Matter and Form :

and the like. If we compare mere Being to the cell in its simple state, we may say that in the second sphere of Logic a nucleus has been formed,—that a distinction has sprung up between two elements, which are still in closest interconnexion. We have penetrated behind the seeming simplicity of the surface : and in fact discovered it to be mere seeming in the light of the substratum, cause, or essence, upon which it is now reflected. In immediate Being one category, or specificate, or dimension of thought passes over into another, and then disappears : but in mediated Being one category has a meaning only by its relation to another,—only by its reflection on another,— only by the light which another casts upon it. Thus a cause has no meaning except in connexion with its effect : a force implies or postulates an exertion of that force : an essence is constituted by the existence which issues from it. Instead of ' is ', therefore, which denotes resting-upon-self, or connexion-with-self, the verb of the second sphere is ' has ', denoting reference, or connexion-with-something-else : e. g. the cause *has* an effect : the thing *has* properties. Instead of numerals, come the prepositions and pronouns of relation, such as which, same, like, as, by, because. The only conjunction in the first stage or Being was ' And ',—mere juxtaposition ; and even that conjunction was perhaps premature, and due to reflective thought, going beyond what was immediately before it, and tracing out connexions with other things. The first stage, as we have seen, treated of the terms of natural thought present in the action of the senses : the second stage—that of Essential Being—deals with scientific, reflective, or mediate thought. What, why, are the questions : comparison and connexion the methods : the establishment of relations of similarity, causation, and co-existence, the purpose in this range of logical method. Its categories are those most familiar to science in its reflective and comparative stage. It is the peculiar home of what are known as Metaphysical subtleties. The natural but delusive tendency of reasoning is to throw the emphasis on one side of the relation, and to regard the other as accessary and secondary. Contrasts between *essentia* and *existentia : substantia* and *modi* : cause and effect : real and apparent : constantly occur.

If the first branch of Logic was the sphere of simple

Being in a point or series of points, the second is that of
difference and discordant Being, broken up in itself. The
progress in this second sphere—of *Essentia* or Relative
being—consists in gradually overcoming the antithesis and
discrepancy between the two sides in it—the Permanent
and the Phenomenal. At first the stress rests upon the
Permanent and true Being which lies behind the seeming—
upon the essence or substratum in the background, on
which the show of immediate Being has been proved by
the process in the first sphere really to rest.   Then, secondly,
Existence comes to the front, and Appearances or Phenomena are regarded as the only realities with which science
can deal.   And yet even in this case we cannot but distinguish between matter and form, between the phenomena
and their laws, between force and its exercises : and thus
repeat the relativity, though both terms in it are now
on the whole transferred into the range of the Phenomenal
world.   The third range of Essential Being is known as
Actuality, where the two elements in relation rise to the
level of independent existences, essences in phenomenal
guise—bound together, and deriving their very characteristics from that close union.   Relativity or correlation is
now clearly apparent in actual form, and comprises the
three heads of Substantial Relation, Causal Relation,
and Reciprocal Relation.   In this case while the two
members of the relation are now indissolubly linked
together, they are no more submitted to each other than
they are independent.   According to Reciprocity everything actual is at once cause and effect : it is the meeting-
point of relations : a whole with independent elements in
mutual interconnexion.   Such a total is the Notion.

This brings us to the third branch of Logic,—the theory
of the Notion, or Grasp of Thought.[1]   The theory of
Causality, with which the second branch closed, continued
to let the thought fall asunder into two unequal halves—
always however in relation or connexion with each other.
But in the present part of the Logic the two halves are
re-united, or in their difference their identity is also recog-

---

[1] No doubt, as Dr. W. T. Harris remarks, *Notion* (used by Dr.
Stirling) is a quite insignificant rendering of Hegel's *Begriff* :—for
which he proposes Self-activity.   But, as he admits, that is just
Hegel's way :   he coins brand-new the old terms, and forces us, if
we will follow him, to think full meaning into them.

nised. Instead of a cause of a thing (which is separate from it in order), we have a concept which is its principle of unity, its universal in which it is individualised. Instead of incessant and endless Relativity, we have Development. By development is meant self-specification, or self-actualisation : the thing is what it becomes, or while it changes it remains identical with itself. The Category of Development is the category or method of philosophic or speculative science : just as Being corresponded to natural thought, and Relativity or Reflection to metaphysical and realistic science. According to the law of Development diversity and unity both receive their due. Mere unity or Being reappears now as Universality or Generality. Mere diversity, or the relativity of essence, re-appears as Particularity, or the speciality of details. And the union of the two is seen in the Individualised notion or real object. In other words, the true thought which really grasps and gets all round its object, which is a real whole, is a Triplicity : it is first seen all as the ground or self-same, the possibility —secondly, all as the existence in details, and difference, the actuality or contingency—and thirdly, all as the self-same in difference, and the possible in actuality. Every object in its full reality is an innate movement ; and to grasp it wholly we must apprehend it as such a self-evolving and self-involving unity of elements, in each of which however it is whole and entire. Thus the Notion embraces the three elements or factors of universal, particular and individual. These three elements first rise to independence and get their full significance or explication in the syllogism, with its three terms and judgments, exhibiting the various ways in which any two of these elements in thought are brought into unity by means of the third. This adequate form is a system or organic unity which contains in itself the premisses of its conclusion or the means to its realisation,—which is a process within itself, and when complete and self-supporting perforce gives itself reality.

The Notion or *Begriff* is where Hegel makes his special mark on Logic. Schelling, even, following on Kant, had (like Schopenhauer after him) lauded the merit of the Intuition at the expense of the mere notion,[1] and expressed himself surprised at Hegel's use of the word. But what Hegel wants first to insist upon is that the Intuition or

[1] See vol. ii, Notes and Illustrations, p. 408.

Perception (*Anschauung*) is built upon the Notion—that it is only because there is a universal principle in its details that the individual reality of the percept is assured. That we can elicit a notion from a perception is only possible because it is implicitly dominated by a universal. Secondly, Hegel wishes to note (as elsewhere) that the full adequate notion, the notion as self-explaining and self-constituting, is all that is meant by the object. Thus the Notion or Subject—*Causa Sui*—when it is fully realised in the plenitude of its elements or differences,—when each element has scope of its own, is the Object—the actual and individualised total of thought, or syllogism in reality. This objective world or Object appears in three forms. An Object is either a mechanical, a chemical, or a teleological object. The terms mechanical and chemical are not to be understood in the narrow sense of a machine or chemical compound. They are to be taken in an analogical sense, just as J. S. Mill speaks of a chemical or geometrical method of treating social problems. The object or realised notion is mechanical, when the unification of the members in the totality comes or seems to come from without, so that the whole or universal they form is external and almost indifferent to the particulars, and only arranges them. An object is chemical, when the connexion or genesis of the compound from its factors is not evident : when the elements are as it were lost, and only give rise to a fresh particular. An object is teleological, when the universal is, though not distinctly conceived as realised, still always as tending to be realised by the particulars. And in each of these grades the object comes more and more to be seen to be a self-enacting, self-legislating being ; more and more a due pendant to the subject-notion. Modern science is a vehement opponent of teleology : and with justice, so far as in teleology, means and end fall apart. But it is mistaken in supposing itself to return to the mechanical point of view. On the contrary its success is most generally secured by rising to the point of view given by the Idea of Life, and by looking upon the objective world as an Organism, that is, as the notion in objectivity, soul indissolubly united with body. But even the Idea of Life, in which we enter the third stage of the notion, is defective as a representation of the truth of Objectivity : for body and soul must part. The conception of an Organism or

living being is too crude.   Reality is no doubt well described
as alive :   the Absolute well defined as Life.   But here
again Life is taken in a higher than its sense of *mere* Life :
it is life as intelligent and volitional energy.   If the universe—the Absolute—can be said to be living, it must be
said also that it is more than Living.   Such a Life—such
existence—is what Aristotle has called θεωρία and ἐνέργεια
of the highest in man.   It is mental and spiritual life.
In its consummation it is the Idea—the absolute Idea—the
totality which is and is aware of itself,—the developed
unity of the Notion with Objectivity.   This unity thus
presented is what lies implicit to our perception in Nature :
and thus the Idea, as developed in Logic, forms the pro-
logue and presupposition to the Philosophy of Nature.

CHAPTER XXIX

THE SEARCH FOR A FIRST PRINCIPLE

IF there be one thing which, more than another, distinguishes Modern Philosophers from the Ancient Philosophy of Athens, it is the desire to discover a First Principle of certainty, a handle by which they may get hold of and set in due order the perplexed mass of reality. They find themselves born to an inheritance of tradition, a mass of belief and lore which overwhelms where it does not support. The long watches of the Middle Ages had been a time of preparation—even if the ' cerebration ' had been somewhat unconscious. The mind had been by discipline trained to freedom. As it worked amid the material and tried to order it and defend it, the intellect grew to recognise its lordship over the load of authority. Overt revolts indeed against coercion by decrees and by canons of dogma had never been wanting even in the quietest of the so-called ' ages of faith '. But it is not in the loudest outcry or the most rampant dissent that progress shows its most effective course. The ' catholic ' and ' orthodox ' tradition equally bears witness to a movement to emancipation, to self-centred intelligence. Such an emancipation however cannot be complete and self-realised without a sharp and painful wrench at the moment of mental birth. The great word of disruption, of self-assertion, of defiance to the past and to the dominant, must be said : and, as human beings are constituted, it will be said in a tone of acerbity for which neither the revolutionist nor the reactionary are severally alone responsible.

Thus to hear the brave words and the bold defiance hurled out by the thinkers of the sixteenth and seventeenth centuries, one might fancy they, like Archimedes, sought a supernal vantage-ground from which they could move the world. Yet, unlike the material earth, the intellectual globe is a burden we each carry with us,—which we find upon us when—if ever—we begin to shake ourselves out of the slothful unconsciousness of our merely vegetative life. For though we all carry it, we do not all feel its weight. In some individuals and in some ages there is so accurate a proportion between the inner power and the outer pressure that the load of belief and custom is but a well-fitting garb, almost a second nature. To others there is a felt disproportion, a sense of superincumbent clothes and uncongenial, unnatural trappings. Out of such struggles to be free, grow, occasionally, philosophers, and reformers. To the former the burden is the burden of the unintelligible : to the latter the burden of the unbearable and intolerable. To the philosopher the removal of the burden consists in such a re-adjustment of the intellectual world that it shall be no longer a foreign thing, but bone of his bone and flesh of his flesh. But, to re-adjust and to re-organise, one must stand back from the objective : one must cast it forth, and look about for a clue to an exit from the maze of confusion. The given and subsistent is put on probation : not rejected, but for the moment declined : not denied, but asked to present its credentials.[1] This is the ἐποχή of the sceptical schools of later Greece ; the invitation to doubt addressed by Descartes to his own soul. It is the protest against that vulgar precipitancy which in primitive and modern credulity is ready to give itself away to any doctrine which has the voice and the garb of outward authority. Or it is the assertion of the royal and inalienable sovereignty of the Subjectivity to be *certain* of whatever claims to be objective and *true* : the assertion that what is true must be seen and experienced to be true. Or it is, in another way, the principle of Socrates : that the beginning of knowledge, the first step in the way of wisdom, is to know that you know nothing— to realise the absolute supremacy of self-consciousness.

It is in short the same demand as Augustine's. There is indeed a wide gulf of temperament and circumstances dividing the bishop of Hippo from the mathematician Descartes and the rationalist Spinoza. But in the cry for the knowledge of ' God and my Soul ' as the first, the indispensable, the sole knowledge : as the *one* knowledge which binds the finite and the infinite together,—the knowledge on which turns the truth of science, and the reality of experience, the great thinkers of these diverse

[1] Cf. p. 68.

ages are at one.[1] They turn their backs upon the external that they may find rest in the truly internal, on the inner certainty, which is not a mere subjective but a very objective also : not a mere *anima mea*, but in close unity therewith *Deus meus*. This is perhaps more explicit in Spinoza, in some points, than in Descartes, and in many respects more decisively put by Augustine than by either. But this is what is really meant by the initial concentration of suspense : this is what is sought when a Principle is sought. Nothing short of this unity of subjective and objective in an Absolute—we may say—Ego, is a principle.

But ' principles ' like other terms are sometimes lightly taken ; and can be in the plural—just as in lower levels of religion and society there can be gods many and lords many. Nor in a way wrongly. For, as has been before pointed out, a principle is the unity of beginning and end : it is only caught hold of by approaching from different directions : it loses its life and power when cut off from the many organs by which it distributes itself so as to grasp reality. If it be essentially one, it is not a bare unit : it cannot, without injury, be reduced to utter simplicity, and accepted in the shape of a single term. And yet this is what almost inevitably happens to every so-called principle.

Like a *deus ex machina*, or a trick of the trade, it is applied to unloose every knot, and to clear any difficulties that arise. But a principle of this stamp possesses no intimate connexion or organic solidarity with the theory which it helps to prop. It is always at hand as a ready-made schema or heading, and can be attached to the most incongruous orders of fact. Thus in the works of Aristotle, the principle of ' End ' or ' Activity ' has sometimes seemed to be applied to whatever subject comes forward, and like a hereditary official vestment to suit all its wearers equally well or equally ill. What is true ' on the whole ' is not always true ' of each ': the καθόλου never quite equals the καθ' ἕκαστον. The modern principle of Utility is equally flexible in its application to the problems of moral and social life. It costs no trouble to pronounce the magic word, and even ' such as are of weaker capacity ' may make something out of such a formula. But an abstract

[1] Augustin. *Soliloq.* i. 7. ' Deum et animam scire cupio. Nihilne plus ? Nihil omnino.'

formula, which is equally applicable to everything, is not particularly applicable to anything. While it seems to save trouble, and is so plain as to be almost tautological (as when the worth of a thing or act is explained to mean its utility), it really suggests fresh questions in every case, and multiplies the difficulty. Having an outward adaptability to every kind of fact, the principle has no true sympathy with any : it becomes a mere form, which we use as we do a measuring-rod, moving it along from one thing to another. We are always reverting to first principles as our last principles also. Even Aristotle, when he remarked that an object had to be criticised from its own principles and not from general formulae, saw through the fallacy of this style of argument.

This is like asking for bread and getting a stone. The philosopher, who ought to take us through the shut chambers of the world, merely hands us a key at the gate, telling us that it will unlock every door, and then the insides will speak for themselves. But we would have our philosopher do a little more than this. Not being ourselves omniscient, we should be glad of a guide-book at the least, and perhaps even of the services of an interpreter to explain some peculiarities, some startling phenomena, and sights even more unpleasant than those which appalled the spouse of the notorious Bluebeard. Or, dropping metaphor, we wish the formula to be applied systematically and thoroughly. When that is done the formula loses its abstractness ; it gains those necessary amplifications and qualifications, as we call them, without which no theory explains much or gives much information. And thus, instead of fancying that our initial formula contains the truth in a nutshell, we shall find that it is only one step to be taken on the way to truth, and that its narrow statement sinks more and more into insignificance, as its amplified theory gains in significance.

But an adequate principle must have other qualities.[1] What has been said up to this point, only amounts to a condition, that our principle must cease to be abstract and formal, and must become concrete and real. What

[1] ' A Principle,' says Herbart (*Psychologie als Wissenschaft*, Einl.), ' should have the double property of having originally a certainty of its own, and of generating other certainty. The way and manner in which the second comes about is the Method.'

we want, it may be said, is a Beginning. But a beginning is not exactly the same thing as a principle : a beginning is to a large extent a matter of choice and convenience,— a matter depending on the state and prospects of the beginner ; and the main point is not where we should begin, but that we should be thorough in our treatment. It is otherwise, however, in the present case. For the skill of the expositor simply lies in the exactitude with which he reproduces the spontaneous movement of growth in his object. His art is *celare artem :* to retire, as it were, into the background, and seem to leave the object to expound itself. In a dramatic work it is no doubt the hand of the dramatist that seems to set the whole of the characters in motion, that weaves destinies and snips the thread of life. And yet in a perfect work of dramatic art everything must seem to flow on by a necessity of character, a consecution of inner fate. The true artist dare not act or allow the *deus ex machina.* So every genuine work of science—which is more than a compilation, a school-book, a bundle of notes, and contributions towards a subject— must be a self-determined unity—a self-justifying scheme in which the personality of the worker enters into and is absorbed in the system of his work.

If this is generally true, it is above all a canon to rule the logician. He at least must follow the Logos and the Logos alone. His theme must be a law unto itself : all its movements must be freely and nobly objective. For his subject-matter is at least an organism, and develops according to an inward law. But it is even more than an organism : it must not merely develop, as organisms do,— not merely live and grow—but *know* that it develops and as it were *will* its own development—and in that harmony of being, willing, and knowing, be essentially one. In Hegelian language it must not merely be implicit—*an sich* or *für uns*—the subject of a change which it undergoes and feels, but without definitely realising,—the subject of a change which we (the historians) perceive. It must also be *für sich* : aware of its modifications, an agent in bringing them about : and yet withal in so looking forth and willing, be self-possessed, and self-enjoying.

The principle of Hegelianism is the principle of Development, the principle of the Notion—but a Notion which is objective as well as subjective—the Idea. That principle then determines the beginning of Logic. We must know the whole course of growth and history before we can say where is the true commencement. It must be that out of which the end can obviously and spontaneously issue. In a sense, it must implicitly contain the end. It must show us the very beginning of thought, before it has yet come to the full consciousness of itself,—when the truth of what it is still lurks in the background and has to be developed. We must see thought in its first and fundamental calling. As the biologist, when he describes the structure of a plant, rests upon the assumption of a previous development of parts, in an existing plant, which has resulted in a seed,—but begins with the seed from which the plant is derived: so the logician must begin with a point which in a way presupposes the system to which it leads. But in its beginning this presupposition is not apparent : and in fact, the presupposition will only appear when the development of the system is complete. The first step in a process, just because it is a step, may be said to presuppose the completed process. Thus the beginning of Logic presumes the fullest realisation of Mind, as the beginning of botany can only be told by one who knows the whole story of the plant. It is from this circumstance that Hegel describes philosophy as a circle rounded in itself, where the end meets with the beginning, or says that philosophy has to grasp its original grasp or conceive its concept. In other words, it is not till we reach the conclusion that we see, in the light thus shed upon the beginning, what that beginning really was. From the general analogy of the sciences we should not expect that the beginning of thought would be full-grown thought, or indeed seem to the undiscerning eye to be thought at all. In many cases, the embryonic organism shows but little similarity to the adult, and occasionally a violent abruptness seems, on cursory glance, to mark off one stage of a creation's growth from the next. Who that knew not the result could in the seed prefigure to himself the tree ? The beginning is not usually identifiable with the final issue, except by some effort to trace the process of connexion. The object of science only appears in its truth when the science has done its work.

The beginning of philosophy must hold a germ of development, however dead and motionless it may seem. But it

must also to some extent be a result,—the result of the
development or concentration of consciousness ;—of the
other forms of which it is the hypothetical foundation,
or, of which it is (otherwise viewed) the first appearance.
The variety of imaginative conception, and the chaos of
sense, must vanish in a point, by an act of abstraction,
which leaves out all the variety and the chaos,—or rather
by an act of distillation, which draws out of them their
real essence and concentrated virtue.   This variety, when
thoroughly examined and tested, shrivels up into a point :—
it only *is*.   Everything definite as we call it, the endless
repetitions of existence, have disappeared, and have left
only the energy of concentration, the unitary point of
Being.

We may describe the process in two ways.   We may
say that we have left out of sight all existing differences,—
that we have stripped off every vestige of empirical conceptions, and left a residue of pure thought.   The thought
is pure, perhaps, but it is not entire.   In this way of
describing it, pure thought is the most abstract thought,—
the last outcome of those operations which have divested
our conceptions of everything real and concrete about
them.   But thus to speak of the process as Abstraction
would be to express half of the truth only :   and would
really leave us a mere zero, or gulf of vacuity.   In the
beginning there would then be nothing—the mere annihilation of all possible and actual existence.   And it is certainly true that in the beginning there can be nothing.—
On the other hand, and secondly, there is affirmation as
well as negation involved in the ultimate action by which
sense and imagination pass into thought.   They are not
left behind, and the emptiness only retained :   they are
carried into their primary consequence, or into their
proximate truth.   They are reduced to their simplest
equivalent or their lowest term in the vocabulary of thought :
which is Being.   The process which creates the initial
point of pure thought is at once an abstraction from everything, and a concentration upon itself in a point :—which
point, accordingly, is a unity or inter-penetration of positive
and negative.   This absolute self-concentration into a
point is the primary step by which Mind comes to know
itself,—the first step in the Absolute's process of self-
cognition—that process which it is the purpose of Logic to

trace, so far as it is conducted in the range of mere thought.

The bare point of Being and nothing more is the beginning in the process of the Absolute's self-cognition : it is, in other words, our first and rudimentary apprehension of reality,—the narrow edge by which we come in contact with the universe of Reason. For these are two aspects of the same. The process of the self-cognition or mani-festation of the Absolute Idea is the very process by which philosophers (not philosophers only) have built up the edifice of thought. What the one statement views from the universal side or the totality, the other views in con-nexion with the several achievements of individual thinkers. Of course the evolution of the system of thought, as it is brought about by individuals, leaves plenty of room for the play of what is known as Chance. The Natural History of Thought or the History of Philosophers has to regard the action of national character upon individual minds, and the reciprocal action of these minds upon one another. The History of Organic Nature similarly presents the dependence of the species upon their surroundings, and of one species upon another in the medium of its conditions. Gradually Physical Science reduces these conditions to their universal forms, and may try to exhibit the evolution of the animal through its species in all grades of develop-ment. So in the Science of the development of this Idea the accidents, as we may call them, disappear : and the temporary and local questions, which once engrossed the deepest attention, fade away into generalised forms of universal application. Philosophy, as it historically pre-sents itself in the world, is not an accidental production, or dependent on the arbitrary choice of men. The accident, if such there be, is that these particular men should have been the philosophers, and not that such should have been their philosophy. They were, according to their several capacity for utterance, only the mouth-pieces of the Spirit of the Times,—of the absolute mind under the superficial limitations of their period. They saw the Idea of their world more clearly and distinctly than other men ; and therein lies their title to fame : but really their words were only a reflex,—an almost involuntary and necessary movement, due to the pressure of the cosmical reason. The great philosophers are, like all men in all estates, and

according to their measure, the ministers of the Truth,—
apostles charged to bring about that consummation of the
times in which reality is more fully apprehended and more
adequately estimated. Necessity is laid upon them to
consecrate themselves to the service of the Idea, and to
devote their lives to the noble but austere work of speculation—the work which seeks *sine ira et studio* to reconstruct that city of God which is the permanent, if it often
be the hidden, foundation of human life.

CHAPTER XXX

THE LOGIC OF DESCRIPTION : NATURAL REALISM :
BEING

THE antithesis between thought and being, between idea and actuality, between notion and object, is almost a commonplace of criticism. Between the ideas of the subject and objectivity a great gulf seems to yawn fixed and impassable. Thinkers, like Anselm and Descartes, have (it is asserted) attempted by a trick which cheated themselves to get from the notion to the object. But—as Kant is supposed to have for ever shown—these *decepti deceptores* are now universally discredited.[1] Yet the same Kant had shown that the ' things ' of ordinary experience are only ideas or appearances in consciousness. These latter ideas, however, were verified by the necessity of interdependence in which they stood, as given by sense. From the notions which Anselm and Descartes proposed to invest with objectivity, there was absent the feature of sense-perception. They were not limited and real ideas, but synthetic laws, general and abstract aspects of reality, modes of conception. They were not definite and individualised things, but terms or conditions for all concepts and realities. They were forms,—forms essential to the explication of reality—and never mere parts of reality.

With such ' forms ' or ' thought-terms ', such abstractions, Logic (*à la mode de Hegel*) has to deal. And in dealing with them it has to counteract this popular distinction (which Kant inclines toward) which sets up an insuperable division between thought and being, between reality and syllogism, between is and is known. Certain of these denominators which thinking employs to describe reality the popular mind wholly identifies with reality. That being is a thought, that force and thing are only modes of conception, sounds to the untrained intellect

[1] What he did show was that these Ideas were not objects in the vulgar sense of reality, or things.

only a verbal quibble. Things, beings, are there—*out there*, it says : force is ' ultimate reality '. It is perhaps ready to allow that *substances* are only mental figments: but it is more doubtful about causes, and inclines to assume them to be in outside nature, and to generate a real necessity in things. On the other hand, it has little doubt that concepts and syllogism are only our ways of looking at reality,—the reality of substances and phenomena, with quality and quantity: that ' final cause ' is a mere subjective principle of explanation : and that ideas and knowledge are altogether additions superinduced on a real world.

Now what the Logic shows is that, on one hand, all these terms are ideal and regulative ; and on the other that they are real, because constitutive of reality. Showing— or shall we say, reminding us—that being is after all a form of thought, it shows us that knowledge, at the other end, contains or implies reality. It is the business of logic as a fundamental philosophy to dispel the illusion that sensations are fixed reality : that causes and effects are an absolutely real order ; whereas concepts and sciences and still more aesthetic and moral principles are not. Its doctrine is that all our thought-terms, the most vulgar and the most delicate, are, as we may put it, symbolical of reality : explications and manifestations of it. Absolutely real—if that means utterly unideal—none of them are. On the other hand, absolutely ideal,—if that means utterly unreal—none of them are either. If you call them real, their reality is that of thought. If you call them ideal, it is an ideality of a real. Being is not a fixed and solid substratum, a hard rock of reality, on which we may build our relations and further determinations. It also is a thought : it also lives in relation, and becomes more real by further determination.[1] But the habit comes natural to the majority to attribute essential and independent reality (total reality) to the thought-modes it is familiar with in practice : whereas the modes familiar to more advanced intelligence are put aside as merely ideal.

Thus in proportion as Logic insists on the reality of idea, it insists also on the ideality of being. Being is after all a thought : when separate from the relations of experi-

[1] Cf. the controversy between Schiller and Goethe as to idea and observation, quoted by Whewell, *Scientific Ideas*, i. 36.

ence, a very poor thought. A 'supreme being' even is
a thought. And the question of questions for Logic is
what degree of reality, what amount of truth does each
result of unification express. Is it self-consistent and
complete, or does it imply further elements, and if so, in
what direction does it suggest and receive completion?
But at the best the reality of a logical term is an abstract
or formal reality, and consists in its power to interpret, to
expound, to define the Absolute. Its more concrete and
material reality it has in Nature and in Mind. There
however Philosophy has in a further measure to repeat its
earlier lesson and show that Nature is not without its ideal
aspect, and that Mind is founded on physical reality.

All science tends to carry us over the hard lines of separation which practical interests treat as if ultimate disruptions.
The sciences of Nature, for instance, in their completed
circle must carry us from the inorganic to the organic:
must in some way make a path from the lifeless to the alive.
The science of thought has a corresponding task. It has
to show that the incommensurability between thought and
being, or between the idea and actuality, disappears on
closer examination. When we trace the development of
thought sufficiently far, we see that Being is an imperfect
or inadequate thought,—certainly not inadequate to the
Idea, but not for that reason generically differing from it.
The fixity of Being as more than, and superior to, mere
Thought is a habit of mind, due to the same worldly-minded
immobility as leads us all to believe (and, within the limited
practical range, to believe rightly) that the earth is solidly at
rest, notwithstanding all the demonstrations of the Coper-
nicans. But Thought has not deposited all its burden, or
uttered all its meaning in Being. Being is the veriest
abstraction,—the very rudiment of thought—meagre as
meagre can be. It is on one side the bare position or
affirmation of thought: on the other hand it is the very
negation of thought,—if thought be only possible under
difference. For a mere ' Is ' is a mere indescribable without-
difference. There is no such thing as mere Being: or mere
Being is mere nothing: *mere* Being is not.

The first category of Ontology is that of Being. It is
the merest simplicity and meagreness, with nothing definite
in it at all: and for that very reason constantly liable to
be confused with categories of more concrete burden. It

denotes all things, and connotes next to nothing. It does not however mean something which has being ; it does not mean definite being : still less does it mean permanent and substantial being. Ordinary language certainly uses being in all these senses. But if we are to be logical, we must not mix up categories with one another : we must take terms at their precise value. Mere Being then is the mere ' Is ', which can give no explanation or analysis of itself : which is indescribable in itself : which is an ' Is ' and nothing more. The simplest answer to those who invest Being with so much signification, is to ask them to consider the logical *copula.* ' Every school-boy knows ' that the ' Is ' of the copula disappears in several languages : that it is far from indispensable in Latin : that in Greek e.g. the demonstrative article serves the same purpose. In Hebrew too the pronouns officiate for the so-called substantive verb : and the same verb probably does not exist in the Polynesian family of languages, where its place is supplied by what we call the demonstrative pronoun.[1] In the copula, which according to M. Laromiguière, as quoted by Mr. Mill, expresses only ' *un rapport spécial entre le sujet et l'attribut* ', we encounter the mere undeveloped and unexplained unifying of thought, the very abstraction of relativity.[2]

In the beginning, then, there is nothing and yet that nothing is. Such is the fundamental antithesis of thought : or the discrepancy which makes itself felt between each

---

[1] The use of the substantival form *Being* for the verbal (participle, infinitive, or indicative) suggests an idea of permanence and substance, or essence. So potentiality seems much more real than *may* or *can.* And yet the phrase He knows δυνάμει is only equivalent to He can or may know (δύναται or ἐνδέχεται).

[2] When it is said that : ' It is strange that so profound a thinker as Hegel should not have seen that the conception of definite objects, such as a *dog* and *cat*, is prior no less in nature than in knowledge to the conception of abstract relations, such as *is* and *is not*,' it is difficult to say what the writer meant. Had he ever heard of geometry ? Both in nature and in knowledge (i. e. in the natural process from sense to thought) chairs and tables are prior to lines and surface. The mathematical point and line are abstractions, i. e. thoughts, and no image of sensuous reality. It is also true that the ordinary conception of the sun's movements was ' prior no less in nature than in knowledge ' to the theory of the earth's rotation. And no doubt Hegel, sedate though his boyhood was, had made the acquaintance of dog and cat in his pre-logical days : as of balls and windows before he was turned upon Euclid. See Mansel's *Letters, Lectures,* &c., p. 209.

several term of thought and the whole Idea of which they
are the expression. Being is the term emphasised as
absolute by understanding : then the dialectical power,
or the consciousness of the whole, steps in to counteract the
one-sided element. In other words, thought, the total
thought, asks what is Being, mere and simple ; and answers
mere nothing.[1] The one aspect of the point is as justifiable
as the other. In other words the two aspects are indissoluble : they are in one. The term ' Unity ', applied to the
relation of Being and Not, may perhaps mislead : and it is
therefore better to say that the two points of view are (as
Mr. Spencer puts it) at once ' antithetical and inseparable '.
An unrelated being, an ' absolute ' (i.e. separate and
transcendent) reality is an Unknowable, i.e. an ineffable, an
unspeakable of which we can legitimately predicate a
not-   , leaving imagination to fill up the blank after
the hyphen. A mere Not, with no substratum which it
negatives, is mere Being : and a mere Being, which has
no substratum, is a mere Not. The movement upward
and the movement downward are here illustrated : and it
is evident that they are the same movement,[2]—the same
unrest, only differentiated as up and down by some *termini*
not yet explicitly brought into view. Each—Is and Not—
as it seeks to differentiate itself, to make itself clear, passes
into the other. In fact, the very vocation, calling, or notion
of Being and Nothing, is not Being and Nothing, but the
tendency of each to pass into the other. Their truth, in
short, is not in themselves, but in their process,—and that
process by which the one passes into the other is ' To
become '. Try to get at mere Being and you are left with
Nought : of mere Nought you can only say it is. The two
abstractions have no truth except in the passage into
one another : and this passage or transition is ' To become '.
Take reality apart from what it leads on to, and from what
it has come from, apart from its end or purpose and from its
cause, take it as mere being : then this being in its supposed

[1] As *Being* to ordinary unthinkingness seems to mean a great deal
it cannot expound, so the mind full of the mystic depths of time
and space is disgusted to find them turn so empty and shallow
when it would set forth its wealth. See Augustin. *Confess.* xi. 14.

[2] This may be illustrated by saying that to *affirm* is the same
energy of thought as to *deny*, and that the difference lies in the
terms related by the judgment. *In themselves*, the one act is as
empty or meaningless as the other.

singleness and self-subsistence is really annihilated : *stat magni nominis umbra* : but it is the name of nothing. True being is always on the way to or from being : to stop is fatal.

This unity or inseparability of opposite elements in a truth or real notion is the stumbling-block to the incipient Hegelian. The respectable citizens of Germany were amazed, says Heine, at the shamelessness of J. G. Fichte, when he proclaimed that the Ego produced the world, as if that had cast doubts on their reality ; and the ladies were curious to know whether Madame Fichte was included in the general denial of substantial existence.[1] If easy-going critics treated Fichte in this way, they had even better source for amusement in Hegel. That Being and Nothing is the same was a perpetual fund for jokes, too tempting to be missed. Now, in the baldness, and occasionally paradoxical style, of Hegel's statements, there is some excuse for such exaggerations. Being and Nothing are not merely the same : they are also different : they at least tend to pass into each other. In the technical language of logicians, the question is not what being denotes, but what it connotes. The word ' is ' had, it may be, originally a ' demonstrative ' meaning, a ' pronominal ' force, which in course of time passed from a local or sensuous meaning to express a thought. No doubt ' is ' and ' is not ' are wide enough apart in our application of them as copula of a proposition : but if we subtract the two terms and leave only the copula standing, the difference of the two becomes inexpressible and unanalysable. In both there is the same statement of immediacy or face-to-faceness : that two things are brought to confront each other,—united, as it were, without producing any real or specific sort of union. If Thought be unifying, Being is the minimum of unification : if Thought be relating, Being is the most abstract of relations. So abstract, indeed, that its relativity is completely lost sight of : so utterly one, that it vanishes in a point. And just because it *is* (as it seems) out of relations, it must be nothing. No doubt, between the two terms Being and not-Being a difference is meant ; when they are employed, a difference is thrown into them ; and then they are not the same : but if we keep out of sight what is meant, and stick to the ultimate point which is said, we shall find that mere being and mere

[1] Heine, *Ueber Deutschland (Werke)*, v. 213.

nothing are alike inapprehensible by themselves, and that to institute a difference we must go out of and beyond them. Perhaps some approach to the right point of comprehension may be made, if we note that when two people quarrel and can give no reason or further development to their opposite assertions, the one person's ' is ' is exactly equal (apart from subsequent explanations) to the other's 'is not'. The mere ' Is ' and ' Is not ' have precisely the same amount of content : a mere affirmation or assertion, which is mere nothing,—because connecting, where there is nothing to connect.

The truth of ' is ' then turns out ' become ' : nothing *is* : all things are coming to be and passing out of being. This illustrates the meaning of the word ' truth ' in Hegel. It is partly synonymous with ' concrete ', partly with the ' notion '. With concrete : because to get at the truth, we must take into account a new element, kept out of sight in the mere affirmation of being. With notion : because if we wish to comprehend being, we must grasp it as ' becoming '. For truth lies in transcending the first or merely given. We have to go forward, and to go backward, as it were : forward from being, backward to being : we look before and after. The attempt to isolate the mere point of being is impossible in thought : it would only lead to the ' representation' of being,—i.e. the notion of being would be arrested in its development, and identified probably with a sensible thing, i.e. with *something*, and some concrete thing said to be.

If being, however, is truly apprehended as a passage from the unknown to the known, or as emergence from bare vacuity, then it implies a definiteness, which we missed before. Somewhat has become : or the indeterminate being has been invested with definiteness and distinct character. Mere being (mere *Is*) is nothing : to be something *is* must be not something else. The second step in the process to self-realisation therefore is reached : Being has become Somewhat ; which is more, because it professes less. The fluid unity or movement from ' is ' to ' is not ', and *vice versa*, has crystallised : and ' There is ' is the still imperfectly unified result precipitated. By this term we imply the *finitude* of being,—imply that a portion has been cut off from the vague, and contrasted with something else. In the ordinary application of the word, Being is especially employed to denote this stage of definite being.[1] Thus we speak of bringing something into being : by which we mean, not mere being, but a definite being, or, in short, reality. Reality is determinateness, as opposite to mere vagueness. To be real, it is necessary to be somewhat,— to limit and define. Whatever is anything or is real, is *eo facto* finite. Even an infinite therefore to be real must submit to self-limitation. This is the necessity of finitude : in order to be anything more and higher, there must come, first of all, a determinate being and reality. But reality, as we have seen, implies negation : it implies limiting, distinction, and dependence. Everything finite, every ' somewhat ', has somewhat else to counteract, narrow, and thwart it. To be somewhat (*esse aliquid*) is an object of ambition, as Juvenal implies : but it is only an unsatisfactory goal after all. For somewhat always implies something else, by which it is limited : whereas mere being, just because it is nothing, is free from the check of an other.

This, then, is the price to be paid for rising into reality, and coming to be somewhat : there is always somewhat else to be minded. The very point which makes a ' somewhat ', as above a mere ' nothing ', is its determinateness : and determinateness, as at first determinateness from outside, a given and passive determinateness, is also a negation and limit. Now the limit of a thing is that point where it begins to be somewhat else : where it passes out of itself and yields to another. Accordingly in the very act of being determined, somewhat is passing over into another : it is altering, and becoming somewhat else. Thus a ' something ' implies for its being the being of somewhat else : its being is as it were only to be beside something else,—it is finite, and alterable, a *this* with a *that* always in the neighbourhood. Such is the character of determinate being. It leads to an endless series from some to an other, and so on *ad infinitum* : everything as a somewhat, as a determinate being, in reality, presupposes a something else, and that again has some third thing ; and so the chain is extended with its everlasting *And*, And, And, (as in the children's way of telling a story). Somewhat-ness is always vexed by the fact that it is not somewhat else : and for that very reason, ceasing to be the primary object, it becomes somewhat else becomes the somewhat.

---

[1] πᾶσα οὐσία δοκεῖ τόδε τι σημαίνειν (Ar. *Cat.* 5).

And so the same story is repeated in endless progression, till one gets wearied with the repetition of finitude which is held out as infinite.

Thus in determinate being as in mere being we see the apparent fixity resolved into a double movement—the alteration from some to somewhat else, and *vice versa*. But a movement like this implies after all that there is a something which alters : which is alterable, but which alters into somewhat. This somewhat which alters into somewhat, and thus retains itself, is a being which has risen above alteration,which is independent of it because including it : which is *for itself*, and not for somewhat else. Thus in order to advance a step further from determinate and alterable being, we have only to keep a firm grasp on both sides of the process, and not suffer the one to slip away from the other. We must not merely *say*, but energise the unity of the two ' antithetical yet inseparable ' elements we are naturally disposed to take and leave only as One *and* an Other. Something becomes something else : in short, the one side passes on to the other side of the antithesis, and the limitation is absorbed. The new result is something *in* something else : the limit is taken up within : and this being which results is its own limit, i. e. no restrictive limit at all, but self-imposed characteristic and definiteness. It is Being-for-self :—the third step in the process of thought under the general category of Being. The range of Being which began in a vague nebula, and passed into a series of points, is now reduced to a single point, self-complete and whole.

This Being-for-self is a kind of true infinite, which results by absorption of the finite. The false infinite, which has already come before us, is the endless range of finitude, passing from one finite to another, from somewhat to somewhat else, until *satiety* sets in with weariness. The true infinite is *satisfaction*,—the inclusion of the other being into self, so that it is no longer a limit, but a constituent part in the being. Such inclusion in the unity of an idea, of elements which are realistically separate,is termed ' ideality '. The antithesis is reduced to become an organic and dependent part. It still exists, but as no longer outside and independent. Thus in determinate being the determinateness is found in somewhat else : in being-for-self the determinateness is self-realisation. Being-for-self may be

shortly expressed by 'one' or 'each': as determinate
being a, or an, or by 'some': and Being simple has no
nominal equivalent. As 'some' is always fractional or
partial, 'each' is always a whole or unit. Mere Being has
not the consistency of any noun or pronoun : it is the bare
(impersonal) verb.

But 'each for self' expresses the sentiment of an armed
neutrality with implicit leanings to universal war,—the
bellum omnium contra omnes. Each is self-centred, independent, resting upon self, and not minding anything else,—
which is now thrown out as indifferent into the background.
Each is centripetal ; anything else is for it a matter of no
moment. If determinate being was something to be explained by something other, this is or professed to be self-
explanatory, and rests upon itself. It seems purely affirmative, and promises to give a definite unity. But we
cannot free thought from negation in this sphere, any more
than in the earlier. We may, if we like, assert the absolute
self-sufficingness, primariness, and unalterability of each ;
but a very little reflection shows the opposite to be true.
The very notion of each is exclusiveness towards the rest :
a negative and, as it were, polemical attitude towards
others is the very basis of Being-for-self. One after one,
they each rise to confront each, each excluding each, until
their self-importance is reduced to be a mere point in a
series of points, one amongst many. When that is clearly
seen, their qualitative character has disappeared : and
there is left only their quantity.[1] The negative attitude
of each to each forms a sort of bond connecting them. If
to the reference which connects we give the name of attraction, then we may say that the repulsion of each against
each is exactly equal to their mutual attraction. And thus,
in the language of Hobbes, the universal quarrel is only
the other side of the general union in the great Leviathan :
repulsion, in the shape of mutual fear, is the principle of
attraction. Thus each for self is repeated endlessly :
instead of the atom or unit we have a multitude, utterly
indifferent to what each is for itself. The mere fact that
it is, entitles it to count, and so constitutes quantity.

Here we may shortly recapitulate the categories of
Quality or Being Proper. It forms three steps or grades :

[1] Hence the disparaging sense in which the term 'individual'
may be used.

those of indeterminate being : determinate being : self-
determined being : or if we speak of them as processes, we
have becoming : alteration : attraction and repulsion.[1]
From the extreme of abstraction and concentration thought,
under the form of Being, passes on to greater determinateness and development. The fixity of mere Being is seen
to imply a distinction of elements, and a dependence of
one upon the other : where the ' is ' and ' is not ' part from
each other sufficiently to let us distinguish them. This is
the stage of finitude : when we say that there is somewhat,
but there are others, and imply that any one has an end,
a limit, a negation in its nature. These words describe the
finite scene,—a fragmentary being which makes an advance
upon indeterminateness, but loses its wholeness and is
always and necessarily leading on to something else. It is
the revulsion from the vague and yet unspecified universal
to definite and limited particulars. In the third stage the
limit is uplifted and included in the particular, which now
contains its negation in itself,—is (by accepting its dependence) independent, is its own ground, and may be called
an individual. But an individual, again, implies an aggregate of ones, or a multitude. This being-for-self is an
individual or atom : it is the basis of those higher developments known as subjectivity and personality. These are,
as it were, higher multiples of it.

This first sphere of thought, apparently so abstruse and
unreal in its abstractions, had to be thus narrowly discussed
because it presents all the difficulties and peculiarities of
Hegel in their elementary form. They are clearly the
fundamental problems of ancient Greek philosophy—of that
first or fundamental philosophy which discusses Being and
its intrinsic attributes or accidents. Modern superficiality
has sometimes reproached these old thinkers (who, forsooth,
' knew no language but their own ') for their tiresome
insistence on this problem of Is and Is not. Compared,
indeed, with what are called topics of interest, e.g. the Soul
and the Hereafter, or the origins of the Cosmic process,
tiresome such inquiry is. But it is the bitter lesson of
experience that till such fundamentals are at least critically
surveyed, the interesting topics will still (and in more than
one sense) belong to the Unknowable. Herbart not less
than Hegel sees it is the prime business of philosophical

[1] These latter terms being used in a metaphorical sense.

criticism (i. e. of philosophy) to examine thoroughly those
primary notions on which the whole structure of thought
rests. It is on the comprehension of the radical limitations
latent in the seemingly simplest terms of thought, that the
profoundest problems of human interest ultimately turn.

Thus, in the first place, the process of Being, as seen
in the light of the whole system of Logic, shows that reality
is truly known only as a trinity,—or perhaps rather as a
duality in unity. This is the ' Notion ' or ' Grasp ' of Being.
First, reality seems an unspecialised and self-centred being,—
and that by itself is mere nothing : a mere *universal*.
Second, it appears a specialised and differentiated being of
some and other : a mere *particular*, limited by other particulars, and so finite. Third, as a combination of the two
earlier stages : as wholeness with determinateness, as
unity ; and so an *individual* which is the *true* or complete
and authentic character of all being. In the *metaphysics*
of Being these three elements follow, one after another : but
in the *logic* of the notion they interpenetrate, and each of
them is the others and the total. The truth or the notion
of being takes it in Being-for-self as a universalised particular
or as an individual.—In the second place : the sphere of
mere Being is that of *mere* identity : that of determinate
being is the sphere of otherness, difference : that of self-
determined being is the sphere of well-grounded existence.—
Thirdly : the first sphere may be illustrated by the freedom
of indeterminateness, expressed by the word ' may ' : the
second by necessity or determinateness, expressed by the
word ' must ' : and the third, by the freedom which even
in its determinateness is self-determining, expressed by
the word ' will '.—Fourthly : these steps illustrate the
meaning of the Hegelian technical terms *setzen : aufheben :
an sich : für sich : Idealität : Realität*. Thus Determinate
Being or somewhat is *an sich* or implicitly (by implication)
somewhat else : and the process of determinate being is
to lay it down or express (*setzen*) it as such. When this
explicitly-stated ' other ' or limit is included in the Being,
and reduced into a unity with somewhat in each Being-
for-self, it is said to be ' *aufgehoben* '—uplifted, as it were,
so that it is no longer a separate existent, but is still an
efficient element. As being partly *this*, and partly *that*, now
one, and now an *other*, which limits and is limited, determinate being is *Realität*. The characteristic of reality is

externality of its parts, which are thus left side by side quasi-independent : that of ideality is unity and solidarity of function. When the mutual dependence of elements is tightened till it becomes equivalent to unity and totality, these elements are seen in their Ideality (*Idealität*). Such a total has the others in it as elements (*Momente*) ; they are there ideally (*ideëller Weise*), as it were (in the loose analogical use of that term) organically : that is, they are denied the privilege, which their total has, of being-for-themselves. They do not enjoy the benefit of their own being, though their presence is felt.—Fifthly : Being-for-self is absolute negativity; i.e. the negation of negation. Determinate being was a negation of Being mere and simple : Being-for-self is the negation of this, and so a return to true affirmation, as including the element of negation.

Being seemed to describe a complete reality. But its latent limitation has become explicit. It only retains itself by a self-assertion which leaves it a mere abstract unit, or atom,—a unit with nothing in it to be united, and where it matters not whether it be somewhat or other. The quality of Being, in which all qualitative attributes are lost and sunk, is Quantity : the characteristic of which is to be a matter of no importance to Being, as it originally presents itself. In other words, whilst Quality is identical with Being,—while Being means qualitativeness, and the Being of a thing means its quality, or constitution ; Quantity is external to Being, and a thing is, while its quantity undergoes all sorts of variation. At least this is true within certain limits : for quantity is not an ultimate category any more than quality. But for the present the truth of quality is quantity ; or, in other words, if a thing is to be anything definite it must ultimately rest on a solid atom : must be a unit and amenable to measurement. First come qualities, such as sweet, green, and the like : these seem to be truth and reality to the senses and the natural mind : and in their universality are represented by the abstract terms of qualitative being. The first step in the progress of knowledge consists in seeing that quality presupposes quantity. Number, in short, is the proximate truth to which the vague qualitative distinction of *a*, *some*, and *each* is to be reduced. The qualitative differences of sounds are reduced to relations or ratios of number : and so are the other data of sensation. We see this truth recognised in the Atomic School, which may be taken to represent the summing-up of that period of thought which begins with the ' Being ' of Parmenides, and the ' Becoming ' of Heraclitus. When Democritus says that, although bitter and sweet are conventional distinctions, yet in reality there is only atoms and void,[1] he is introducing a distinction between real and apparent. But again the irregular and sporadic appearances of species of quality are replaced by a gradual and regular series of quantities. With mere Being you have a conception quite unfit for describing the manifold reality. But by breaking up the whole Being into a countless number of atoms of being, you get the means of establishing an equation between a given sensible and some multiple of the atomic unit. Thus Atomism, with its many bits of being and its interfluent non-being in which they can unite, replaces the total and complete universe of being and its attendant shadow of unreality, the world of opinion. Still the *Is not* clings to the *Is* : if each atom seems complete, they are subject to a necessity which forces them by negation, i.e. by the void (as Atomism figuratively calls the repulsion of the atoms) to meet each other and form apparent unities. Before a step could be made to higher problems, it was necessary to see that the proximate truth of the qualitative world,—or world of sense proper (ἰδία αἴσθησις), is in its simplest terms a quantitative world, or world of common sensibles (κοινὰ αἰσθητά), universalised sensibles, number and quantity.

The sphere of quantity need only be briefly sketched. It has its three heads : (1) quantity in general,—the universal and vague notion of quantitativeness, the mere conception of reality as the Great and the Little, or the More and Less : [2] (2) Quantum, or defined quantity, expressed in the shape of a number : and (3) the quantitative ratio or degree, which is the individualisation or self-determination of numbers, or their application to one another,—which gives the real meaning and value of numbers. The fundamental antithesis, which we found in quality, comes before us here more definitely as the opposition of many ones in one number. In every quantity

---

[1] νόμῳ γλυκὺ καὶ νόμῳ πικρόν· ἐτεῇ δὲ ἄτομα καὶ κενόν, Democritus ap. Sext. Empir. *adv. Math.* vii. 135.

[2] Aristotle's μᾶλλον καὶ ἧττον : see *Metaph.* i. 6 τὸ μέγα καὶ τὸ μικρόν.

there are the two elements : the ' one ', unity or solidarity, which renders a total number possible, and the ' many ' or multiplicity, which gives it real body and character. By this quantitative law, reality must always be both Continuous and Discrete. Thus when I regard a line as consisting of a number of points I treat it as a discrete quantity : as many in one. When, on the other hand, I regard the line as the unity of these points, it becomes a continuous quantity. These distinctions are not so trivial as they may appear : they lie at the bases of paradoxes like those by which Zeno disproved the ordinary representations of motion, and when a M.P. informs the House of Commons that it is impossible to divide 73*l*. 1*s*. 6*d*. by 1*l*. 2*s*. 6*d*., he is, like Zeno, and perhaps more unconsciously, forgetting that these quantities are not merely continuous but discrete.

The Pythagoreans, according to the tradition of antiquity, philosophised number. In it they found the reality, or the principle of things,—the characteristic feature which dominated existence, and by which the world in all its multiplicity could be made coherent and intelligible. They saw it composed of two elements : a limit or limiting, and an unlimited : the latter as it were a dark ground, measureless and endless, on which definiteness was gradually marked out. Such a limiting principle would be e. g. the unit of number. But the full definiteness of number only comes out when a numerical scale is fixed on, in which each number bears a definite ratio to what goes before and what comes after. Each number in such a scale is really a multiple of its unit : a product of its unity into its multeity, of the monad into the indefinite duad. It is this view of each number, as the product of its prime unit with the ratio, which comes explicitly to the fore in Degree, or quantitative ratio. Each so-called quantitative statement is thus a ratio between a given quantity in the object and an assumed standard or unit of number.

These implications latent in quantitative order or determination come out in mensuration. If quantitative or numerical precision is to have a real basis, it presupposes the existence of a qualitative atom or unit which shall be the Measure. Measure is therefore the truth and the unity of quantity and quality : each refers forward and backward to the other, and both lead up to or imply a modulus, or standard unit. Such a standard unit may seem, at first sight, to be a matter of arbitrary choice and imposition. There seems to be no ultimate reason for taking the foot or the cubit as unit of measurement : and if the original foot or cubit be the king's limb, it is easy to say that the whole thing is conventional and artificial. But it is evident on further reflection, first that the foot or the pace is the natural and primitive measurer of lengths of space for the human being, and secondly that the particular foot which is imposed as the measure is taken as being normal and typical. So too it is partly arbitrary choice which fixes upon the starting-point for the scale of temperatures : but here also the range from freezing-point to boiling-point of the commonest of liquids affords a sufficient standard from which naturally to carry on the scale above or below it.

What happens is therefore that what is the rule, the standard,—we may also say, the test of being, is the natural mean or average. The measure presents itself as the permanent and regular proportion of quantity and quality. It is the amount or quantity at which things settle down in equilibrium and produce the quality or characteristic feature of the object. To say that Measure is the supreme category or the truth of being—of that superficial being which merely is—of the mere fact of perception—is to say that the prime or governing feature of reality, its obviously dominant characteristic in this sphere, is a self-imposing harmony and proportion. It naturally arranges itself—defines and describes itself in rhythmic series, in regular scales, in symmetrical schemes. All things are in geometrical proportion, self-defined and uniformly graded. Such a conception and category of reality may be said to be peculiarly Greek. The doctrine of the Mean is well known as a principle of their popular Ethics. But the Mean is an average which is regarded as a Normal,—a regular and permanent mode of being which is equivalent to a standard. The rule is given by the logic of facts and of nature. There is in it an apparent optimism—a belief that what is predominant and fundamental is right : a doctrine of immanent symmetry and order. The mere habitual custom is as such held to be the right and good. It is true, no doubt, that Protagoras came to point out that this Measure was not inherent in things, but came from Man, the measure of all things : and that the later philosophy had to show how the conception of reality should be re-construed, if the objectivity of Measure and symmetry in the universe were still to be maintained. Still even with this correction the belief remained down to the Stoic School that being is essentially self-ordering : that Nature is immanent proportion.

The Measure thus emerging as the Mean, which stands out as the permanent background or recurrent same amidst varying extremes, is set against these divergencies and used to measure them. It has to serve as a denominator for all of these : or each of these differences has a definite ratio to it. For that purpose it must be so graded or present such a scale that the smallest difference from it that exists may be measured, estimated and defined in terms of it. It is here out of place to consider how this can be accomplished,—how mensuration in any case is solved as a problem of scientific determination. What is more important is to note the fact that appearances everywhere start up to testify to the incompatibility of the two elements in measure,—to their tendency to fly away from each other. It is only within certain ranges that quantity and quality change proportionately to each other. The colour spectrum, the scale of musical notes, the series of chemical combination, the order of the planets, all are found in experience up to some point to follow a symmetrical order, and exhibit a measure. But after that point is reached, a sudden change or transition occurs. There is a break in the continuity of being : without warning, a new series of physical manifestation, having a new rule or measure, emerges by a sort of catastrophe. So also, it is only to a certain portion of the process of physical order in the human body that psychical changes are found to correspond. Everywhere the correspondence or harmony or proportion of immediate fact has its breaks,—its sudden emergencies into a new range of being.

It is on the repeated evidence of this fact—the discontinuity of immediate being, the inexplicable gulfs which separate its ordered provinces from one another, that we rise to the distinction of two orders or grades of being : a double aspect of reality. The primitive consciousness is, we may suppose, confined to one level of being, one world. And so long as the facts remain within limits there is no need to go further. The measure is the rule. But the uniformity breaks down abruptly : [1] the rule has its inevitable exceptions : it is no law or principle, but only the factual majority within a fixed range. Thus the measure, to fulfil all that is expected of it, and be a full expression or definition of reality, must go beyond a mere measure : must become the essence, or rather give place to the essence. In order to explain the irregularity and want of measure which turns up if we exceed the narrow provinces of being, we are forced on the conception of a being, one permanent and the same, set in relation, antithetical but inseparable, to an other being, manifold, changing, and different. The undying rhythm, the ceaseless symmetry retreat into the further region—the world beyond : while the older surface-being, as set against it, comes to be a mere phenomenon or appearance, a derivative and dependent something, which has its roots of being in the underlying law and essential reality. But the two planes are still in intimate connexion, in a correlation which becomes more and more palpable as its implications are disclosed and realised.

This change from Measure to Essential Being is one which Greek philosophy seems to exhibit in the step from Pythagoreanism to Platonism. Plato himself has noted the passage from what have been called the mathematical to the metaphysical categories, and insisted on the essential and higher truth to which mathematics only point. Mathematical terms give the supreme definiteness to the world of being ; they show it as in its several compartments a world immanently ordered and measured. As in Greek Art, all seems to be fully brought to the surface : as the image suggests no further and deeper meaning, but affords an absolute identity of aspect and purport ; so the natural and semi-popular philosophy of Greece was satisfied for its ethics with the proportionate, the becoming, the beautiful. Plato however passes beyond the surface, and reflects the apparent fact on a deeper permanent reality behind. That reality is still, in name, only the ' form ' or ' shape '—only the regular and permanent type—only the measure. But it is called the really real, the ὄντως ὄν,—the being of being. In it the truth is clear, transparent, one and systematic, which in the sensible or immediate world is

[1] Thus, the sharp break at death suggests the reference of vital phenomena to a substantial soul.

obscure, confused, multiple.   It is the key to explain the
difficulties and irregularities of the first and visible scene.
Yet even Plato never for a moment forgets the essential
correspondence of the two realms, however he may insist
upon their separation, and however hard he may find it to
explain how being can be duplicated, how the one can be
many and yet not cease to be one, how appearance has
part in reality.

This indeed is not a difficulty confined to Plato.   It is,
after all, the same antithesis as we found in the beginning :
the Is which lapses into the Is not.   It now becomes the
play of positive and negative—of perpetual relativity : of
a known dependent on an unknown, and an unknown interpreted by a known : an essence guaranteed by its show or
seeming and a *Schein* which supposes permanent *Sein.*
How can a thing be, and yet not be true ? How can pleasures
seem and not be real ? Aristotle, taking up the Platonic
antithesis of true and apparent being, carries it on into
greater detail.   Matter and form : possibility and actuality :
are amongst his cardinal pairs of correlatives.   But he is
anxious to maintain their essential relativity : to show
that reality only is and maintains itself as the unity of the
two poles of universal and particular, reason and sense, or
as a syllogism and a development.   So far as he succeeds in
doing this, Aristotle rises above the correlational view of
reality into the comprehension of it as a unity, which carries
itself through difference into self-realisation.

CHAPTER XXXI

THE LOGIC OF EXPLANATION AND REALISTIC METAPHYSICS: ESSENCE

THE coherence and consistency of being was, it appeared in the last chapter, only to be maintained by assuming it to fall into two planes, or orders, always however relative to each other. The need of a measure forced itself upon even the superficial student. In the ordinary business of economical life one commodity of common use or of general acceptability steps into the place of a common measure. At first it is no more than one amongst many, a more suitable and convenient means of discharging the task of mensuration. But gradually it draws away into a world of its own, and acquires in common estimation a unique and peculiar dignity. It becomes a commodity of a higher order than the common, and is even treated as if it had intrinsic and inherent worth, apart from all relations of exchange. In a further stage it rises to rank as an invariable and almost supersensible standard, which amid all the fluctuations of currency tends to remain unchanged. One loses sight of the movement out of which it grew and in which it exists—the social give and take, the interaction of individual needs and general opinion.

The characteristic feature of this sphere of thought is the perpetual antithesis of terms. And its tragedy is the result of the tendency to separate the terms, and treat them as independently real. It matters not how often this error may be detected. Each side of the antithesis no doubt reflects itself upon the other. But we as constantly fail to note that reflection. Even the philosopher who most loudly preaches relativity falls into the common trap, and speaks of relatives as ultimate and absolute. He talks of an Unknowable, as if it could be without a Known (or Knowable): whereas no such term fully manifests itself. Each term owes its distinct existence to its correlative: each gives itself over to the other, and invests it with meaning and authority. Accordingly when even the ordinary mind, which takes these categories as they are given, is asked what each means, it can only reply by referring to the other. A cause is *that* which has an effect. The dialectic in the nature of thought,—its self-revising self-conscious nature—which was concealed in the First Part of Logic, where one term, when carried to its extreme, passed over into another, is made obvious in the Second Part, where each term postulates and even points to its correlative, and, however it may be contradistinguished, cannot be thought without it. Thus, force is a meaningless abstraction without the correlative expression or utterance of force : and matter means nothing except in its distinction from, and yet reflection on, form. These, it may be said, are simple and tautological statements. They are princi- ples, however, which every day sees disregarded. Have they, for example, been remembered by those theorists who tell us that everything is ultimately reducible to matter, or who propose to improve upon that theory by explaining that matter is after all only another name for force ? Forgetting how this reduction is made, they are dealing with abstractions or mental figments, and losing their way in an endless maze of metaphysics. Do those who speak so confidently of laws of nature as something real and effective ever reflect that the two terms are more or less relative to each other, and that there is some latent metaphor in the phrase ? Or if they prefer to speak of laws of phenomena, on which word is the accent to be laid ? Those who thus speak of matter and force, really speak of a matter which is formed and form-possessed, capable of determining its own form, and of a force which can rule its own exertions : and for such conceptions the words in question are scarcely adequate representatives. They use the language of the Second, to express notions which pro- perly belong to the Third branch of Logic.

The whole range of Essence or Relativity exhibits a sort of see-saw : while one term goes up in importance, the other term goes down. The several antitheses, too, have their day of fashion, and give place to others. Those inquirers who speak of the phenomena of nature shrug their shoulders at the very mention of essences : and the practical man, whose field is actuality, acquires a very pronounced con- tempt for both abstractions. One class of investigators glories in the perpetual discovery of differences, and stigmatises the seekers after identity and similarity as dreamers : while the latter retort, and name the specialisers empiricists. One intellect considers an action almost solely by its grounds or motives : another almost solely by its consequences. Some console themselves for their degradation by piquing themselves on what they might have been : others despise these ' would-be ' minds for what they practically are. What a wealth there lies in each of us, which our nearest friends know nothing of, and which has never been made outward ! But in this mode of thought, it is the persistent delusion, misleading science no less than metaphysics and the reflective thinking of ordinary life, to suppose that either of two relative terms has an existence and value of its own. In Germany paper-money is sometimes known as ' Schein ' or Show. That term marks its relativity to the gold or silver currency of the realm : and it would be as absurd to pay with Austrian paper-money in Persia, as to take one term of Essence apart from its correlative. The disputes about essences, about matters and forces, about substance, about freedom and necessity, or cause and effect, are generally aggravated by a forced abstraction of one term from another on which its meaning and existence depend.

The essence may be roughly defined as that measure or standard which corresponds to the variation of immediate being, and yet remains identical in all variation. Or, if we like, we may say that this immediate being, which, as derivative, may now be called existence,[1] has its ground in the essence. The essence is the ground of existence : and essence which exists is a ' thing '. Such an existing essence or thing subsists in its properties ; and these properties are only found in the thing. Thus the essence, when it comes into existence as a thing, turns out to be a mere phenomenon or appearance.—Such briefly stated is the development of essence proper into appearance.

With the idea of essential being—a permanent which yet changes, there emerge the problems connected with the double aspect of relation as identity and difference,—the favourite categories of reflection. These terms indeed the

---

[1] *Existence*, as opposed to *Dasein*, should thus imply the emergence into efficient being from a state of quietude or passive latency (*Wesen*).

popular logician would fain avoid as savouring of pedantic
accuracy, and prefers the psychological titles of similarity
and contrast. These, he tends to insinuate, are unique
experiences, direct feelings, beyond which it is impossible
to go in analysis. The logician, on the other hand, must
insist on dealing with the more radical phase of the terms.
And he must note their essential interdependence and their
intrinsic contradictoriness. Abstract sameness, or sameness which does not presuppose a tinge of difference, is
a fiction of weak thought, which wishes to simplify the
subtlety of nature. Identity is a relative term, and for
that very reason presupposes difference : and for the same
reason difference presupposes identity and is meaningless
without it. The whole dispute about ' Personal Identity ',
as it descends from one English psychologist to another, is
enveloped in the obscurity which springs from failure to
grasp the logical antinomy on which the question turns.
When I feel that my friend whom I have not met for years
is still the same, should I take the trouble to express myself
in this manner, unless with reference to the difference
betwixt Then and Now ? If I remark that two men are
different, would the remark be worth making or hearing
unless there was some identity which made that difference
all the more striking ? The essence is, in short, the unity
of sameness and difference : and when so apprehended,
it is the ground by which we explain existence. The
essence, ground, or possibility, is at once itself and not
itself : if it is self-identical, it is for the same reason self-
distinguishing. If it is to be itself, it can only be so by
negativing what in it is other than itself. The affirmation
of self implies the negation of the other of self,—the redintegration (though not the blank absorption) of the other in
it. This is the *crux* which lies in *Ex nihilo nihil fit* : what
exists must not be other than the essence (the effect not
more than the cause), and yet unless it is other and different,
there has been no passage from essence to existence.

The tendency to identify, and the tendency to distinguish,
alternate both in scientific thought and in general culture.
But whichever prevail for the moment, it is only as a re-action
and a protest against the one-sided predominance of the
other. And thus both ultimately rest upon and presuppose
a ground of existence which is neither mere sameness nor
mere difference. It is only when the two tendencies meet

and interpenetrate that science accomplishes its end, and discovers the ground of existence. In the first instance the world presents to incipient science the aspect of mere identity and of mere difference. Likeness is confounded with sameness, and unlikeness with diversity. The popular and the infant minds do not draw fine distinctions. Things to them are either the same or different : one point of sameness may in certain conditions obliterate whole breadths of difference ; and tiny divergence may make as nothing all the many points of agreement, purely and simply, i. e. abstractly. But the process of comparison, setting things beside each other, teaches us to refine a little, and speak of things as Like or Unlike. One thing is like another when the element of identity preponderates : it is unlike, when the difference is uppermost. Thus while we distinguish things from one another, we connect them. From mere variety, and mere sameness, we have risen, secondly, to distinctions of like and unlike. But, thirdly, this distinction of same and different is in the thing itself. Everything includes an antithesis or contradiction in it : it is at once positive and negative. One can only be virtuous, so long as one is not utterly virtuous.[1] To be a philosopher, implies that you are not wholly or merely a philosopher. The rational animal is so, because of an inherent irrationality, and is so, only as rising upon and superseding it. Every epithet, so to speak, by which you describe any reality, presupposes in it the negative of the quality. Not only does every negation presuppose an attempted or surmised affirmation, but an affirmation is always, it may be said, a re-affirmation against an incipient doubt. Every stage of reality involves the presence of antithetical but inseparable elements : every light implies a shadow to set it forth. The epithet of each real is only *a potiori*. While it retains itself, it must lose itself. Its positivity is only secured by its self-negation and its identity is based upon its self-distinction. Every proposition which conveys real knowledge is a statement that self-sameness is combined with difference. Every such proposition is synthetical : it unites or identifies what is supposed to be implicitly different; or differentiates what seemed only identical.

[1] As Aristotle says, The brave man stands his ground, yet fearing : (cf. Tolstoi : *Siege of Sevastopol*). If he does not fear, brave is not the word for him.

Here we have that *coincidentia oppositorum*, which is the truth of essence. Thus, e.g. the essence of the Self is the contradiction between its self-centred unity and its existence by self-differentiation into elements.

Essence, thus comprehended as the unity of identity and difference, as that which is and is not the same, is the Ground, from which an Existence comes as the Consequent. Or, otherwise expressed, the ground is the source of the differences,—the point where they converge into unity, and whence they diverge into existence. Everything in existence has such a ground : or, as it is somewhat tautologically stated in the common formula, a sufficient ground. On that account, it is no great matter to give reasons or grounds for a thing, and no amount of them can render a thing either right or wrong, unless in reference to some given and supposedly fixed point. For the ground only states the same thing over again in a mediate or reflected form. It carries back the actual fact to its antecedent : and thus deprives it of its abruptness or inexplicability, by showing you it was there implicitly ; and therefore as you accepted the ground you cannot complain of what but serves to continue it. To refer to the ground is to say there is really nothing new : and as you raised no objection before, you need raise none now.

The Existent world—a world of existents, each conditioning and conditioned—is popularly described as a world of Things. These Things are the solid hinges on which turns our ordinary conception of change and action. They act, and exhibit properties. Being is partly substantive, partly adjective. The Thing itself is the ground of its properties : i. e. each thing is looked upon as a unity in which different relations converge, or an identity which subsists through its changing states. This is the side emphasised in ordinary life, when a thing is regarded as the permanent and enduring subject, which has certain properties. But a little science or a little reflection soon turns the tables upon the thing, and shows that the properties are independent matters, which, temporarily it may be, converge or combine into a factitious unity which we term a thing. But these very matters cannot be independent or whole, just because they interpenetrate each other in the thing. The thing, which from one point of view seemed permanent, and the properties, which from another point of view seemed self-subsistent matters, are neither of them more than appearance. For they must be at one, and at one they cannot be. And if we reduce the various matters to one, and speak of Matter in general, we have a mere abstraction—a something which only becomes real by being stamped with a special form. *Mere* Matter like *mere* Thing (thing in itself) is a knowable Unknowable.

In this way we pass from the talk about essence, things, and matter into an other range of the sphere of relativity. We no longer have one order of being behind or in the depth, and another referring back to it. We now speak (as Mill does) of Phenomena :—not phenomena of an unknown, but, simply disregarding the background, we find all we want upon the surface. For neither is thing more real than property, nor essence than existence. Each is exactly equal in reality to the other, and that reality is its relation to the other. The thing and the essence with their claim to truth disappear. Nothing truly is : but only appears to be. The semblance (*Schein*) may refer to an essential. But the appearance (*Erscheinung*) only refers to another appearance, and so on. The phenomenal world is all on one level :—as was the world of immediate being. But, there, each term of being presented itself as independent : here, nothing is independent—nothing ever really *is*, but only represents something else, which is in its turn representative. Yet even here there is a pretence of hierarchy in existence. In the phenomenon a certain superiority is attributed to its Law. But the conception of Law is hard to keep in its proper place. Either it assumes a permanency—even were it but a permanent possibility—as contrasted with the coming and passing phenomenon : and then it is apt to be confounded with a real Essence. Or, on the other hand, it comes to be looked on as a mere way of colligating phenomena,—as a mere appearance in the variety of appearance (as it were an iris in the rain-drops)—a phenomenon of a phenomenon. Such a distinction between the phenomenon and its law, therefore, is and must be illusory, or itself only an appearance. As such it is described as the difference of Form and Content : two terms, which are incessantly opposed, but which more than most antitheses reveal when pressed the hollowness of their opposition. For true or developed Form is Content, and *vice versa*.

Instead however of this practical identification of the law

of the phenomenon with the duly-formulated phenomenon itself, it is more natural to emphasise the discordance of the two aspects of reality, and yet to acknowledge their essential relativity. This essential relativity in the phenomenon has a threefold aspect : the relation of whole and parts ; of force and the exertion of force ; of inward and outward. The relation of whole and parts tends to explain by statical composition : the relation of force and its exertion, by dynamical construction. According to the former the parts are constituted by their dependence upon and in the whole, and yet the whole is composed by the addition of the several parts together. Each extreme is what it is only through the other. Only those parts can make up a whole, which somehow have the whole in them : and to become the whole, they must contrive to wholly obliterate their partitional character. A better exhibition of the inner unity and the difference between form and contents is seen in the relation of a force to its exertion. Here the contents appear under a double form : first, under the form of mere identity, as force,—secondly, under the form of mere distinction, as the manifestation of that force. Yet a force is only such in its utterance or manifestation, while in that utterance, if abstracted from the force it carries forth, all energy has been superseded. This separation of content and form, or of content as developed in two forms, appears still more clearly in the third relation : that of outward and inward. This is a popular distinction of very wide application in reference to phenomena. But neither outside nor inside is anything apart from its correlative. If the elements implied in the conception of phenomena are to have full justice done them, it must be expanded so as to give expression to these two phases, to include the outward and the inward. But at first only by reverting to something like the old distinction of essence and existence,—an essence however which is existent or phenomenal, and an existence which stands independent, though in correlation. Such being is Actuality—being, i.e. which is what it must be, and must be what it is.

Actuality, though it comes under the general head of Essence, tends to pass away into another sphere. Here, as elsewhere, we see that the general rubric of a sphere is only partially applicable to some of its subordinate sections.

In essence proper there were, or were assumed to be, two grades of being—a real or essential, and an unessential or seeming : or being was regarded (contradictorily) both as ideal (as one thing) and real (as having several properties). In Appearance or Manifestation the aspects of being are supposed to lie on a level ; but they are always a pair of aspects, one side of which is entirely dependent for its explanation on a reflection from the other, e.g. whole and parts, the favourite category for explaining the larger unities. But in the category of actuality there is nothing so merely potential, so unessential as mere essence recognised : and each actual is something firm and self-supporting which does not, like a phenomenon, merely borrow its reality from its antithesis or correlative. Thus we have, in a way, got back to the characteristics of immediate being : only, as we find it, we have this affirmation of the self-subsistence of reals contradictorily accompanied with the conviction of their necessary interdependence. It is a reflective (or correlated), not an immediate reality. There is no other world of being to have recourse to for explanation now : nor can we play back and forward from aspect to aspect of a reality which never comes forward itself, but only as a reflection on or from another. The world of reality is a self-contained world : its parts and phases are each hard realities : and for that reason they bear hard upon each other in the bond of necessity.

The total actuality falls naturally in our conception into three elements. We separate first the central fact —the nucleus of the business, the concentrated reality in reality : the fact in its mere identity and inner abstractness : the ultimate drift or inner possibility of things. Then we turn to the rest of the concrete fact—all without which the fact would not be itself—the detail and particularity : this we treat as a sort of materials or passive conditions from which the real fact is to be produced, on which it is dependent and which precede it in time. Lastly, in order to get back the unity of the fact from these two unconnected elements, we refer to some agency which puts them together. The End—or thing to be realised— (so to speak) has to be brought out by a motive agency (efficient cause) which imposes the form (or general character) on the matter and makes these one. By this analysis, however, we have only put asunder what is one experience and introduced a mechanical (external) unifier needlessly. The name of *conditions* is given to the particulars or details, considered apart from the rest of the fact, and hypothetically invested with an existence anterior to it, with the implication, first, that they are self-subsistent, and secondly, that they to some extent involve the rest of it. Again, the general fact, the fact in its mere nominal or abstract generality or essence, its mere possibility, does not exist separately : every fact when in thought completed has its so-called conditions not outside it, but as constituent elements, aspects, or factors in it. Lastly, the so-called agency is the active element itself in the act, an aspect or factor in the totality : the aspect which keeps actuality together as a self-energising fact—a *Thathandlung* and not a mere *Thatsache* (to quote Fichte's phrase). Our practical and technical habits, where the agent is other than his materials and aims, lead us to draw the same distinctions in the realm of total Nature : they are aspects useful *in ordine ad hominem* which we, without due modification, apply *in ordine ad universum*.

It is originally in our practical operations that the distinctions of necessary and possible emerge,—with a view to the accomplishment of our desires and purposes. That is necessary which is required and needed if some bare plan is projected and is to be actualised : it is the condition or conditions without which the end cannot be attained. It is an epithet of the means. Possible, on the contrary, is an epithet of the end or plan, and denotes that there are means for its attainment, without however always specifying that this is known of the present or given instance. It is clear that everything as regards the application of these terms will depend on the definiteness with which the plan is conceived, both in itself so to speak and in its relations with the rest of the circumstances. On the other hand, when a result emerges without being included in the purpose, and without any means having been employed for attaining it, it is said to be a chance, accident, or contingency.

These terms are applied by analogy to the uses of theoretical explanation. Just as in will you have a general aim to begin with, which becomes more and more determinate as it moves forward in the volitional process to execution ; so in the attempt to understand the world you suppose it first of all the mere shadow or phantom of itself, a promise and potentiality of things to come : a next-to-nothing, which however you credit with a magic wealth of potential being. So much indeed may this possibility be emphasised that nothing more is needed : it is possible, and, without a thought of difficulties and counteractives, you could swear that it is actual.[1] Being removed above this solid land of actuality, cut off from the ties and bonds of conditions, it fancies itself moving in its vacuum ; and being free from all bonds of actuality fancies itself actually free, or self-disposing, whereas it can only claim this *liberum arbitrium indifferentiae*, so long as it remains bare and powerless possibility—a mere may-be, which, apart from all conditions, would exist only by a mere contingency, or freak of chance. This mere potentiality—being only an ante-dated, presupposed, and hypothetical actuality—being only a substance or substratum—must be raised out of its supposititious existence into reality by means of appropriate conditions. These conditions are necessary to its resuming its place or reaching a place in actuality. Thus each object becomes actual or real from a presupposed possibility by means of an external necessity. As in the former case the possibility was identified with power, and conditions were left out of sight as comparatively unimportant : so here the possibility—taken to lie at the root of the thing—is made a mere susceptibility, which would be nothing actual unless stimulated and necessitated from outside.

This necessity in the very heart of actuality (which is its characteristic to the reflectional mode of mind) thus arises from the separation and hypostatisation of its elements into independent powers which are so far in stress and opposition. This is the climax of metaphysics—if metaphysics be the investiture of the dynamic factors of the notion with the power and character of supposed agents or forces. It appears in three phases, with the three categories of substance, cause, and reciprocity. To the first, reality is regarded as dominated by its mere underlying potentiality : the reality of the mere superficial contingents is controlled by the necessity of its latent or substantial being. To explain event or incident, here, is

---

[1] Put into Greek, the mere ἐνδέχεται (*licet*, or *forsitan*) is taken as equivalent to δύναμαι (*possum*).

merely to bind it to the generic nature or the intrinsic doom, which—unexplained and inexplicable—manifests itself in an extrinsically fluctuating appearance of facts : e.g. the single crime is explained as the product of social conditions. Under the conception of Causality, each thing is a mere might-be which owes all its actuality to a definite antecedent or cause,—an antecedent termed for the moment unconditional, but anon reduced to dependence on further conditions. The effect is as a fact : but would not have been so unless for an earlier fact—i.e. unless the effect in a supposed earlier stage of its growth had been helped on by certain conditions or circumstances to acquire actual and full being in the effect. And cause and conditions can change places, according to what we happen to regard as the central nucleus or inner possibility of the effect. Lastly, the conception of reciprocity recognises that causality is rather an arbitrary simplification of reality into strands of rectilinear event ; it remembers that Substance emphasises the dependence of each non-independent element on the supposed totality which they grow from, and doing so, it lays down the reversibility and essential elasticity of the causal relation. The cause in causing re-acts upon itself, and the effect is itself a cause of the effect, active as well as passive. The dependence in short is all-environing : nowhere is there any loop-hole to escape from necessity. Motives act on purpose, and purpose acts on motives : the stone hurls back the hand that hurled it.

Explanation is thus baffled and thus forced to recognise its own limitations. The simplest fact is beyond all the powers of explanatory science to do full justice to : for to know fully the ' flower in the crannied wall ' after this method of explanation would involve endless multiples of action and re-action. The antinomy between necessity and contingency arose by following out the antithesis, so natural to us, between selfsame and different, essence and existence, substance and accidents, till they were invested with a right to independent place and function. But the separation of the abstract receptacle of possibility, selfsame and essential, from the equally abstract conditions which fill it up and make it actual, is only the great human instrumentality of comprehension, which however is not reached until each thing is realised and idealised as an

individual, which has universality and has particularity,
but never either alone. Its universality is possibility—its
particularity the aspect of contingency : but these aspects
are in submission to an inclusive unity. The real when
ill known seems contingent ; when somewhat better known
it seems necessary by external (physical) compulsion ; in
its truth to intelligence, the real is a self-active, a *causa sui*,
or it is necessary by that self-determination which is the
freedom of autonomy.

The view of the world under the category of actuality
(Reality), and as dominated by the law of causality, is the
culminating stand-point of scientific or reflective realism.
It began with a mere descriptive science, naming and
qualifying the successive aspects of being,—with description
which passed through numeration into the definiteness of
measurement. But all such determination was found to
imply the existence of a permanent reality, or at least to
involve the reference of one reality to another, outside of
it, and yet not independent of relations to it, which had
to make part of its nature. To the scientific realist the
sum of fact presents itself independent of consciousness,
as a complicated mass of real elements governed by laws
and subject to necessities. Each thing or state of a thing
is explained by reference to something outside it, which
is its cause, and measured by something inside it which
is its unit or atomic standard. Alternately the reference,
and the unit are designated arbitrary (contingent) and
necessary (essential) : i.e. they are sometimes considered
as only a way of looking at reality [1]—and sometimes as
inevitable implications and conditions of reality.

All this is Objective Logic : or, so far as it does not
realise its implications, it is Metaphysics. Its terms of
thought [2] are in practice treated as elements of a reality
which is what it is, apart from thought-conditions, apart
from consciousness. As Hegel exhibits them in their
interdependence, they hint their underlying thought-
nature, which in their empirical applications is hardly
apparent. For to the realistic stand-point mind and
subjectivity are left out of account as only passive onlookers. The realist may no doubt speak of a Subject :
but he means a real, a corporeal self, an actual amongst

---

[1] Herbart's *Zufällige Ansicht*, or contingent aspect.
[2] ' Denkbestimmungen.'

other actuals. If he speaks of mind and will, such mind
and will are parts and ingredients in a general scheme of
causes and effects ; they are points of transition through
which passes the moving stream of event. They also are
things and substances. They are agents and patients,
always both, no doubt ; but the chief circumstance to note
is that they are actuals, and that even knowledge and will
are regarded as species of action and motion.

When Protagoras laid down his maxim that *Man is
the measure of all things*, he stated, apparently in an ambiguous manner, that the fact of measure (and all that
mensuration implies), and (we may add) the existence of
correlation in actuality, presupposed for their explanation
the assumption of Mind and subjectivity. Mind thus
became the basis of all actuality which claimed to be
objective—claimed, in short, to be actual. The truth and
objectivity of the objective lies in the subjective ; Mind
is its own measure, i.e. the absolute measure, and it is
self-relation. So Kant had taught and Fichte enforced.
The basis of objectivity is the subjective ; but a subjective
different from that so-called by the plain man or by the
naive psychologist. By the subjective he does not, as the
plain man, understand the compound of body and soul,
the living and breathing organism amid outer objects—
nor, as the psychological idealist does, a psychical process,
a series or bundle of states of consciousness, always contrasted with a reality, *the* reality outside consciousness.
It is true that his language resembles the language of
psychology : as Herbart and others have said, that is to
be expected, for he talks of mind and consciousness. But
the consciousness he speaks of is a unity that includes all
space and all time : it is one and all-embracing, infinite,
because not as individual (psychological) consciousness set
in antithesis to reality, as the other half of the duality
of existence. It is consciousness generalised—*Bewusstsein
überhaupt*—an eternal, i.e. a timeless consciousness, an
universal i.e. not a localised, mind :—a necessary Idea,
but with an inward self-regulating necessity. Such a
consciousness Fichte called the Absolute Ego : but as we
saw before, the adjective transforms the substantive.
Such a consciousness, which is absolute self-consciousness,
is the Idea :—no psychical event, but the logical condition
and explanation of reality whether physical or psychical.

The Idea is the presupposition of epistemology, but of an epistemology which claims to occupy the place of old usurped by metaphysics. Metaphysics has no higher category than actuality : transcendental logic shows that actuality rests in the Idea,—reality conceived and conception realised.

CHAPTER XXXII

LOGIC OF COMPREHENSION AND IDEALISM : THE NOTION

THE distinction between the psychical or psychological idea and the logical concept has been more than once alluded to. The idea or representation is under psychical form exactly equivalent to the undigested and passively accepted thing to which we give the title of physical or external. It is the ideal, in the sense of the psychical, pendant to the real : and hangs up in the mental view in the same way as the real object to the physical perception. It is in brief the crude object, considered not as existing, but as a state of consciousness—it is a reduplication in inner space of the thing in outer space. If we cannot say it is altogether mythological, we must however note that it is simply a psychical reflex, which has an existence only through abstraction, and is neither more or less than the object apprehended without comprehension.

The concept or notion is more than an image, and less than an image. An idea-image is symbolical of the unanalysed totality of the thing. But the notion is in the first instance due to an analysis, and secondly, a reconstruction of the thing. It takes up the thing in its relations : it thinks it, i. e. it abstracts and mutilates it, and artificially recombines. It implies analysis and synthesis. It produces a sort of manufactured thing : a mental construction. But the construction—as contrasted with the passivity that says first A and then B and a connexion of them—has the traces of subjective or mental violence about it : for violence there is in the act of comprehension. We have however got together in unity what actuality in the process of history let fall asunder, and could only, at the best, show as independent reals held against their will in ubiquitous relations of reciprocity. But the unity in which the individual sets the universal and the particular is an imported unity, which though it gives place and explanation to the elements of reality, seems to impose its synthesis upon reality. So far the concept is subjective only. It is an ample explanation including the facts, but not quite self-explanatory. *We* conceive, and judge, and reason: but all this is alien to the object.

But there is a counterpart almost in antagonism to this. There is a concept, i.e. a grouping of existence into totals mediated by necessary links, which presents itself as embodied in things: and this embodied concept is the objective world. That world, apart from our interpretation and conception, offers itself as a synthesis of universal, particular and individual. It groups itself into systems, mechanical, chemical, and teleological. But in all of these there is lacking the evidence of the inward and subjective principle of unification. The unity is external, the members are held in a vice: their unity is given as a fact: it follows through certain laws and does not reveal itself. There is a want of perspicuity of connexion: logic—the need of inner explanation—in short, is not satisfied by this logic of facts. It is rather a realm of necessity than of freedom. It wants life; wants true self-activity. As in the subjective notion, the facts resented the hand of the logician (for here is the sphere of logic proper in the old Aristotelian sense), and refused to show themselves in the simple and transparent transitions of his argument: so the objective synthesis of the members of a mechanical system, or of a kingdom of means and ends, lacks the freedom and lucidity of inner movement which logical insight demands. Objectivity—the logic of fact—is a syllogism of necessity, so hardened and fixed that the necessity of the conclusion is more obvious than the self-determination by the syllogism.

The third stage of the Notion shows the union of the pellucidity and ideality of the syllogistic progress with the necessity and reality of the objective order. Here actuality and the concept are at one. At first as a mere fact—or more fact than idea. Life, organic life, is no doubt development: a totality which is in all its parts, and where parts have their being in the total. But life as such, the so-called vital principle, does not emancipate itself to a true universal: it is immersed in its particulars. Intellectual life, on the contrary, the form of consciousness —rises independent and distinct from the totality of life. Psychology follows Biology. But as such—under the

form of intellect and will—it has an antithesis no less fatal
to its absoluteness than the opposite one-sidedness of life.
There is—to put it in language more familiar to the present
day—there is an analogue of life in all nature ; and all
reality, even the rock and the crystal, has its life-history.
There is, properly speaking, no mere inorganic reality:
organic life is universal. And then, going a step further,
we attribute to all reality something analogous to a soul,
or a consciousness. We talk, in rash moods, of ' mind-
stuff ' and feelings, even in molecules. But as Spinoza has
reminded us, terms like Will and Intellect have about
them something finite, because they imply an antagonism
to an object : they are predominantly subjective. The
reality in its final truth must be a subject-object : the
adequacy of thought and being, the equation of real and
ideal, the intellection which is life. And this is called
Absolute Idea. It is natural to translate such an equation,
when made a result, into a mere blank. And a blank it
would be, if we suppose all that has gone before obliterated,
and only the result left. Then, in the coincidence of
opposites, we have only a zero of a gulf of negation. A life
which *is* consciousness may seem to fade away like a vague
ideal with no reality. A consciousness which *is* life can
be no consciousness at all. The *is* and the *is known* dare
not coincide or they perish both.

A categorical proposition, says Hegel, can never express
a speculative truth. That is to say : the subject over-
rides the predicate, or the predicate makes you ignore the
subject. The affirmation keeps out of sight the negation.
To say that life *is* consciousness makes us forget that the
very assertion would not and could not be made, unless
also life were other than consciousness. In its full proportion of meaning, therefore, the proposition must imply
a return to unity through difference, to identity through
otherness. Affirmation, fully realised, is re-affirmation
through negation. Cognition is but recognition deepened
by contrast. This law which governs—or rather which is—
logic ; the principle of identity through contradiction—
must not be lost sight of in the supreme struggle of thought.
The Idea is the unity of life and consciousness : but it is
a unity in which they are (*aufgehoben*)—not a zero in
which they utterly collapse.

We may illustrate in two ways. In the first we may

compare the Ἐνέργεια of Aristotle.   That is his formula of
reality.   Nominally it only means activity and actuality :
and sums up the metaphysical formula for what really is,—
the hard fact of being.   But through it there glimmers the
meaning of consciousness.   It not merely is, but it means
what it is.   Energy of Soul is the end of life—the supreme
fulfilling of desire, and consummation of tendency.   As
such it is, and feels that it is.   It is the virtuous deed,
which is its own reward.   But Aristotle seems sometimes
to fall from that identification of being and consciousness.
The world of *praxis* parts from the world of *Theoria*.   In
that case the activity is a mere activity—the outward
shell of action :   and then, as a supplement or complement
to the abstract result of the activity the consciousness of
achievement gets a distinct position as Pleasure :   and the
activity, now no consummation, but only a means to an
end, get its completion from this arbitrarily abstracted
shadow of reality.[1]

The second illustration may come from Mr. Spencer.

' We can think of Matter only in terms of Mind.   We
can think of Mind only in terms of Matter.   When we
have pushed our explorations of the first to the uttermost
limit we are referred to the second for a final answer :
and when we have got the final answer of the second we
are referred back to the first for an interpretation of it.'
Beyond this see-saw indeed we cannot go, so as to leave it
behind :   but in reality we transcend it.   The Mind that is
in terms of Matter is partly the region of psychic event,
partly the world of science, art and religion.   And psychic
event is always antithetical to physical reality.   But the
spiritual world already includes the antithesis of psychical
and physical, and including it keeps it as a principle of life
and consciousness.   The supreme or absolute mind does
not indeed rise above Physis and Psyche so as to have no
antagonism :   but it is the unity of antitheses.

What those who crave for something higher than this
rest in unrest, this life in consciousness and consciousness
in life, want, would destroy the very condition of reality.
Still philosophising, they would be above philosophy.
They want an objective reality in which they may still
their beating hearts,—a ' repose which ever is the same '

---

[1] Cf. the quaint phrase by which *Eth.* x τελειοῖ τὴν ἐνέργειαν,
sinks below *Eth.* i τέλος ἡ ἐνέργεια.

and yet is not annihilation :—to sink into the great sea of being, and leave consciousness with its radical division behind. Such a craving philosophy, in Hegel's hands, has no power of satisfying. It cannot, in the sense in which Jacobi and Schelling used the words, reveal Being. It cannot get at the *That* except by means of the *What*, and is the eternal antithesis and correlation of these two. It will always be rational and logical—for it is its function to think being : and it will re-affirm that an unthought and a-logical being is a mere name, which in the language of humanity at least has no meaning, whatever it may stand for in the Volapük of imagined gods. To go beyond this correlation of Being and Thought is therefore no advance, but a relapse into the *Natura Naturans*, which, in its abstract completeness, *is*, but dare not be anything. Philosophy therefore in its supreme Idea is still the Ἐνέργεια of Θεωρία, and not bare Οὐσία. For it mere Being is always Nothing. And to be actual it must live in antithesis and live victorious over antithesis. It follows the law of humanity (*Und das heisst ein Kämpfer sein*)—which can only exist in warfare as a church militant, but for continuous existence must also be a church triumphant. Like religion and art, it sometimes craves for utter union in the fullness of Being. Such a fullness is the unspeakable and the vain,—which we may picture as the apathy of Nirvana ; but which is the absorption of Art, Religion and Philosophy,—the cease of consciousness and an abyss. We may call it—it matters not—Being.

These stages of the Notion must be examined in somewhat fuller detail. The subjective notion is the effort at the comprehension (at first subjective) of the two correlated elements into which actuality as such has been seen to fall— and to fall again and again without end. It brings out, or explicates (and with some opposition to the divisions of reality) the unity which was presupposed by the antagonist and inseparable reals. Hitherto we have had two things or aspects in relation and move from one to the other by an act of reflection. But to get two points in relation, they must belong to or exist in a unity. The divided reality of cause and effect must, if it is to be intelligible, submit to a unification of its elements. It is comparatively easy to get on if we are always allowed to have one foot on solid ground, and can move the other. Give us a standing-point, and explanation is simplified. But to get a notion of things is, it may seem, to transcend them, or get beneath them, and take a stand-point outside actuality which shall unify them. If we added to immediate being a further element to explain it, it may be said we now superadd a third to explain the two others. Over and above the different and related elements, there is assumed to be a unity. And at first it is certainly such a superimposed element, added to the facts, and regarded as our way of looking at them, as a subjective notion or grasp, holding together what is in itself reluctant to be unified.

The three aspects or factors in a Concept are the Universal, the Particular, and the Individual. These are what Hegel calls the ' moments ' or ' vanishing factors ' of the notion. They are ' vanishing ', because in their logical mobility they form a pellucid union : if they are distinct, yet they refuse to be independent of one another. Or, we may say, each in its truth is the meeting-ground and unification of the two others, thus forming a sort of cycle of perpetual movement. And in this way we may see that the addition of the third has really been a simplification : it has made two one. For the Unit which welds together is not a *tertium quid*, but simply the explicit statement and assertion of the truth implied in the antithesis, which was yet insepara-bility, of the two others. And for the same reason, neither mere universal nor mere particular nor mere individual are full reality, when taken apart. One can understand how Hegel could speak of the ' Bacchante-like intoxication ' of the concept. It may be illustrated by the following utter-ances in which a modern psychologist labours to express the complex unity of mental fact. First we are told that a ' nervous shock ', e.g. the awakening caused by a sudden blow, or a simple sensation (so-called), is the ultimate unit of consciousness. And if this were all, it would correspond to the qualities of immediate being, which we can suppose measurable : we should get a science of purely empirical psychology based on psychical atoms. But, immediately after, it appears that the ' relational element ' is never absent from the lowest stage of consciousness. Accordingly, besides feelings, there *must be* relations between feelings. And that means a good deal : especially if we also note the proposition that, in truth, ' neither a feeling nor a relation is an independent element of consciousness.' Evidently you cannot have either without both, and it seems difficult

to have both when neither is independent. Nor does it
mend matters to learn that ' a relation is a momentary
feeling ' : for that only seems a way of implying that it is,
and yet is not, a feeling. Such are the difficulties that beset
the sincere attempt to comprehend. The fixed points of
explanation stagger under the burden of truth ; and their
unsteadiness shows that they lack the full foundation. Yet
that foundation—it must be repeated—is not something
extra : it is the underlying unity which gives life to the
relativity of the separates.

For the peculiarity of the Notional stand-point is that
it insists on thorough comprehension. The usual explanation refers us from a later to an earlier, from a strange to
a familiar, from a complex to a simple, from compound to
elements. It keeps analysis and synthesis, induction and
deduction apart. To comprehend is, on the other hand,
to light up earlier by later and later by earlier, and carry
both into their unity. It does not merely refer existence
to its ground, phenomenon to law, or effect to cause ; because
beyond these it has still to reveal the unity of nature which
carries on one of these into the other. Thus, the explanatory method in Social Science may either refer us to the
simple elements or parts out of which the total is composed,
or to an earlier stage in the same institution's life. The
analytical sociologist does the former : the historical the
latter. Neither really faces the problem. For if the whole
is made up of parts, it is made up of parts which have been
characterised by the whole. If the later has come from
the earlier, that only shows that the nature of the earlier
was inadequately ascertained. Development—which implies a permanent which changes, an identity which is also
different,—is thus more than mere reference to an antecedent ; because the antecedent must also figure as a simul-
taneous. *Cessante causa, cessat et effectus.* But here, in
the concept (or λόγος) or syllogism, the permanent exists
as the—may we call it—consciousness which binds together
the elements of reality, as the life and the history, which is
ideally continuous through real changes, and is a real unity
through the distinctions of appearance.

Such a comprehension e. g. of the State would show that
though it must have a universal aspect, a particular, and
an individual, yet these are not severally identifiable with
the divisions of sovereign, executive, and people, but that

in each of the latter the three moments of the notion must
appear, and that e.g. the people is not mere people, but
also executive and sovereign, just as the sovereign is no
mere sovereign, but also executive and of the people. The
same may be illustrated in the so-called individual. A man
in his special department and sphere of action may very
likely lose the sense of his wholeness and his integrity,—
perhaps in more senses than one ! He may reduce himself
to the limits of his profession. But in so doing he becomes
untrue, or, in Hegelian parlance, abstract : he fails to
recognise the universality of his position. All work, however petty, which is done in the right spirit, is holy.

> ' One place performs, like any other place,
> The proper service every place on earth
> Was framed to furnish man with : serves alike
> To give him note, that through the place he sees
> A place is signified he never saw.'

It is a false patriotism, for example, which is inconsistent
with the spirit of universal brotherhood : and there is
something radically wrong with the religion, on the other
hand, which cannot be carried into act amid the pettiness
of ordinary practical interests. The universal, again, is
not a world beyond this world of sense and individuals : if
it were so, it would itself be a mere particular. It is rather
the world of sense unified, organised, and, if we may say
so, spiritualised. And an individual which is merely and
simply individual is an utter abstraction, which is quite
meaningless, and in the real world impossible. Or, if we
prefer to express the same thing in connexion with the
mind, sensation apart from thought is an inconceivable
abstraction. Sensation is always alloyed with thought,
and we can at the most *suppose* pure sensation to exist
amongst the brutes. The mere individual opens out and
expands : and in that expansion we see the universal :
(sensation is thought in embryo). But, on the other hand,
the developed universal concentrates itself into a point :
(thought returns into the centre of feeling).

The same process of particular, individual and universal,
which thus goes on under the apparent point of the notion,
is more distinctly and explicitly seen, with due emphasis
on the several members, in the evolution of the notion into
the Judgment and the Syllogism. The judgment is the
statement of what each individual notion implicitly is, viz.

a universal or inward nature in itself, or that it is a universal which individualises itself. The judgment may, therefore, in its simplest terms be formulated as : The Individual is the Universal. The connective link,—the copula ' is ', expresses however at first no more than a mere point-like contact of the two terms, not their complete identity. By a graduated series of judgments this identity between the two terms is drawn closer, until in the three terms and propositions of a syllogism the unity of the three factors of the notion finds its most adequate expression in (subjective) thought.

It may be a question how far syllogisms as they are ordinarily found are calculated to impress this synthesis of the three elements upon the observer. The three elements there tend to bid each other good-bye, and are only kept together by the awkward means of the middle term, and the conjunction ' therefore '. In these circumstances it becomes easy to show, that the major premiss is a superfluity, not adding anything to the cogency of the argument. But under the prominence of this criticism of form, we are apt to let slip the real question touching the nature of the syllogism. And that nature is to give their due place to the three elements in the notion : which in the syllogism have each a quasi-independence and difference as separate terms, while they are also reduced to unity. The syllogism expresses in definite outlines that everything which we think, or the comprehension which constitutes an object, is a particular which is individualised by means of its universal nature. As always, thought refers to reality ; and a notion has to be carried out into objectivity. But as Aristotle complained, matter is recalcitrant to form. The objective appears at first only as an opposite, and instead of revealing, it rather obscures and condenses the features of subjectivity.

Objectivity, or the thought which has forgotten its origin and stands out as a world, may be taken in three aspects : Mechanical, Chemical, and Teleological. That is to say, the mode in which groups or systems naturally present themselves in the objective world, is threefold. The contradiction which stands in the way of comprehending objectivity comes from the fact that it contains subjectivity absorbed in it. In other words, the object is at once active and passive ; as thought and subjectivity it should be its own synthetiser, as objectivity it is necessitated to inter-dependence, and the subjectivity, at this stage, is in abey-ance. Consequently, either the two attributes co-exist, or they cancel each other, or they are in mutual connexion.

(1) In the first case the objects are independent, and yet are connected with one another. Such connexion is an external one, due to force, impulse, and outward authority. The principle of union is implied : but the objects are mutually determined from without. The more, for example, an object acts upon the imagination, the more vehement is the reaction of the mind towards it.—(2) But if the object is independent, as has been allowed, then the determination from without must really come from within. Thus desire is a turning or bent towards the object which draws it. The desiring soul leans out of itself. It gravitates towards a centre : and it is its own nature to be thus centripetal. The lesser objects of themselves draw closer around the more prominent object.—(3) But if this gravitation were absolute, the objects would lose their independence alto-gether, and sink into their centre. Accordingly if the independence of these objects is to remain, there must be, as it were, a double centre, the relative centre of each object, and the absolute centre of the system to which it belongs. In each of these three forms of mechanical com-bination, the objects continue external and independent. A mechanical theory of the state regards classes as inde-pendent, seeks to produce a balance between them, sepa-rates individuals and associations from the state, and, in short, conceives the state as one large centralising force with a number of minor spheres depending upon it, but with a greater or less amount of self-centred action in each of them.

The fact is that an object cannot really be thought as thus independently subsistent. Its real nature is rather affinity,—a tendency to combine with another : it requires to receive its complement. Every object is naturally in a state of unstable equilibrium, with a tendency to quit its isolation and form a union. This theory, which is called the Chemical theory of an object, regards it as the reverse of indifferent : as in a permanent state of susceptibility. When objects thus open and eager for foreign influences combine, there results a new product, in which both the constituents are lost, so far as their qualities go. The qualities of the constituents are neutralised. A man's mind, for example, prepared by certain culture, meets a new stimulus in some strange doctrine, and the result is a new form of intellectual life. But at this point the process, which such a form of objectivity represents, is closed : all that remains is for the product to break up one day into its constituent factors. There is no provision made for carrying it on further. Hence if we are to have a self-regulating system of objectivity, we must rise above the Chemical theory of objects. And to do that, the first course is to look at the objective world as *regulated* (though not immanently constituted) by the Notion.

The Notion as regulative of objectivity,—as independent and self-subsistent, but as in necessary connexion with Objectivity,—is the End, Aim, or Final Cause. According to this, the Teleological and practical theory of the Universe,[1] the object is considered as bound to reproduce and carry out the notion, and the notion is looked upon as meant to execute itself in reality. The two sides, subjective and objective, are, in other words, in necessary connexion with each other, but not identical. This is the contrast of the End and the Means. By the ' Means ' is meant an object *which is determined by an End*, and which operates upon other objects.—(1) The End is originally subjective : an instinct or desire after something—a feeling of want and the wish to remedy it. It is confronted by an objective mass, which is indifferent to these wishes : and manifests itself as a tendency outwards,—an appetite towards action. It seizes and uses up the objective world.—(2) But the End in the second place reduces this indifferent mass to be an instrument or Means : makes it the middle term between itself and the object.—(3) But the means is only valuable as a preparation to the End regarded as Realised, which thus counts as the truth of the thing. These are the three terms of the Syllogism of Teleology : the Subjective End, the Means, and the End Realised. It is the process of adaptation by which each thing is conceived as the means to some end, and which actively transforms the thing into something by which that end is realised. In the last resort it presents us with an objective world in which utility or design is the principle of systematisation : and in which

[1] Teleology meaning here not an immanent teleology, such as is found in organism.

therefore there is an endless series of ends which become means to other and higher ends. After all is done, the object remains foreign to the notion, and is only subsumed under it, and adapted to it. We want a notion which shall be identifiable with objectivity—which shall permeate it through and through, as soul does body. Such a unity of Subjective and Objective—the Notion in (and not merely in relation to) Objectivity—is what Hegel terms the Idea.

The first form of the Idea is Life, taking that as a logical category, or as equivalent to self-organisation. The living, as organisms, are contrasted with mere mechanisms. The essential progress of modern science lies in its emphasis on this aspect of the Idea : which includes all that the teleological period taught about adaptation, and only sets aside the externality of means to ends there found. The savant of the last century and the beginning of the present dealt with the object of his inquiries as a mechanical, chemical, or teleological object. The modern theorist tends to see the world as one self-evolving Life. According to the naturalist of last century, kinds of animals and plants were viewed as convenient, and perhaps arbitrary arrangements : according to the moderns, these kinds represent the grades or steps in the life of the natural world.

What, then, is the nature of the process which we call Life ? Is it adequately or definitely defined as ' a continuous adjustment of internal to external relations ' ? Or is it a good deal more than anything the word ' correspondence ' implies ? According to Hegel it is nothing so simple, but a syllogism with three terms, and a syllogism moreover which permutates its terms and premisses. There is, in the first place, the term, which is also a process, of self-production. The living must articulate itself, create for itself limbs and members, and keep up a perpetual re-creation of morphological and structural system of parts. Secondly, there is the assimilation of what is external to the living individual. If there is to be life, spiritual or bodily, there must be a physiological intus-susception of foreign elements. Without this the first term or process is impossible. Thirdly, there must be a term or process of Reproduction or generation by which the living being passes itself on as a new unit. All life, mental or bodily, involves Reproduction.—These are the three terms of the process of vitality.

But such a life, considered as merely organic, the life studied in Biology, is only a fragment. The truer life is in the genus, not in the individual : the consciousness, the sensation which inwardly unifies the diversity of organic processes. The universal has become the medium in which the Idea exists : it exists no longer in immediacy. The mere natural life gives place to the life of the Spirit. The life of the Spirit has the double form of Cognition and Will : —the theoretical and the practical action of the Idea : or Truth and Goodness. In short, the Idea divides into two halves, which yet remain the same at bottom : Reason and the World : but yet there is reason in the world. The action of the Idea, or its process at this stage, is to bring these two terms into connexion, and show their ideal unity. Beginning with Reason, it goes on to discover reason in the World. Truth consists in the adequacy of object to notion. Such adequacy is the Idea : and an object which thus corresponds with its notion is an ideal object. The ideal man is the True Man. Truth is the revelation of rationality from the objective world : and Cognition is the name for that process. On the other hand, Goodness is the realisation of rationality in the objective world : and the Will is the name for that process. Truth proceeds from the Objectivity : Goodness from the Subjectivity. But truth can only proceed (analytically) from the objective world, in so far as it is produced (synthetically) by the subjectivity. And, on the other hand, when the good is realised in objectivity, it is submitted to the process of Cognition.

With the unity of Life and Consciousness, the Absolute Idea, we reach the supreme effort of Logic. In Bacon's words, ' the truth of being and the truth of knowing is all one ' (cf. p. 171). That is the absolute condition of comprehending reality : the principle of Absolute Idealism, so far apart from its psychological wraith, and yet compelled to employ the same language. But after all it is Logic, i.e. only the supreme logical condition of the reality of the physical and psychical world. And it gains reality at the cost of the disruption of its elements : it lets the Is slip from the Is known—the *est* from the *cogitatur*—Being from consciousness. Or, in less mysterious language, fundamental philosophy, or Logic, gives place to the concreter system of Philosophy—the Philosophy of the Outward and of the Inward actuality,—of Nature and Mind.

The reader of the *Divina Commedia* may hardly need to be reminded that, at each of the grander changes of scene and grade in his pilgrimage, Dante suddenly finds himself without obvious means transported into a new region of experience. There are catastrophes in the process of development : not unprepared, but summing up, as in a flash of insight, the gradual and unperceived process of growth. There is birth and death in the spiritual world : and such are moments of sudden lapse, abrupt conversion, when the waters of Lethe close around, and thereafter all things are new. There are such moments of accumulated and abnormal intensity also in the Hegelian philosophy when a new cycle of idea suddenly appears. Such are the epochs of change at the great crises from Being to Essence, and from Essence to Notion. There is a revulsion, a sharp turn of the path which dialectic can enforce but cannot smooth away,—on that path which dialectic indeed, as opposed to the old logic of identity, shows not to be a mere smooth continuity. All development is by breaks, and yet makes for continuity.

This is again exemplified in the passage from Logic to Physics. The reality which presents itself to the philosopher as Nature is a world of reason—but, as it stands, it only lives as some speechless work of art. It is, so to speak, the picture on the wall—the reflection that is cast by the fuller reality of experience. Reason here is in the garb of sense-perception. Nature is the silent image—the *tableau vivant*—which becomes intelligent, speaking, and real, in the observing and comprehending mind. It is the statue of Condillac, not yet invested with the minimum of sensibility and consciousness. Nature is or shows all that the Idea contained, but contained only in possibility, as a logical condition of reality. It shows it in reality— and that is a reality spread through endless times and spaces. Its unity, its meaning, its continuity are broken up into fragments. Yet as Nature, i.e. in its structural unity, and not in the dispersion of things and elements, it is all a unity of development and has a life-history written in its organism for intelligence to read and to reconstitute, on the assumption that all its accident and irregularity is but the inevitable imperfection of reality as given in parts and successions.